Governing the Frontiers in the Ottoman Empire

The Ottoman Empire and Its Heritage

POLITICS, SOCIETY AND ECONOMY

Edited by

Suraiya Faroqhi
Hakan Karateke
Derin Terzioğlu

Founding Editor

Halil İnalcık†

Advisory Board

Fikret Adanır – Antonis Anastasopoulos – Idris Bostan
Palmira Brummett – Amnon Cohen – Boğaç Ergene
Jane Hathaway – Klaus Kreiser – Hans Georg Majer
Ahmet Yaşar Ocak – Abdeljelil Temimi

VOLUME 79

The titles published in this series are listed at *brill.com/oeh*

Governing the Frontiers in the Ottoman Empire

Notables, Tribes and Peasants of Muş (1820s–1880s)

By

Gülseren Duman Koç

BRILL

LEIDEN | BOSTON

Cover illustration: Map of Bitlis. Source: Istanbul Metropolitan Municipality, Atatürk Library.

The Library of Congress Cataloging-in-Publication Data is available online at https://catalog.loc.gov
LC record available at https://lccn.loc.gov/2023042470

Typeface for the Latin, Greek, and Cyrillic scripts: "Brill". See and download: brill.com/brill-typeface.

ISSN 1380-6076
ISBN 978-90-04-68303-7 (hardback)
ISBN 978-90-04-68304-4 (e-book)
DOI 10.1163/9789004683044

Copyright 2024 by Koninklijke Brill NV, Leiden, The Netherlands.
Koninklijke Brill NV incorporates the imprints Brill, Brill Nijhoff, Brill Schöningh, Brill Fink, Brill mentis, Brill Wageningen Academic, Vandenhoeck & Ruprecht, Böhlau and V&R unipress.
All rights reserved. No part of this publication may be reproduced, translated, stored in a retrieval system, or transmitted in any form or by any means, electronic, mechanical, photocopying, recording or otherwise, without prior written permission from the publisher. Requests for re-use and/or translations must be addressed to Koninklijke Brill NV via brill.com or copyright.com.

This book is printed on acid-free paper and produced in a sustainable manner.

To Yener and Derin

Contents

Acknowledgements XI
List of Illustrations XIII
A Note on Transliteration XIV

1 **Introduction** 1
   1.1 Frontiers, Tanzimat and Provincial Studies 7
   1.2 Historical Geography of Muş 16
   1.3 About the Sources 21
   1.4 Structure of the Book 22

2 **Emin Pasha of Muş: A Negotiation of Power in the Periphery of the Ottoman Empire** 26
   2.1 Notables of Muş and the Nature of Their Political and Economic Power 31
      2.1.1 *The Yurtluk-Ocaklık System* 32
         2.1.1.1 Historicizing the Yurtluk-Ocaklık Status of Muş 37
   2.2 The Rise of Emin Pasha 44
      2.2.1 *The 1828–29 Ottoman Russian War* 46
         2.2.1.1 The Revolt of Timur Pasha and the Consolidation of the Power of Emin Pasha 50
   2.3 Utilization of Frontier Tribes 52
      2.3.1 *The Case of the Tribe of Sıpkî* 53
         2.3.1.1 The Cases of the Tribes of Cemaldini and Haydaran 60
   2.4 Conclusion 65

3 **The Revolt of Emin Pasha: Punishment and Cooptation** 67
   3.1 Preparation for the Revolt: In the Pursuit of Allies 69
   3.2 Between Negotiation and Contest 74
      3.2.1 *The Tribes and the Pashas* 79
   3.3 The Contours of Negotiation 82
   3.4 The Reappointment of Emin Pasha 84
   3.5 Muş in the Course of Centralization Efforts: The First Phase of the Abolition of Yurtluk-Ocaklıks 88
      3.5.1 *The Exile of Emin Pasha to Vidin* 95
         3.5.1.1 Struggle for Power to the End 97
   3.6 Conclusion 100

4 The Tanzimat State in Muş: Collaboration with and Punishment of Local Actors 102
  4.1 On the Eve of the Application of Tanzimat Reforms: A Network of Exploitation 106
  4.2 The Tanzimat State in Muş 113
  4.3 Old Actors and the New Regime 121
     4.3.1 *The Settlement of Accounts* 126
  4.4 Şerif Bey as Mediator: The Beginning of the End 129
  4.5 Exile of Alaaddin Pashazades from Muş 134
  4.6 Conclusion 140

5 Aftermath of the Exile of the Yurtluk-Ocaklık Holders 142
  5.1 Confiscation of the Yurtluk-Ocaklık Villages of Şerif Bey and His Brothers and Its Implications 145
     5.1.1 *Debate on the Revenue and Boundaries of the Yurtluk-Ocaklık Villages of the Alaaddin Pashazades* 148
  5.2 Limits of the Villages and the Determination of Salaries 154
  5.3 Struggle for Forgiveness 162
  5.4 Debate over the Yurtluk-Ocaklık Villages of Emin Pasha 168
  5.5 Future of the Yurtluk-Ocaklık Salaries 171
  5.6 Conclusion 173

6 The Post Tanzimat Era: Evaluation of the Reforms through the Petitions of Ordinary People 176
  6.1 Conflicting Viewpoints Regarding Governors 181
  6.2 New Administrators, Old Habits 186
  6.3 Socio-Economic Results of the Crimean War for Muş's Locality 194
     6.3.1 *The Case of Ömer Pasha* 195
        6.3.1.1 The Edict of Reform and Its Results for the Armenian Population 204
  6.4 Council Members, Tax Farmers, Moneylenders and Peasants 208
     6.4.1 *The Migration and Depopulation* 215
     6.4.2 *Migration from Crimea and Caucasia* 221
  6.5 Conclusion 225

7 Governors, Tribes, and Peasants 227
  7.1 Implications of the Tanzimat Reforms for the Nomadic Groups 232
  7.2 Peasants and the Nomads: Settlement of the Tribes 235
  7.3 Nomadic Tribes in the Vicinity of the Sanjak of Muş 245

8 The Hesenan Tribe: The Cases of Rıdvan and Kulihan Aghas   252
   8.1 The Tribes in Dispute: Conflicts between the Tribes of Muş and Those of Its Vicinity   264
   8.2 In Lieu of a Conclusion   270

9 Conclusion   274

   Bibliography   279
   Index   296

Acknowledgements

This long journey would not be possible without the assistance and support of many individuals and institutions. I am grateful "to be brought up" at Boğaziçi University. The interdisciplinary curriculum of my undergraduate years broadened my vision, nurtured my interests and guided me in finding the right place for my focus. From the beginning of my graduate studies, the Atatürk Institute provided the necessary intellectual environment for improving and shaping my academic skills and perspective. I would like to express my deepest gratitude to my mentor, Nadir Özbek. Without the theoretical and historical perspective that I have gained from him, a study such as this could not mature. His encouragement, comments, questions, and patience were important for finishing my dissertation on the same topic. I am indebted to Cengiz Kırlı, not only because he was one of the jury members for my dissertation from its initial phase, but also because of his lectures and his comments which have shaped my way of thinking. I also owe a debt of gratitude to Şevket Pamuk, Çağlar Keyder, Ayşe Buğra, Asım Karaömerlioğlu and Yücel Terzibaşoğlu for guiding my academic life. I would also like to thank the jury members for my dissertation, Fehmi Yılmaz, Can Nacar, and Ali Sipahi, for their invaluable suggestions and comments. I have to thank Hamit Bozarslan whose suggestions and directions in relation to sources and archives in France, during a semester stay at the EHESS, were very illuminating. Istanbul Medeniyet University was my scholarly home when this project was completed. I am also heartily thankful to Turhan Kaçar and Recep Karacakaya for their help, support and understanding. My thanks are also due to Alp Yücel Kaya for his help and kindness.

The research, writing and re-writing process of this study were possible with the help of many archives and libraries. I am grateful to the staff of the Ottoman Archives of the Office of the Prime Minister who were very helpful during my research. The staff of Boğaziçi Library were also very kind, helpful and thoughtful in their dealings with me, I would like to thank all of them. The staff of the National Archives of the United Kingdom and the Archive Diplomatiques du Ministère des Affaires Étrangères facilitated my research. My thanks are due to the staff of the Atatürk Kitaplığı of Istanbul Municipality for the visual materials used in this study.

My trip to Diyarbakır, Muş and Bitlis was possible thanks to Seren Üstündağ and Ayşe Batgi, along with the hospitality of their families. I am thankful to Seren for sharing joys and sorrows of life, though we are miles apart. My deepest gratitude is due to Tayyip Yıldırım and his late father Abdurrahman Yıldırım, who were generous in sharing their family history with me. My conversations with them enabled me to imagine what took place almost two hundred years ago.

I am profoundly grateful to Brill for this great opportunity. I feel fortunate in having the comments and extensive reading of two anonymous reviewers, which enabled me to turn a dissertation into a monograph. I am grateful to Suraiya Faroqhi for her valuable comments and drawing my attention to some of the finer details. I am thankful to the assistant editor, Franca de Kort, for making the whole review and publication process easier for me and for her quick replies to my endless questions. My thanks are also due to Ester Lels for supervising the production process. I would like to express my gratitude to Jonathan Philips and Barry Stocker who respectively copy-edited the initial and last versions of this project.

During my years at Boğaziçi University, I had the good fortune to have many friends whose companionship made the dissertation-writing process enjoyable. I am thankful to Uğur Bayraktar for his companionship during our archival research in the Ottoman Archives of the Office of the Prime Minister. The friendship and moral support of Alp Kadıoğlu, Başak Akgül, Ramiz Üzümçeker, Seval Gülen, Özkan Akpınar, İbrahim Kuran, Erhan Bektaş, Faruk Yalçın, Hüseyin Sert, Çiğdem Oğuz, Ozan Gürlek, Özlem Kinaş, Berna Kamay, Melike Sümertaş, Ezgi Burcu Işıl, and Şahika Karatepe have always been valuable for me.

Özlem Dilber has always been more than a friend for me. I am grateful for her unconditional help, encouragement, enthusiasm, and good judgement. I am heartily thankful to Ceren Ünlü and Fatma Özkan who have been wonderful colleagues and friends and with whom I have shared the feeling of solidarity. Yıldız Yıldırım is the sister who deserves huge thanks for her invaluable support and true friendship.

Lastly, I would like to express my gratitude to my parents, Sevgi and Mehmet Baki and my brother Semih who always unquestioningly supported me during my academic journey. My thanks also are due to my cousins Gizem, Ebru, Şeyma and Ceren for supporting me and making me laugh.

This book is dedicated to the two men of my life. I am profoundly indebted to Yener, my companion and husband, who was the closest witness of the writing and re-writing of this project, critically reading each word of it. His emotional support, love, and care sustained me through the writing of this book and for every single day. In September 2020, my beloved son Derin was born, and he has become the sun and the mirth, the source of gratitude and inspiration for my life. I am grateful to him for teaching me endless love and the joy of being curious about everything.

Illustrations

Figure

1   Şerif Bey Hill in Bitlis   2

Maps

1   The map of Bitlis province, late 19th century   17
2   The locations of some villages which the family controlled after the abolition of the yurtluk-ocaklik status of Muş   158

Tables

1   The values of yurtluk-ocaklik villages of the three brothers in 1850   155
2   Two-year revenues of the yurtluk-ocaklik villages of Şerif Bey   156
3   Two-year revenues of the yurtluk-ocaklik villages of Murad Bey   156
4   Two-year revenues of the yurtluk-ocaklik villages of Hurşid Bey   157
5   The amount of money embezzled by Ridvan Agha from the inhabitants of Malazgirt   255

A Note on Transliteration

In the transliteration of the Ottoman Turkish materials, only the *'ayn* and *hamza* are kept throughout the text, and circumflexes are used to signify lengthened vowels. Unless otherwise noted, all translations and transliterations in the book are my own.

The archival documents are generally cited according to dispatchment dates, but in the case of huge discrepancies, the dates of individual documents are cited instead and footnoted. The Hicri (Lunar) and Rumi (Julian) dates of the cited documents are presented along with Gregorian equivalents in the footnotes. All the archival documents are cited in abbreviated form in the footnotes. The extended versions of them are presented in the bibliography.

All place names are provided with their contemporary equivalents upon their first appearance in the book, except for those I could not identify.

CHAPTER 1

Introduction

Among the four sanjaks of the province of Bitlis, Muş is certainly the most important. The importance of the sanjak stems first from natural resources like the abundance of its agricultural land, and second from political causes like its multiethnic and multi-religious population. In fact, the plain of Muş extending from the north to the south of the district center, the town of Muş, is a pleasant plain, unique in Kurdistan, which is surrounded by mountains. [Moreover] the most important branch of the Euphrates River, the Murat River flows across the plain and watering it with various streams large and small, flowing from the high mountains all around. The vast plain takes ten hours to cross from west to east, and twenty hours from north to south. With reference to its outstanding capacity for agriculture, there is a local saying that "the plain of Muş is the source of gold." The foothills of the surrounding mountains are of equal importance due to their abundance and variety of fruit trees and wide pastures suitable for the grazing of large flocks of livestock as well as relatively high population density. Similarly, the administrative and political significance of the sanjak stems from its being situated in a geography contiguous with the provinces of Erzurum and Van and adjacent to Russia, and its being inhabited mostly by Kurds and Armenians.[1]

The author of the quotation above is Ahmed Mâcid, the *mutasarrıf* (administrator of a sanjak/sub-province) of Muş, who wrote these lines in 1909. The report of the mutasarrıf is significant in that it indicates the geopolitical and socioeconomic conditions, and peculiarities of a sanjak in an eastern province of the Ottoman Empire in the eyes of an Ottoman bureaucrat. It is also meaningful to the context of this book, which attaches importance to the effects of the geography and the local dynamics of a region for the implementation of reforms throughout the nineteenth century. Being in the middle of an agriculturally fertile plain surrounded by high mountain ranges, Muş was also geopolitically situated in a frontier zone contiguous with the Ottoman, Russian and Persian empires. Besides, demographically the prominence of Muş in the eastern frontier of the Ottoman Empire stemmed not only from its ethnic and religious diversity but also from its different life patterns. Armenian and Kurdish

---

[1] Ahmed Macid, "Kürdistân Ahvâli ve Mesele-i Islahât," Mülkiye, no. 8 (1 Eylül 1325).

FIGURE 1   Şerif Bey Hill in Bitlis
ISTANBUL METROPOLITAN MUNICIPALITY, ATATÜRK LIBRARY

peasants constituted the majority of the settled population, while nomadic and seminomadic Kurdish tribes spent summers in the mountains surrounding the plain of Muş and wintered in the villages on the plain.

In this demographically and socioeconomically outstanding sanjak, the roles and functions of the local ruling power-holders were also important. The sanjak was governed by a local Kurdish dynasty, known as Alaaddin Pashazades, as a *yurtluk-ocaklık* since from the early eighteenth to the middle of the nineteenth century. Muş, like many regions especially in the eastern frontier of the empire, held a yurtluk-ocaklık status which refers to hereditarily enjoyed land grants with large fiscal and administrative immunities. This book explores the characteristics and transformations of this type of land tenure during the nineteenth century.

Covering a period starting with the pre-*Tanzimat* (literally, re-organization) reforms era and going up to the 1880s, this book scrutinizes the social, economic, and political transformation that the sanjak of Muş went through between the 1820s and 1880s. Focusing on the plains of Muş and Bulanık, it explores the effects of the fiscal, administrative, and military reforms culminating in the Tanzimat in the sanjak throughout the nineteenth century. The book sheds light on local network relations by uncovering a variety of local actors like Muslim and non-Muslim notables, governors, tribal leaders, tax farmers, usurers, and peasants. The milestones of this era affected all local groups in different ways. The military and administrative transformations inaugurated by Selim III, the wars with Russia and Iran, tribal conflicts between the Ottoman and Persian empires, and internal developments like the rise of Mehmed Ali Pasha in Egypt set the stage for many local actors to become involved in local politics. Similarly, the fiscal, military, administrative, and judicial reform package that culminated in the Tanzimat including the formation of local councils, abrogation of the usufruct rights of large tracts of land under the control of Kurdish notables, new systems of land tenure, taxation, and conscription, transformed the locality of Muş as it did in other localities around the empire. Lastly, the conjuncture that began with the Crimean War not only led to acceleration in the pace of the reforms, but also brought to the fore the issue of immigrants, which deepened with the Ottoman-Russian (1877–8) and Balkan Wars.

In this era of reforms, especially from the 1830s to the 1850s the Ottoman governments applied to the mediation of yurtluk-ocaklık rulers of Muş to govern the region better. One of the main arguments of the study is that although the central government gradually curtailed the power of local dynasties, depriving them of their economic and political power, the administrative, fiscal, and military reforms on the agenda could not be implemented without the collaboration of local power holders. Although their power was curtailed through the eradication of their economic power, yurtluk-ocaklık holders were also incorporated into the administrative system. With their local knowledge and experience, local notables continued their intermediary role between the provincial/central authorities and local society, combining it with new official duties that emerged as a result of the Tanzimat reforms.

The yurtluk-ocaklık holders of Muş were local notables (*ayan, eşraf, ilerigelen*). Albert Hourani defines the notables as those "who can play a certain political role as intermediaries between government and people (...)."[2] Nonetheless, the local notables were not a uniform, static group, but contained variations. They also contested, contended and collaborated among themselves. Which of the notables took up the role of intermediary between the central government and the locality varied according to administrative and fiscal transformations. In her examination of Jalilis in Mosul, Dina Rizk Khoury explains how the hegemony of this political group was brought to an end with the help of different sections of Mosuli society, like the gentry and

---

2 Albert Hourani, "Ottoman Reforms and Politics of Notables," in William R. Polk and Richard L. Chambers eds, *Beginnings of Modernization in the Middle East: The Nineteenth Century* (Chicago: University of Chicago Press, 1968), 48.

the merchants.³ In the sanjak of Muş, despite the fact that comparable commercialization leading to the rise of a merchant class did not take place, secondary power holders⁴ who had been overshadowed by the yurtluk-ocaklık holders had great interest in the decrease of the power of the local dynasty. The yurtluk-ocaklık holders, the traditional Kurdish nobility, were exiled in the middle of the nineteenth century, but a new kind of local actor emerged. These new actors were either local council members, or tribal leaders who not only became district administrators but also became more influential in the absence of local dynastic families. Tax farmers, tribal aghas, stewards of former governors, and religious leaders became more influential after the exile of the notables of Muş and the novelties of the Tanzimat, like local councils, became platforms from which they exercised power.

The reforms and transformation era of the Ottoman Empire has long been discussed as a top-down process. However, recent studies show how the nineteenth century reforms were negotiated, shaped and transformed according to local dynamics. For instance, Dina Rizk Khoury underscores that Tanzimat reforms cannot be regarded only as a project imposed from the imperial center; rather, some parts of Mosuli society had an interest in breaking the power of local households and were involved in the reformation of the provincial administration.⁵ Similarly, Yonca Köksal's comparative study of the implementation of Tanzimat reforms in the core provinces of Edirne and Ankara also sheds light on how the local networks, geopolitical location, and economic prosperity affected the outcomes of the same reforms.⁶ These examples show that the Tanzimat was a not a top-down process, but was negotiated, changed and adapted according to the necessities and peculiarities of different regions. As Jens Hanssen, in his piece on center-periphery relations in the Arab East during the Tanzimat era, argues:

> Focusing specifically on certain imperial strategies of crisis management in the Arab provinces, such as imperial inspection tours, local petitions and councils, and model provinces, there emerged distinct and subtle

---

3 Dina Rizk Khoury, *State and Provincial Society in the Ottoman Empire*: Mosul, 1540–1834 (Cambridge: Cambridge University Press, 1997), 212.
4 Secondary power holders including ulema, local influential people can be referred to as "lesser ayans." Here I borrow these terms from Robert Zens. Robert W. Zens, "The Ayanlık and Pasvanoğlu Osman Paşa of Vidin in the age of Ottoman Social Change, 1791–1815" (PhD diss., University of Wisconsin, 2004), 31.
5 Khoury, State and Provincial Society in the Ottoman Empire, 212.
6 Yonca Köksal, *The Ottoman Empire in the Tanzimat Era: Provincial Perspectives from Ankara to Edirne* (Abingdon: Routledge, 2019). For a study that analyzes Tanzimat reforms in an Anatolian town, Tokat, see John K. Bragg, *Ottoman Notables and Participatory Politics: Tanzimat Reform in Tokat, 1839–1876* (London: Routledge, 2014).

modes of contestation, appropriation and co-optation in the provincial peripheries that determined the application of *Tanẓīmāt* reforms. Moreover, what has consistently been considered as instances of impositions of state power, malicious or benevolent, under closer scrutiny turned out to be attributable to socio-political processes and agencies in the provincial peripheries that were then adopted in Istanbul as imperial legislation.[7]

Similarly, the implementation of direct rule through the Tanzimat reforms, that is to say, the increase in "state capacity," did not occur in a sudden or linear process. Similarly, the implementation of direct rule did not necessarily exclude local intermediaries like notables, religious leaders, and community representatives. As Yonca Köksal argues by comparing Edirne and Ankara, nineteenth-century reforms took place through "a combination of direct and indirect rule."[8] In Mosul, Khoury underscores the following "the government attempts succeeded in the frontier area because it relied on elites who had successfully struck local roots while maintaining their loyalty to the central state. Where it was unable to do so …, the governors' prerogatives remained limited."[9] Similarly, in Vidin, as Safa Saraçoğlu notes, after the abolition of *gospodarlık* (the landlord system in the Balkans), the descendants of *gospodars* were able to exert their influence through the administrative and judicial councils that were products of Tanzimat reforms.[10] The case of Muş was similar, as the mediation and collaboration of Alaaddin Pashazades was required to maintain order, control tribes, and implement reforms. Even after the

---

7 Jens Hanssen, "Practices of Integration: Center-Periphery Relations in the Ottoman Empire," in *The Empire in the City: Arab Provincial Capitals in the Late Ottoman Empire*, eds. Jens Hanssen, Thomas Philip, and Stefan Weber (Beirut: Orient-Institut der DMG, 2002), 74.
8 Köksal, "Local Intermediaries and Ottoman State and Ottoman State Centralization: A Comparison of the Tanzimat Reforms in the Provinces of Ankara and Edirne (1839–1878)" (PhD diss., Columbia University, 2002), 55–56. "Indirect rule" broadly means "the cooptation of local and regional power holders to the state rule without utterly transforming their bases of power." On the other hand, "direct rule refers to unmediated intervention of the state in the lives of local communities, households, and productive enterprises." Charles Tilly, *Coercion, Capital, and European States, AD 990–1992* (Cambridge: Blackwell, 1992), 24–103. Quoted in Köksal, "Local Intermediaries and Ottoman State," 56.
9 Dina Rizk Khoury, "The Ottoman Center versus Provincial Power-Holders: An Analysis of the Historiography," in The Cambridge History of Turkey, ed. Suraiya Faroqhi (Cambridge: Cambridge University Press, 2006), 143.
10 M. Safa Saraçoğlu, "Resilient Notables: Looking at the Transformation of the Ottoman Empire from the Local Level," in *Contested Spaces of Nobility in Early Modern Europe*, eds. Matthew P. Romaniello and Charles Lipp (Burlington: Ashgate, 2011), 257–77.

liquidation of the yurtluk-ocaklık system and their exile, some of the family members returned to participate in provincial politics and administration.

This book is not only confined to the provincial notables' roles in the reform process. As Muş was a demographically heterogenous sanjak, it was one of the best examples for showing how the different ethnic groups received the reforms and how the reforms were shaped according to this demographic heterogeneity. This book provides snapshots of intercommunal relations as well. The nineteenth century also witnessed transformations in intercommunal relations, including massacres, demographic changes, along with dispossession and property transfers. The commercialization and commodification of land led first to the development of an "agrarian question,"[11] which turned into an ethnic problem when the contours of class and ethnicity overlapped in certain cases.[12] By focusing on a region populated by Armenian and Kurdish sharecroppers and Kurdish tribes, this book provides a better context for the terms of the conflict among them, which left its mark on the last decade of the nineteenth century. By focusing on the role of overtaxation, corvée and debt for the migration and dispossession of Armenian and some Kurdish peasants in the pre-Tanzimat and Tanzimat eras, this book contributes to the studies of intercommunal relations in the eastern provinces of the Ottoman Empire, while most such studies cover only the late Hamidian era and thereafter.

Finally, the study contributes to the studies of seminomadic and nomadic tribes. Geopolitically, the frontier tribes were always at the core of the politics and socioeconomics of Muş. In the early nineteenth century, the influence of the notables of Muş over frontier tribes constituted one of the main pillars of their power. The tribes were also actively involved in the politics of the region. Muş was an important pastureland for the tribes of the province of Diyarbakır who spent summers in the mountains to the south of the plain. Similarly, the seminomadic tribes of Muş spent summers in the mountains surrounding the sanjak and spent winters in villages on the plain, that were mostly inhabited by Armenians. The reforms of the nineteenth century more fervently embarked

---

11 For the "agrarian question," see the pioneering study by Janet Klein, Janet Klein, "Power in the Periphery: The Hamidiye Light Cavalry and The Struggle over Ottoman Kurdistan, 1890–1914" (PhD diss., Princeton University, 2002); *The Margins of Empire, Kurdish Militas in the Ottoman Tribal Zone* (Stanford Stanford University Press, 2011). Similarly, Nadir Özbek shows that how the taxation policies of the Hamidian era affected the development of the Armenian Question. Nadir Özbek, "The Politics of Taxation and the 'Armenian Question' during the Late Ottoman Empire, 1876–1908," Comparative Studies in Society and History 54, no. 4 (2012): 770–97.

12 For a study of the transformation of the Armenian land question, see Mehmet Polatel, "Armenians and the Land Question in the Ottoman Empire, 1870–1914" (PhD diss., Boğaziçi University, 2017).

upon the settlement of nomadic and seminomadic groups, not only to turn them into taxpayers and conscripts but also to diminish the burden on the settled population. As those tribes were not accustomed to agricultural cultivation they had to rely on peasants for their subsistence and that of their livestock. In that sense, this book examines two important system, *kışlakiye* and *hafirlik* to understand the relations among nomads and peasants; in the case of the former, notables were also at the corner. Kışlakiye or winter quartering was an ancient regime in which peasants provided the nomads with shelter, hay, raw and straw during winters.[13] In return, nomads were paying an amount of money which gone certainly in the pockets of notables not of peasants.[14] In that sense, winter-quartering became corvée for the peasants of Muş. This custom was supposed to be abolished with the Tanzimat. However, since the mid-1850s, the practice of *hafirlik*, the protection tax paid by peasants in grains and similar other goods to nomads emerged. This practice of hafırlık indicates the root of the aggravated relations between peasants and nomads, as discussed thoroughly in Chapter 7.

1.1 Frontiers, Tanzimat and Provincial Studies

Muş's political and socioeconomic prominence mainly derived from its being in a frontier zone of the Ottoman Empire contiguous with Iran and Russia. This book treats the sanjak of Muş as a frontier region, in that it was geopolitically close to the Russian and Iranian empires and consequently the sanjak was affected by the political and military developments in the frontier. In addition, the sanjak was ruled as a yurtluk-ocaklık which referred to an indirect rule. "A frontier," in Khodarkovsky's terms, "is a *region* that forms the margins of a settled or developed territory, a politico-geographical *area* lying beyond

---

13 The tax of *kışlak* or *kışlakiye* was an ancient tax collected from nomads and seminomads. Cengiz Orhonlu, *Osmanlı İmparatorluğu'nda Aşiretlerin İskânı* (Istanbul: Eren Yayıncılık, 1987), 24. As Ahmed Akgündüz emphasizes, the *resm-i kışlak* (the tax for winter quarters) was taken from *reʿâyâ* (commoners) who came to a specific land from outside, not from those reʿâyâ who were already paying the sheep tax (*resm-i ağnam*), tithe (*aʿşâr*) and some other taxes. Ahmed Akgündüz, *Osmanlı Kanunnameleri ve Hukuki Tahlilleri*, vol. 1 (Istanbul: Fey Vakfı, 1990), 186–7.

14 Consular reports from the nineteenth century described kışlakiye as an imposition on villagers. For instance, in Hınıs, where one of the members of Alaaddin Pashazades Murad Bey, enjoyed power, peasants were paying a kışlakiye, which was depicted as the heaviest tax. Brant, "Notes of a Journey," 348.

the integrated region of political unit."[15] Similarly, drawing a distinction between "urban centers" and "remote rural areas," Eugene Rogan emphasizes that "remote areas," like Eastern Anatolia and Arab provinces, "are treated as frontiers inasmuch as they represented socio-political orders apart from the institutions of the Empire at large."[16]

Frontiers had great variations. As Karpat underscores, "the Ottoman borderlands cannot be grouped in one single category." Both "internal" and "international" reflections determined each borderland's relation with the Ottoman Empire.[17] A variety of dimensions, like "the autonomous local elites, the degree of intervention of European interest in a given area and local perceptions of the benefits of Ottoman rule" shaped the "Ottoman experiences" in frontier areas.[18] Thus, the "centralist approach," which neglects borderlands, and the center-periphery dichotomy, which neglects "the great variation of centers and borderlands" can be misleading.[19] The centralist approach and center-periphery dichotomy has long dominated Ottoman historiography. The center was regarded as the sole agent which shaped the periphery from top-down and this account was read through the lens of achievement and failure. Recent studies have challenged this dichotomy and indicate that the relations between center and periphery are more complicated.

In this respect, the concepts of "poly-centricity" and "poly-activity" employed by Jongerden and Verheij are crucial. "Poly-centricity" proposes that there were "regional centers" in the Ottoman Empire that shaped the social, economic, and political transformations that society went through. The outstanding provinces like Diyarbekir and Erzurum in the Ottoman East might be examples of "regional centers." Similarly, "poly-activity" refers to "a range of actors and dynamics, networks and interactions, not of just one group or class."[20] Along the same lines, Joel Migdal, offers a "state-in-society approach"

---

15 On the contrary, the author continued, a border "is a clearly demarcated boundary between sovereign states." Michael Khodarkovsky, *Russia's Steppe Frontier: The Making of A Colonial Empire, 1500–1800* (Bloomington: Indiana University Press, 2004), 47.

16 Eugene L. Rogan, *Frontiers of the State in the Late Ottoman Empire, Transjordan, 1850–1921* (Cambridge: Cambridge University Press, 1999), 5–6.

17 Kemal H. Karpat, "Comments on Contributions and the Borderlands," in *Ottoman Borderlands: Issues, Personalities and Political Changes*, eds. Kemal H. Karpat and Robert W. Zens (Madison: University of Wisconsin Press, 2003), 1.

18 Rogan, *Frontiers of the State*, 6.

19 Karpat, "Comments on Contributions," 4.

20 Joost Jongerden and Jelle Verheij, "Introduction," in *Social Relations in Ottoman Diyarbekir, 1870–1915*, eds. Joost Jongerden and Jelle Verheij (Leiden: Brill, 2012), 3.

as a response to state-centered theories.²¹ "States are parts of societies. States may help mold, but they are also continually molded by the societies they are embedded." His argument is important as it falsifies the notion of "large collectivities called states against large collectivities called societies," focusing instead on the relations and variations between "different segments" of both states and societies.²²

Instead of studies in which there is a binary opposition between state and society, or a statist approach empowering the state as the only agent and confining society to a static, ineffective position, it is better to use studies that point out blurred state-society, center-periphery distinctions and emphasize that historical contexts, power relations, and negotiations are important to elaborate the "state-in-society" perspective.²³ Following the point of departure of Krohn-Hansen and Nustad, "we need to set the construction of states as the outcome of complex sets of practices and processes. A state formation is the result of myriads of situations where social actors negotiate power and meaning."²⁴ Thus, as Özbek illustrates, one can insist on examining "the state

---

21 The theoretical tenets of this statist approach is framed in Peter B. Evans, Dietrich Rueschemeyer, and Theda Skocpol, eds., *Bringing the State Back in* (Cambridge: Cambridge University Press, 1985).
22 Migdal proposes four claims to frame the "state-in-society approach:" "states vary in their effectiveness based on their ties to society; states must be disaggregated; social forces, like states, are contingent on specific empirical conditions; states and other social forces may be mutually empowering." Joel S. Migdal, "Introduction: Developing A State-in-Society Perspective," in *State Power and Social Forces: Domination and Transformation in the Third World*, ed. Atul Kohli Joel S. Migdal, Vivienne Shue (Cambridge: Cambridge University Press, 1984), 2–4. For more details on the state-in-society perspective, see *State in Society: Studying How States and Societies Transform and Constitute One Another* (Cambridge: Cambridge University Press, 2004). Michael Meeker follows a similar approach in his study of the Ottoman province of Trabzon, particularly the district of Of. Emphasizing the "necessity of a theory of a society within, rather than against, the state," he argued that the aghas, mansions, clans, and parties "were country extensions of the imperial military and administrative establishment." Michael E. Meeker, *A Nation of Empire: The Ottoman Legacy of Turkish Modernity* (Berkeley: University of California Press, 2002), 32–3.
23 For instance, Nadir Özbek points out "a dynamic political sphere, yet one not categorically distinct from public authority, but rather in the context of a blurred boundary between state and civil society, public and private" in the context of Second Constitutional Period philanthropic activities. Nadir Özbek, "Defining the Public Sphere during the Late Ottoman Empire: War, Mass Mobilization and the Young Turk Regime (1908–1918)," Middle Eastern Studies 43, no. 5 (2007): 797.
24 Christian Krohn-Hansen and Knut G. Nustad, "Introduction," in *State Formation: Anthropological Perspectives*, eds. Christian Krohn-Hansen and Knut G. Nustad (London: Pluto Press, 2005), 13.

through its particular concrete and material effects in people's lives."[25] This conceptualization enables us to analyse the state-society relations better, to acknowledge the agency of a variety of actors including their role in the reformulation and implementation of Ottoman rule throughout the Empire.

The implementation of Ottoman rule in remote areas in Syria, Yemen, Çukurova in the east and south, and Albania and Walachia in the west differed as much as they were similar. Hence, the implementation of direct rule in the sanjak of Muş, which was situated on a frontier, was determined by a variety of factors, both internal and external. Being irrigated by the Murat and Karasu rivers, the sanjak of Muş, particularly the plain named after it, had always been fertile and populous, and it had the potential to be a principal grain supplier if the necessary infrastructure, like transportation facilities, was provided. Moreover, Muş was on a frontier that was suitable for transition between the winter and summer pastures of the Kurdish tribes, so it was an appropriate place for their settlement. The richness of the land together with the human resources, which would be the result of the settlement of nomadic and semi-nomadic Kurdish tribes, turned the region into a site of struggle over resources between various actors. In this struggle over the men, resources and surplus, a comprehension of the roles and functions of the local beys of Muş is crucial. The functions of the local notables are particularly at the core of the land politics of the empire before the nineteenth century – that is to say, the large tracts of land under their control.

Especially on the frontier with Iran, the centuries-long Safavid-Ottoman rivalry shaped policies in Ottoman Kurdistan of which Muş was a significant part. As Sabri Ateş argues, "failing to extend their authority on a permanent basis, the competing imperial powers engaged in a continuous process of conciliation and coercion with local elites, which provided ample opportunities for 'localized political autonomy and relative freedom of socioeconomic borderland movement.'"[26] Thus, as a frontier region, Muş had been granted to its mutasarrıfs who were mostly from a local Kurdish dynasty, the lineage of Alaaddin Pasha, as *yurtluk-ocaklıks* until the second half of the nineteenth

---

25   However, Özbek also accentuates the reality that "one cannot deny the logistical difficulty of studying the local and the everyday without relying, to some extent and by default, on an abbreviated view of the state as a more or less solid and integrated political actor." Özbek, "The Politics of Taxation," 774.

26   Richard Schofield, "Narrowing the Frontier: Mid-Nineteenth Century Efforts to Delimit and Map the Perso-Ottoman Boundary," in *War and Peace in Qajar Persia*, ed. Roxane Farmanfarmaian (New York: Routledge, 2008), 150. Quoted in Sabri Ateş, *The Ottoman-Iranian Borderlands: Making a Boundary, 1843–1914* (New York: Cambridge University Press, 2013), 1–2.

century when this type of land holding was abrogated. Nevertheless, the elimination of this system was a gradual process that culminated with the implementation of the Tanzimat. *Yurtluk-ocaklıks* and their counterpart *hükûmets* were forms of hereditary land usufruct, but the latter had more autonomy. In addition, they had been widely used before Ottoman rule was asserted in the Kurdish periphery and were common in Safevids and Turkoman states, as well. Thus, the granting of yurtluk-ocaklık lands was neither specific to Ottoman Kurdistan nor a particularity of the Ottoman Empire. It was among the strategies of the imperial states ranging through: force, economic concessions, ranks and titles applied in the remote, peripheral areas. This book provides an account of the features of the yurtluk-ocaklık status of Muş, its change over the course of time, and finally, its gradual abrogation – first in the first half of the nineteenth century and then with the implementation of Tanzimat reforms in the province of Erzurum – and its aftermath.

The nineteenth century has been considered as an age of reforms in the Ottoman Empire. Rogan argues that during the nineteenth century, "the Ottomans came to place a new premium on their frontier regions as untapped resources which could contribute taxes and manpower if put under direct rule."[27] In the case of the Ottoman East, this "new premium" required many detailed reforms ranging from the cooptation and incorporation of Kurdish notables through a myriad of means, to the settling of nomadic and semi-nomadic Kurdish tribes, to the introduction of a new taxation and land tenure system. It is possible to contextualize the reforms of the long nineteenth century of the Ottoman Empire, as a development of infrastructural power by the central government. Michael Mann defines "infrastructural power" as "the capacity of the state to actually penetrate civil society, and to implement logistically political decisions throughout the realm."[28] However, this does not mean that the infrastructural power of the state increased immediately; rather, it was a gradual process shaped by geographic diversities and local power relations. Nevertheless, the reforms of the long nineteenth century including those during the reigns of Selim III and Mahmut II were an important phase. The modest attempts at military reform by Selim III, called *Nizâm-ı Cedîd* (New Order[29]), followed the military, administrative, and judicial reforms of the

---

27 Rogan, *Frontiers of the State*, 5.
28 Michael Mann, "The Autonomous Power of the State: Its Origins, Mechanisms and Results," *European Journal of Sociology* 25, no. 2 (1984): 189.
29 However, "new order" was not confined to military reforms. In Carter Findley's words, "the perception that the New Order required planning and regulation marks the transition from 'traditional' towards 'rational-legal authority.'" Carter Vaughn Findley, "The

era of Mahmut II.[30] Bureaucratization, the division of labor, and the establishment of ministries and advisory councils were watersheds in the course of reform. Similarly, the nineteenth century was a period during which the central government took responsibility in myriad fields in which it had not previously claimed any responsibility like health, education, and public transport. Thus, the improvement of communication channels – like the establishment of postal services – or developments to reach and obtain the consent of and penetrate the everyday life of the subjects – like the first official newspaper and the census – were integral parts of the infrastructural power of the Ottoman government.[31]

The reform era known as the Tanzimat[32] was not only the first solid attempt to provide Muslim and non-Muslim equality and safeguard the lives, property, and honor of all subjects, it was also the most important phase of the development of infrastructural power. Among other aspects, the efforts to ameliorate the taxation system and the administrative innovations inherent to those efforts were crucial. The tax farming system was reorganized, and *muhassıls* (centrally-appointed officials) were dispatched to collect the "tax," a system which was enabled through the register of the incomes, properties, and population of the subjects.[33] The second mission of the muhassıls was to establish

Tanzimat," in *The Cambridge History of Turkey*, ed. Reşat Kasaba (New York: Cambridge University Press, 2008), 12.

30 For an evaluation of nineteenth century reforms, see Roderic H. Davison, *Essays in Ottoman and Turkish History, 1774–1923* (Austin: University of Texas Press, 1990).

31 Nilay Özok-Gündoğan evaluates census-making not as a top-down but as a social process. She focuses on role of the different provincial actors in the planning and implementation of the census-making in the Ottoman Kurdistan between 1830 and 1850. Nilay Özok-Gündoğan, "Counting the Population and the Wealth in an 'Unruly' Land: Census Making as a Social Process," *Journal of Social History*, 53 (3) 2020: 763–791.

32 The periodization of the Tanzimat era is controversial. For an evaluation of the historiography of this era, see Yonca Köksal, "Tanzimat ve Tarih Yazımı," Doğu Batı: Osmanlılar I 51 (2010): 193–216. Similarly, the reign of Abdülmahit II has led to many debates in the literature with respect to the continuity and discontinuity of reforms. For a discussion of the historiography of this era, see Nadir Özbek, "Modernite, Tarih ve İdeoloji: II. Abdülhamid Dönemi Tarihçiliği Üzerine Bir Değerlendirme," Türkiye Araştırmaları Literatür Dergisi 2, no. 1 (2004): 71–90.

33 For the taxation system of the Tanzimat era, see Abdüllatif Şener, *Tanzimat Dönemi Osmanlı Vergi Sistemi* (Istanbul: İşaret Yayınları, 1990); Nadir Özbek, *İmparatorluğun Bedeli: Osmanlı'da Vergi, Siyaset ve Toplumsal Adalet (1838–1908)* (Istanbul: Boğaziçi Üniversitesi Yayınları, 2015); Tevfik Güran, "19. Yüzyıl Temettüat Tahrirleri," in *Osmanlı Devleti'nde Bilgi ve İstatistik – Data and Statistics in the Ottoman Empire*, eds. Halil İnalcık and Şevket Pamuk (Ankara: T.C. Başbakanlık Devlet İstatistik Enstitüsü, 2000); Coşkun Çakır, "Tanzimat Dönemi Vergi Uygulamalarında Karşılaşılan Güçlükler ve Vergi İhtilalleri," İktisat Fakültesi Mecmuası 51, no. 1 (2001): 71–95.

local councils, which would become the locomotive for the implementation of reforms in the locality.[34] In the same vein, compulsory military service and fixed terms of service were important parts of the Tanzimat. Furthermore, the Provincial Law of 1864 (*Vilâyet Nizâmnamesi*) and ensuing regulations were important phases of provincial bureaucratization.[35] Although its effects were substantially felt in the 1870s in the region under study, the Land Code of 1858 brought about many changes, especially its contribution to the exclusive ownership of land helped to individualize the relations of the state with local groups.[36] All these developments were milestones of the nineteenth century and were important phases of the increase of the infrastructural power of the state.

The path of the Tanzimat reforms were not the same all through the empire. A variety of factors, like geopolitical condition, local networks, and economic prosperity affected the results of the same reforms.[37] Thus, provincial studies are important and necessary to understand the unique process that each province experienced as well as the encounters with local context. The provincial literature on the Anatolian and Arabian lands of the Ottoman Empire is vast.[38] Recent studies have contributed to the social, political, and economic

---

34 Jun Akiba, "The Local Councils as the Origin of Parliamentary System in the Ottoman Empire," in Development of Parliamentarism in Modern Islamic World, ed. Sata Tsugitaka (Tokyo: Toyo Bunko, 2009); Stanford J. Shaw, "Local Administrations in the Tanzimat," in 150. Yılında Tanzimat, ed. Hakkı Dursun Yıldız (Ankara: Türk Tarih Kurumu Yayınları, 1992).

35 İlber Ortaylı, *Tanzimat Devrinde Osmanlı Mahalli İdareleri (1840–1880)* (Istanbul: Türk Tarih Kurumu, 2011; repr., 2).

36 Ömer Lûtfi Barkan, "Türk Toprak Hukuku Tarihinde Tanzimat ve 1274 (1858) Tarihli Arazi Kanunnamesi," in Tanzimat I (Istanbul: Maarif Matbaası, 1940), 321–421; Roger Owen, ed. New Perspectives on Property and Land in the Middle East (Cambridge: Harvard University Press, 2000).

37 Yonca Köksal, *The Ottoman Empire in the Tanzimat Era: Provincial Perspectives from Ankara to Edirne* (Abingdon: Routledge, 2019), p. 30.

38 If I name a few: Lisa Anderson, The State and Social Transformation in Tunisia and Libya, 1830–1980 (Princeton: Princeton University Press, 1986); Ussama S. Makdisi, The Culture of Sectarianism: Community, History and Violence in Nineteenth-Century Ottoman Lebanon (Berkeley: University of California Press, 2000); Beshara Doumani, Rediscovering Palestine: Merchants and Peasants in Jabal Nablus, 1700–1900 (Berkeley: University of California Press, 1995); Khoury, State and Provincial Society in the Ottoman Empire; Rogan, Frontiers of the State; Ebubekir Ceylan, The Ottoman Origins of Modern Iraq: Political Reform, Modernization and Development in the Nineteenth-Century; Middle East (London: I.B. Tauris, 2011); Köksal, The Ottoman Empire in the Tanzimat Era; John K. Bragg, Ottoman Notables and Participatory Politics: Tanzimat Reform in Tokat, 1839–1876 (London: Routledge, 2014); Meltem Toksöz, Nomads, Migrants and Cotton in the Eastern Mediterranean: The Making of Adana Mersin Region 1850–1908 (Leiden: Brill,

history of the Ottoman East by focusing on the different regions and revealing the agencies of the Kurdish, Armenian nobility, peasantry and transhumant communities. Özok-Gündoğan, focusing on the transformation of the yurtluk-ocaklıks in Palu, claimed that Tanzimat state-making by the empire, used means other than military suppression, like "administrative reorganization" and "economic policies in land and taxation."[39] In so doing, she also criticized the representation of the Ottoman state and Kurdish notables as two antagonistic sides. Similarly, focusing on the transformation of yurtluk-ocaklık lands in the hands of Zirki Beys in Tercil, Hani, and Atak Uğur Bayraktar Uğur Bayraktar also problematizes the exclusion of Kurdish notables from the literature on Ottoman provincial notables.[40]

Challenging the positioning of the central state and notables/tribes as two opposing camps was the common point of these studies. Yaşar Tolga Cora uncovers the role and participation of the Armenian notables in Tanzimat reforms in Erzurum. He offers to look at "the ways in which the central(izing)/modern(izing) Ottoman state and Armenian notables were simultaneously constructed as a result of their continuous interaction over that period."[41] In so doing, he acknowledged the agency of Armenians and especially of Armenian notables not only during the Tanzimat period but also in previous and later periods.[42] Bringing the story of the pastoral nomadic tribes living at the intersection of the Ottoman, Russian and the Persian Empires, Yener Koç also argues that the projects and policies of the modernizing imperial powers were reshaped in the local context according to tribal responses and border politics.[43] In a similar vein, Talha Çiçek, through focusing on the tribal confedarations of Anezeh and Shammar, argues that how the modernizing Ottoman state adopted its policies in the desert to the tribal peculiarities. Thus, he

---

2010); Mahmud Yazbak, *Haifa in the Late Ottoman Period, 1864–1914* (Leiden: Brill, 1998); Maurus Reinskowski, *Düzenin Şeyleri, Tanzimat'ın Kelimeleri: 19. Yüzyıl Osmanlı Reform Politikasının Karşılaştırmalı Bir Araştırması*, (Istanbul: Yapı Kredi Yayınları, 2017).

39   Özok-Gündoğan, "The Making of the Ottoman Modern State in the Kurdish Periphery," 2, 23.
40   Uğur Bayraktar, "Yurtluk-Ocaklıks: Land, Politics of Notables and Society in Ottoman Kurdistan, 1820–1890" (PhD diss., Boğaziçi University and École des Hautes Études en Sciences Sociales, 2015), 21.
41   Yaşar Tolga Cora, "Transforming Erzurum/Karin: The Social and Economic History of a Multi-Ethnic Ottoman City in the Nineteenth Century" (PhD diss., The University of Chicago, 2016), 4.
42   Ibid., 29.
43   Yener Koç, 'Nomadic Pastoral Tribes at the Intersection of the Ottoman, Persian and Russian Empires (1820s–1890s)' (Phd. diss., Boğaziçi University, 2020), 1–2.

defines the state-tribe relations as a partnership which was based on a constant negotiation in which both parties give concessions and are conciliated.[44]

This book contributes to this recent literature by focusing on a frontier region populated by mostly Armenians and Kurds, which is outstanding given its fertile land in a mountainous zone and given that it was a transition zone between the summer and winter quarters of nomadic and seminomadic groups. Similarly, the study depicts nineteenth-century Muş by exploring administrative, fiscal, and military transformations. It emphasizes that these transformations were negotiated, contested, and shaped in the local context. Thus, geopolitical position, geography, the nature of local power-holders, and the tribal and Armenian-Kurdish demography affected not only the course but also the outcomes of the reforms of the long nineteenth century in the locality of Muş. The principal military and fiscal transformation that Ottoman Kurdistan went through was the abolition of the yurtluk-ocaklık system. The abolition of this system in Muş was based on negotiation. While local notables sought to keep their privileged position during this process, they became involved in the reforms.

It was not only the notables who became parts of centralizing and modernizing reforms of the nineteenth century in Muş's locality. A variety of actors, Kurdish, Armenian, nomadic communities played politics during this process. Kurdish and Armenian peasantry took part in the reforms through new institutions of the Tanzimat. As elaborated in Chapter 6, they made their opinions, complaints or satisfaction about their administrators, about taxation and problems regarding settlement of the tribes heard through the politics of petitioning. Central and provincial authorities took the position of the peasantry into consideration while making policies, albeit not always. Similarly, pastoral nomadic tribes who were pasturing and/or wintering in the sanjak negotiated the policies regarding their settlement, taxation and conscription. Some of these tribes were among the disputed tribes between the Ottoman and Qajar empires like the Zilan, Sıpkî and Haydaran who played politics in Muş's locality by establishing alliances with imperial and transimperial agents. Acknowledging the agency of a variety of actors in the reforms of the nineteenth century in the locality of Muş, this book hopes to contribute to the state-in-society perspective.

Focusing on a sanjak in the eastern frontier of the Ottoman Empire, this book also hopes to contribute to Tanzimat studies. All through the nineteenth century, the centralizing state sought ways to control the surplus of the region

---

44 Talha Çiçek, *Negotiating Empire in the Middle East: Ottomans and Arab Nomads in the Modern Era, 1840–1914* (Cambridge: Cambridge University Press, 2021), 8–9.

from which it hardly benefited in the previous eras. The confiscation of hereditarily enjoyed large tracts of lands was a part of this aim. While eradicating the economic-cum political power of the yurtluk-ocaklık holders, the central authorities both applied administrative and fiscal transformations and when necessary military operations. However, yurtluk-ocaklık holders had a power that stemmed not only from the large tracts of lands under their exclusive control, but also from their relations with tribal leaders, with other provincial notables as well as with state and interstate actors. In this way, governing the region was based on bargains between central authorities and provincial power-holders as well as their networks.

1.2 Historical Geography of Muş

The city of Muş[45] neighbors the districts of Patnos, Tutak (in Ağrı) and Ahlat, Adilcevaz (in Bitlis) to the east; Solhan and Karlıova (in Bingöl) to the west; Hınıs, Tekman, Karaçoban and Karayazı (in Erzurum) to the north; and Kulp (in Diyarbakır), Sason (in Batman) and Güroymak and Mutki (in Bitlis) to the south. Its surface area is 8,196 square kilometers.[46] The current districts of Muş are Bulanık, Malazgirt, Varto, Hasköy, and Korkut. In the nineteenth century, the sanjak of Muş included the districts of Bitlis and Huyut (contemporary Kavakbaşı in Mutki/Bitlis); and in some parts of the century it also included Ahlat, Sason, and Genç, in addition to Varto, Bulanık, and Malazgirt.[47] For most of the period under study, Muş was a sanjak of the province of Erzurum.

---

[45]   The etymology of the name "Muş" is controversial. In Persian, it means "mouse" or a "small ship" and in Arabic "thin, transparent and brilliant." Nevertheless, its most plausible etymology given its fertile plains is in Hebrew, meaning that "well-watered, grassland territory." Gökşen Yıldırır, Saim Erdem, and Hüseyin Erol, eds., *Muş İl Yıllığı* (Elazığ: Bingöl Matbaası, 1973), 1. It is also possible that the name of Muş derived from the name of Muşel, a ruler from the Armenian Mamikonian dynasty. Mithat Eser, "Muş Adına Dair Bir Soruşturma," in Muş *Tarihi*, ed. Murat Alanoğlu, Mustafa Alican, and Mehmet Özalper (Istanbul: İdeal Kültür Yayıncılık, 2021), 30. In Armenian, it is called Taron/Daron. As Robert Hewsen states the name of Taron refers to the plain itself, to an Armenian principality established on this plain and to a larger area including some other principalities. Robert H. Hewsen, "The Historical Geography of Baghesh/Bitlis and Taron/Mush," in *Armenian Baghesh/Bitlis and Taron/Mush*, ed. Richard G. Hovannisian (California: Mazda Publishers, 2001), 42.

[46]   Yıldırır, Erdem, and Erol, *Muş İl* 1.

[47]   See Naci Okcu and Hasan Akdağ, *Salnâme-i Vilâyet-i Erzurum* (1287/1870–1288/1871–1289/1872–1290/1873), *Erzurum İl Yıllığı* (Erzurum: Atatürk Üniversitesi Yayınları, 2010), 442.

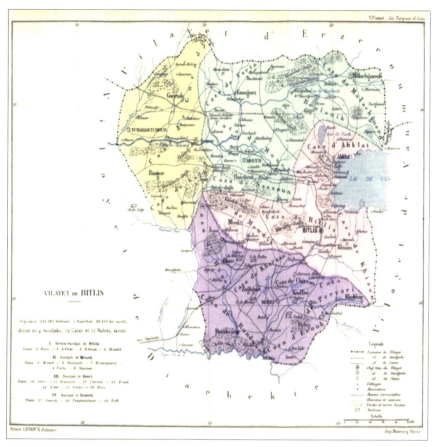

MAP 1   The map of Bitlis province, late 19th century
         SOURCE: BIBLIOTHÈQUE NATIONALE DE FRANCE (BNF)

The current city is in the Upper Murat-Van part of Eastern Anatolia, characterized as a vast plateau surrounded by depressions, among the most prominent of which is the depression of Muş.[48] The city of Muş is situated on the northern slopes of Mount Kurtik, to the south of the city, which is among the most important summits of the Haçres (Karaçavuş, Çavuş) Mountains, which spread out in the southwest as an extension of the South-East Taurus. In the

---

48   Sırrı Erinç, *Doğu Anadolu Coğrafyası* (Istanbul: Sucuoğlu Matbaası, 1953), 79.

north-west of the Muş Plain are Şerafettin Mountains. The Otluk Mountains also spread out in a northwest–southeast direction to the north of the plain.[49]

The most prominent landforms in the city of Muş are certainly plains, which led to the rise of Muş's prominence in a region dominated by several mountain ranges. The plain of Muş starts from the foothills of Nemrut Mountain in the east and extends over eighty kilometers. Its width is around thirty kilometers, and its surface is around 1650 square kilometers. The plain of Muş has the most attractive thermal conditions of the Upper-Murat region. Its thick, fertile soil led to its being known as an important agricultural area.[50] Together with the plains of Bulanık, Liz, and Malazgirt, the plain of Muş is significant in terms of agriculture and husbandry. Irrigation of the plain of Muş is facilitated by the Murat River, a branch of the Euphrates, which rises from the Aladağ Mountains to the north of the city of Van and runs around 600 kilometers. Through its journey, the Murat River unites with many small streams, but the most important one is its branch, the Karasu River (Black Water), which, rising from Güroymak (in Bitlis) and entering the city from the south, flows for 68 kilometers.

Travelers, consuls, and missionaries who passed through the region throughout the nineteenth century describe the plain of Muş as fertile which made possibile the cultivation of a range of products, especially good quality wheat and barley.[51] In addition, rye, millet, lentils, and chickpeas were among the products cultivated. For everyday life, peasants were consuming rye and particularly millet – most probably because of poverty –, which did not require much cultivation as well as barley for feeding a variety of livestock of the region.[52] Nevertheless, the plain included some stony and arid parts. Moreover, its climate was not as severe as that of Erzurum; despite having the same amount of snowfall, it was not as cold.[53] The winters lasted five months[54] and the summers were warm, "sultry,"[55] and healthy.[56] The town did not lack any kind of fruit or vegetable. The entrance of city was densely cultivated, as

---

49 Yıldırır, Erdem, and Erol, *Muş İl* 12.
50 Erinç, *Doğu Anadolu,* 86–88.
51 Ibid., 86.
52 Vital Cuinet, *La Turquie d'Asie: Géographie Administrative: statisque, descriptive et raisonnée de chaque province de l'Asie Mineure*, 4 vols., vol. 2 (Paris: E. Leroux, 1891), 577–79.
53 James Brant, "Notes of a Journey through a part of Kurdistan, in the Summer of 1838," The Journal of the Royal Geographic x (1841): 352.
54 Horatio Southgate, "Narrative of a Tour through Armenia, Kurdistan, Persia and Mesopotamia: With an Introduction, and Occasional Observations upon the Condition of Mohammedanism and Christianity in those Countries," vol. 1 (New York: D. Appleton, 1840), 207.
55 Brant, "Notes of a Journey," 352.
56 Cuinet, La Turquie d'Asie, 2, 575.

observed from various vegetable gardens and vineyards.[57] The variety of fruits, pears, apples, cherries, and melons were abundant. In the vineyards on the hillsides, grapes were grown with which non-Muslims made wine.[58] In the mountains surrounding the town, there were oak forests with various kinds of oak like the ones producing gall nut and manna.[59]

As to the scale of products grown, empirical data on commercial activities in Muş is scarce for the first half of the century. Nonetheless, based on traveler accounts, consular reports, especially those on trade in Erzurum, and Ottoman archival documents, it is possible to draw a picture. Moreover, as the archival research conducted for this study demonstrates, the sanjak of Muş was a major grain store for the imperial troops deployed in the eastern front during the wars with Russia. Towards the end of the nineteenth century, Vital Cuinet emphasized that the plain of Muş and the district of Bulanık were the main places where wheat and barley were cultivated.[60] In addition to grain, tobacco was also stated to be the principal product suitable for export to Europe.[61] On the banks of the Karasu, a large amount of tobacco was cultivated and some of the produce was even taken to market in Istanbul.[62]

The landscape of the sanjak of Muş was also suitable for animal husbandry. It was an important economic and commercial activity in the region. The peasantry was also engaged in animal husbandry, but Kurdish tribes had the predominant role in this kind of economic activity – sheep and goat farming. Consul Brant mentions that traders bought sheep in Muş and brought them to Syria or Constantinople.[63] In the same vein, tribes coming from Diyarbekir to the summer pastures in the mountains to the south of the town of Muş also brought dairy products and wood to the local market for barter and profit.[64]

When it comes to trade, the American missionary Horatio Southgate reports that there were five hundred horses (for pulling caravans) in the town of Muş, used mainly for trade originating elsewhere.[65] Trade in the town was generally with Erzurum, Bitlis and Diyarbekir – that is to say, it was mainly regional.

57   Southgate, "Narrative of a Tour through Armenia, Kurdistan, Persia and Mesopotamia," 1, 202.
58   Ibid., 207; Brant, "Notes of a Journey," 352.
59   "Notes of a Journey," 352.
60   Cuinet, *La Turquie d'Asie*, 2, 536.
61   Brant, "Notes of a Journey," 352.
62   Richard Willbraham, "Travels in the Trans-Caucasian Provinces of Russia and Along the Southern Shores o the Lakes of Van and Urumiah in the Autumn and Winter of 1837" (London: J. Murray, 1839), 332.
63   Brant, "Notes of a Journey," 352.
64   Southgate, "Narrative of a Tour through Armenia, Kurdistan, Persia and Mesopotamia," 1, 205.
65   Ibid., 206.

However, it was possible to observe that there was a transit trade via Erzurum. British Consul Dalyell reports that the neighboring districts of Erzurum also had a share of the exports and imports of the province. For instance, grain, sheep and cattle were generally provided from Kars, Van, and the southern districts of the province. Accordingly, there were regular caravans from Erzurum to Erzincan, Kars, Muş, Bitlis, Van, Harput, and Diyarbakır.[66] Similarly, Cuinet notes that the cultivation of wheat and barley on the plains of Muş and Bulanık normally exceeded the needs of the region. Nevertheless, due to lack of transportation facilities, the surpluses of the villagers sometimes rotted while in storage.[67] In the same vein, the time to get from the city of Muş to the city of Erzurum was about thirty-six hours,[68] so it is possible to imagine the transportation difficulties between those cities. Although Ottoman governments implemented various methods for the building of the road between Trabzon and Erzurum, it was an "inconclusive process," some parts of it remained unrepaired even after the fall of the Ottoman Empire.[69]

Armenian and Kurdish peasants consisted the majority of the settled population of Muş throughout the nineteenth century. The whole sanjak had approximately four hundred villages. Armenians were the majority in the plain villages, yet beyond the plain, both Kurdish and Armenian peasants lived either in separate or in common villages. Brant also notes that excluding tent-dwelling Kurdish tribes, Armenian peasants exceeded Kurdish ones in number.[70] The plain of Muş consisted of at least a hundred villages, mostly Armenian villages,[71] which were approximately "a day's ride" from the town of Muş.[72] Those plain villages also sheltered a great many Kurdish tribal families during the winters. In 1840, Southgate argues that even though the plain had a

---

66 FO 78/1669, No: 9, Consul Robert Dalyell, "Report on Eyalet of Erzurum," February 28, 1862.
67 Cuinet, *La Turquie d'Asie*, 2, 536.
68 *Salnâme-i Vilâyet-i Erzurum*, 1290(1873), 136.
69 Fulya Özkan, "A Road in Rebellion, A History on the Move: The Social History of the Trabzon-Bayezid Road and the Formation of the Modern State in the Late Ottoman World" (PhD diss., State University of New York, 2012), 174.
70 Brant, "Notes of a Journey," 351.
71 According to the report of General Mayevsky, more than half of the villages in the plain of Muş were Armenian. *Bayram Bayraktar, 20. Yüzyılın Dönemecinde Rus General Mayevsky'nin Türkiye Gözlemleri: Van-Bitlis Vilâyetleri Askerî İstatistiği (Istanbul: İnkılâp Kitabevi, 2007)*, 83. Vladimir Mayevsky was a Russian general who had also been Russian consul in Van and Bitlis. His reports on these two provinces were translated into the Ottoman Turkish by a Turkish major from the military intelligence service. Ibid., 8. Mayevsky's reports include great details about the demographic, geopolitic, and socioeconomic peculiarities of these two regions in the Ottoman East.
72 Southgate, "Narrative of a Tour through Armenia, Kurdistan, Persia and Mesopotamia," 1, 209.

considerable population, it had the capacity to sustain a much larger population. Large plots of land were still uncultivated, some parts of it were marshes. Starting from the late nineteenth century, the government tried to improve the irrigation system in the Muş plain.[73] Less productive parts of the plain could also be used as pastureland for the herds which were already scattered all over the plain.[74]

In the first half of the century, the population of the town, according to Consul Brant, consisted of 700 Muslim families and 500 Armenian ones, and the latter were claimed to be the wealthier part of the population.[75] However, from the 1840s to the 1860s, one of the main issues for the Armenian peasants of Muş was the decrease in their population. Peasants had to migrate, especially to Russia, for a set of reasons like over taxation, forced labor, and indebtedness. Chapter 6 of this book will discuss this vital problem through an analysis of consular reports and the collective petitions of the Muslim and non-Muslim peasants of Muş.

1.3 About the Sources

Several groups of sources have been examined for this study. The most important research has been carried out in the Ottoman Archives in Istanbul. The main collections utilized in this study were *Hatt-ı Hümâyûn* (imperial orders), *Meclis-i Vâlâ* (the Supreme Council), *Sadaret* (the Grand Vizirate) and *İrade* (Imperial Order). The Hatt-i Hümâyûn collection is important for the narrative of the pre-Tanzimat era, as most of the documents are from the eras of Selim III and Mahmut II. Accordingly, chapters 2 and 3, which explore the context of the power relations of the notables of Muş in the pre-Tanzimat era, are based on this collection. The documents collected in İradeler serve the same purpose for the period after 1832, offering insight into the process of the discussion of a matter among various administrative bodies and the final opinion of the sultan. Both the documents and books (*defter*) in the collection of Meclis-i Vâlâ, named after the most significant institution of the Tanzimat, are valuable for ascertaining the implementation of the new reform package and the reaction to and reception of it in the sanjak of Muş and its vicinity. In addition,

---

73   BOA. DH.MKT 1491/112, 22 Cemaziyelahir 1305 (6 March 1888).
74   Ibid., 209–10.
75   Brant, "Notes of a Journey." At the beginning of the twentieth century, the population of the town was not less than 20 thousand according to Lynch. H.F.B. Lynch, *Armenia, Travels and Studies*, vol. 2 (London: Longmans, 1901), 172.

Meclis-i Vâlâ also includes the collected petitions written by both notables and inhabitants of Muş. For the period after the abolition of the Supreme Council, the collection of Şûrâ-yı Devlet (Council of State) serves the same purpose.

Using petitions was a significant part of this study. Besides a good bunch of petitions by the notables, governors, and bureaucrats, the ones by the commoners of Muş contributed substantially to this book. Muslim and Armenian peasants of Muş filed common petitions to make preferences about their rulers, to be heard about their socio-economic problems like taxation and immigration. Despite its limits like to be forged by the local council members, these petitions, as examined in Chapter 6, were distinguished sources to grasp the agency and discursive strategies of the peasantry of Muş.

In addition to Ottoman archival documents, this book is based on research in the National Archives of the United Kingdom in London. The Foreign Office collections include reports of the consulates of the British Empire established around the Ottoman Empire. The reports of the Consulate of Erzurum are detailed for a depiction of the geography, population, economy, commerce, and politics of the province in general and the sanjak of Muş in particular. Limited research was also carried out in the Archive Diplomatiques du Ministère des Affaires Étrangères in Paris. In a manner similar to the British consular reports, the reports of French Consulates in Erzurum and Trabzon provide detailed information about the province which is being examined.

Apart from Ottoman, British, and French archival documents, this study also significantly benefits from accounts by British, American, and French travelers and missionaries and the reports of the Ottoman bureaucrats, which are important materials for a depiction of the historical geography, population and socioeconomic situation of the sanjak of Muş. Lastly, although it is impossible to conduct a fieldwork for a study of the nineteenth century, a journey through the region under study to observe the vastness of the plain of Muş helped me to imagine the struggle over its resources almost a century and a half ago. Moreover, I carried out several interviews in Muş with the descendants of the notables of Muş. Those with the grandchildren of Murat Bey, conducted in Istanbul and Muş, were especially helpful in providing details about the Alaaddin Pashazades.

1.4 Structure of the Book

Together with this introduction and conclusion, this book consists of nine chapters. The book examines different historical moments from the pre-Tanzimat and Tanzimat eras and their aftermath in the plain of Muş. The chapters are structured accordingly. Chapters 2 and 3, explore the nature, components, and transformation of the power and influence that the local dynasty of Muş enjoyed from the 1750s to the 1830s. Based on the general literature on provincial notables of the Ottoman Empire, chapter 2 discusses the nature of land usufruct called yurtluk-ocaklık, together with the related economic, social and political rights, possessed by the notables of Muş. The local dynasty known as Alaaddin Pashazades had exclusive right over agricultural surplus and great political power over nomadic and seminomadic groups. However, the nineteenth century witnessed the gradual abrogation of this kind of land ownership along with the immunities and rights it entailed. The story of Emin Pasha, from the Muş dynasty, exemplifies this process. The reforms of Mahmut II were curtailing the power of provincial notables around the empire. Kurdish notables were not exempt from this, however, geographical, demographic, and political differences led to different experiences. Focusing on the career of Emin Pasha of Muş, the rise of a provincial notable through collaboration, negotiation, and adaptation to the changing conjuncture will be analyzed.

Nevertheless, collaboration and negotiation did not imply lack of contention. Emin Pasha rebelled against provincial authorities by leaning on the collaboration of notables in the vicinity when his negotiation efforts became deadlocked. Accordingly, chapter 3 inquires into the revolt of Emin Pasha in 1833; the motivations, reasons, and the components of his allies and the league constituted against him. An analysis of the rebellion of a notable in a peripheral zone reveals certain important facts about the power of the yurtluk-ocaklık holders, the influence of the tribal population, and the clash of interests between the yurtluk-ocaklık holders and provincial governors. Second, the chapter will focus on the first phase of the abolition of the yurtluk-ocaklık lands of the notables of Muş through novel military and administrative reforms, contributing to the argument that the abrogation of such types of land ownership was a gradual process. The second phase of this process took place with the inclusion of the sanjak of Muş in the Tanzimat program.

The remaining chapters examine the account and aftermath of the Tanzimat reforms with different thematic focuses. Chapter 4 starts with a depiction of Muş on the eve of the inclusion of the sanjak in the Tanzimat program in 1845. Shedding light on local actors, the chapter presents the overtaxation, corvée, and indebtedness that the peasants of Muş endured under an exploitative system of tax-farmers, local administrators, and governors. Because of this, the inhabitants of Muş received the news of the promulgation of the Tanzimat with anxiety mixed with fear as they regarded it as a new kind of taxation. However, the geographical delicacy and tribal social structure of the province of Erzurum resulted in population and income surveys – which were the principal steps in the implementation of Tanzimat reforms – being postponed. In the town of Van, reaction to Tanzimat reforms started, creating anxiety about the possible emergence of a revolt around the Kurdish periphery. Thus, the chapter continues with an account of the employment of the notables of Muş in order to inspect the gradual implementation of reforms and mediate the Bedirhan Bey Revolt which was affecting the region from Cizre-Bohtan to Van, as well. Nevertheless, after the suppression of the Bedirhan Bey Revolt in the summer of 1847, the most senior among the notables of Muş were exiled and their lands were confiscated. This account of the notables of Muş indicates that there was also a progressive subordination of Kurdish notables.

Since the beginning of the nineteenth century, some Ottoman bureaucrats had been drawing attention to the surplus in eastern provinces from which the imperial treasury never benefited. Thus, the subordination of Kurdish notables through the elimination of their economic and political power and through governance of the region by centrally-appointed officials was supported by various central and provincial authorities, and considered to be essential for proper administrative and fiscal transformation to take place. Thus, chapters 5 and 6 focus on the aftermath of the second phase of the annulment of the yurtluk-ocaklık system in Muş. Chapter 5 is an inquiry into the fate of the yurtluk-ocaklık villages of Emin Pasha and his brothers. The many peculiarities of the yurtluk-ocaklık system in Muş were uncovered during the process of confiscating the villages. From the moment the yurtluk-ocaklık lands of the family were confiscated, struggles over its boundaries, revenues, and over the landed properties of the family – like vineyards, orchards, mills, and mansions – started and lasted for a long time. The chapter will also explore the struggle of the family members to obtain imperial pardon, and their taking advantage of each opportunity to reclaim their rights and properties.

Chapter 6 examines the reflections of the implementation of Tanzimat reforms in the petitions of the local inhabitants of Muş. By analyzing the complaints of the common people, the chapter will shed light on the ways that administrative and fiscal reforms shaped, affected, and transformed the politics, demography and socioeconomic situation of the sanjak with respect to its centrally-appointed *kaimakams* (administrator of a sanjak), local councils, and new tax regime. The grievances of the commoners of Muş can be grouped into two categories; on the one hand, petitions against the system of exploitation that included a coalition comprising kaimakams, local council members, tax farmers, usurers (*murabahacı*), moneylenders, and Armenian notables; and on the other hand, tribal members, who constitute the focus of chapters 7 and 8. As most of the complaints were from the plain villages, they present important clues not only about the aftermath of the annulment of yurtluk-ocaklık villages, but also about the dispossession of Armenian peasants through a system of extortion, over taxation, forced labor, and indebtedness. Then the chapter will scrutinize the conjuncture that started with the Crimean War and continued with the *Islahat Fermanı* (Reform Edict) and settlement of immigrants. The complaints of the peasantry regarding overtaxation and corvée increased during the war conditions and the Armenian peasantry especially left their villages. The immigrants were thought to populate the region vis-à-vis the decrease in the Armenian population.

Chapter 7 and 8 examine one of the most important demographic components of the locality of Muş and its vicinity: the tribes. Although nomadic and seminomadic groups constitute an inherent part of this book, these two chapters deal with the seminomadic tribes of Muş and nomadic tribes in its vicinity whose pasturelands were in the mountains lying to the south of the sanjak. The settlement of nomadic and seminomadic groups was among the main tenets of Tanzimat reforms. Thus, the process of settling the tribes of Muş and its vicinity as well as their relations with governors and peasants will be discussed. Similarly, Chapter 7 will provide important details about the tribal economy, and the agency of tribal members. Chapter 7 underscores the emergence of the *hafırlik* system (taxes and services that settled populations provided to tribes in return for protection), which contributed to the aggravated relations between Kurdish tribes and Armenian peasants towards the end of the century. Chapter 8 provides a case study of one of the most important tribes of Muş, the Hesenan.

CHAPTER 2

Emin Pasha of Muş: A Negotiation of Power in the Periphery of the Ottoman Empire

the Serai (palace), situated at a village called Mogiyunk [Mongok], rather more than a mile eastward of the town. It was a large quadrangular building with an irregular tower at each corner, in the same style as the old residence of former Pashas near our camp. This new Serai was built by Emin Pasha, a short time since, and Khurshid Beg had a residence close by not yet finished. I was ushered into an elevated Kiosk (Koshk), over one of the corner towers, which was entered by crossing the terrace of the palace: The view from it was extensive, and its height made it accessible to every air that stirred, and very cool and pleasant.[1]

Consul James Brant thus described the palace of Emin Pasha, the eldest of four brothers of the Muş dynasty, during his visit in 1838. Emin Pasha, the mutasarrıf of Muş, felt the necessity to build a new palace instead of living in the ruined one of the former pashas of Muş in Mongok [Soğucak], a village that was green, breezy, and famous for its vineyards and that was close to the center of the city of Muş. The need to build a new and spectacular residence was to epitomize Emin Pasha's power, which he had been trying not only to maintain but also consolidate throughout the 1830s.[2] Together with his other brothers, Şerif Bey of Bitlis, Murat Bey of Hınıs, and the youngest Hurşid Bey, Emin Pasha enjoyed remarkable influence in Muş, which was rooted in their lineage, monopoly on the agricultural surplus of the region, and ability to bargain for power at every turning point.

Emin Pasha was from a local dynasty of Muş known as the Alaaddin Pashazades. John Bragg makes a distinction between "dynastic" and "non-dynastic" notables, the former "had gained notoriety over generations by acting in concert to run the affairs of the town," and "developed their bases of wealth and power by taking up local military, religious and tax collection posts" and worked "as intermediaries between state officials, local institutions

---

1 Brant, "Notes of a Journey," 350.
2 Michael Meeker establishes a correlation between mansions of local notables and those of state officials, where the governmental functions were performed. Meeker, *A Nation of Empire*, 194.

and sub-groups."[3] Similarly, Margaret Meriwether argues that "the consistent use of these family names over several generations in official sources is clear evidence that the families were identifying themselves as members of the social notability and that the wider society recognized their 'claim.'"[4] In that sense, Alaaddin Pasha was a provincial notable (*â'yân*)[5] who enjoyed the heyday of his power during the second half of the eighteenth century in an era that would later be called the "age of the â'yâns."[6] *Â'yânlık*, or â'yânship, has been the focus of a variety of studies given its socioeconomic, political, and institutional attributes.[7] However, a regional inattention, if not necessarily a bias, has prevailed in the literature with respect to the provincial notables in that they exclusively deal with those of the Balkans and Anatolia, and not the other parts of the empire, especially Kurdistan.[8]

The socioeconomic transformation that the Ottoman Empire went through, especially the wars with the Habsburgs and Safavid Iran from the sixteenth to the eighteenth centuries was the main force that triggered the emergence and

---

3   Bragg, *Ottoman Notables and Participatory Politics*, 13. Similarly, Uğur Bayraktar also states that "dynasticisation" by attachment of the suffix "-zades," meaning literally "son," also points to the Ottoman government's acknowledgement of provincial notables. Bayraktar, "Yurtluk-Ocaklıks," 24.

4   Margaret L. Meriwether, *The Kin Who Count: Family and Society in Ottoman Aleppo, 1770–1840* (Austin: University of Texas Press, 1999), 35.

5   The term âyân had been used for influential people in cities, towns, villages, and several layers of the state and army since the early years of the Ottoman Empire and these people were called mostly as "âyân-ı vilâyet," "âyân ve eşraf," "âyân ve vücuh." Yücel Özkaya, *Osmanlı İmparatorluğu'nda Âyânlık* (Ankara: Türk Tarih Kurumu, 1994), ix.

6   Bruce Mcgowan, "The Age of Ayans, 1699–1812," in *An Economic and Social History of the Ottoman Empire, 1600–1914*, eds. Halil İnalcık and Donald Quataert (Cambridge: Cambridge University Press, 1997). "An Ottoman official of that time," as Suraiya Faroqhi suggests, "did not view the Empire as divided into a stable set of regions, distinguished by the services they rendered to the central government. Rather, the Ottoman lands must have appeared as a congeries of domains controlled by different local power holders." Suraiya Faroqhi, "Coping with the Central State, Coping with Local Power: Ottoman Regions and Notables from the Sixteenth to the Early Nineteenth Century," in *The Ottomans and the Balkans: A Discussion of Historiography*, ed. Fikret Adanır and Suraiya Faroqhi (Leiden: Brill, 2002), 366.

7   Özkaya, Osmanlı İmparatorluğu'nda; Ali Yaycıoğlu, *Partners of the Empire: The Crisis of the Ottoman Order in the Age of Revolutions* (Stanford: Stanford University Press, 2016); Yuzo Nagata, Muhsin-zâde Mehmed Paşa ve Âyânlık Müessesesi (Tokyo: Institute for the Study of Languages and Cultures of Asia and Africa, 1982).

8   In a study, Uğur Bayraktar challenges this prevalence and emphasizes the "commensurability" of the provincial notables of the Balkans and Anatolia with the emirs of Ottoman Kurdistan. Bayraktar, "Yurtluk-Ocaklıks," 1. Bayraktar further notes that the absence of the yurtluk-ocaklık and hükûmet holders in the literature on Ottoman provincial notables is the result of the decentralization paradigm that links the rise of ayans to the decline of the Ottoman Empire. Ibid., 19.

rise of the â'yâns. The *tımar* (fief) system,[9] "the backbone of both the military and fiscal structure of the Ottoman state" since the early fourteenth century, proved insufficient to subsidize the "new modes of warfare" by the mid-sixteenth century.[10] In the same vein, the military constituent of the tımar system, the *sipahi* (cavalrymen), could no longer compete either with firearms or infantry armies.[11] The outdatedness of the cavalry and the urgency of establishing an infantry in turn led Ottoman governments to expand the janissary units and the use of mercenaries.[12] The need for tax revenues to meet the expense of paying for soldiers together with the devaluation of the *akçe* (coin) at the end of the sixteenth century required a change to the tax-collecting system, and the replacement, the tax farming system quickly spread.[13] Both the expansion of the tax farming system and *mâlikâne* (life-long tax-farms), which was applied after 1695, led to the rise of provincial notables.[14] Mâlikâne-*mukatâ'as* (mukatâ'as were revenue units of the Treasury) under the exclusive authority of provincial notables constituted the bases of their material power together with *çiftlik* (large farms) type land ownership.[15]

9   In this system taxes were collected by sipahis (cavalries) to whom the tımars were assigned in the provinces. "Tımar-holding sipahis" constituted the main body of the Ottoman army during the classical period. Halil İnalcık, "Military and Fiscal Transformation in the Ottoman Empire, 1600–1700," Archivicum Ottomanicum VI (1980): 311.

10 Zens, "The Ayanlık and Pasvanoğlu Osman Paşa of Vidin," 14–15. Yücel Özkaya also notes that in the seventeenth and eighteenth centuries, fiefs were granted to everyone regardless of their capability. When fiefs were granted by the local authorities like *kadı* or *naib*, provincial notables and officials took them to profit from them. Özkaya, Osmanlı İmparatorluğu'nda, 94.

11 İnalcık, "Military and Fiscal Transformation," 288; Zens, "The Ayanlık and Pasvanoğlu Osman Paşa of Vidin," 18.

12 İnalcık, "Military and Fiscal Transformation," 288–92; Musa Çadırcı, "II Mahmut Döneminde Mütesellimlik Kurumu," DTCF Dergisi XXVIII, no. 3–4 (1970): 287. Furthermore, protracted wars of the eighteenth century and the assignment of multiple posts to the same official led to the expansion of *mütesellimlik*. Yücel Özkaya, "XVIII. Yüzyılda Mütesellimlik Müessesesi," Ibid.: 371. Ali Yaycıoğlu, in the same line, asserts "three major institutional transformations" in the Ottoman provinces, namely "localization, privatization and communalization of authority." Those three transformations provided a favorable environment for the participation of local actors in provincial administration. Besides, all were closely related to the "consolidation of three major offices": deputy-governorship, intendantship, and ayanship. Yaycıoğlu, "The Provincial Challange," 189.

13 İnalcık, "Military and Fiscal Transformation," 312–13.

14 For mâlikâne, Mehmet Genç, *Osmanlı İmparatorluğu'nda Devlet ve Ekonomi* (Istanbul: Ötüken, 2000); Erol Özvar, Osmanlı Maliyesinde Mâlikane Uygulaması (Istanbul: Kitabevi, 2003); Ariel Salzmann, "An Ancien Régime Revisited: Privatization and Political Economy in the Eighteenth-Century Ottoman Empire," Politics & Society 21, no. 4 (1993).

15 For a discussion of çiftliks, Halil İnalcık, "The Emergence of Big Farms, Çiftliks: State, Landlords, and Tenants," in *Landholding and Commercial Agriculture in the Middle East*,

Similarly, from the seventeenth century onward given not only the obsolescence of the fief system but also the increasing number of high-ranking officials, many sanjaks were assigned as *arpalık* (allowance) to high officials who had not necessarily ever set foot there. In those cases, the governor appointed a *mütesellim* (deputy) to administrate in their place. As those mütesellims were among "the men on the spot," the â'yân, the prominence of the latter increased.[16] By the eighteenth century, the most prominent â'yân families in Anatolia, from the Karaosmanoğulları of Manisa to the Nakkaşzadeler and Müderriszadeler of Ankara, consolidated and maintained their power and strength through *mütesellimlik*. Overcoming their rivals in the struggle over the mütesellimlik, many â'yân families managed to "hold it on a hereditary basis."[17]

The story of the local dynasty of Muş resembles that of the provincial notables in the rest of the Ottoman Empire. As Hacı Mustafa Agha of the Karaosmanoğulları family was increasing his power by holding the mütesellimlik of Saruhan in the 1740s, Alaaddin Pasha, as will be discussed in the following pages, was also consolidating his power by enjoying the position of the mütesellimlik of Muş.[18] His grandson Selim Pasha was a contemporary of Tepedelenli Ali Pasha. Kurdish begs, like contemporaneous provincial notables, increased and consolidated their power through exploiting the circumstances created by the empire's wars with Russia and Iran, holding tax-collection rights and mâlikâne-mukâta'as, and being mütesellims and mutasarrıfs.

The similarities should not lead to underestimation of the divergences. Two important and intrinsic points about the provincial notables of Rumelia and Anatolia were the issues of the institutions of "âyânship" and confiscation (*müsadere*). Many seminal studies deal with â'yânlık as an institution that emerged in the middle of the eighteenth century. As an institution â'yânlık implies an election process by the local inhabitants.[19] Despite the complexities

---

    ed. Çağlar Keyder and Faruk Tabak (Albany: State University of New York Press, 1991); Gilles Veinstein, "On the Çiftlik Debate," Ibid. See especially chapters 2 and 5 in Bruce McGowan, *Economic Life in Ottoman Europe: Taxation, Trade, and Struggle for Land, 1600–1800* (Cambridge: Cambridge University Press, 1981).

16   Faroqhi, "Coping with the Central State, Coping with Local Power," 351.

17   Halil İnalcık, "Centralization and Decentralization in Ottoman Administration," in Studies in *Eighteenth Century Islamic History, Papers on Islamic History* ed. Thomas Naff and Roger Owen (Carbondale: Southern Illinois University Press, 1977), 32–33.

18   For a study of Karaosmanoğulları, see Yuzo Nagata, *Tarihte Âyânlar: Karaosmanoğulları Üzerine Bir İnceleme* (Ankara: Türk Tarih Kurumu, 1997).

19   Studies by Nagata, Özkaya, and Yaycıoğlu were the leading ones. Nagata, *Muhsin-zâde Mehmed Paşa*; Özkaya, *Osmanlı İmparatorluğu'nda*. Especially Yaycıoğlu differentiates between ayanhood and ayanship, the former of which refers to "natural leadership" and

of the institutional aspects of â'yânlık for Anatolia and Rumelia â'yâns, I have not come across any indication of an electoral process for the Kurdish begs of Muş. This is because of the fact that the Kurdish nobility had been powerful enough before the Ottoman system had incorporated them. This was also the case for the confiscation system – the confiscation by the central treasury of the property of discharged or deceased officials. The central government applied the confiscation system as a means of control over officials. However, the properties of Kurdish notables were not confiscated.[20] Nevertheless, new yurtluk-ocaklık holders were required to pay the *muhallefât* (payment for assets and estates of a late official). It is possible that this stems from the peculiarities of the districts and sanjaks under the rule of Kurdish begs as yurtluk-ocaklıks and hükûmets.

The political and economic power of Emin Pasha's lineage, the Alaaddin Pashazades, stemmed from the large tract of land under their control. Emin Pasha's ancestors were holders of yurtluk-ocaklık, which, together with its counterpart, hükûmets, is an imperial system of delegating power to notables or chieftains on the frontiers by granting not only land but also fiscal, administrative, and judicial privileges and immunities. Nevertheless, the characteristics of yurtluk-ocaklık lands were different from sanjak to sanjak and in different periods.[21] As Nilay Özok-Gündoğan argues, the vantage point of most studies of yurtluk-ocaklık and hükûmet types of land are their range of autonomy and they barely examine how the rights over those lands were actually practiced.[22] Emin Pasha's story in the first quarter of the nineteenth century – which I will

---

the latter of which to the "office of overseers." Yaycıoğlu, "The Provincial Challenge," 145–151.

20   Yet, cases of execution were not absent. For instance, a former mutasarrıf of Muş and cousin of Emin Pasha, Selim Pasha, was executed in 1827, yet no traces have been found regarding the confiscation of his property. BOA. HAT. 892/39382, 25 Safer 1243 (17 September 1827). Further research and comparative studies of Kurdish notables would be necessary to make certain claims about the availability of the confiscation system to yurtluk-ocaklık and hükûmet holders. Nevertheless, available sources point out that lands and properties of notables in Muş were not confiscated until the abolishment of the yurtluk-ocaklık system altogether. Similarly, Yaycıoğlu annotates that except remote areas like Crimea, Caucasus, Kurdistan, Bosnia and Hecaz, the provincial notables did not hold their offices or contracts as "hereditary rights," as their properties could be confiscated and even their lives were put to an end. *Partners of the Empire: The Crisis of the Ottoman Order in the Age of Revolutions* (Stanford: Stanford University Press, 2016), 67.

21   Orhan Kılıç, "Ocaklık Sancakların Osmanlı Hukukunda ve İdari Tatbikattaki Yeri," Fırat Üniversitesi Sosyal Bilimler Dergisi 11, no. 1 (2001).

22   Özok-Gündoğan, "The Making of the Ottoman Modern State in the Kurdish Periphery," 166.

focus on throughout this and following chapters – was also a story of his keeping inherited yurtluk-ocaklık lands intact. Therefore, his story contributed to the functioning of yurtluk-ocaklık lands particularity in Muş in the nineteenth century during the course of their gradual liquidation.

Similarly, as it sheds light on a periphery of the Ottoman Empire and on the capacity of its elites to negotiate on the eve of the Tanzimat reforms, an account of Emin Pasha also serves as an introduction to the reforms that were implemented during the Tanzimat era. Therefore, the starting point of Huri İslamoğlu is significant for the present chapter. She refutes arguments that the Ottoman state of the nineteenth century excluded any kind of negotiation in contrast with that of the early modern era. Rather she offers "to distinguish the historical context in which negotiation took place."[23] In the same vein, this chapter will focus on center-periphery relations, not by regarding them as binary oppositions, but rather by looking at the coalitions and bargaining for power between them.[24]

The source of Emin Pasha's strength also stemmed from his ability to adapt to the transformations that the Ottoman Empire was going through during the first quarter of the nineteenth century. While central authorities sought to break the power of the notables in the vicinity of Muş, Emin Pasha used a set of strategies to turn them to his own advantage. The turning points of this era by which Emin Pasha increased his power were the wars with Russia, tribal and frontier issues with Iran, and later, the threat of Mehmet Ali Pasha of Egypt. Emin Pasha manipulated each of these three matters as well as some regional circumstances (e.g., the revolt of Timur Pasha of Van) to consolidate his power during the first half of the nineteenth century. After elaborating the discussion of yurtluk-ocaklık types of land and historicizing the family of Emin Pasha, the following pages will discuss the rise of Emin Pasha in the 1830s.

2.1 Notables of Muş and the Nature of Their Political and Economic Power

The administrative and political status of Muş had changed from the sixteenth to the nineteenth century. Although the history of Alaaddin Pasha's ancestors before the eighteenth century was not clear, they were from Bilbasi clan of the

---

23 Huri İslamoğlu and Peter C. Perdue, "Introduction," Journal of Early Modern History 5, no. 4 (2001): 278.
24 Jongerden and Verheij, "Introduction," 3.

Rojki tribe.[25] Moreover, based on the individual petitions of family members and the fact that Alaaddin Bey was the steward of khans of Bitlis in the early eighteenth century and was appointed as mütesellim of Muş by the Burhan Han of Bitlis, it is obvious that they enjoyed some privilege under the influence of the hükûmet of Bitlis, as the sanjak of Muş was generally part of Bitlis in the early eighteenth century.[26] Since the middle of the eighteenth century, Alaaddin Pasha's sons and grandsons held the mutasarrıflık of sanjak of Muş as yurtluk-ocaklık. Nevertheless, the sanjak also included tımars and mâlikânes, and family members expanded the range of their economic autonomy by taking several mukâta'as, such as Hınıs, Tekman, and Malazgirt.[27] To better comprehend this what follows will introduce a discussion of the yurtluk-ocaklık system in general, and of Muş's status in particular.

2.1.1 The Yurtluk-Ocaklık System

Yurtluk-ocaklık and hükûmet types of land were granted to notables of newly conquered, geographically remote and, politically delicate places. Such grants mainly targeted the loyalty and collaboration of local power holders. Therefore, Kılıç states, this type of land was seen in Bosna, Anatolia, Diyarbekir, Van, Kars, Çıldır, Rakka, Damascus, and Baghdad, but it was much more common in Van and Diyarbekir due to the Ottoman-Iranian wars starting in 1578.[28] The encounter of the Ottoman Empire with Safavids in the east and Habsburgs in the northwest shaped its "administrative strategies" on both frontiers.[29] Yurtluk-ocaklık and hükûmet types of land were an integral part of this administrative strategy. Nevertheless, as Ágoston asserts, one must be cautious about referring to "lands grants" in the legal texts of the sixteenth and seventeenth centuries. They were, in fact, recognition of the rights of pre-Ottoman rulers

---

25 Interview with Tayyip Yıldırım, from the lineage of Alaaddin Bey, 19 July 2014, Istanbul.
26 BOA. C. DH. 270/13478, 13 Cemâziyelahir 1160 (22 June 1747).
27 The assignment of tımars and zeamets was implemented under the influence of yurtluk-ocaklık holders, and so, their relatives and supporters were generally assigned these appanages. Mehmet Ali Ünal, "XVI. Yüzyılda Palu Hükümeti," On Dokuz Mayıs Üniversitesi Eğitim Fakültesi Dergisi, no. 7 (1992): 1072; Ömer Toraman, "Tanzimat'ın Yurtluk-Ocaklık ve Hükümet Sancaklarda Uygulanması (1839–1864)" (PhD diss., Fırat Üniversitesi, 2010), 9.
28 Orhan Kılıç, "Yurtluk-Ocaklık ve Hükümet Sancaklar Üzerine Bazı Tespitler," OTAM, no. 10 (1999): 124. For this analysis, Kılıç makes use of two lists of sancâks, the one from Kanunname-i Sultan Süleyman and the other from Sancâk Tevcih Defteri dates to 1631–1632.
29 Gábor Ágoston, "A Flexible Empire: Authority and its Limits on the Ottoman Frontiers," in Ottoman Borderlands: Issues, Personalities and Political Change, eds. Kemal H. Karpat and Robert W. Zens (Madison: University of Wisconsin Press, 2003), 18.

over the traditional pastures of Turkmen and Kurdish tribes in the region "as a consequence of a political deal that reflected the balance of power and mutual interdependence in the frontier zones."[30] As Ágoston argues it was the existing power structure and aristocracy rather than inter-imperial wars that gave rise to this system.

"Ottoman pragmatism and flexibility"[31] cannot be limited to the conquest methods of the fifteenth century, which were regarded as effective during their time: Ágoston argues that it continued in the following centuries. Likewise, yurtluk-ocaklıks, with their "special administrative status" were indicators of continuing pragmatism and flexibility.[32] It was a "condominium," Ágoston further argues, "that is, the joint rule of the former power elite and Ottoman authorities." Nevertheless, the peculiarities of this joint rule differed according to place and time.[33]

More importantly, such land grants were not specific to the Ottoman Empire. İnalcık asserts that "in the states founded by the Turkish and Mongol dynasties in Iran, Azerbaijan, Central Asia, and the *Dasht* (the Eurasia steppe region), the *temlîknâme* (a grant showing the freehold) type of land grant was called *soyurghal*."[34] "Soyurghals always involved full exemption and immunity from administrative control, state taxes and services."[35] In the same vein, based on an analysis of the soyurghal of a ruler of Aqqoyunlu in the fifteenth century, V. Minorsky accentuates the fact that "the document is a typically feudal act by which the suzerain delegates to the grantee a part of his sovereign rights within a defined territory."[36]

---

30 Ibid., 19. Bayraktar also draws attention to this point. See Bayraktar, "Yurtluk-Ocaklıks," 50.
31 For a critique of using the term "pragmatism" in Ottoman historiography, see Murat Dağlı, "The Limits of Ottoman Pragmatism," History and Theory 52, no. 2 (2013): 194–213.
32 Ágoston, "A Flexible Empire," 18. For a further discussion of the fact that yurtluk-ocaklık system was not a Kurdish peculiarity but a peripheral strategy, see Bayraktar, "Yurtluk-Ocaklıks," 59–75.
33 Ibid., 23. Similarly, Karen Barkey defines empires as "negotiated enterprises," between the state and social actors. Karen Barkey, *Empire of Difference: The Ottomans in Comparative Perspective* (Cambridge: Cambridge University Press, 2008), 68.
34 Halil İnalcık, "Autonomous Enclaves in Islamic States: Temlîks, Soyurghals, Yurdluk-Ocaklıks, Mâlikâne-Mukâta'as and Awqaf," in *History and Historiography of post-Mongol Central Asia and the Middle East: Studies in Honor of John E. Woods*, ed. Judith Pfeiffer and Sholeh A. Quinn; in collaboration with Ernest Tucker. (Wiesbaden: Harrassowitz, 2006), 119.
35 Ibid., 113–14.
36 V. Minorsky, "A Soyūrghāl of Qāsim b. Jahāngir Aq-qoyunlu (903/1498)," Bulletin of the School of Oriental and African Studies 9, no. 4 (2009): 945. A soyurghal was occasionally in the form of granting an amount of revenue. Not only notables but also religious classes could enjoy this right. See Ann K.S. Lambton, "Two Ṣafavid Soyūrghāls," Ibid. 14, no. 1. In

The main source that elaborated the specificities of yurtluk-ocaklık lands and clarified their differences from hükûmets was the *Kanunname-i Hümayun* (Imperial Law Book) prepared during the reign of Süleyman I. Based on these sources, Ayn-i Ali Efendi, a custodian of the Imperial Registers (*Defter-i Hakani*), prepared another book of law at the beginning of the seventeenth century. Ayn-ı Ali Efendi, regarding the province (*eyâlet*[37]) of Diyarbekir, states that when the lands were conquered they were assigned to Kurdish beys as yurtluk-ocaklık. He emphasized that unlike other kinds of official post, the beys could not be discharged and reappointed (*azl ve nasb kabul eylemezler*), and their lands were handed down from father to son. No one from outside could be appointed in their place. However, as in other sanjaks, their incomes were registered. They included fiefs (*tımar*) and *zeamet* (large fiefs). He then continues by describing the responsibilities of yurtluk-ocaklık holders: In the case of a war, they should join in like the beys of other sanjaks. If Kurdish beys did not obey this rule, their sanjaks would be taken from them and assigned to their sons or other relatives. Then he clarified the difference between yurtluk-ocaklık and hükûmet sancâks: In hükûmet sancâks, there was no tımar or zeamet. They were regarded and used as freehold property (*mülk*) and were *mefruz'ul kalem and maktu'al kadem*,[38] emphasizing the autonomous status of hükûmets and literally translated by Rhoads Murphy as "separated from treasury account" and "off limits to all trespass."[39] This article clarifies the freehold status of hükümets which also refers to some sort of autonomy.

Along the same lines, referring to the law book of Ali Çavuş of Sofya, Midhat Sertoğlu states that *ocaklık* was a kind of land tenure system and if the revenues of a place were granted to someone for life, it was then called *yurtluk* (family property). In addition, if this right was handed down from father to son, it was

---

this context, Bayraktar links the predominance of the soyurghal system in the Aqqoyunlu and Safavid Empires to the "pragmatism" of Ottomans who recognized "pre-conquest" practices in the Kurdish periphery. Bayraktar, "Yurtluk-Ocaklıks," 51.

37   According to Ömer Toraman "eyâlet" was used instead of beylerbeyliği (governorship) to denote the regional autonomy of Kurdish beys. Toraman, "Tanzimat'ın Yurtluk-Ocaklık ve Hükümet" XXI. In the same vein, Metin Kunt emphasizes that "eyâlet" entails more regional autonomy than "sancâk" and "vilâyet." Metin İ. Kunt, Sancaktan Eyalete: 1550–1650 arasında Osmanlı Ümerası ve İl İdaresi (Istanbul: Boğaziçi Üniversitesi, 1978), 28.

38   Ayn-ı Ali Efendi, Kanunname-i Âli Osman: Osmanlı Devleti Arazi Kanunları, trans. Hadiye Tuncer (Ankara: Resimli Posta Matbaası, 1962), 6–7.

39   Rhoads Murphey, ed. *Kanûn-nâme-i Sultânı li Aziz Efendi = Aziz Efendi's Book of Sultanic Laws and Regulations: An Agenda for Reform by a Seventeenth-century Ottoman Statesman* (Cambridge: Harvard University Press, 1985), 58.

called *ocaklık* (hereditary family estate[40]) or yurtluk and ocaklık. As Sertoğlu was mainly interested in the issue of autonomy, he argues that those granted with the yurtluk-ocaklıks were not owners or proprietors of those places. In other words, they could not sell, donate, or endow their yurtluk-ocaklık lands. They only had the fifth provision of ownership: the right to legate. Nonetheless, they had rights over *şer'î* (Islamic) and *örfi* (customary) taxes on those lands. The difference of yurtluk-ocaklık from fiefdoms or other land types was the fact that they were not necessarily granted in return for a service and they persisted and could not be taken back until no heir remained. Furthermore, the holders of yurtluk-ocaklık lands had some administrative and judicial rights.[41] They also had *tabl-u alem* (a drum and flag), signifying a *beylik* (principality) not only for Ottomans but also the for the Seljuks.[42]

Evaluations of the law books of the seventeenth century only shed light on the theory and logic of the land tenure system. They neither explain the practical outcomes and regional differences nor the continuities and discontinuities in time. It is possible to invalidate the rights of yurtluk-ocaklık holders – which were strictly defined in these law books – with respect to whether they could sell, donate, or endow their villages. As an example, Fatih Gencer argues that there were instances in which Kurdish beys sold their yurtluk-ocaklık villages. For instance, in the early nineteenth century, Musa Bey, one of the Mahmudi beys, disposed of some of his villages in the sub-district (*nahiye*) of Kotur, giving them to Iranians because of his indebtedness. Musa Bey used the imperial order as a proof of his proprietorship, yet his act led to a cross-border problem.[43]

Moreover, the status of yurtluk-ocaklık and hükûmet lands changed over time. As Tom Sinclair argues, the Ottoman Empire's attempts "to marry the sancak system with the tribal principalities and their hereditary institution resulted in something unstable and difficult to control."[44] In addition, the

---

40 For the English versions of "yurtluk" (family estates) and "ocaklık," (hereditary autonomous appanage, ancestral lands) see Ateş, *The Ottoman-Iranian Borderlands*, 39.
41 Midhat Sertoğlu, ed. *Sofyalı Ali Çavuş Kanunnamesi: Osmanlı İmparatorluğu'nda Toprak Tasarruf Sistemi'nin Hukukî ve Malî Müeyyede ve Mükellefiyetleri* (Istanbul: Marmara Üniversitesi Yayınları, 1992), 15.
42 Ibid., 32–33.
43 Fatih Gencer, "Merkezileşme Politikaları Sürecinde Yurtluk-Ocaklık Sisteminin Değişimi," Ankara Üniversitesi Dil ve Tarih-Coğrafya Fakültesi Tarih Bölümü Tarih Araştırmaları Dergisi 30, no. 49 (2011): 79.
44 Tom Sinclair, "The Ottoman Arrangements for the Tribal Principalities of the Lake Van Region of the Sixteenth Century," in *Ottoman Borderlands: Issues, Personalities and Political Change*, eds. Kemal H. Karpat and Robert W. Zens (Madison: University of Wisconsin Press, 2003), 142.

provision that in hükûmets tax and population surveys could not be carried out was also challenged by the example of the Bitlis hükûmet, which was surveyed a few times between 1535 and 1578.[45]

Similarly, there were examples where the term yurtluk-ocaklık was used to define both hükûmet and yurtluk-ocaklık lands in the course of time. In Palu, as Nilay Özok-Gündoğan discusses, the term yurtluk-ocaklık was used to identify the hereditary lands of the Palu Beys in the nineteenth century, but it was known that they had been granted as hükûmets in the sixteenth century. The reason for this preference was, according to her, "what the central Ottoman state was seeing as a problem in the nineteenth century was the broad category of yurtluk-ocaklık type of land ownership, that is hereditary ownership of the Kurdish emirs."[46]

The discussion of the autonomy of yurtluk-ocaklık and hükûmet types also concerns their place in Ottoman land tenure, in other words, whether they were *mülk* (freehold property) or *mîrî* (the state-owned lands only the usufruct rights of which are possessed by the holder). What was the essence of freehold property? Was it the land or the right to collect taxes?[47] Based on the *temlîknâmes* (conveyance deed) given to the beys of Palu during the sixteenth century, Özok-Gündoğan argues that they enjoyed the lands granted to them as mülk, or freehold property.[48] Bayraktar also argues that the status of the lands of the Zirki Beys was between mîrî and mülk, yet closer to the latter.[49] These examples show that there were variations within categories of yurtluk-ocaklık and hükûmet lands. It is also certain that their political and economic autonomy changed over the course of time. In fact, neither central nor provincial authorities thoroughly knew the revenues and worth of yurtluk-ocaklık lands in Muş in the second half of the nineteenth century. This both blurs

---

45 Ibid., 124. Sinclair also acknowledges that except for this difference, all hükûmets in the Van region (those of Bitlis, Hakkari, Mahmudi, and Hizan) enjoyed "the same rights and responsibilities." Ibid., 138.

46 Özok-Gündoğan, "The Making of the Ottoman Modern State in the Kurdish Periphery," 104–05. Similarly, throughout this book, the term yurtluk-ocaklık was used for hereditary land holdership in general in the context of the nineteenth century.

47 For instance, Ömer Toraman was certain that although hükûmets were granted by the way of freehold, the *rakabe* (the absolute ownership) of this type of land belonged to the state. He asserts that freehold was exclusive of the tax revenues which were supposed to be collected by the state. Toraman, "Tanzimat'ın Yurtluk-Ocaklık ve Hükümet" 8.

48 Özok-Gündoğan, "The Making of the Ottoman Modern State in the Kurdish Periphery," 169. Nevertheless, she also emphasized that further research is needed to draw a "definitive conclusion" about the change in the status of the lands of the Palu Beys in the course of time.

49 Bayraktar, "Yurtluk-Ocaklıks," 241.

the distinction made in the law books between hükûmet and yurtluk-ocaklık lands – which emphasize the absence of land surveys for the former and their existence in the latter – and calls for more local studies that cast light on what happened in practice. For instance, the yurtluk-ocaklık status of Muş changed over the course of time. Regardless of the property relations, the survival of the yurtluk-ocaklık system into the nineteenth century shows that it was a hereditary family estate and further shows the existence of "landed provincial elite" on the eastern periphery of the Ottoman Empire.[50]

2.1.1.1 Historicizing the Yurtluk-Ocaklık Status of Muş

In *Sharafnama*, Şeref Han, the hereditary governor of Bitlis, states that the khanate of Bitlis was composed of Bitlis, Ahlat, Hınıs, Muş and their environs.[51] However, the administrative situation of Bitlis was volatile in those times, as Mehmet Öz argues. Although, after the incorporation of the eastern provinces during the campaign of Selim I, Bitlis had the status of eyâlet and was later termed as a hükûmet, when members of the hereditary ruling family left Bitlis and took the side of the Safevids in 1530s "it became an ordinary Ottoman district or sanjak." The province of Van was established in 1548, and Bitlis became a district of it. However, after 1579, the district was granted to Şeref Han as an ocaklık, thus regaining its hereditary status.[52] Also, in 1584, the sub-district of Muş together with some of its *has* (appanage) villages were annexed to Bitlis in return for 200 thousand *akçe* (Ottoman silver coin). The khan kept half of the taxes collected in Bitlis and the other half was sent to the bey of Van. In 1635, the khan of Bitlis was allowed to keep poll taxes levied on the plain of Muş.[53] In the seventeenth century, Evliya Çelebi emphasized that "the kharac on the Muş plain is entirely the Khan's private estate and provides him 26.000 piasters annually."[54]

---

50   Ibid., 59.
51   Şeref Han, *Şerefname*, trans. Mehmet Emin Bozarslan (Istanbul: Yöntem Yayınları, 1975), 485.
52   Mehmet Öz, "Ottoman Provincial Administration in Eastern and Southeastern Anatolia: The Case of Bidlis in the Sixteenth Century," in *Ottoman Borderlands: Issues, Personalities, and Political Changes*, eds. Kemal H. Karpat and Robert W. Zens (Madison: University of Wisconsin, 2003), 151.
53   Han, *Şerefname*, 579.
54   Robert Dankoff, *Evliya Çelebi in Bitlis: The Relevant Section of the Seyahatname*/edited with translation, commentary and introduction (Leiden: E.J. Brill, 1990), 61. Evliya Çelebi used "guruş" (piaster) for the currency of kharac, yet peasants of Muş were paying their tax in "akçe" (Ottoman silver coin) during that period. Evliya Çelebi, *Günümüz Türkçesiyle Evliya Çelebi Seyahatnamesi*, ed. Seyit Ali Kahraman and Yücel Dağlı, vol. 4 (Istanbul: Yapı Kredi Yayınları, 2010), 128. The Ottoman guruş first appeared in the end of the seventeenth

Besides the accounts in *Sharafnama* and *Seyahatname*, it can be inferred from the phrase "our four-hundred-year dynasty" which was widely used by Emin Pasha and his brothers in their letters and petitions that the notables of Muş enjoyed rule under the governance of the khans of Bitlis for a while. Given that both the khans of Bitlis and the ancestors of Alaaddin Bey were from the Rojki tribe, there might be a connection between the two families if not necessarily kinship. However, by the eighteenth century, the khans of Bitlis were not as powerful as they used to be. Therefore, it is no coincidence that Alaaddin Pasha,[55] the grandfather of Emin Pasha, was known as the man who consolidated the authority and power of the begs of Muş in the eighteenth century.

Alaaddin Bey was the steward (*kethüda*) of the khans of Bitlis.[56] The well-known story about him concerned his resistance to provincial authorities while he was the mütesellim of Muş. In 1747, the governor of Erzurum, İbrahim Pasha reported that Alaaddin Bey, the mütesellim of Muş was attacking and plundering both Erzurum and Bitlis. The khan of Bitlis, Burhan Han attempted to punish him, but Alaaddin Bey repelled the forces sent against him. İbrahim Pasha emphasized how Alaaddin Bey was getting stronger, day by day, in allying with Kurdish tribes and building forts.[57] The Ottoman archival documents point out that there were seven fortresses under the administration of Alaaddin Pasha.[58] The strongest of those forts was near an Armenian village in the plain of Muş, called Sakavi [Mercimekkale], where Alaaddin Bey successfully resisted the forces of Burhan Han of Bitlis.[59] Consul Brant interprets this event as a turning point, after which the relatives of Alaaddin Bey maintained the *pashalık* (used for provincial and sub-provincial governorships) of Muş with few interruptions and with "greater or less independence."[60]

---

century. At first, 1 guruş was fixed as 120 akçes. Şevket Pamuk, *A Monetary History of the Ottoman Empire* (Cambridge: Cambridge University Press, 2000), 160.

55 There is no information in the Ottoman archives proving that Alaaddin Bey was granted the title of 'pasha.' However, the family was defined as 'Alaaddin Pashazades' afterwards. Thus, throughout the book I have used 'pasha' and 'bey' interchangeably for Alaaddin Bey/Pasha.

56 BOA. C. DH. 187/9340, 29 Safer 1152 (7 June 1739).

57 BOA. C. DH. 270/13478 13 Cemaziyelahir 1160 (22 June 1747).

58 BOA. C. DH. 65/3220, 11 Zilhicce 1167 (29 September 1754).

59 Near this village was also a small hill, which, according to Consul James Brant, was called Osp-polur in Armenian, meaning "the mountain round as a lentil." After the confrontation between Aladdin Bey and Ottoman forces, the hill got its name: Mercimek Tepesi. Brant, "Notes of a Journey," 348–49.

60 Ibid., 350. The term of 'pashalık' was used in the British consular reports of the era for the mutasarrıflık of Muş.

After the victory of Alaaddin Bey over Burhan Han, İbrahim Pasha warned the imperial center that immense precautions were needed to control Alaaddin Bey and asked for permission to suppress him with the mobilization of forces in the sanjaks and nahiyes (sub-district) of Erzurum.[61] This clarifies how Alaaddin Bey became powerful and was considered as a threat to the authority, not only of the khans of Bitlis, but also of the governors of Erzurum. Meanwhile, the local people and ulema of Muş and Bitlis tried hard for the pardon of Alaaddin Bey and they offered a payment for his pardon and their request was accepted.[62] This shows that Alaaddin Bey had support from among the 'lesser notables' of Muş and Bitlis and his authority was respected.

Alaaddin Bey with the seven forts he munified, and the tribal members he allied with, remained as a threat to the local power holders. The main allegations towards Alaaddin Bey were from some people from Van who had been granted shares from the poll-tax of Muş. They could not benefit from this, because of obstruction by Alaaddin Bey.[63] Because of the incessant complaints against him, in 1754, the new governor of Erzurum Abdullah Pasha commanded forces to suppress the revolt of Alaaddin Bey, who had been deployed in seven forts. After the clash, Alaaddin Bey and his sons ran away, the forts were demolished, and the ammunition in those forts was sent to the fort of Erzurum.[64]

Although it cannot be discerned from archival documents whether Alaaddin Bey was caught or not, it is certain that his sons and grandsons maintained his rule in Muş, Bitlis and Hınıs from that time onward. Both Alaaddin Bey and his sons and grand-sons left their marks to these cities by establishing pious foundations along with their mosques, bathhouses, and madrasahs.[65] In addition, the phrase "our four-hundred-year dynasty" or "our four hundred years of servitude to the Ottoman Empire" are common in the scripts of Emin Pasha and later in those of his brothers. Therefore, it is possible to infer that before Alaaddin Bey reinforced his power in the 1750s, his relatives had posts in Muş under the authority of the khans of Bitlis. However, the successful resistance of Alaaddin Bey at Mercimek Hill paved the way for the consolidation of power in the hands of his dynasty. From this time onward, it is unsurprising that while

---

61   BOA. C. DH. 270/13478 13.06.1160 (22 June 1747).
62   BOA. C. DH. 98/4864 29 Muharrem 1161 (30 January 1748).
63   Fatih Gencer, *Bitlis ve Muş'un Son Beyleri: Alaaddin Paşazadeler*, (Istanbul: Libra Kitap, 2019), 27. The imperial soldiers in the sanjak of Van had shares from the poll-tax of Muş and Bitlis. However, the administrators of Muş and Bitlis were opposing this situation and when they were powerful enough, they did not send the shares of those soldiers. For instance, BOA. HAT. 728/34650, 29 Zilhicce 1245 (21 June 1830).
64   BOA. C. DH. 65/3220, 11 Zilhicce 1167 (29 September 1754).
65   Bilal Yılmaz, "Muş Vakıfları" (master's thesis, Yüzüncü Yıl Üniversitesi, 2009).

Alaaddin Bey's dynasty enlarged its power over the domain, surrounding notables were subordinated to the growing power of this family. For instance, by the nineteenth century, Selim Pasha, the grandson of Alaaddin Bey and cousin of Emin Pasha,[66] gained power over the beys of Bitlis who were already in decline in the eighteenth century. Selim Pasha subdued the beys of Bitlis and attached the beylik to Muş.[67]

After Alaaddin Bey's death, his son Maksud Bey became the mütesellim of Muş. In the beginning, there were complaints about Maksud Bey claiming that he was rebellious and following the path of his father.[68] However, the 1768–1777 Ottoman-Russian War paved the way for Maksud Bey to be recognized by the Ottoman authorities. In return for his joining the army under the authority of the commander-in-chief of Kars, Maksud Bey was granted the rank of *mirimiran* (brigadier general) and so became a pasha.[69] This was not the last time when Alaaddin Pashazades established political and economic alliances with imperial authorities during the inter-imperial wars.

During these times, it was not only through promotion in rank that the Alaaddin Pashazades had benefited. The lands under their exclusive use as yurtluk-ocaklık also expanded. In the last decades of the eighteenth century, Maksud Pasha was granted Malazgirt first for lifelong tax-farming, then as yurtluk-ocaklık.[70] During the rule of Murat Pasha, who became the mutasarrıf of Muş after his father, Maksud Pasha's death, the yurtluk-ocaklık lands of Muş's begs expanded thanks to their political alliances with the provincial and central authorities. Maksud Pasha, together with the governor of Trabzon, Tayyar Pasha was nominated to catch the rebellious Gürcü Osman

---

66   James Brant claims that Selim Pasha was the father of Emin Pasha; however, many archival documents state that Yusuf Pasha was his father. Furthermore, in my personal interviews with the grandsons of Alaaddin Bey it became clear that Yusuf Pasha was the father of Emin Pasha. Selim and Emin pashas were cousins.
67   Brant, "Notes of a Journey," 380. From some archival documents it can also be understood that Selim Pasha extended the range of his power by eliminating some of his relatives. For instance, although it was recorded that Hınıs and Tekman had been yurtluk-ocaklık lands of Ali Bey's father, Selim Pasha managed to get rid of him (pederinin üzerinden def' itdirmiş olduğundan). BOA. HAT. 819/37339C, 3 Safer 1237 (30 October 1821). Fatih Gencer also noted that Selim Pasha attacked the administrator of Ahlat and Adilcevaz, Şeyh Ahmet, who was said to have been his enemy, and took control over his lands. Lastly, he attacked Şirvan and plundered the villages. See Gencer, "Merkezileşme Politikaları Sürecinde," 80.
68   BOA. C. DH 279/13938, 29 Safer 1178 (28 August 1764).
69   Fatih Gencer, Bitlis ve Muş'un Son Beyleri: Alaaddin Paşazadeler, (İstanbul: Libra Kitap, 2019), 32–33.
70   Gencer, *Bitlis ve Muş'un Son Beyleri*, 35.

Pasha, the ex-governor of Rumelia.[71] In the suppression of Gürcü Osman Pasha's rebellion, his capture and finally execution, Murad Pasha and his family played a great role. In return, the sanjak of Hınıs and Tekman were added to the yurtluk-ocaklık lands of Murad Pasha.[72] Besides, his son Mirza Beg and his brother İbrahim Beg, who had also joined the forces against Gürcü Osman Pasha, were granted the ranks of *mir-i miranlık* (brigadier general) and *silahşörlük* (knight) respectively.[73]

After Murad Pasha's death, his son Mirza Pasha was appointed as the mutasarrıf of Muş.[74] However, his uncle, Yusuf Kamer Pasha – the father of Emin Pasha – thought that as the elder of the family he had the right to be the mutasarrıf of Muş. His claim was recognized by the provincial and central authorities and he became the mutasarrıf of Muş.[75] His brother, Elhac Şeyho Bey was appointed as the steward of the khan of Bitlis, and his other brother İbrahim Bey became the mütesellim of Hınıs and Tekman. The mukataa of Hınıs and Tekman was shared by Yusuf Pasha and Şeyho Bey as a life-long tax farm.[76] The case of Yusuf Pasha indicates that the yurtluk-ocaklıks were not necessarily handed down from father to son. The uncles, cousins and brothers of the Alaaddin Pashazades became rivals for acquiring governing of Muş as yurtluk-ocaklık.

In this rivalry over being the ruler of Muş, the payment of an amount of money, which was known as the cost of the *muhallefat* (assets and estates of a late official) for being appointed as the new yurtluk-ocaklık holder of Muş became critical for the family members. This point provides provincial and central authorities with a leverage to replace family members with each other as the mutasarrıf of Muş. In the case of Yusuf Pasha, for instance, he was discharged from the mutasarrıflık of Muş as he did not pay for the *muhallefat* of Murad Pasha, the previous mutasarrıf of Muş.[77] Yusuf Pasha also did not pay for the *muaccele* (the lump-sum payment for the life-long taxfarms) of the mukataas of Hınıs and Tekman.[78] Thus, another son of Murad Pasha, Selim Bey was granted with the sanjak of Muş as yurtluk-ocaklık – and became a 'pasha'

---

71   BOA. HAT. 96/3885, 29 Zilhicce 1218 (April 10, 1804). For details about the career and rebellion of Gürcü Osman Pasha, see Lütfiye Sevinç Küçükoğlu, "Power Politics in Ottoman Provincial Administration: A Case Study of Gürcü Osman Pasha (1789–1807)" (PhD diss, Bilkent University, Ankara, 2019).
72   BOA. HAT. 175/7583 E, 29 Zilhicce 1218 (April 10, 1804).
73   BOA. HAT. 96/3885, 29 Zilhicce 1218 (April 10, 1804).
74   BOA. HAT. 1364/53898, 29 Zilhicce 1222 (27 Şubat 1808).
75   BOA. C. DH. 133/6650, 29 Ramazan 1223 (18 November 1808).
76   BOA. C. DH 217/13539, 13 Recep 1225 (14 August 1810).
77   BOA. C. DH. 229/11448, 29 Rabiülevvel 1226 (23 April 1811).
78   BOA. C. ML. 280/11486, 29 Muharrem 1226 (23 February 1811).

with the rank of mîr-i mîrânlık – on the condition that he paid the amounts which Yusuf Pasha did not.[79] In the following years, his rank was specified as the governor-general of Rumelia.[80]

The rule of Murad Pashazade Selim Pasha in Muş coincided with historical moments for both the locality of Muş, and the empire in general. In the 1810s, Selim Pasha played a crucial role in the cross-border migrations of the nomadic tribes of Haydaran, Sıpkî and Zilan who were known as 'disputed tribes' between the Ottoman and the Qajar empires. The crossing border of these tribes and their provision with winter quarters in the Ottoman lands led to problems, both at imperial and inter-imperial levels. At the imperial level, the local administrators of Muş, Van and Bayezid laid claim over the nomadic tribes and got into conflict among themselves specifically on the winter quartering of these tribes. At the inter-imperial level, the tribal dilemma caused the 1821–1823 Ottoman-Iranian War. The inter-imperial wars also created an environment for the local rulers of the borderlands to establish inter-imperial agencies.[81]

The Ottoman-Iranian War of 1821–1823 was such an occasion when the trans-imperial agency of the notables of Muş became apparent. During the war, Selim Pasha was accused of playing both sides by the Ottoman authorities.[82] When the attacks of Iranian forces on the domains under his control intensified, Selim Pasha accepted Iranian suzerainty.[83] Nevertheless, in the course of war his asking for pardon was welcomed by the Ottoman authorities. Selim Pasha's alliances with the tribes of the borderlands, especially the irregular units he recruited from the Haydaran and Sıpkî, which attacked Iranian lands, were great contribution to the Ottoman military forces during the war. As a return for his services to the Ottoman army, he was granted the title of 'tribal

---

79   BOA. HAT. 721/34384, 29 Safer 1226 (25 March 1811).
80   BOA. C. DH. 201/10011, 12 Şevval 1234 (4 August 1819).
81   Gülseren Duman Koç, "A Negotiation of Power during the Age of Reforms in the Ottoman Empire: Notables, Tribes and State in Muş (1820–1840)," *Middle Eastern Studies* 57/2 (2021), 212–213. For, the details regarding the role of the local notables of the Ottoman eastern borderlands – specifically Selim Pasha of Muş – in the defection of these 'disputed' nomadic tribes to the Ottoman side and its consequences, see Yener Koç, 'Nomadic Pastoral Tribes at the Intersection of the Ottoman, Persian and Russian Empires (1820s–1890s)' (Phd. diss., Boğaziçi University, 2020), 91–106.
82   BOA. HAT. 793. 36838 B, 25 Zilkade 1237 (13 August1822). Ahmed Cevdet Paşa, *Tarih-i Cevdet*, trans. Dündar Günday, 6 vols., vol. 6 (Istanbul: Üçdal Neşriyat, 1983–1984), 2652–3.
83   BOA. HAT. 826/37442 A, 24 Safer 1237 (20 November 1821); BOA. HAT. 818/37320 F, 7 Safer 1237 (3 November 1821); BOA. HAT. 819/37340 M, 19 Muharrem 1237 (16 October 1821).

chieftainship' (*aşiret başbuğluğu*), along with a fur and horse.[84] However, it is highly possible that Selim Pasha's attitudes during the war led to his execution a few years later. The governor of Erzurum, Galip Pasha asked for the replacement of Selim Pasha through accusing him of being a drunk and careless in his duties.[85]

Such kinds of accusations resulted in Selim Pasha's escape from Muş, so that for a while he searched for alliances and fought to get control over Muş and its environs again.[86] The guardian of Van İshak Pasha, the mutasarrıf of Bayezid Behlül Pasha helped the new mutasarrıf of Muş, Seyyid Ahmed Pasha to fight against and obtain the surrender of Selim Pasha. In the correspondence of these pashas, Selim Pasha was stigmatized as a traitor to the sultan.[87] Similarly, the *naib* (deputy judge) of Bitlis, Mustafa Efendi penned a petition accusing Selim Pasha of being irreligious, drunk and cruel to people.[88] Having lost the support of an important section of the local power holders, Selim Pasha asked for help from the Qajars. The governor of Revan, Hüseyin Han, informed the Ottoman authorities that although Selim Pasha offered money in return for aid, they did not accept it as they were committed to maintain good relations between the two states.[89] Meanwhile, Seyyid Ahmed Pasha, the mutasarrıf of Muş, was assassinated by the supporters of Selim Pasha, and instead of him, Abdurrahman Bey, the nephew of Selim Pasha was appointed as the mutasarrıf of Muş.[90] Although Selim Pasha tried hard to get control again in Muş, his efforts achieved no result. Finally, Selim Pasha had to negotiate with the governor of Erzurum, Galip Pasha, and he accepted life in Sivas, as a place of exile. Apparently, his exile was a pretext, as he was executed on his way to Sivas in 1827.[91]

Although an influential member of the Alaaddin Pashazades fell into disfavor, the sanjak of Muş remained within the family. The successor of Selim Pasha, his nephew Abdurrahman Pasha would be murdered, too; yet, this time it was a result of intrafamilial rivalry. The story of Emin Pasha unfolded with this account of murder.

84   BOA. HAT. 795/36863 N, 13 Muharrem 1238 (30 September 1822) Koç, "A Negotiation of Power ...," 213.
85   BOA. HAT. 811/37220 C, 7 Rebiülahir 1241 (19 November 1825).
86   BOA. HAT. 735/34903 21 Cemaziyelevvel 1242 (21 December 1826).
87   BOA. HAT. 736/34932 B, 9 Cemaziyelevvel 1242 (9 December 1826); BOA. HAT. 736/34932 C, 11 Cemaziyelevvel 1242 (11 December 1826); BOA. HAT. 736/34932 D, 14 Cemaziyelevvel 1242 (14 December 1826).
88   BOA. HAT. 770/36176, 29 Zilhicce 1242 (24 Temmuz 1827).
89   BOA. HAT. 736/34932 F, 7 Cemaziyelevvel 1242 (7 December 1826).
90   BOA. HAT. 1229/47949, 25 Şaban 1242 (24 March 1827).
91   BOA. HAT. 892/ 39382 B, 25 Safer 1243 (17 September 1827).

2.2 The Rise of Emin Pasha

Emin Pasha was one of the last members of the Alaaddin Pashazades who enjoyed power stemming from the characteristics of the yurtluk-ocaklık land tenure system. Both consular reports and Emin Pasha's references to his own dynasty unfold a story of a powerful family that had negotiated its power in the framework of the socioeconomic and political circumstances and transformations of the era. Emin Pasha followed the same path, yet he first had to stand out among his relatives who also claimed power. The first occasion, which brought Emin Pasha and his brothers (also known as Yusuf Pashazades) to the center in Muş during the late 1820s was an intrafamilial – but at the same time a political – murder of Abdurrahman Pasha, the mutasarrıf of Muş.[92] Although being part of the dynasty of Muş, it seemed that Emin Pasha did not take a turn as mutasarrıf until the late 1820s. Yet he used his own means – which were deeply-rooted in the political relations of the region – to take the reins of power.

In 1828, the cousin (*emmizade*) of Emin Bey, Abdurrahman Pasha, was the mutasarrıf of Muş, and Emin was his *kethüda* (steward). Abdurrahman Pasha dismissed his cousin from this post though the reason was not clarified.[93] A group of people from Muş filed a petition claiming that Abdurrahman Pasha was angry with Emin Bey, because he had arranged for his brother Murad Bey to become engaged to the daughter of the sheikh of Gümgüm. Allegedly, they

---

92   Among the four brothers, Emin Pasha was described as the most commanding figure, yet the other three brothers also shared a great role in the region. Murad Bey resided in Hınıs which was defined as part of the sanjak of Muş in 1838. Brant, "Notes of a Journey," 345. Furthermore, Şerif Bey was defined as the *mütesellim* of Bitlis, and under his exclusive authority there were eighty villages. He had also built a new residence in Bitlis two years earlier, as Emin Pasha had in Muş. Ibid., 381. J. Shiel's description of appearance of Şerif Bey might offer a visualization of traditional rulers of Bitlis and Muş in the nineteenth century: "He was a dashing Kurd of twenty-five years of age, and chiefly remarkable for his dress. It consisted of short yellow boots, blue cloth trousers of prodigious dimension, three jackers of silk and cloth of different colours, and one of them with sleeves two yards in length; a wide silks sash round his waist, and an enormous turban of silk of every colour: a white Arab cloak was thrown round him, and a dagger, long pistols in belt, and a sword completed his equipment," J. Shiel, "Notes on a Journey from Tabriz, through Kurdistan, via Van, Bitlis, Seert and Erbil to Suleymaniyeh, in July and August 1836," *Journal of the Royal Geographical Society of London*, vol. 8 (1838)," 75.

93   BOA. HAT. 1088/44264 B, 29 Şevval 1243 (14 May 1828). For a shortest version of the story of Emin Pasha, see Gülseren Duman Koç, "A Negotiation of Power during the Age of Reforms in the Ottoman Empire: Notables, Tribes and State in Muş (1820–1840)," *Middle Eastern Studies* 57/2 (2021), 209–226.

had to break off the engagement.⁹⁴ Abdurrahman Pasha might have opposed this marriage, because he saw Emin Pasha as a rival and so prevented him from forming matrimonial alliances with powerful religious figures. Soon afterward, the governor of Erzurum, Galip Pasha, informed the *Sadaret* (Vizirate) about the murder of Abdurrahman Pasha by his cousin Emin Bey and his brothers on his way from Bitlis to Muş. Upon Abdurrahman Pasha's death, Galip Pasha suggested that the sanjak of Muş be governed as a mütesellimlik for a time, and he searched for proper candidates, all of whom were family members, as was characteristic of the yurtluk-ocaklık system.⁹⁵

Galip Pasha's report which presents information about each candidate is significant for underlining the deep-rooted power relations in the region. The first and most powerful candidate for the mütesellimlik of Muş was Mehmed Bey, the brother of a former mutasarrıf of Muş, the deceased Selim Pasha. Mehmed Bey was the kethüda of the khan of Bitlis at the time, which also points to the strong relations between the khans of Bitlis and the mutasarrıfs of Muş.

The other two candidates were İbrahim Bey among the Maksud Pashazades who was in Istanbul and Hacı Ahmed Bey who was in Halep. Both were notorious, as the former was the uncle of the Emin Bey and the latter was their eldest brother. The last candidate, the brother of Abdurrahman Pasha, Abdülfettah Bey, had died of natural causes. Therefore, the best candidate, according to Galip Pasha, was Mehmed Bey, whom the sheikhs of Bitlis also supported. The circle of coalitions of each candidate would pave the way for their coming to power. As Zens argues, "a coalition of lesser notables including members of the *ulema* and other locally influential people, and government officials, such as *kadı*s and *ağa*s from the local janissary garrison," could support their candidate ayan to become mütesellim either through "issuing recommendations" or through pressure.⁹⁶

The crucial question is why a mütesellim from outside was not appointed given that the family members had a bad reputation from the state authorities' perspectives. According to Galip Pasha, abolishing the yurtluk-ocaklık and appointing a mütesellim from outside was an option. Yet the pasha further argued that yurtluk-ocaklıks were a long-standing tradition and that Muş was part of Kurdistan where maintaining control (*taht û rabta idhâli*) was a long, thorny process. The second obstacle was the war with the Russian Empire and the need for soldiers.⁹⁷ Therefore, it was best to choose the mütesellim from

---

94   BOA. HAT. 1088/44264 C, 20 Şevval 1243 (5 May 1828).
95   BOA. HAT. 1087/44245, 01 Zilkade 1243 (15 May 1828).
96   Zens, "The Ayanlık and Pasvanoğlu Osman Paşa of Vidin," 31–32.
97   Ibid.

among the family members. Galip Pasha's explanation contains two nuances regarding Muş and its rulers. On the one hand, situated on the borderlands of the empire, Muş was a source of human power during the wars with the Russians and Persians. On the other hand, his explanation points to the struggle of the notables of Muş to maintain and consolidate their autonomy during the nineteenth century. The oscillation between mütesellimlik and mutasarrıflık was a formulation of this struggle. As discussed above, provincial notables increased their influence by securing the post of mütesellimlik. However, the post of mütesellimlik was responsible to provincial governors. In mutasarrıflık, which was used for administration of sanjaks,[98] it was possible to have greater autonomy.

Emin Bey sought to be the mutasarrıf of Muş, as discussed throughout this chapter, mütesellimlik was a transitory stage for him. In the particular situation of the sanjak of Muş, being its mutasarrıf meant to have power over the sanjak which consisted of approximately four hundred villages and included the districts of Malazgirt, Hınıs, and Tekman as yurtluk-ocaklık. In the view of local, and central authorities mütesellimlik was also for a trial period. For instance, when Mehmed Bey was appointed as the mütesellim of Muş, it was explained as being provisional in order to discover his behavior and ability to govern.[99]

2.2.1 *The 1828–29 Ottoman Russian War*

While the governor of Erzurum was trying to find a proper mütesellim for Muş and in the end decided on Mehmet Bey, Emin Bey, who had escaped to Diyarbekir with his brothers after having killed his cousin, looked for opportunities to be forgiven. His ultimate goal was to be the mutasarrıf of Muş. According to Mehmed Salih Pasha, the new governor of Erzurum, Emin Bey promised one thousand five hundred purses (*kese*)[100] to the treasury in return for his forgiveness and nomination as mutasarrıf of Muş. He also guaranteed that he would let his brothers and children be held as hostages. Emphasizing his connections with tribal leaders and the notables of Muş, Emin Bey also promised that he would support the army with a great number of cavalrymen if he was summoned for service in the war (the 1828–9 Ottoman-Russian War) and would go to wherever he was commanded.[101]

---

98 Orhan Kılıç, 18. Yüzyılın İlk Yarısında Osmanlı Devleti'nin İdari Taksimatı: Eyalet ve Sancak Tevcihatı (Elazığ: Şark Pazarlama, 1997), 25.

99 "… bir müddetcek harekâtı sûret-i idâresi anlaşılmak üzere Muş sancâğının mütesellimlik vechile zabtı …" BOA. HAT. 1087/44245, 01 Zilkade 1243 (15 May 1828).

100 One kese equals 50,000 akçe. See footnote 21 in Şevket Pamuk, *A Monetary History of the Ottoman Empire*, 97.

101 BOA. C. DH. 142/7060, 29 Zilkade 1243 (12 June 1828).

This would not be the last time for Emin Bey would bargain with Ottoman governments by taking advantages of the delicate moments. His efforts yielded results at such conjunctures. The war with the Russian Empire was the determining factor in Emin Pasha's pardon.[102] As the Ottoman Empire was mobilizing all its resources and energy to fight the war against Russia, it could not deal with additional trouble that was on the frontier of another rival empire. Meanwhile, Emin Bey allied with the Silvanlı tribe in Diyarbekir, the leaders of which also penned a solicitation (*ricâname*) for Emin Bey's pardon. The governor of Erzurum was anxious as that tribe was neither small nor totally under control. The best choice was to negotiate with Emin Bey; otherwise his subordination would require a lot of effort.[103]

Together with concerns about Emin Bey's alliances, the need for soldiers and, most importantly, the closeness of the region to the frontiers of the Empire paved the way for his pardon and his appointment as the mutasarrıf of Muş with the title of 'pasha'. P.İ. Averyanov argues that although the emir of Hakkari announced his neutrality when the war started in 1828, the pashalıks of Van, Erzurum, and Muş as well as the Kurds of Bayezid later support the Ottomans.[104] In addition, as Ottoman archival documents show, when the Russian army attacked from Eleşgird, it was Emin – now a pasha and the mutasarrıf – along with the mütesellims of Hınıs, Tekman and Hısn-ı Mansur, who counter-attacked with about four or five thousand soldiers.[105]

Based on military reports submitted to the czar, Averyanov also describes how Emin Pasha played both sides during the war. He also highlights General Paskoviç's efforts to gain the support of Kurds in the region. Emin Pasha, while bargaining with Ottoman authorities for the mutasarrıflık of Muş, also contacted Russian authorities to achieve the same goal. It was reported that in 1828, before the war began, Emin Pasha sent an Armenian mediator to Tbilisi to General Paskoviç, who pledged to him, in return for his full support against the Turkish troops, the rank of pashalık and financial aid for troops that Emin Pasha promised to recruit from among the Kurdish tribes. Allegedly, Emin Pasha reached a deal with Paskoviç. However, it turned out that he did not provide the Russian army with the promised Kurdish cavalry. Nevertheless, Averyanov argued that his hesitance and passiveness at critical moments

---

102   Similar to the rise to power of the Karaosmanoğlu family which benefited from circumstances created by the Ottoman-Russian Wars of 1768 and 1787. Nagata, *Tarihte Âyânlar*, 33.
103   Ibid.
104   P.İ. Averyanov, *19. Yüzyılda Osmanlı İran Rus Savaşlarında Kürtler*, trans. İbrahim Kale (Istanbul: Avesta, 2010), 54–5.
105   BOA. HAT. 1011/42437A, 5 Rebiülevvel 1244 (15 October 1828).

during the war was for the good of Russia.[106] Similarly, British Colonel Francis Chesney also notes that the pasha of Muş was persuaded by the offers of the Russian general, which led to a loss of 12,000 Kurdish cavalry for the Ottoman troops.[107] Yet, as stated above, Emin Pasha eventually fought against the Russian troops that attacked Eleşgird. Following this, according to Averyanov, Genereal Paskoviç decided to punish Emin Pasha for his double-dealings by invading Muş in 1829.[108]

In this story, Emin Pasha's effort to take advantage of the war between two empires is not extraordinary. Bargaining for power by utilizing their location at the frontiers of Russian, Ottoman and Iranian empires was at the core of the role played by Kurdish notables. Alaaddin Pashazades had always played crucial roles during the inter-imperial wars, as well. For instance, the rule of Selim Pasha in Muş, a cousin of Emin Pasha, coincided with the Ottoman-Iranian War of 1821–23. In the course of the war, Selim Pasha first fought with Ottoman forces, then he changed side and accepted Iranian subjecthood. Finally, he asked for the Ottomans' forgiveness and gave service to the Ottoman army by sending members of Haydaran and Sıpki tribes as 'raid units' to the Iranian lands. In return, he was awarded gifts and the title of 'tribal chieftainship.'[109]

In the case of Emin Pasha, he also changed his alliances in the course of the war, not because he was changing his mind but because he was meticulously evaluating and manipulating each new development. When he decided not to help Russia by providing Kurdish cavalry, rumors about a peace agreement between Russia and the Ottoman Empire had already spread in the region.[110] Besides, he might use a possible coalition with Russian authorities as a trump card against the Ottoman authorities, strengthening his hand later on. The cases of Selim and Emin pashas among Alaaddin Pashazades during the inter-imperial wars indicate that local Kurdish beys regarded themselves as autonomous rulers, who could play politics like any other actors and negotiate their interests accordingly.

During the war, neither Ottoman central authorities nor the governors of Erzurum Province were content with the services of Emin Pasha. The successor of Galip Pasha, Salih Pasha wrote to the imperial center that although Muş was expansive and significant (*cesim bir mahal*), it could not be governed

---

106　Averyanov, *19. Yüzyılda Osmanlı* 65–7.
107　Francis R. Chesney, *The Russo-Turkish Campaigns of 1828 and 1829: With a View of the Present State of Affairs in the East* (New York: Redfield, 1854), 204.
108　Averyanov, *19. Yüzyılda Osmanlı* 75–6.
109　BOA. HAT. 795/36870, 11 Muharrem 1238 (28 September 1822), BOA. HAT. 795/36863 N, 13 Muharrem 1238 (30 September 1822).
110　Averyanov, *19. Yüzyılda Osmanlı* 75–6.

properly. During the governorship of his predecessor, three mutasarrıfs came and left Muş in three years' time; finally, Emin Pasha came to rule it. However, he reported the misbehavior of Emin Pasha, stating that the pasha trusted in the Kurds (that is to say, Kurdish tribes) and thought that they were the guarantors of his future in the region. Relying on his coalitions with the tribes of the region, Emin Pasha played politics with freedom. Therefore, the governor of Erzurum claimed that Emin Pasha acting on such a belief, behaved improperly, and so his governorship in Muş was unfavorable.[111] Although Salih Pasha suggested other candidates, Emin Pasha managed to keep his post in Muş.

It was not only provincial governors that complained about local power holders. For instance, in 1830, the representative of Russia in Istanbul informed the central government that some Ottoman officials in the eastern provinces were provoking revolts in the region. After investigation, the commander in chief of the east (*Şark Seraskeri*), Osman Pasha, stated it could not be no one other than Emin Pasha who would dare to do such a thing. Although such allegations could not be proved, the exile of Emin Pasha to Erzincan or Karahisar for a while was discussed.[112] Nevertheless, even this discussion did not diminish Emin Pasha's power. This is mainly because of the aforementioned peculiarities of the geography, which prevented the abolishment of land tenure system, yurtluk-ocaklıks. Such an obstacle disables the local and central authorities through appointing an administrator from outside the long-established Muş dynasty.

In addition to the Russian-Ottoman War of 1828–1829, two other developments stemming from the geopolitical location of Muş shaped Emin Pasha's sphere of influence. The first one was his service in the suppression of the revolt of Timur Pasha, the *muhafız* (guardian) of Van. As it occurred on the border with Iran, the possibility of the spread of the revolt caused anxiety among both central and provincial authorities. Emin Pasha, in return for his services, was granted the *berat* (imperial certificate) of Muş as a yurtluk-ocaklık.

---

111 "… kendünün bekâsı ekrâdın iânesine mahsûsdur zannıyla uygunsuz harekete ibtidâr ve mûmâileyhin bu hâl ile Muşda bekâsı muzırr görünûb …" BOA. HAT. 1016/42520, 17 Cemaziyelevvel 1244 (25 November 1828). The struggle between the two pashas did not last. Emin Pasha asked for a steward (*kapukethüdası*) for himself, but the governor of Erzurum stated that the mutasarrıfs of Muş did not have important missions in Istanbul, so it was unnecessary. Claiming a steward shows Emin Pasha's vision of himself and how he cared about his role in the region. BOA. HAT. 724/34457, 18 Şevval 1244 (23 April 1829).

112 BOA. HAT. 1023/42698 F, 6 Zilkade 1245 (29 April 1830). Kemal Beydilli also accentuates the fact that Emin Pasha should have controlled Kurdish tribes in Muş and Hınıs during the war. However, his ignoring the warnings resulted in the complaints of Russian authorities. Kemal Beydilli, *1828–1829 Osmanlı-Rus Savaşında Doğu Anadolu'dan Rusya'ya Göçürülen Ermeniler* (Ankara: Türk Tarih Kurumu Basımevi, 1988), 385–6.

The second development was not a specific event; rather, it stemmed from the tribal social structure of Muş. Emin Pasha would play the card of settling the nomadic and semi-nomadic tribes, and the conscription of tribesmen for the *Asakir-i Mansure-i Muhammediyye* (Victorious Soldiers of Muhammad; hereafter, Mansure Army, the army Mahmud II established after the abolishment of Janissaries in 1826) to extend the domain where he had effective power. Specifically, he requested to be contracted with the mukâta'as of Hınıs, Tekman and Malazgirt, which would be a long lasting matter of debate between the notables of Muş and the provincial authorities of Erzurum.

2.2.1.1 The Revolt of Timur Pasha and the Consolidation of the Power of Emin Pasha

Emin Pasha was not the only Kurdish notable who sought to strengthen his power in this period. The muhafız of Van, Timur Pasha – who was also local – had previously demanded to be part of the Mansure Army, which the commander in chief considered appropriate.[113] However, Timur Pasha, a year after his dismissal from the *muhâfızlık* (guardianship) of Van, was trying to get the support of Kurds and some tribes around Van (which the official documents defined as 'provocation') with the help of his brother, Fazıl Bey, with the aim of being granted the province of Van. Ottoman authorities were alarmed about this revolt, as they were worried about cross-border troubles. Therefore, they formed coalitions in the region, appointing other pashas of the Kurdish region to suppress the revolt. Emin Pasha was among those pashas. In line with this, the suppression of Timur Pasha's revolt – or "issue of Van" (*Van maddesi*) as it was called in the Ottoman documents – resulted in the promotion of Emin Pasha to the rank of *mirliva* (major general).[114]

"The issue of Van" led to the rise of Emin Pasha but it also provides clues about the nature of different kinds of alliances in the region, variously comprised of Kurdish tribes, notables, and Ottoman and Persian authorities. While central authorities formed a coalition against Timur Pasha, he had a meeting with Cihangir Mirza, the son of Qajar crown prince Şahzade Abbas, near the border. The Pasha allegedly offered gifts to Cihangir Mirza, and some correspondence were exchanged between them. Ottoman authorities warned the Iranians about Timur Pasha, reminding them not to infringe on the cordiality and tranquility between the two states and especially to prevent tribal

---

113   BOA. HAT. 308/18189, 29 Zilhicce 1245 (21 June 1830).
114   It was a newer title for *sanjak beyi*. Stanford J. Shaw and Ezel Kural Shaw, *History of the Ottoman Empire and Modern Turkey*, 2 vols., vol. 2 (Cambridge: Cambridge University Press, 1976–77), 499.

involvement in his revolt. However, Timur Pasha did not step back and kept on "provoking tribes and spreading news from Bagdad to Rumeli regarding his power and possible turmoil he could create." Istanbul was concerned that the revolt would spread in the region.[115]

Apprehensive that Emin Pasha could also collaborate with Timur Pasha, the central and provincial authorities agreed that Emin Pasha should be treated well and granted him the berat of Muş as a yurtluk-ocaklık, which he had long demanded. In return, Emin Pasha was charged with helping the new *kâimakâm* (administrator of a sanjak) of Van, Adil Bey, who was the steward of Esad Pasha, the governor of Erzurum. Emin Pasha would join him in Malazgird with four to five thousand troops constituted of the tribes of Muş. The coalition of Timur Pasha was about the same size, and a crucial part of it was the tribe of Haydaran together with some others. Therefore, it was important to break this coalition by persuading some tribal members to join the other camp. This aim was realized; the Haydaran chief Kasım Ağa's brother, Sultan Agha, defected to the side of Emin Pasha and Adil Bey together with four hundred families (*dört yüz hâne*) and the armed men of the tribe.[116] This was a major blow to Timur Pasha's coalition. The last blow to the revolt came from Şerif Bey, the brother of Emin Pasha. With the help of Emin Pasha and his brothers, the revolt of Van was suppressed. Timur Pasha left his brother Fazıl Bey in Van and took shelter in the Castle of Hoşap (Mahmudi).[117] In the defeat of the rebellion of Timur Pasha, the dissolution of the league he formed from the Haydaran was crucial. Nomadic and semi-nomadic Kurdish tribes continued to provide manpower for both rebelling local actors and for the imperial forces.

Upon the suppression of Timur Pasha's revolt, Adil Bey, 'an outsider' as stated in the Ottoman documents was dismissed. Instead, Esad Pasha asked Ishak Pasha to take on the mission. The reason for this change also includes some important clues regarding administrative practices in Ottoman Kurdistan. The appointment of a kaimakam from the center was not desired due to the Kurdish and tribal social structure of the region, and because this required a large number of soldiers to maintain security and order in the region. Such security measures were an extra financial burden on the treasury.[118] In addition, someone with knowledge of the locality was chosen. In the first quarter of the nineteenth century, from the standpoint of many central and provincial

---

115   BOA. HAT. 703/33795, 17 Cemaziyelevvel 1247 (24 October 1831).
116   Ibid.
117   Ibid.
118   "… havâlî-i mezkûre ekrâd ve 'aşâir yatağı yerleri olduğundan hâricden kâimakâmla idâresi kâimakâm bulunanların külliyetlû 'asker istishâbına tevkîf ideceğine ve bu sûret masârîf-i külliyeye icâb ideceğinden başka yine sızıldısı kesmeyeceğine …" Ibid.

authorities, the best way of governing Ottoman Kurdistan was direct rule, yet the issue of security and control were major obstacles to realizing it, as they consistently emphasized. Therefore, until the source of the power of local beys was transformed, the region would be governed as it had been. Such a transformation became partially possible with the application of Tanzimat reforms in the eastern provinces in the 1840s. Indeed, their best way of governing might have conflicted with the interests of the local population. As discussed in Chapter 6, after the exile of Kurdish notables, the peasants of Muş filed petitions for the return of their traditional leaders.

Upon suppressing the revolt, Emin Pasha was granted arms, robes of honor (*hil'ats*), and the rank of *mirlivâlık*, which is lower than that of *ferik* (major-general) and higher than *miralaylık* (colonel), so is equivalent to a brigadier general.[119] Most importantly, he was granted with the berat of the sanjak of Muş as a yurtluk-ocaklık.[120] The governor of Erzurum, Esad Pasha, reported that the sanjak of Muş had been granted to Emin Pasha during the reign of Salih Pasha, his predecessor, during the war with Russia. By being provided with the berat, Emin Pasha guaranteed his usufruct. As the sanjak had always had the status of yurtluk-ocaklık (*livâ-i mezbûr öteden berû bervech-i yûrtluk-ocâklık tevcîh olunagelmiş*) and as the services of Emin Pasha during the Van revolt were appreciated, he was given the berat of the yurtluk-ocaklık. This instance shows two significant peculiarities of the yurtluk-ocaklık land in Muş: First the berat of yurtluk-ocaklık was renewed for each candidate for the mutasarrıflık of Muş, who must be from the dynasty of Muş. Second, the governors of Erzurum carried out the proposition and declaration (*arz ve inha*) of granting Muş as a yurtluk ocaklık.[121] As will be explained throughout this chapter, the granting of yurtluk-ocaklık lands was also an object of struggle among family members in particular and a dimension of the negotiation among provincial authorities in general.

2.3   Utilization of Frontier Tribes

If the first step for Emin Pasha's promotion was the suppression of Timur Bey's revolt, the second one was his use of the issue of conscription as leverage. Conscription was seen as a significant part of the imposition of order in the region (*silk-i nizâma idhâli*). In this instance, Emin Pasha made two demands:

119 BOA. HAT. 703/33819, 29 Zilhicce 1247 (30 May 1832).
120 Ibid.; BOA. HAT. 659/32173 C, 6 Şaban 1247 (11 December 1831).
121 BOA. HAT. 659/32173 C, 6 Şaban 1247 (11 December 1831).

the contracts of mukâta'as of Hınıs, Tekman, and Malazgird and immunity from the intervention of neighboring governors. In return, he promised to enlist tribesmen for the Mansure Army. Emin Pasha struggled for immunity from the control of the governors of Erzurum. One of the best examples was his direct request to the commander-in-chief about his wish to take part in the Mansure Army and his demand to be exempt from the intervention of the governors of Erzurum. Although the willingness of the pasha to provide conscripts was appreciated, his demands for immunity from the control of Erzurum's governors were seen as improper.[122]

The issue of military conscription is related to human resources. In the case of the eastern provinces, these resources were mainly drawn from the tribal populations – nomadic and seminomadic groups. Therefore, Emin Pasha's suggestion of enlisting tribesmen into the new army went hand-in-hand with the settlement of the tribes.

2.3.1 *The Case of the Tribe of Sıpkî*

Due to the conscription policy of Qajar Crown Prince Abbas Mirza and the advance of Russian armies on the Iranian lands, several semi-nomadic tribes in Iran migrated to the Ottoman side. A significant number of the tribe of Sıpkî had to migrate from Iranian lands to Van and Muş on the Ottoman side with their chief Süleyman Agha when the Russian armies moved towards the Khanate of Revan in the 1810s. Although Ottoman lands on the northeastern frontier were abundant in terms of pasturing grounds, this was not the case for winter grazing. Thus, the semi-nomadic tribes had to negotiate their needs with the Ottoman local authorities and Kurdish dynasties.[123] In the early 1830s, the settlement of the Sıpkî tribe corresponded to the aims of Emin Pasha. The sanjaks of Hınıs, Tekman, and Malazgirt were contracted to Emin Pasha, and in return he offered to carry out the settlement of the Sıpkî and to occupy them with agriculture (*hayme-nişinlikten ferâgat iderek ziraâ't ve harâset ile meşgûl*). However, Emin Pasha did not immediately perform his promise with the excuse that he could still not sort out the matter financially. The question was whether the expense of new conscripts would be covered by the three mukâta'as contracted to him, or directly by the central state.[124] This was the financial side of the issue.

---

122 BOA. HAT. 308/18189, 29 Zilhicce 1245 (21 June 1830).
123 Yener Koç, 'Nomadic Pastoral Tribes at the Intersection of the Ottoman, Persian and Russian Empires (1820s–1890s)' (Phd. diss., Boğaziçi University, 2020), 91.
124 BOA. HAT. 309/18264, 29 Zilhicce 1245 (21 June 1830).

The other side was about the willingness of the Sıpkî to settle. Some people who knew the region argued that it was impossible to settle the Sıpkî without coercion. During the nineteenth century, especially with the Tanzimat reforms, Ottoman authorities applied a set of strategies to settle tribes across the empire. Yonca Köksal, in her article on settlement practices in Ankara, states that the "geopolitical location" of a tribe was a key factor for determining state-tribe relations, especially whether the state used mediation, coercion, or a mix of both.[125] On the frontiers, the best way for governmental circles to proceed was to search for "mediators" to settle tribes.

Emin Pasha was regarded as an appropriate mediator. In one report, he argued that Muş was in the middle of Kurdistan and that the Kurds and tribes of the sanjak would not act without his support or consent. More importantly, the pasha stressed and governmental authorities did not deny that the family of Emin Pasha, the dynasty of Muş, had always been in the service of the empire (*ebâ-'an-cedd devlet-i aliyyenin hizmetinde*). Emin Pasha justified his most important aim from the beginning – joining the Mansure Army by enlisting Kurdish tribesmen – with such a family history. Such a desire underscores that local actors in a frontier region of the empire had appropriated and adapted to military reforms – the constitution of a brand-new army – after the abolition of the Janissaries. Emin Pasha even manipulated the Mansure Army to consolidate his power.

Emin Pasha's aim to settle the Sıpkî tribe was a part of his wish to join the Mansure Army and he was partially successful in settling the tribe. The Ottoman authorities were persuaded by his partial success and so the alliance between Emin Pasha and the government reached one of its golden moments, at least for a short while.[126] As aforementioned, in return for settling the tribes in the region, he obtained the contracts of Hınıs, Tekman, and Malazgird.

Sıpkî was one of the tribes in question and it had long been a matter of debate between the Ottoman Empire and Iran. To understand the contentious situation of the tribes between Iran and the Ottoman Empire, it is necessary to recall the terms of the first Erzurum Treaty of 1823. As Sabri Ateş puts it:

> Because the *casus belli* for Iran was the Haydaran and Sıpkî migration to the Ottoman side, the treaty's third article – the so-called *Ekrâd maddesi* or "Kurdish article" – was especially contentious. ... It was finally concluded that the populations in question could remain where they were

---

125   Yonca Köksal, "Coercion and Mediation: Centralization and Sedentarization of Tribes in the Ottoman Empire," Middle Eastern Studies 42, no. 3 (May 2006): 472.
126   BOA. C. ML. 269/11018, 13 Zilkade 1246 (25 April 1831).

but should be prevented from raiding territory and allowed to return permanently to Iran. If they choose the latter option, Ottoman authorities would refuse them if they tried to return, whereas Iranian authorities would prohibit them from raiding or crossing back over. The fourth article stipulated that in line with previous treaties, neither party would protect fugitives or tribes that crossed the frontier.[127]

However, even after the treaty, debate over those tribes continued, making control and surveillance of cross border movements difficult. One of the dynamics of the bargaining of Emin Pasha was the settlement of the Sıpkî, a tribe on the frontier. In fact, the family of Emin Pasha had played crucial roles in the migration and settlement of tribes on the frontier. For instance, his cousin Selim Pasha, the mutasarrıflık of whom coincided with the 1821–23 Ottoman-Iranian Wars, played a crucial role in the settlement of the Haydaran and Sıpkî.[128] As Sabri Ateş states, Selim Pasha, together with the governor of Erzurum, Celaleddin Pasha, was responsible for the continuing migration of the Haydaran and Sıpkî tribes to Ottoman lands, which resulted in complaints from Iranians.[129] The Sıpkî tribe would be a matter of discussion between Ottoman and Iranian authorities "again" in the early 1830s.[130] The Iranians demanded the return of the tribe which had crossed the border to reside in Ottoman lands. The Ottomans did not approve of the return of the tribe, claiming that no matter the reason, the Sıpkî had come to Ottoman lands and did not want to go back; sending them back could only be realized by means of force and violence. The Ottoman government asked for this excuse to be accepted. However, Iran objected to this argument. If the Sıpkî remained in Ottoman lands, it would cause rumors among other tribes in the Qajar Empire. In other words, the authority of the Qajars over the Kurdish tribes would be shaken, and it could be deprived of the necessary tools to prevent them from going beyond the frontiers.[131] It is clear that for both Ottoman and Iranian authorities, the tribes were sources of manpower, and therefore their mobility had to be controlled.

---

127 Ateş, *The Ottoman-Iranian Borderlands*, 56–7.
128 BOA. HAT. 802/27108, 13 Cemaziyelevvel 1239 (15 January 1824).
129 Ateş, *The Ottoman-Iranian Borderlands*, 50. Although the Haydaran were in good relations with the notables of Muş during the 1820s, in later years they were fell to loggerheads and the Haydaran moved forward to Erciş (Van). Erdal Çiftçi, "Osmanlıdan Cumhuriyet'e Hayalî bir aşiret olarak Heyderan Aşireti ve Değişimi," in *Kürt Aşiretleri: Aktör, Müttefik ve Şaki*, eds. Tuncay Şur and Yalçın Çakmak, (Istanbul: İletişim Yayınları, 2022), 261.
130 Ateş, *The Ottoman-Iranian Borderlands*, 56–7.
131 BOA. HAT. 794/36840 G, 28 Zilhicce 1247 (29 May 1832).

The project of Ottoman governments concerning the Sıpkî was clear: settling the tribe and, in so doing, securing a source of troops. This plan was even negotiated with Süleyman Agha, the leader of the tribe. After the negotiation, it was decided that the tribe should be protected from the intervention of Iranian authorities, as the importance of the tribe was once again realized during the Van issue (that is, the revolt of Timur Pasha). Süleyman Agha proved his loyalty to the Ottoman state (*ibrâz-ı sadakat*) when he collaborated with Emin Pasha to suppress the Van revolt. However, on his return, he allegedly had trouble with Emin Pasha. Then, Süleyman Agha appeared before Esad Pasha and described his situation without complaining about Emin Pasha. After repeating his words of loyalty and his readiness for the service, Süleyman Agha recalled the terms of the previous negotiation, about which Emin Pasha had also informed Esad Pasha. According to these terms, when the Sıpkî tribe was saved from the intervention of Iran and came to be protected by the Ottoman government, the tribe was to be settled in parts of the Hınıs, Malazgird, and Tekman districts (*kazâ*) that remained within the province of Erzurum and were contracted out to Emin Pasha.[132]

However, relying on his role in the suppression of the Van revolt, Süleyman Agha of the Sıpkî sought to strengthen his hand by renegotiating the terms of their settlement. This was the source of debate between Emin Pasha and Süleyman Agha, as the latter claimed parts of Hınıs and Tekman, which remained in Erzurum, as well as the mukâta'a of Malazgird, which had already been contracted out to Emin Pasha. If he was awarded the contracts of these mukâta'as, Süleyman Agha promised that after his tribe abandoned their tents and became engaged in agriculture, he would constitute, within four to five months a battalion (*tabur*) for the Mansure Army, the salary, uniforms and expenses of which would be covered by the government. For the training of the battalion, he also asked for a mentor from Istanbul, but officers (*zâbitân*) would be chosen from among the agha's relatives. As a second option, Süleyman Agha offered that if his tribe settled in Adilcevaz or Erciş in the sanjak of Van, he would form only half a battalion. Consequently, Esad Pasha, not wishing to offend Emin Pasha, who was also instrumental in the suppression of the Van revolt, was of the opinion that other places in Van, Adilcevaz, or Erciş should be allocated to the Sıpkî.[133] By demanding the contracts of the mukâta'as – whether in Erzurum or Van – and by offering to form a salaried battalion from among his tribesmen, Süleyman Agha claimed a place in the web of power relations during the first half of the nineteenth century.

---

132   Ibid.
133   Ibid.

The contracts of the mukâta'as of the parts of Hınıs and Tekman in Erzurum and also Malazgird were awarded to Emin Pasha in exchange for the settlement of the Sıpkî and some other tribes at the end of the Russian-Ottoman War of 1828–1829. However, the settlement of the tribes was thorny due to two main problems. The first problem stemmed from the power relations between the tribes and local pashas, and the second concerned the financial burden of the settlement process. Although Esad Pasha, the governor of Erzurum and commander-in-chief of east, reported that a debate arose between Emin Pasha and Süleyman Agha of the Sıpkî after the suppression of the Van revolt, the relationship between two actors was actually strong. He even argued that because of his close intimacy with Süleyman Agha, Emin Pasha played a central role in the settlement of Sıpkî. Although the settlement of frontier tribes was not a new tendency for the beys of Muş, it is necessary to understand Emin Pasha's specific motivations. Through the settlement of the Sıpkî, Emin Pasha both sought a position in the army by promising the conscription of tribal members and, as mutasarrıf of Muş, he wanted to easily collect taxes from the settled tribe. However, the tribe, as Esad Pasha reported, 'created trouble.' In the previous year, Emin Pasha allowed the tribe to settle in Malazgird as their winter quarters. Soon afterwards, peasants started to send petitions complaining about the burdens and cruelty inflicted by the tribe.[134] Upon hearing about the situation, Emin Pasha claimed that he would carry out what was necessary, punish them and send them back. Yet the pasha never fulfilled such a promise. At this point, Esad Pasha, the governor of Erzurum, recalled initial doubts that the Sıpkî tribe could not be settled without a degree of force. The Sıpkî were said to be notorious for brigandage, and their behavior proved that it was difficult to keep them under control.[135] This also reinforced the idea that the reason for Emin Pasha bringing the Sıpkî from Iran was only to strengthen his position. Certainly, this kind of statements was a sign of established biased view of the provincial authorities against nomadic tribes and Kurdish nobility.

The second part of the problem regarding tribal sedentarization was the financial dimension, which brought the issue of Hınıs, Tekman and Malazgirt mukâta'as back to the agenda. The governor of Erzurum, Esad Pasha was also confused about covering the expenses of the troop that would be recruited

---

134 "... 'aşîret-i mezkûre her ne kadar kazâ-i mezkûre olvechile yerleşdirilmiş ise de bunlar bütün bütün kazâ-i mezkûr fukarâsına tahmîl-i bâr iderek envâ'-i ta'addiyâta ibtidâr itmekde olduklarından kazâ-i mezbûr fukarâsı tarafından tazallüm-i hâl siyâkında ..." BOA. HAT. 718/34245 D, 29 Zilhicce 1247 (30 May 1832).

135 "... 'aşîret-i mezkûrenin mine'l-kadîm ma'rûf oldukları şekâvet ve el-hâletü hâzihi meşhûd olân etvâr ve hareketlerine nazaran usûl-i nizâm üzere rabtı kabûl itmeleri me'mûl olmadığından ..." ibid.

from among the Sıpkî. Would they be met from these mukâta'as, which had been contracted out to Emin Pasha, given that they would be a part of the Mansure Army, or would the salaries and expenses of the troop be covered by the center, as in other places in the empire?[136] The confusion of the governor of Erzurum was a sign of an in-betweenness or a transition from the ancien regime to the new order.

In order to solve the problem of the expense of the troops, Esad Pasha summoned the regiment master (*alay beyi*) of Hınıs, Abdülkadir Agha, to get a detailed information about the revenue of the mukâta'as of Hınıs and Tekman. The mukâta'as of Hınıs and Tekman were composed of eight *nahiyes* (sub-district) nıfs-ı Hınıs, Göksu, Dağönü, Tekman, and Suşehri in Erzurum and Varto, Henderesi, and Amber in Muş. Emin Pasha had "seized" the nahiyes in Muş asserting the title of *pasha of Muş* (*Mûş pâşâlığı cihetiyle zabt û rabt itmekde olduğuna*). To put it differently, as Muş had been granted to Emin Pasha as a yurtluk-ocaklık, said nahiyes were automatically under his control. The parts remaining in Erzurum were contracted out to Emin Pasha, who was paying fifty thousand *guruş* (piasters) annually in return.[137] Esad Pasha's choice of words – *zabt û rabt* (seizure) – to define landholding practices in Muş are remarkable, in showing the perception of provincial officials about these hereditary landholdings.

Accordingly, to understand the debate over the Hınıs and Tekman mukâta'as, it would be beneficial to survey their situation at the beginning of the nineteenth century. During the reign of Selim III, in 1804, Hınıs and Tekman were granted to Murad Pasha, the uncle of Emin Pasha, as a yurtluk-ocaklık.[138] After him, the father of Emin Pasha, Yusuf Pasha was granted the sanjak of Muş, and the sanjaks of Hınıs and Tekman were annexed (*ilhak kılınmış*) to it.[139] The governor of Erzurum also argued that these mukâta'as had been awarded as mâlikâne to the family members of Emin Pasha for twenty to thirty years.[140] Although Hınıs and Tekman at first were granted as yurtluk-ocaklıks, in time they were contracted out to members of Muş dynasty as mâlikâne. Furthermore, it can be inferred that with the establishment of the Mansure Army, some portions of these mukâta'as were confiscated by the treasury and used for the expense of the new army. For instance, the shares of Abdurahman Pasha and Abdülfettah Bey – from among Alaaddin Pashazades – was confiscated in 1243 (1828) once both passed away.[141] However, after the end of

---

136 Ibid.
137 BOA. HAT. 718/34245 D, 29 Zilhicce 1247 (30 May 1832).
138 BOA. HAT. 175/7583 E, 29 Zilhicce 1218 (10 April 1804).
139 BOA. C. DH. 133/6650, 29 Ramazan 1223 (18 November 1808).
140 BOA. HAT. 718/34245 D, 29 Zilhicce 1247 (30 May 1832).
141 BOA. C. ML. 269/11018, 13 Zilkade 1246 (25 Nisan 1831).

the Ottoman-Russian War (1828–1829) the mukâta'as of Hınıs and Tekman together with Malazgird were granted to Emin Pasha who in return, as stated, would settle the Sıpkî and some other tribes, and work for their conscription.

The sub-districts of Hınıs and Tekman were administratively divided between Erzurum and Muş and were contracted out to Emin Pasha. To put it differently, as the mutasarrıf of Muş, Emin Pasha had control over the sub-districts of Hınıs and Tekman which remained within the borders of Muş as a yurtluk-ocaklık. For those remaining in Erzurum, he was paying fifty thousand guruş annually. However, the question of whether the mukâta'as should be united and the sub-districts in both Erzurum and Muş be confiscated and governed by the Mukâta'at Treasury was still valid.[142] The main argument about the unity of the mukâta'as is that the other three sub-districts in Muş were so extensive and productive as to be worth fifty thousand guruş. Emin Pasha's annual payment of fifty thousand guruş was just for the sub-districts in Erzurum. Briefly, if the whole mukâta'as of Hınıs and Tekman, with its eight sub-districts, were confiscated and administered by the Mukâta'at Treasury, the gain would be one hundred thousand guruş.[143] This meant that the treasury was losing around fifty thousand guruş.

Yet the problem was not only a financial loss. Esad Pasha emphasized that the nomination of an official from the Mukâta'at Treasury and the central administration of the mukâta'as would create problems. It would not be a problem in the nahiyes in Erzurum; they would be well governed. However, if an official were to be appointed to govern the nahiyes remaining in the sanjak of Muş, it would be risky. He emphasized that these nahiyes were not only in Kurdistan but specifically in Muş, where Emin Pasha could provoke the Kurds (referring to Kurdish tribes). This would result in great difficulties for the administration of the mukâta'as.[144] Therefore, the idea of the confiscation and administration of the mukâta'as of Hınıs and Tekman by the Mukâta'at Treasury was renounced, and Emin Pasha continued to hold them. After a while, he was promoted to the rank of *mîr-i mirânlık*.[145] It is important that the governor of Erzurum characterized Muş as a specific, fragile place within Kurdistan, emanating from its

---

142 The Mukâta'at Treasury was established in 1826 for the expenses of the new army, and it was then called the Mansure Treasury. Stanford J. Shaw and Ezel Kural Shaw, *History of the Ottoman Empire and Modern Turkey*, 2 vols., vol. 2 (Cambridge: Cambridge University Press, 1976–77), 42.

143 BOA. HAT. 718/34245 D, 29 Zilhicce 1247 (30 May 1832).

144 "... nevâhi-i mezkûre Kürdistân içinde ve bi'lhusûs Muş dâhil-i hükûmeti olan mahallerle ihtilâtda bulunduğundan nevâhi-i mezkûrenin mukâta'ât tarafından müdir ile zabt ve ta'şîri takdirinde pâşâ-yı mûmâileyh ekrâdı tahrîk iderek idâresine ..." Ibid.

145 BOA. HAT. 727/34640, 29 Zilhicce 1248 (19 May 1833). Mîr-i mirân was new title for *beyler beyi*. Stanford J. Shaw and Ezel Kural Shaw, *History of the Ottoman Empire and Modern Turkey*, 499.

being at the frontier and from the strength of local dynasties. It also shows that the debate about administrating Ottoman Kurdistan from the center had already begun in the first quarter of the nineteenth century, but Istanbul opted not to do so due to geopolitical and socioeconomic circumstances.

In the aftermath of the decision regarding Emin Pasha's administration of the mukâta'as of Hınıs and Tekman, his *haznedar* (treasurer) was questioned about the number of conscripts and their expenses. The haznedar suggested that including the Sıpkî and some other nomadic (*hayme-nişin*) tribes in Muş, the number amounted to four to five thousand. Their settlement would commence in winter, and in summer, new villages would be established in proper places. They would be exempt from taxes for a time during their settlement. After that, they could be compelled to pay taxes; and more importantly, if they attempted to resist, their locations would be known (since they would have abandoned their tents), and they could be easily suppressed.[146] This more or less similar to the strategies of sedentarization that Ottoman authorities had applied to other nomadic groups all over the empire. For instance, Köksal argues that during the Tanzimat, tax exemption continued to be a strong "incentive" for settlement, as it had been prior to that.[147] It is also remarkable that Emin Pasha's treasurer portrayed a sedentary tribe as one more easily suppressed in case of unrest, showing the dimension of control which was an aim of their settlement. By such arguments, Emin Pasha appealed to the aims of the state that in the end, overlapped with his own. The pasha asked that the expenses be covered by the center claiming that he could not afford it. With such arguments, Emin Pasha intended to benefit from the opportunities that emerged in the establishment of a modern army. Although the mukâta'as of Hınıs, Tekman and Malazgird had been awarded to him in return for the settlement and recruitment of the Sıpkî, he tactically tried to dispense with the expenses of military conscripts since he was aware of the fact that the central treasury was covering the expenses of the new army.

2.3.1.1 The Cases of the Tribes of Cemaldini and Haydaran

In the Ottoman archives, provincial authorities describe Emin Pasha as the kind of man who could clear himself of any allegations with various tricks. No matter how much he was warned, he went his own way. In May 1833, Esad Pasha reported that Emin Pasha was again involved in a tribal issue, which would

---

146 "… olvakt muhâlefet sûretine düşseler bile çadır altından çıkmış ve yerlu yurdlu bulunmuş olacaklarından icrâ-yı idâre mümkün olunacağına …" BOA. HAT. 718/34245 D, 29 Zilhicce 1247 (30 May 1832).

147 Köksal, "Coercion and Mediation," 479.

endanger relations with Iran. Offended by the prince of Khoy, Cihangir Mirza, Koro Agha of the Cemaldini [Cemaleddin, Cemadanlı] tribe had migrated Muş with a hundred and fifty families and Emin Pasha gave them shelter. Upon this, Cihangir Mirza, sent an envoy (*elçi*) to submit a letter to the governor of Erzurum. Referring to the good, strong relations between the two states, the prince demanded the return of Koro Agha and his tribe accompanied by some men of Esad Pasha. When Emin Pasha was informed of this request, he replied that refraining from causing a trans-border problem he did not allow the agha to stay longer in Muş and Koro Agha went to Köroğlu Plateau in Kars, which was on the border with Russia. The governor of Erzurum informed Cihangir Mirza once Koro Agha was summoned from Kars, he would be returned to Iran. However, Esad Pasha believed that Emin Pasha lied when said that he had not allowed Koro Agha to remain in Muş.[148]

The Cemaldini was not the only tribe over which Emin Pasha had claimed control. The Haydaran, in the migration of whom the Alaaddin Pashazades played a crucial role was among the disputed tribes (*münâzaün-fih aşair*) between the Ottoman and Iranian empires. In 1820, the migration of the Haydaran from Iranian lands to the Ottoman side had become a matter of contention between two empires during the rule of Selim Pasha, the cousin of Emin Pasha, in Muş. The Iranian authorities blamed Selim Pasha, and the governor of Erzurum, Celaleddin Pasha.[149] First, in 1818, 500 hundred families of the Haydaran with their chief Mehmed Agha, then 1000 families of the tribe under the leadership of Kasım Agha migrated to Ottoman lands, specifically to Muş and its environs.[150] Another branch of the Haydaran under the chieftainship of Ferhad Agha also came to Muş with the help of Selim Pasha in 1819.[151] The reasons behind the migration of the Haydaran to the Ottoman side were the same with those of the Sıpkî: the precariousness stemming from the advancing Russian armies in northwestern Iran, and as precaution to this, the increase in the efforts of Abbas Mirza to conscript and tax tribes.[152]

148   BOA. HAT. 721/34364 L, 29 Zilhicce 1248 (19 May 1833), BOA. HAT. 789/36774, 20 Rebiülahir 1249 (6 September 1834). Later, Esad Pasha called Koro Agha to Erzurum with the aim of sending him back to Iran accompanied by a few men. Yet allegedly, Cihangir Mirza sent a letter to Koro Agha threatening that if he had arrived with the men of Esad Pasha, he would have been executed. Although Koro became afraid of going to Iran, Esad Pasha managed to persuade him. BOA. HAT. 789/36774, 20 Rebiülahir 1249 (6 September 1834).
149   Ateş, *Ottoman-Iranian Borderlands*, 50.
150   Koç, 'Nomadic Pastoral Tribes at the Intersection,' 95.
151   Erdal Çiftçi, "Fragile Alliances in the Ottoman East: The Heyderan Tribe and the Empire, 1820–1929," (Phd. diss., Bilkent University, 2018), 105.
152   Koç, 'Nomadic Pastoral Tribes at the Intersection,' 97.

The Haydaran became a matter of contention again in the early 1830s. Apart from the aforementioned Sıpkî tribe, two thousand families from the Haydaran tribe had been spending their winters in Muş. However, the issue became more complicated when the Prince of Khoy went to the tent of Kasım Agha, the leader of the tribe, to persuade the agha to return with him to Iran. Kasım Agha accepted the prince's offer, yet the younger brother of the agha, Sultan Agha stayed in Muş with a thousand families. The other thousand families migrated with Kasım Agha to Iran.[153]

The meeting and the bargaining of an Iranian prince with a tribal leader provides significant clues about the function of these tribes for Iran. Lois Beck emphasized that tribes in Iran were "constant," as the states in Iran needed the power of the tribes for "levies, revenues and regional security."[154] Beck's remarks also explain the perception of these tribes in the Ottoman Empire; not only did government authorities regard the tribes as sources of recruitment and taxation, local actors pursued opportunities to secure and reinforce their negotiating positions in power struggles by using the tribes.

In the same vein, Emin Pasha, given his support of the Sıpkî tribe, was accused of pursuing only his own interests from the beginning. This so-called "interest" was concretized when Emin Pasha collected twelve hundred purses of guruş from Sultan Agha of the Haydaran in the name of *kışlakiye* (the tax for winter quarters) in return for the tribe's having spent winters in Muş. As Esad Pasha had reported, the tribe could not have the power and opportunity to oppose him during the winter and Emin Pasha manipulated this situation.[155]

Emin Pasha later would defend himself by arguing that although it was true that he had taken six hundred purses from the Haydaran, it was a long-standing rule for the mutasarrıfs of Muş to take *sâlyâne* (annual tax) from the said tribe (salyane here refers to kışlakiye). In addition, according to his defense, the Haydaran had long been troublesome, so he could not levy taxes on them. Instead the common people (re'âyâ *and* berâyâ) were obliged to pay taxes. The taxes that could not be collected from the Haydaran had been imposed on

---

153   BOA. HAT. 721/34364 L, 29 Zilhicce 1248 (19 May 1833).
154   Lois Beck, "The Tribes and the State in Nineteeth and Twentieth Century Iran," in *Tribes and State Formation in the Middle East,* eds. Philip S. Khoury and Joseph Kostiner (Berkeley: University of California Press, 1990), 202.
155   BOA. HAT. 721/34364 L, 29 Zilhicce 1248 (19 May 1833). To put it differently, tribes had to pay the tax of kışlakiye to local authorities in return for sheltering there and provisioning of themselves and their livestock during the winters. However, the problem here is that local authorities, who were generally notables, did not share this tax with peasants, who were the actual providers. As a result, winterquartering of nomads became a burden on peasants who were not paid for their services like providing tribes with food and shelter along with their livestock in their villages.

local inhabitants of Muş. Emin Pasha explained himself by arguing that, in this case, he had collected the sâlyâne from Haydaran and thus rescued the poor inhabitants from this obligation. He also added that if he had been informed about the abolishment of the sâlyâne, he would not have taken even a single piaster.[156] Although the tax called kışlakiye had not been abolished, it was not allowed for it to be levied on frontier tribes like the Haydaran as they were among the disputed tribes between Iran and Ottoman Empire. However, Emin Pasha insisted on being exempt from compensating for the kışlak tax with the excuse that the Haydaran had paid it to him in return for winter quarters and the income of certain villages in Muş.[157]

Emin Pasha's interest in the settlement of the Haydaran in Muş became clear with the imposition of a tax on the tribe, yet he got into trouble when Sultan Agha informed his brother Kasım Agha – who had already left for Iran with Cihangir Mirza – about the money issue. Upon Kasım Agha's complaint, Cihangir Mirza sent a letter to Esad Pasha demanding both the repayment of the tax and the return of Sultan Agha to Iran, claiming that the Haydaran were in fact a tribe of Iran and that the eldest brother, Kasım Agha, who was the chief of the tribe, was already there.[158] Upon receiving the correspondence, the governor of Erzurum, Esad Pasha wrote to Emin Pasha emphasizing that the situation of the Haydaran was still a dispute between the two states. Once it was decided whether the tribe would stay in Iranian or Ottoman lands, necessary steps would be taken regarding the repayment of the tax. More importantly, Emin Pasha was warned to avoid giving rise to a problem between the two states and to be careful about his deeds. However, according to Esad Pasha, Emin Pasha was not leaving his habit of deceitfulness and ignoring any advice.[159]

Upon further inquiry, Emin Pasha sent the governor a letter in the name of Sultan Agha with his treasurer along with a tribal notable (*torun*) of the Haydaran informing him that Sultan Agha had voluntarily given Emin Pasha six hundred purses, not twelve hundred, in the name of kışlakiye. In return,

---

156 "… Hayderânlûdan altı yüz kise alındığı vâki' ise de eslâfımız olân Muş mutasarrıfları dâhi 'aşîret-i merkûmeden olvechile sâlyâne aldıkları usûl-i sabikadan idüğü ve 'aşîret-i merkûme sinîn-i vefîreden berû fermânber olmayub kutta-üt-tarîk olduklarından re'âyâ ve berâyâ kullarının üzerlerine mu'tâd olan sâlyâne …" BOA. HAT. 722/34418 D, 29 Zilhicce 1249 (9 May 1834). Although at the beginning the amount of kışlakiye taken from Haydaran was specified as 1,200 kese, later documents mentioned an amount of half that. However, the reason of the discount was not specified.

157 Ibid.

158 BOA. HAT. 721/34364 L, 29 Zilhicce 1248 (19 May 1833).

159 "… mu'tâd olduğu hilekârlıkdan bir vechile ferâgat ve bir sûretle kabûl-i nasihat itme-yerek …" Ibid.

Emin Pasha claimed that he provided the tribe with villages to inhabit and, bestowed ceremonial robes, and provided them with grain. Emphasizing that although Kasım Agha had gone to Iran, the Haydaran were a tribe of the Ottoman state; thus the letter argued that Iran did not have the right to interfere in its affairs.[160] However, it turned out that the situation was more complicated. While Emin Pasha was sending a letter allegedly from Sultan Agha to Esad Pasha, the agha at the same time had a letter delivered by one of his men to Esad Pasha, claiming that he had given that letter to Emin Pasha unwillingly. The agha also informed the envoy of Iran that he should not trust the letter, which he had written under duress. Furthermore, Sultan Agha stated that if Esad Pasha called him to his presence and supported him, he would say that his was a tribe of the Ottoman state and Iran did not have any rights in that regard. And he would want compensation for the money from Emin Pasha. To grasp the details of the situation, Esad Pasha called for Sultan Agha and other influential tribal members.[161]

Two important points are revealed in this case. First, Sultan Agha, by sending letters to both Esad Pasha and the envoy of Iran, did not want to risk his situation in either of the states. He did not dare do this in the presence of Emin Pasha, either. After guaranteeing the support of Esad Pasha, he could ignore the role of Emin Pasha. Second, this story points out how the tribes were not passive objects over which government authorities bargained and implemented their policies. Rather, they had an active, decisive role in the policies of the region. As Sabri Ateş states, their "indigenous agency" should be brought back into history.[162]

The concerns of the governor of Erzurum became justified, the deeds of Emin Pasha resulted in a crisis on the frontier, leading to a furious conversation between local authorities, Esad Pasha, and the Iranian envoy. Emphasizing the unpleasant acts of Emin Pasha in this interstate matter, the Iranian envoy implied that neither the central nor local authorities had the capability to control this subject of the imperial state. Herewith, he offered that the Iranians could deal with Emin Pasha, and take both the money and the tribe from him if Ottoman authorities committed to not becoming involved.[163] The speech of the envoy clearly pointed out the delicacy of the issue.

Having become irritated by the attitude and tone of the Iranian envoy, Esad Pasha emphasized that the situation of the Haydaran was still uncertain – that is, it had not been decided whether it was a tribe of the Ottoman Empire

---

160 Ibid.
161 Ibid.
162 Ateş, *The Ottoman-Iranian Borderlands*, 6.
163 BOA. HAT. 721/34364 L, 29 Zilhicce 1248 (19 May 1833).

or of Iran. Thereafter, he warned Emin Pasha again, stating that his disobedience was becoming clearer day by day and so his being brought into line was becoming more and more necessary. Therefore, Esad Pasha ordered Emin Pasha to send him both Koro Agha of the Cemaldini and Sultan Agha of the Haydaran along with some tribal notables. If he did not obey, the attack on Muş by Iran would be unavoidable.[164] Such an order shows the control and influence of Emin Pasha over the frontier tribes. Despite being the governor of Erzurum, Esad Pasha needed the mediation of Emin Pasha to control nomadic and semi-nomadic Kurdish tribes. Emin Pasha was manipulating the mobility and disputed situations of those tribes.

2.4 Conclusion

The beys of Muş, like provincial notables all over the Ottoman Empire, enjoyed tremendous political and economic power especially during the eighteenth century. Large tracts of hereditary lands from which they benefited and the great immunities of yurtluk-ocaklıks – the right over agricultural surplus and to tax nomadic groups – constituted the main contours of their power. Although it was a part of imperial pragmatism and not peculiar to Ottoman Kurdistan, the yurtluk-ocaklık type of land usufruct provided great autonomy to such provincial leaders. In particular, the wars with Russia and Iran and the porous nature of the frontier, provided Kurdish notables with the ground to negotiate and consolidate their range of political and economic power.

Nonetheless, both the power of Kurdish notables and the status of yurtluk-ocaklıks changed in the course of time. The Khanate of Bitlis enjoyed its heyday during the sixteenth century due to the Ottoman-Safavid rivalry, but started to falter in the eighteenth century. Therefore, it was no coincidence that Alaaddin Bey of Muş consolidated his power by assuming the deputy-governorship of Muş in the mid-eighteenth century. Despite the scarcity of sources about Alaaddin Bey's pre-eighteenth century lineage, it is possible that they were a local family enjoying either yurtluk-ocaklık lands or mâlikâne-mukataʿas, but overshadowed by the khans of Bitlis.

However, starting with the deputy-governorship of Alaaddin Bey, his sons and grandsons held the sanjak of Muş through mutasarrıflık and increased their range of power by extending those lands – taking for instance the mukataʿas of Hınıs, Tekman, and Malazgirt as either mâlikâne or as yurtluk-ocaklıks. Thus, the boundaries of yurtluk-ocaklıks also changed during this time. As will be discussed in chapter 5, neither the boundaries nor the revenues of the villages

164 Ibid.

held by Emin Pasha and his brothers in the second half of the nineteenth century can be accurately known.

Emin Pasha might be the last member of his family to enjoy political and economic autonomy in a frontier zone of the Ottoman Empire. Although the abolition of the yurtluk-ocaklık type of land usufruct and the economic and political privileges it entailed were accelerated after the promulgation of Tanzimat reforms, this process was gradual and actually started in the first half of the nineteenth century. Therefore, the story of Emin Pasha was important for the assertion of Ottoman state control over these lands on its eastern frontier and the strategies and maneuvers of local notables to keep these lands intact. To achieve this primary aim, Emin Pasha benefited from inter-imperial wars, manipulated the status of frontier tribes, took advantage of local uprisings, took part in the century's military and economic reforms, and when necessary did not hesitate to rise up. The next chapter will introduce the story of Emin Pasha's revolt and his fall from power, albeit temporarily.

CHAPTER 3

The Revolt of Emin Pasha: Punishment and Cooptation

The Spring and summer of 1833 were eventful for Emin Pasha and his brothers. Esad Pasha, the governor of Erzurum ordered Emin Pasha to send the tribal elders of the Haydaran and Cemaldini to Erzurum, as recompense for the money taken from the Haydaran in the name of kışlakiye, and to leave Muş and accept his place of exile which would be announced later. Esad Pasha, was clear in presenting two options for Emin Pasha: either obey the rules or accept the results of his disobedience. Emin Pasha chose the second. When another member of the Alaaddin Pashazades, one of his cousins, Hüseyin Bey was granted Muş instead of him, Emin Pasha did not recognize this decision. Taking shelter in the house of beys of Atak in Diyarbekir, Emin Pasha sought to establish a web of alliances from among provincial notables and Kurdish tribes, with the help of whom he hoped to seize power in Muş again. However, in the course of time, Emin Pasha lost a great portion of his allies with whom the governor of Erzurum, Esad Pasha was in confidential contact. Nevertheless, in the end, he will be pardoned and reincorporated into the Ottoman administrative system, thanks to the military and administrative reforms of the era.

It was no exception for Ottoman central authorities to resettle a local actor in a place far from his sphere of power, as a means of control and surveillance. Likewise, it was no exception for provincial notables to pursue alliances and to revolt to negotiate and accomplish their aims. Nevertheless, the rebellion of Emin Pasha is important to contextualize yurtluk-ocaklık holders of Muş in the network of rebel provincial notables.[1] This chapter will focus on Emin Pasha's rebellion and his search for allies, which spanned borders and circumstances that paved the way for his pardoning. Similarly, Esad Pasha sought coalitions benefiting from the tribal social structure of the region and the rivalry within the Alaaddin Pashazades. Provincial authorities interpreted Emin Pasha's behavior as "trouble," (*gaile*), an "inappropriate attitude" (*harekât- nâmarziye*), "sedition" (*fesad*), "wrong" (isaet) "revolt" (*isyan*), "insubordination" (*tuğyan*)

---

1 For a study of the career of a bandit/rebel, Kara Feyzi, and his transformation into an imperial official and then a recognized a'yân, see Tolga U. Esmer, "A Culture of Rebellion: Networks of Violence and Competing Discourses of Justice in the Ottoman Empire, 1790–1808" (PhD diss., The University of Chicago, 2009).

and as an action to "conquer" (*zabtetmek*) Muş and they described the pasha as a rebel (*bagi*) and a traitor to religion and the state (*hain-i din û devlet*). Did Emin Pasha really intend to "conquer" Muş or just aim to maintain the rights from which his ancestors had benefited? For a better comprehension of the claims, it would be beneficial to keep in mind the practice of rebellion in the pre-Tanzimat context. Hamit Bozarslan argues, "the Ottoman state tradition conceived of rebellion, or at least resistance as a means of bargaining or negotiation by the subordinate peripheral groups for improving their status within the state."[2] In a similar vein, Karen Barkey argues that if early seventeenth-century Ottoman elites rebelled, "they did so to demand that they be incorporated into the state's privileged structure once again."[3] In line with such arguments, Emin Pasha, and later his brothers employed the expression that they were in servitude to the Sublime Porte for generations (*eba'an ced devlet-i aliyyenin hizmetinde*), while negotiating their interests. It is possible to interpret such a statement as a reminder of their status instead of as breaking with imperial center, even if they were not obeying orders.

In the following lines, the peculiarities of the coalitions on both sides – the one around Emin Pasha and the one constituted against him – will be introduced first. Then, Emin Pasha and his brothers' pardon will be elaborated upon together with the respective appointments of Reşid Mehmed and Hafız pashas to the *müşirlik* (military governorship) of Sivas. The submission of many provincial notables of the Balkans and Anatolia in the 1810–1820s enabled the central government to deploy talented officials to subdue Kurdish beys. In this process, one prominent strategy was to employ notables in the vicinity of the region where operations were initiated. The pardoning of Emin Pasha and his brothers can be understood in this context, as well.

The military operations and reforms of both Reşid Mehmed and Hafız pashas also brought a significant transformation to the yurtluk-ocaklık status

---

2   Hamit Bozarslan, "Kurdish Nationalism in Turkey: From Tacit Contract to Rebellion (1919–1925)," in *Essays on the Origins of Kurdish Nationalism* ed. Abbas Vali (Costa Mesa: Mazda, 2003), 186. Bozarslan explains this tradition of rebellion, borrowing from Şerif Mardin, in terms of "tacit contract" (zımnî sözleşme) between the sultan and his subjects. The former had to abide by the contract to protect his reign. In the same vein, rebellions by subjects generally were based on the belief that the ruling class was not standing by their promises. For tacit contract, see Şerif Mardin, *Türk Modernleşmesi*, 22 ed. (Istanbul: İletişim Yayınları, 2013), 106–20.
3   Karen Barkey, *Bandits and Bureaucrats: The Ottoman Route State Centralization* (Ithaca Cornell University Press, 1997), 55–6. Nevertheless, Barkey's approach was also criticized as approaching the Ottoman Empire "as an omnipotent manipulator of the society." Tolga U. Esmer, "Economies of Violence, Banditry and Governance in the Ottoman Empire Around 1800," Past & Present 224, no. 1 (2014): 172.

of Muş. Disclaiming or being compelled to disclaim the sanjak of Muş as a yurtluk-ocaklık, Emin Pasha sought to secure for himself and his relatives twenty-four villages in the most productive parts of the sanjak. His situation fluctuated and was shaped by regional developments, as well. Even his participation in the forces sent to fight Mehmed Ali Pasha of Egypt did not rescue him from his exile in Vidin at the end of the defeat at Nizip. Nevertheless, he managed to return after two years.

3.1 Preparation for the Revolt: In the Pursuit of Allies

While the provincial and central authorities were discussing the control and submission of Emin Pasha, precautions were taken against any turmoil in Muş that could spread to the provinces in its environs, especially to Van – where it could easily turn into a border matter with Iran. The preliminary measure was to determine another mutasarrıf who would be chosen from among Emin Pasha's relatives. As discussed in the previous chapter, in spite of awareness of the necessity of appointing an administrator other than local notables, because of the peculiarities of the region (its being on the frontier, land tenure practices, and tribal social structure) the required infrastructure for such an option did not exist. Moreover, a mutasarrıf from the local family, with a refined knowledge of the region and influence over the tribes and other notables, could also be helpful in constituting a coalition against Emin Pasha.[4]

For provincial authorities, who were certainly afraid of new troubles in a frontier region, the only good news was overcoming the "trouble of Arabistan" (the revolt of Mehmet Ali Pasha of Egypt, which was delayed for a while with the Agreement of Kütahya in 1833). With such an opportunity, Esad Pasha argued that Emin Pasha could no longer get away with his disobedience as it was then possible to allocate every means to pacify him. The only option was for him to settle in a place determined by the governor of Erzurum.[5]

However, Emin Pasha had no thought of submitting easily; rather, he applied a variety of strategies to sustain his position. On one hand, he tried to consolidate his power; on the other, he contacted local authorities to request a pardon. Hitherto, the pivotal pillar of his power had been the tribes of Muş. Therefore, having arranged a meeting with some tribal leaders in Hınıs, Emin Pasha offered them financial aid and villages in return for their collaboration. His revolt was partially motivated by tribal issues. And due to the geopolitical

---

4 BOA. HAT. 790/36808 B, 3 Rebiülahir 1249 (20 August 1833).
5 Ibid.

location of Muş, the pasha could pursue trans-border allies, as well. He crossed the border, came together with Cihangir Mirza, the governor of Khoy, and allegedly said to him that he would conquer lands as far as Sivas for rule by Iran in return for their backing.[6] The details of this meeting are not clear, but he must have secured the support of the prince, as he felt comfortable bargaining with Ottoman authorities. Accordingly, he delivered a letter to Esad Pasha containing two options. He affirmed that he would be at the service of the Sublime Porte if he was pardoned and presented with a robe of honor. Otherwise, he threatened to create trouble in the region with the help of his allies, the tribes and mîrs[7] of Kurdistan. Meanwhile, Emin Pasha allegedly deployed more than five thousand soldiers to Hınıs, where he had already gone.[8]

Provincial authorities were cautious about this coalition, especially regarding the involvement of Cihangir Mirza. Refraining from causing a trans-border problem, the governor of Erzurum carefully tried to dispel this alliance of Emin Pasha. He believed that only then would his dismissal and pacification be possible. The plan was to secretly contact the tribes of the region to win them over. In line with this cautious plan, Esad Pasha did not step back vis-à-vis Emin Pasha's threats. Rather, he set the conditions for his pardon: recompensing the money (kışlakiye) taken from the Haydaran and sending the fugitive Koro Agha (of the Cemaldini) back to Iran. Thus, Esad Pasha challenged Emin Pasha's previous statement that he had not allowed Koro Agha to remain in Muş. The insistence of provincial authorities on sending back fugitive tribal members was because of their concern for causing interstate trouble. For Emin Pasha, a local actor whose subsistence was based on the extraction of surplus from the people over whom he claimed control and influence, tribes were resources through which he could consolidate both political and economic power. Therefore, it is possible to speculate that the pasha levied taxes on Koro Agha as he had on Sultan Agha of the Haydaran.[9]

Emphasizing that Emin Pasha should give up cruelty and his oppression of the people and obey the rules, Esad Pasha – as a final condition – warned him to pay the money he had promised to the Armenian karabaşı (priest) for the Çanlı (Surp Garabet) Monastery that he had plundered during "the invasion."[10] Despite a lack of information about the "invasion," it is possible he was referring

---

6   BOA. HAT. 789/36774, 20 Rebiülahir 1249 (6 September 1833).
7   Mîr is the Kurdish name for the 'bey.' In their correspondeces the Kurdish nobility used also this term to define themselves. In this book, I used both interchangeably.
8   BOA. HAT. 790/36808 B, 3 Rebiülahir 1249 (20 August 1833).
9   Ibid.
10 Ibid.

to the Ottoman-Russian War of 1828–9.[11] Afterwards, Emin Pasha promised to pay the loss, which totaled a few thousand purses, in installments. However, as stated above, the pasha had not yet paid any installments.

Instead of fulfilling the demands of Esad Pasha without laying down conditions, he sent eighty thousand guruş to the Armenian priest. Emin Pasha declared that he would recompense the Haydaran after his pardon and the grant of a robe of honor. Apparently, he sought to first guarantee his position. However, such a demand drew suspicion as Emin Pasha, together with his three brothers, were amassing men and preparing for a revolt. Thus, for Esad Pasha, acceptance of Emin Pasha's clauses would just play into his hands. Emin Pasha had already allegedly spread rumors in the region that he would take robes of honor and a promotion from Esad Pasha by force. From the perspective of the governor of Erzurum, if Emin Pasha received what he requested, he would be feeling more spoiled. Similarly, he would continue to fabricate news that although the commander-in-chief was going to discharge him, he did not dare to do it. Furthermore, Esad Pasha's efforts to make contact with tribal members from Muş could run aground, if Emin Pasha was forgiven without punishment. At this point, the contest between the two actors should also be emphasized. As governor of Erzurum and general commander of the eastern front, Esad Pasha was concerned about any harm to his influence and honor vis-à-vis Emin Pasha's challenge.[12] Needless to say, Esad Pasha was also an actor guarding his own interests in this game.

In addition, Esad Pasha emphasized the necessity of the strengthening of the bond with tribes with whom he had been in confidential contact for a while. According to this plan, after guaranteeing their support, the sanjak of Muş would be granted to Hüseyin Bey, a cousin of Emin, along with the rank of mîr-i mîran. For the voivodeship of Hınıs, cavalryman Mirza Bey from among the Alaaddin Pashazades was seen as appropriate. Furthermore, propaganda was also carried out among the inhabitants of Muş. Men were recruited from among the neighboring districts. For example, under the command of the Beys of Kığı, there were fifteen hundred soldiers. Hüseyin Bey's brother, Sadık Bey led the troops that were deployed in Muş, instead of Hınıs where

---

11 Kemal Beydilli also states that Kurdish tribes plundered the Armenian villages of Pasin, Muş, and Hınıs after the Russian invasion of Erzurum. Beydilli, *1828–1829 Osmanlı-Rus Savaşında*, 386.

12 Ibid. Esad Pasha's treatment of Emin Pasha and of his other brothers cannot be interpreted merely as a reflection of the central state's position. As Özok-Gündoğan also emphasized, despite being state agents in the locality, provincial governors had their own agendas as they became prominent parts of local power relations. Özok-Gündoğan, "The Making of the Ottoman Modern State in the Kurdish Periphery," 32.

Emin Pasha had already been positioned along with his forces. It was known that the ultimate aim of Emin Pasha was Muş, his ancestral stronghold.[13] The composition of the coalition against Emin Pasha and his allies is striking. All were members of the Muş dynasty, Ibrahim Pashazade Hüseyin and the Sadık beys as well as the Murad Pashazade Maksud and the Mirza beys were cousins of Emin Pasha looking for opportunities to rise to power.

Having constituted a coalition from among Emin Pasha's intrafamilial rivals, Esad Pasha sent him a messenger delivering the imperial order for his dismissal from the mutasarrıflık of Muş, asking him to obey the orders. However, Emin Pasha, who was in Hınıs at that time, detained and jailed the man and according to Esad Pasha started the rebellion which he had been preparing for a while. Emin Pasha uttered threats by swearing that he would go to Erzurum with more than five thousand men (whom the governor of Erzurum described as *haşerat*, insects) and that he would conquer the lands from Erzurum to Sivas. He sent his brother Murad Bey to a point half an hour distant from Erzurum with five hundred tribal members. Attacking villages and passengers, Murad Bey, as Esad Pasha stated, sent "mischievous" (*fesadengiz*) letters to the *miralay* (colonel) of the Mansure Army, Salih Bey and some other local notables and aghas.[14] It appears that Emin Pasha tried to gain the support of the Mansure Army in Erzurum by offering financial support to its commander.

In their letters, Emin Pasha and Murad Bey suggested that if the Miralay, Salih Bey, left Erzurum and joined Emin Pasha with the soldiers under his command, they would have given each recruit two hundred guruş and the Miralay himself five thousand guruş.[15] Yet Salih Bey, as Esad Pasha emphasized, did not accept this appealing offer. Appreciating the loyalty of the Miralay who submitted the said letters to him, Esad Pasha repelled Murad Bey from Erzurum. After Murad Bey was driven back, he escaped to Pasinler. More importantly, after his defeat the tribal cavalries under his command started to disperse and went piecemeal to Esad Pasha, asking for mercy. This made controlling Muş easier. When the men collected under the command of Kığı's Bey approached Muş, they united with those of Maksud Bey from among the Murad Pashazades to whom a letter was secretly sent in advance. Maksud Bey had also established confidential relations with some tribal people and villagers. They together attacked the residence of the mutasarrıfs of Muş, outside of the city itself

---

13 "… mukaddemen mühürmân-i mekâtibe vuku' bulan umerâ-yı 'aşâirle bigâyet hafî olarak mukâvele-i sâbıkaya istihkâm virildikden sonra …" BOA. HAT. 790/36808 B, 3 Rebiülahir 1249 (20 August 1833).

14 Ibid.

15 BOA. HAT. 789/36774, 20 Rebiülahir 1249 (6 September 1833).

where Emin Pasha's brother Hurşid Bey, resisted with a few hundred men. In the end, Hurşid Bey could not keep resisting and fled to Hınıs. Having heard of this failure, Emin Pasha met with the tribal leaders and told them of the situation. Emphasizing his power by claiming that he had been in an alliance with the Kurdish tribes of Iran and Diyarbekir and suggested sending some of their armed men to Muş and some others under his command to attack Erzurum.[16]

Emin Pasha could not realize this plan as tribal leaders did not support him. Esad Pasha's correspondence and contacts with local tribes and notables was effective. The principal actor who broke Emin Pasha's coalition was Faris Agha of the Hesenan tribe. As Esad Pasha stated, Faris Agha came out and said to Emin Pasha that if they moved together, became involved in inappropriate acts without the consent of the commander-in-chief, and revolted against the state, then they would be in trouble not only in this life but also in the afterlife. The agha continued by emphasizing that Hüseyin Bey had been granted Muş, and Emin Pasha was warned and was ordered to surrender. Therefore, what was essential for the pasha was to pull himself together and to obey the rules. Otherwise, the results would be dreadful for both the pasha and the people who had allied with him. The other tribal leaders approved this statement by Faris Agha and so, as argued, the alliance of Emin Pasha was peacefully dissolved.[17]

Having lost a huge part of his support, Emin Pasha attentively took the side of Faris Agha and called his brothers to him – Şerif Bey from Bitlis and Murad Bey from Pasinler. Upon his brothers' arrival, the pasha emerged from Hınıs and spent a night in the house of Faris Agha near Muş. Afterwards, with his three brothers and a hundred of his subjects, he escaped to the houses of Telli Bey, Hüseyin Bey, and Melik Bey in the districts of Lice, Hazro, and Hiyan which were in Diyarbekir and, as described, long known for their "insurrectionism and banditry."[18] Following the escape of Emin Pasha, his men who had been left behind in Erzurum were easily driven back. Yet Emin Pasha did not easily abandon his ambitions regarding Muş.

It was no coincidence Emin Pasha escaped to Diyarbekir; when he killed Abdurrahman Pasha he had run there, as well. Mostly referred to as the notables of Diyarbekir, the beys of the Zirki, namely, Hüseyin, Telli, Receb, and Behram Beys as well as Mirza Agha were influential figures in Emin Pasha's

---

16   BOA. HAT. 790/36808 B, 3 Rebiülahir 1249 (20 August 1833).
17   Ibid.
18   Ibid.

coalition.[19] Provincial authorities described the notables of Diyarbekir as the "equivalents" of him, and blamed them for being in collaboration with the dream of "conquering Muş."[20] As is stated often in the Ottoman archival documents, these aghas and begs had to be punished, as well.[21] Confirming these suspicions, Emin Pasha and Şerif Bey at first harbored at the houses of their those reliable friends and then they started to enhance their alliance network.

3.2 Between Negotiation and Contest

Having sheltered in Atak, Emin Pasha searched for new channels to guarantee his pardon. In order to maximize his chances of success he tried to bypass regional governors, writing directly to Istanbul. His tone shows that he was capable of using minute details to legitimize himself. Having stated that he had received the letter ordering him to leave Muş when he was still there, Emin Pasha emphasized that upon receiving this order he disbanded the armed men around him and left for Atak. As the place to which he was required to go was not specified in the order, he came there rather than any other place as he had deep-rooted relations with the Atak beys. In other words, Emin Pasha tried to justify his departure for Atak as if he were obeying the order to leave Muş. Furthermore, according to the pasha, even if he had accepted the offer of Esad Pasha and moved to a place in Diyarbekir, Keban, or Malatya, because the pasha was angry with him, it would not have changed the result. Esad Pasha would have again wanted to exile him further away, which would have led not only to his own great disadvantage but also to that of his brothers. Furious with Emin Pasha because he still used the signature "mutasarrıf of Muş" despite having been dismissed, Esad Pasha reminded him of his existing debts regarding kışlakiye and compensation for the Çanlı Monastery.[22]

Although Emin Pasha was forced to leave Muş, the provincial authorities always emphasized that as long as he stayed in Atak which was in close proximity to Muş, Muş and its environs would not recover from trouble and conflict, as he was still in contact with the region. This turned out to be true. Correspondence between Emin Pasha and his brothers, which was intercepted

---

19 BOA. HAT. 450/22351 C, 5 Cemaziyelevvel 1249 (20 September 1833). For the beys of Zirki, Bayraktar, "Yurtluk-Ocaklıks."
20 "… Muş mutasarrıf-ı sâbık Emin paşa dinilan hayinin mu'âdili olan Diyârbekir ekrâdı …" BOA. HAT. 446/22291, 9 Cemaziyelahir 1249 (24 October 1833).
21 BOA. HAT. 450/22351 D, 5 Cemaziyelvel 1249 (20 September 1833), BOA. HAT. 450/22351 E, 5 Cemaziyelevvel 1249 (20 September 1833).
22 BOA. HAT. 790/36808 J, 3 Rebiülahir 1249 (20 August 1833).

and sent to the new mutasarrıf of Muş, Hüseyin Pasha, showed that the brothers were trying to ally with the beys of Diyarbekir in various ways. Furthermore, the brothers were sending letters to tribal people to secure their assistance, once they took power again in Muş with the help of the beys of Atak. These letters are rare historical documents including significant clues about not only the family members seeking alliances, but also their perception of their power. For instance, Şerif Bey in a letter dated July 1833 informed various Kurdish aghas about their preparations for an attack and the components of their coalition. He further stated that he was in the fortress of Boşat (to the north of contemporary Silvan, Diyarbekir), in the house of Mirza Agha of Silvan, and that Emin Pasha was in Atak, in the house of Hüseyin Bey. Emphasizing the tribal components of their front, Şerif Bey tried to convince other tribes to join their alliance. He stated that all these tribes were sending countless men with the aim of returning their government (hükûmet) to the way it used to be. It is significant that Şerif Bey used the term hükûmet to refer to their land. As discussed in chapter 2, hükûmets were more autonomous compared to yurtluk-ocaklıks. The members of the family used hükûmet and yurtluk-ocaklık interchangeably, saw no categorical difference between these two types of land tenure as they regarded themselves as traditional leaders of Muş, and saw the sanjak as the place of their ancestral lands.

The details of the letter of Şerif Bey are important in illustrating the scope of the revolt and the nature of local relations. The beys of Atak, Hiyan, and Kırçıl, the voyvoda of Diyarbekir, the aghas of Silvan, and the *emin* (superintendent) of Ma'den-i Hümâyûn were in alliance with him.[23] Şerif Bey sent the same letters to Resul, İsmail, Şakir and Bozu aghas, too, claiming that they had extensive support from Diyarbekir to Ma'den-i Hümâyûn.[24] Technically the tone of the letters fantastically overemphasized their power as a means of persuasion; for instance, in a letter to a certain Hamza Agha he claimed support from Diyarbekir to Mosul and from the tribes of Muş and Bitlis; including the Rojki, Hesenan, and Cibran.[25]

Apart from Kurdish aghas and begs, there were also Armenian moneylenders in Emin Pasha's network of power relations.[26] Emin Pasha was in contact with their family's moneylender Keşişoğlu Ohannes, who was in Erzurum.

---

23   BOA. HAT. 450/22351 H, 13 Rebiülevvel 1249 (31 July 1833).
24   BOA. HAT. 450/22351 I, 19 Rebiülevvel 1249 (6 August 1833).
25   BOA. HAT. 450/22351 J, 19 Rebiülevvel 1249 (6 August 1833).
26   Unfortunately, it is not possible to hear the voices of the commoners, Armenian and Kurdish peasants, vis-à-vis Emin Pasha's revolt from the archival documents dated to the early nineteenth century. Fortunately, as will be discussed in Chapter 6 of this book, the voices of commoners will be heard through their petitions especially after the Tanzimat.

Emin Pasha was trying to get information about Esad Pasha's alliance from Ohannes. He was specifically concerned with the nature of relations between his cousins – the sons of İbrahim Bey – with Esad Pasha.[27] Although his brother was spreading news around Ottoman Kurdistan that they were preparing for widespread revolt from Diyarbekir to Muş, Emin Pasha, at the same time, was sending letters, asking for mercy with reference to his service to the Ottoman state and to how he was ready to compensate for his mistakes. He emphasized that he took shelter in the house of the bey of Atak because of the attacks on him and the difficulties he was going through.[28] However, his request for mercy does not mean that he was willing to break up the alliance that he had circumspectly constituted, given the fact that both he and his brothers continued to write letters to the tribal leaders and local begs and aghas. Rather, he needed to keep on consolidating his alliances, in order to reinforce his hand in bargaining with both central and provincial authorities.

In line with this aim, Murad Bey, another brother of Emin Pasha, tried to get in touch with Rıdvan Agha, expecting to exchange news. Rıdvan Agha was the nephew of the aforementioned Faris Agha of the Hesenan, who broke their coalition. In fact, Murad Bey had not heard anything from the agha for a while, as he expressed his resentment with the words that if someone was out of sight, he was also out of mind.[29] Yet, Rıdvan Agha did not send the expected response to the brothers in Atak. After a while, Emin Pasha himself wrote a letter addressed to Rıdvan Agha including many requests. First, he asked why Hüseyin Pasha, the new mutasarrıf of Muş, had met with the leader of the Cibran. Second, he asked to be informed about the tinniest matters concerning Muş, Hüseyin Pasha and other tribesmen like Süleyman Agha of the Sıpkî or the Haydaran, as well as anything about Bitlis.[30] In firing off questions, Emin Pasha intended to ascertain the strength of his coalition. However, these efforts to get news from Rıdvan Agha were in vain, as it turned out that Rıdvan Agha would take part in the league against Emin Pasha.

Unable to get the support of the Hesenan, Emin Pasha sought other mediators. Ishak Pasha – who was both the governor of Diyarbekir and the emin of Ma'den-i Hümâyûn – sent a letter to Esad Pasha requesting Emin Pasha's pardon and his reappointment to Muş. However, Esad Pasha insisted that Emin Pasha should settle in Keban-Maden-i Hümâyûn, Diyarbekir, or Malatya.

---

27   BOA. HAT. 721/344364 B, 29 Zilhicce 1248 (19 May 1833); BOA. HAT. 721/344364 C, 29 Zilhicce 1248 (19 May 1833).
28   BOA. HAT. 790/36808 O, 27 Rebiülevvel 1249 (14 August 1833).
29   BOA. HAT. 450/22351 U, 1 Rebiülahir 1249 (18 August 1833).
30   BOA. HAT. 450/22351 T, 2 Rebiülevvel 1249 (19 August 1833).

Later, he could also be nominated to a post if he behaved properly and did not get involved in any trouble.[31] Having failed to get the consent of Esad Pasha, Ishak Pasha wrote the same demands directly to Istanbul. Yet he received the same reply.[32] In addition, Ishak Pasha was ordered to surrender Emin Pasha as he was being sheltered in territory under his governance.[33] If Emin Pasha remained in Atak and created trouble in Muş, Ishak Pasha would also be held responsible.[34]

Emin Pasha also reached out to Timur Pasha of Van. He sent letters to Timur Pasha through the leader of the Sıpkî tribe, Süleyman Agha. However, Timur Pasha submitted the letters to Esad Pasha, which the latter regarded as a sign of loyalty.[35] In these letters, Emin Pasha tried to persuade Timur Pasha with the promise of the return of his brother, Fazıl Bey, who was being kept in Erzurum due to his participation in the Van revolt.[36] As discussed before, Emin Pasha had played a key role in the suppression of Timur Pasha's revolt and refrained from helping him. Thus, Timur Pasha, probably, used this matter to transform it into a chance for himself as Emin Pasha had done before.

While Emin Pasha was ceaselessly trying to enhance his strength, and ask for mercy, efforts to expel him from Atak yielded no results. He did not agree to move away to Malatya, Keban, or Diyarbekir. Moreover, the beys of Atak emphasized that their doors were open and that they could not send anyone away who was in need of help. Therefore, they also requested a pardon for Emin Pasha and his brothers. However, provincial authorities interpreted such appeals as tactics to gain time and to gather strength.[37]

These kinds of doubts turned out to be right; it was reported that Emin Pasha had gathered around eight to ten thousand men. The basis of this information was the intercepted letters. Upon this, the new mutasarrıf of Muş took precautions, and in the end, the two sides confronted each other in a place called Bükilân, a village between Diyarbekir and Muş. In this confrontation, which was a death blow to Emin Pasha's ambitions, Sultan Agha of the Haydaran and Faris, Rıdvan and Kulihan aghas of the Hesenan supported the new mutasarrıf, Hüseyin Pasha. The Cibran tribe and the Zirki Beys took the side of Emin

---

31 BOA. HAT. 790/36808 B, 3 Rebiülahir 1249 (20 August 1833). Ishak Pasha was from Çötelizades, a local family of Harput. For details, see Sipahi, "At Arm's Length."
32 BOA. HAT. 789/36774, 20 Rebiüahir 1249 (6 September 1833).
33 Ibid.
34 BOA. HAT. 790/36808 B, 3 Rebiülahir 1249 (20 August 1833).
35 BOA. HAT. 789/36774, 20 Rebiüahir 1249 (6 September 1833).
36 Ibid.
37 BOA. HAT. 450/22351 A, 25 Rebiülahir 1249 (11 September 1833).

Pasha.³⁸ It can be inferred from such a polarization that Sultan Agha probably took sides against Emin Pasha due to the kışlak tax, which Emin Pasha had previously taken from him. Besides, the Hesenan was one of the tribes with whom Hüseyin Pasha, had been in secret contact. Although the terms of their negotiation are not definitely known, Hüseyin Pasha successfully persuaded them.

After the defeat, the beys of Atak and Hani, who comprised a significant part of Emin Pasha's coalition, wrote to the governor of Diyarbekir claiming that they had no intent to launch an assault on Muş but they were trapped by its new mutasarrıf. As proof, they first emphasized that they went to Bükilan with just a few hundred cavalrymen, as if they were peacefully going to a feast. Second, they emphasized that they went for peace and fellowship and that they wanted to carry out trade, but their money was plundered during the clash. Third, they claimed that Bükilan was within Diyarbekir. In other documents, both of Esad and Hüseyin Pashas, Bükilan was said to be a village of Muş. With such claims, the beys of Atak suggested that they did not have any purpose of attacking Muş, as they had met in a village of Diyarbekir.³⁹

Provincial authorities, especially Esad Pasha, the governor of Erzurum, claimed that despite his defeat, Emin was a traitor and deceiver, and would use any opportunity to launch an assault on Muş. In the same way, he claimed that the beys of Atak were long known for their disobedience to the governors of Diyarbekir. Therefore, as a precaution, the emin of Maden, Ishak Pasha, the muhafız of Kars, Ahmed Pasha, and the mutasarrıfs of Muş and Bayezid, Hüseyin and Behlül Pashas were ordered to be ready in the case of any assault by Emin Pasha and his alliances.⁴⁰ However, with a decree of *Meclis-i Şûra* (Assembly of Consultancy) it was stressed that unless Emin Pasha and the beys of Atak attacked, no operation should be carried out against them. Otherwise, it would lead to new expenses that the treasury could not afford at the time. Furthermore, as winter in Erzurum was harsh, it was impossible to deal with new problems.⁴¹ Ottoman provincial governors were disposed to stigmatize traditional local leaders as being 'disobedient' and 'oppressive' when they had clashes of interests with them. The treatment of Emin Pasha and his allies in the official correspondences was an instance of this tendency.

---

38   BOA. HAT. 450/22351 D, 5 Cemaziyelevvel 1249 (20 September 1833); BOA. HAT. 450/22351 B, 17 Cemaziyelevvel 1249 (2 October 1833); BOA. HAT. 450/22351, 25 Cemaziyelevvel 1249 (10 October 1833).
39   BOA. HAT. 450/22351 G, 1 Cemaziyelevvel 1249 (16 September 1833).
40   BOA. HAT. 450/22351, 25 Cemaziyelevvel 1249 (10 October 1833); BOA. HAT. 446/22291, 9 Cemaziyelahir 1249 (24 October 1833).
41   BOA. HAT. 446/22291, 9 Cemaziyelahir 1249 (24 October 1833).

3.2.1 The Tribes and the Pashas

It is impossible to separate the revolt of Emin Pasha from the tribal networks in which he engaged and the possible benefits that he hoped to acquire from this network. It is necessary to recall that one of the pretexts for Emin Pasha's revolt was his reluctance to recompense what he had taken from Sultan Agha of the Haydaran in the name of kışlakiye. Furthermore, Esad Pasha commanded him to return Koro Agha of the Cemaldini back to Iran. Emin Pasha had no intention to lose his financial and military power, which was based on tribal networks. As stated before, the tribes causing problems between the Iranian and Ottoman Empires were the nomadic tribes of the Haydaran, Sıpkî, Zilân, and Cemaldini who were mobile throughout the Ottoman-Iranian borderland. As Sabri Ateş argues, the mobility of those tribes was restricted in time due to a transformation of a borderland into a border.[42] In the Treaty of Erzurum of 1823, although it was stated, that "neither party would protect fugitives or tribes that crossed the frontier,"[43] the mobility of tribes was not totally prohibited. Besides, in archival documents the nomadic Haydaran and Sıpkî tribes were described as "*münâzaün fih* (disputed)" tribes between the Iranian and Ottoman Empires.

Indeed, Emin Pasha managed to gain the support of some of these tribal leaders in his revolt, including Süleyman Agha of the Sıpkî, a large nomadic tribe of the northeastern borderland. Yet not all borderland nomads supported him. Hüseyin Agha of the Zilan and Kasım and Sultan aghas of the Haydaran did not become part of his coalition; rather, they opposed the pasha's regional power. Therefore, the "issue of Muş" and the matter of Iran were discussed together in the Meclis-i Şûra, which provided many significant details about the revolt of Emin Pasha.

To start with the coalition of Emin Pasha, the Sıpkî – as a borderland tribe – was a crucial part of it. Süleyman Agha of the Sıpkî, participated in the suppression of Timur Pasha's previous revolt, together with Emin Pasha. Although his efforts were appreciated, peasants in their winter quarters were complaining about assaults by the tribe. Despite the need of the local authorities to interrogate him, this could not be carried out as the Muş revolt began. Fear of interrogation might be the reason for Süleyman Agha's joining the coalition of Emin Pasha. In addition, Esad Pasha claimed that Mirza Rıza, the Iranian envoy, allegedly frightened Süleyman Agha by implying that Esad Pasha would harm him as much as possible. Mirza Rıza advised Süleyman Agha to join Emin Pasha, and after helping, he could return to the Iranian side and

---

42 Ateş, The Ottoman-Iranian Borderlands, 122.
43 Ibid., 57.

also get financial support. Having been persuaded by the offers of Mirza Rıza, Süleyman Agha took permission from Esad Pasha to leave Erzurum on the pretext that he would welcome the new mutasarrıf of Muş, Hüseyin Pasha. But he went directly to Emin Pasha. Furthermore, with the aim of mustering for Emin Pasha, Süleyman Agha spread news that the dismissing of Emin Pasha was only a means of bringing Kurdistan under control. Süleyman Agha was also said to have become the spokesperson of Emin Pasha during his meeting with Cihangir Mirza.[44] This point also exemplifies the trans-border agency of tribes, indicating that how they could be mediators between authorities of two different states. Besides, Mirza Rıza's pushing Süleyman Agha to ally with Emin Pasha indicates how the agency of local notables spread over the frontiers.

As a vital component of the coalition against Emin Pasha, the Haydaran was motivated by the kışlak tax, which Emin Pasha had taken from Sultan Agha who had remained in Muş though his elder brother, Kasım Agha had crossed into Iran. Sultan Agha informed his brother about the tax which turned into an interstate affair and became a significant factor in Emin Pasha's revolt. Having declared in the presence of the Iranian consul Ağa Hasan and the envoy Mirza Rıza that the Haydaran were a tribe of Ottoman Empire, Sultan Agha took part in the league against Emin Pasha.[45] Moreover, his brother, Kasım Agha, having become angry with Cihangir Mirza, would fall on the Ottoman side during the contest with Emin Pasha. As all energy was spent on confronting Emin Pasha and his coalition, no time remained to solve the situation of Kasım Agha. The agha would also participate in the suppression of the revolt.[46]

In addition to the Haydaran brothers crossing to the Ottoman side, the recompense of the kışlakiye was still a matter of debate. The Iranian officials Ağa Hasan, and Mirza Rıza, argued that if Sultan Agha remained in Ottoman territory, the tax would be taken from Emin Pasha and would be shared between the Iranian and Ottoman states, or else given to the tribe in full. But if Sultan Agha returned to Iran, they would demand all the money from the Ottoman state.[47] Esad Pasha, upon the warnings and petitions of the Iranians, called

---

44 "… Erzurumda olan İrân müdiri ağâ Hasan ile sefîr-i İrân Mirzâ Rıza merkûm Süleymân ağâya Erzurum vâlisi sana şöyle böyle idecektir hemân Emin Pâşâ tarafına firâr ile icrâ-yı muʿâvenetden sonra İrâna gider isen sana şu kadar bu kadar akçe iʿtâ olunur diyerek iğfâl …" BOA. HAT. 789/36774, 20 Rebiülahir 1249 (6 September 1833).

45 "… akçe mâddesini İrânda olan karındâşıma yâzmış isem de maksadım şikâyet değildir ve ʿaşîretimle İrâna gitmeyeceğimi ʿalem bilür ve mevsim-i bahâr gelmeksizin Emin pâşânın şerrinden işbu akçenin iddiʿâsına teşebbüs idemedim şimdi Erzuruma gelmiş olduğumdan vâli maʿrifetiyle iddiʿâ iderim …" Ibid.

46 BOA. HAT. 461/22617 B, 25 Zilkade 1249 (5 April 1834).

47 BOA. HAT. 789/36774, 20 Rebiüahir 1249 (6 September 1833).

Kasım Agha to discuss the issue, yet he did not show up. As the final straw, the Ottoman state apparently would be responsible with the compensation of the kışlakiye since Emin Pasha was reluctant to make redress for this amount.

As tribes were regarded as a source of manpower during uprisings, their importance became more apparent for central and local authorities as well as for the rebels themselves. The Zilân, another pastoral nomadic tribe living at the intersection of Ottoman, Russian and Iranian empires, were among the coalition opposing Emin Pasha.[48] As Hüseyin Agha of the Zilan greatly contributed to Emin Pasha's defeat, the governor of Erzurum, Esad Pasha, asked that the tribe not to be returned to the Iranian state. He was of the opinion that once the tribe was out of Iranian hands, it would be to the benefit of the state if they remained in Ottoman lands. Hüseyin Agha also, allegedly, stated that if his tribe were not protected by the Ottoman state, they would migrate to Russian territory, not to that of Iran.[49] However, as latter correspondence demonstrates, Iranian authorities complained, blaming Esad Pasha for infringing the agreement (*hilâf-ı ahd*) between the two states by not sending Hüseyin Agha back to Iranian lands.[50] In the end, although the tribes – the Zilan and the Cemaldini – were not allowed to remain permanently (*kabul ve sahabet*), they could spend winters in Kars with the consent of the Iranian consul.[51]

As Muş was located in a frontier zone in the transition route between the winter and summer quarters of nomadic and semi-nomadic tribes, the story of Emin Pasha was part of Ottoman-Iranian border making during the 1830s. His narrative shows how local notables made use of lacunas in the web of the power relations. Emin Pasha's role in the settlement of tribes was pivotal, as had been that of his ancestors. He used the settlement card as a way of bargaining for promotion in rank, for enlarging the lands under his exclusive use. Besides, as these tribes were frontier tribes, Emin Pasha's role stretched beyond the border, involving not only the central and provincial authorities of both the Iranian and Ottoman states, but also tribal leaders. Esad Pasha was exposed to the threats of Mirza Rıza and Ağa Hasan, two Iranian officials, because of the non-payment of the kışlakiye and non-return of the said tribes for which Emin Pasha was responsible to a large extent. The Iranians were threatening that if these steps were not taken, Cihangir Mirza would attack the Ottoman lands. In addition, they emphasized that since being in his post in Erzurum, Esad Pasha

---

48 For the Zilan, see Koç, "A Tribal Confederation at the Intersection of the Ottoman, Russian and Qajar Empire: The Zilan Confederation and the Empires (1810–1860)," *Middle Eastern Studies* 59 No. 2 (2023): 181–192.
49 BOA. HAT. 446/22291, 9 Cemaziyelahir 1249 (24 October 1833).
50 BOA. HAT. 789/36774, 20 Rebiülahir 1249 (6 September 1833).
51 BOA. HAT. 461/22617 B, 25 Zilkade 1249 (5 April 1834).

behaved contrary to the orders of the two states (*hilâf-ı rıza-i devleteyn*). They argued that the Ottoman state had already acknowledged that the said tribes were those of Iran. Thus, the deeds of Emin Pasha shook the authority of Esad Pasha in the region.[52]

Esad Pasha also complained about the consul of Iran, Ağa Hasan, who had held that title in Erzurum for more than twenty years. He accumulated wealth by acquiring lands and çiftliks in Erzurum. Moreover, he had had a grasp of each detail of the region. He also protected the vagrant, 'shameless' (*derbeder ve bî edeb*) people who had fled from Iran and become involved in theft and drunkenness. When those vagrants needed to be disciplined, Ağa Hasan prevented the governor from doing so, claiming he would do it himself. According to Esad Pasha, due to his long stay in Erzurum, the agha had learned to use each opportunity to create disturbances from Erzurum to Muş and from Bayezid to Kars. Therefore, Esad Pasha emphasized that with such officials there was no way to resolve frontier matters.[53] Thus, the rebellion of Emin Pasha was part of a broader picture in which local actors such as provincial governors and interstate agents were also playing roles.

3.3   The Contours of Negotiation

As stated above, Emin Pasha and the beys of Atak were to be left untouched unless they attacked Muş. This was necessary not only because of financial reasons but also because of climatic difficulties.[54] Therefore, in the last months of 1833 and the early months of 1834, Emin Pasha had the opportunity to search for channels to obtain a pardon for himself.

As time passed, Emin Pasha away from home, changed his bargaining terms. In a letter addressed to Ishak Pasha, the governor of Diyarbekir, Emin Pasha asked that his debt to the Haydaran tribe, which was six hundred purses be written off. As an explanation, he argued that when he was sent to Van with the mission to suppress the uprising of Timur Bey, he had spent the money for his expenses and for other debts. He added that if he was granted with Muş and he was allowed to return there, he could donate a thousand purses to the treasury, to which he was ready to commit by sending his moneylender. The pasha argued that their properties, belongings, grains, and cultivated lands had been captured; their families were left behind immiserated upon the orders of

---

52   BOA. HAT. 789/36774, 20 Rebiülahir 1249 (6 September 1833).
53   Ibid.
54   BOA. HAT. 446/22291, 9 Cemaziyelahir 1249 (24 October 1833), BOA. HAT. 461/22617 B, 25 Zilkade 1249 (5 April 1834).

Esad Pasha, the governor of Erzurum, after he and his brothers Şerif, Hurşid, and Murad Beys had to leave their houses.⁵⁵ If he were allowed to inhabit one of his villages in Muş, he could work for the settlement of the Kurdish tribes, bringing them under control and levying taxes on them. If he and his brothers were allowed to return, they would not get involved in the affairs of Muş; they would stay at home and not get involved in anything. Moreover, Emin Pasha asked for a guarantee against "any kind of assault or intervention on the part of Esad Pasha."⁵⁶

Convinced of Emin Pasha's argument, Ishak Pasha arbitrated as follows. He was of the opinion that he should not object to Emin Pasha's request regarding his debt to the Haydaran tribe. However, Ishak Pasha did not reaffirm his request to be granted Muş again. As there had been a conflict between Esad and Emin Pashas and as it had resulted in the latter's revolt, the re-nomination of Emin Pasha to Muş would lead to the diminishing of Esad Pasha's influence. Ishak Pasha saw no harm in Emin Pasha's settlement in a village three or four hours from Diyarbekir.⁵⁷ Meanwhile, Esad Pasha was absolutely opposed to Emin's reappointment to Muş, as it would challenge his influence. Although he agreed to Emin Pasha staying in the environs of Diyarbekir, Esad Pasha strongly believed that Emin Pasha and the beys of Atak should be brought into line. He argued that after their defeat and due to their habit of banditry and disobedience, they were seeking revenge. If they attacked Muş again and caused another conflict, it would result in disorder and chaos in the region.⁵⁸

Esad Pasha's suspicions turned out to be right regarding Emin Pasha and his brothers. With Ishak Pasha's support, Emin Pasha was allowed to stay in a village near Diyarbekir. Although he was required to inhabit the appointed place with "honor and civility," Esad Pasha argued, Emin Pasha had sent his brothers to Ibrahim Pasha of Egypt three months before and asked for his help. Esad Pasha condemned this rapprochement, yet, added that how they were to be treated by İbrahim Pasha was not properly known. Upon their return to Atak, Emin Pasha this time sent his brothers to Reşid Pasha, the governor of Sivas. Allegedly, Reşid Pasha gave robes of honor to his brothers and promised to grant Muş to Emin Pasha.⁵⁹ As Esad Pasha reported, this promise resulted in an increase of provocations and riots in Muş triggered by the supporters of Emin Pasha. He further argued that Mehmed Halil of the Cibran tribe, a supporter (*hevâ-dâr*) of Emin Pasha with a thousand cavalry and infantry or "haşarat"

---

55   BOA. HAT. 625/30883, 3 Şaban 1249 (16 December 1833).
56   "... hırkamızı başımıza çekub hânemizde ikâmet üzere ..." BOA. HAT. 722/34418 A, 27 Cemaziyelahir 1249 (11 November 1833).
57   BOA. HAT. 625/30883, 3 Şaban 1249 (16 December 1833).
58   BOA. HAT. 461/22617 B, 25 Zilkade 1249 (5 April 1834).
59   Ibid.

(insects) as the Ottoman documents refer to them, was spreading fabricated news that Muş had been given to Emin Pasha who would be back soon. With such claims, Esad Pasha reported that some tribal members of the Cibran went to the district of Varto and occupied a few villages, leading to disorder. Following on from this, Hüseyin Pasha, the new mutasarrıf of Muş, sent his brother Sadık Bey to defend Varto and upon his request, Esad Pasha sent help.

In addition to these military actions, letters were sent to some notables requesting their help, as a precaution. Esad Pasha was inclined to stigmatize Emin Pasha as a traitor to religion and the state (*hain-i din û devlet*), and argued that he was not among men of honor and decency, so there was no way for him to behave properly. He would cause these kinds of provocations in Muş from time to time, which would result in harm and immiseration for the people. Moreover, Esad Pasha was of the belief that Emin Pasha was preparing a revolt for the end of spring. Even news of his brothers' going to Sivas and making contact with Reşid Pasha had resulted in turmoil in Muş.[60]

Emin Pasha's search for allies – including the ones who were a threat to the Ottoman sovereignty like İbrahim Pasha or Cihangir Mirza – was for reappointment to Muş. He rebelled when his dismissal from Muş became clearer. However, his motivations were not to break with the Ottoman Empire, he sought to show how he was a powerful actor who could play politics. And his negotiations with Reşid Pasha and the latter's promises about Muş were not rumors. Emin Pas was reappointed to Muş, as his negotiations with Reşid Pasha were paid off.

3.4 The Reappointment of Emin Pasha

Emin Pasha's reappointment to Muş as mütesellim coincided with a time when the sanjak was temporarily granted to the governor of Sivas, Reşid Mehmed Pasha, in 1834. To put it differently, Emin Pasha was in Muş again thanks to his negotiations with Reşid Pasha. As discussed before, Emin Pasha's contact with Reşid Pasha dated back to the period when he was sheltered in Atak and in which he had sent his brothers to him. Allegedly, Reşid Pasha promised that Muş will be granted back to Emin Pasha.[61]

Remarkably, the reappointment of Emin Pasha to Muş also corresponds to a period in which pacification of Kurdish beys was on the agenda of the central

---

60 Ibid.
61 Ibid.

administration. Reşid Pasha was engaged in several military expeditions, with the aims of settling nomadic and seminomadic tribes, recruiting their men into the army, and providing "security and order" in Diyarbekir and Ma'den-i Hümâyûn. As is well known, this was part of the centralization policies of Mahmud II. Martin van Bruinessen argued that Sultan Mahmud was determined to bring about centralization and became successful after the 1806–1812 Ottoman-Russian War. He further emphasizes that by 1826, the *derebeyis* (used for rebels and autonomous provincial notables) of Anatolia had been subordinated, allowing the "pacification of the Kurdistan" to begin.[62]

An ex-Grand Vizier, and the governor of Sivas and the emin of Ma'den-i Hümâyûn, Reşid Pasha, was charged with this mission. In his letter to the central administration, Esad Pasha explained the reasons why the sanjak of Muş was given to Reşid Pasha with a special emphasis on its being a must. He drew attention to the fact that the tribes in the Ottoman East were not organized in a few groups; rather, they were dispersed in every part of the region. To maintain order and stability, it was necessary to bring all of them under control at once. Similarly, the winter and summer quarters of the nomadic and semi-nomadic tribes were scattered between Diyarbekir and Muş, so it was proper that both regions be placed under the responsibility of a single person to accomplish the mission.[63]

Esad Pasha, despite his former oppositions to Emin Pasha and his attempts to keep him away from Muş, stated that the important issue was to finalize Kurdish issue with facility. Therefore, despite his former wrongdoings, he emphasized that Emin Pasha would carry out whatever he was ordered to do.[64] This point is important, although Esad Pasha had charged Emin Pasha with betrayal and drawn attention to the flaws in his character, he knew that for the operations to be fulfilled in the Ottoman East, the mediation of the power holders like Emin Pasha was essential. Therefore, in 1834–5 Emin Pasha served in the army under the command of Reşid Pasha and then of Hafız Pasha for the discipline and punishment of the Garzan Kurds. For a while, earlier disputes about the deeds of Emin Pasha were ignored, and he joined in military operations with three hundred cavalrymen from Muş.[65]

---

62   Martin Van Bruinessen, Agha, Shaikh, and State: The Social and Political Structures of Kurdistan (London: Zed Books, 1992), 176.
63   BOA. HAT. 1315/51270 Ç, 21 Cemaziyelahir 1250 (25 October 1834).
64   Ibid.
65   BOA. HAT. 447/22311 A, 10 Şaban 1251 (1 November 1835). However, Reşid Pasha noted that as those places were steep and hilly (*sarb ve sengistan*), it was not possible to fully succeed. Ibid.

Meanwhile, reportedly, the beys of Diyarbekir were spreading news about the operations of Reşid Pasha, claiming that the purpose of the operations was to conscript all men to the Mansure Army so that no one would be left behind. Therefore, the Kurds from Hani to Yezidhan united, and a state of turmoil came to pass. German field marshal Helmuth von Moltke, who accompanied Hafız Pasha's army, gave a narrative of how Kurds resisted conscription. He described the desertion of villages and their inhabitants running away.[66] Muş was in the middle of such a region and was full of tribesmen. It was at that point that Emin Pasha was reemployed. As he knew the region thoroughly, he was ordered to do what was necessary.[67] However, Moltke notes that the reliability of Emin Pasha was also questionable. If the unrest in Garzan spread to Muş it was possible that Emin Pasha would not serve the imperial army.[68] Therefore, the pardon of Emin Pasha could be contextualized in operations against Kurdish notables and tribes in Garzan; apparently the provincial and central authorities sough to secure his support in case of an uprising in Muş, as well. Muş, as home for the tribes, was just the next place for such kind of reforms and operations.

Emin Pasha's usefulness for the Ottoman Empire was also observed in his provision of men for the army. As reported he, along with his brothers Şerif and Murad Beys, commanded five thousand cavalrymen, having recruited them from among their families and relatives and from tribes over which they had influence. This was appreciated. The number of cavalrymen provided by the family was also important to show the continuing influence of the family in the region regardless of their conflicts with provincial governors.

In return for his family's military aid to the Ottoman army, Emin Pasha also took the opportunities to expand the range of his economic power. The matter was again the mukâta'a of Hınıs, from which Esad Pasha was benefiting as governor of Erzurum. Nonetheless, Emin Pasha challenged the usufruct of Esad Pasha by arguing that Hınıs used to be contracted out to them – to the mutasarrıfs of Muş (*öteden berû uhdelerine ihâle*). Emphasizing that Hınıs should be granted to the mutasarrıfs of Muş as it used to be, he argued that if tribes in Hınıs were separated from those in Muş, turmoil would be inevitable on both sides given that the two regions were very close. Besides, the people who were required to be punished in Muş could pass over to Hınıs, and their discipline would fail. Similarly, soldiers under their responsibility

---

66 Helmuth Von Moltke, *Moltke'nin Türkiye Mektupları*, trans. Hayrullah Örs (Istanbul: Remzi Kitabevi, 1969), 190–92.
67 BOA. HAT. 449/22346 F, 27 Şevval 1250 (26 February 1835).
68 Von Moltke, *Moltke'nin Türkiye*, 194.

could escape to Hınıs and could not be recalled. Such a situation endangered the recruitment of the cavalry required.[69] The efforts and arguments of Emin Pasha worked. After an investigation, it was understood that Emin Pasha was right that Hınıs had always been held by the mutasarrıfs of Muş. Although Esad Pasha would be offended by such a decision, Reşid Pasha asked to be awarded Hınıs, as he was the new mutasarrıf of Muş, justifying himself with the claim that it was an obligation to undertake the affairs of state.[70]

Having been offended with this decision, Esad Pasha claimed that his power diminished and affairs in the east (*havâlî-i şarkiye mesâlihi*) were interrupted. However, the real reason for his discontent was the appointment of Emin Pasha as the mütesellim of Muş. Moreover, it became evident that due to previous conflicts between them, Emin Pasha was ignoring Esad Pasha; in other words, he did not act in compliance with administrative hierarchy. Esad Pasha emphasized that, as commander-in-chief of the eastern front, he had to maintain his power. Therefore, his consent should be taken in every issue and Emin Pasha should be warned about this.[71]

Reşid Pasha seemed to be of the same opinion, yet he had his own reasons to stay on the side of Emin Pasha. He believed that unless those regions were freed of the rule of the traditional leaders who were in competition among themselves and were supported by Kurdish tribes, reforms could not be fulfilled. Similarly, unless people like Emin and Hüseyin Pashas were eliminated from Muş and an official from outside was charged with the responsibility, the sanjak would not be brought under control. However, great numbers of irregular cavalrymen (*başıbozuk süvâri*) were necessary for the fulfillment of the reforms and Emin Pasha would be useful in providing men to the army, as Muş was a source of tribes who could be turned into cavalry units. Therefore, the reappointment of Emin Pasha was a necessity rather than a preference.[72] As will be discussed later, when the proper time came, Emin Pasha would be eliminated, which was clearly explained by Reşid Pasha.

In the beginning, Reşid Pasha's operations were benefitting from the collaboration of provincial notables like Emin Pasha. He reported that the "trouble" created by Kurds and tribes could not be resolved in a few months or even in a year. In operations in the environs of Diyarbekir, the help of Emin Pasha was

---

69 BOA. HAT. 377/204876, 29 Şevval 1250 (28 February 1835).
70 Ibid.
71 BOA. HAT. 450/22347 D, 3 Rebiülahir 1251 (29 July 1835).
72 "… bu ekrâd ve ʿaşâir gürûhi tarafgirliğinden kurtarılmakdıkça mesâlih-i mülkiyye lâyıkıyle usûlüne girmeyeceği derkâr olduğu misillû bu Muş sancâğı dâhi Emin Pâşâ ve Hüseyin Pâşâ takımlarından bütün bütün tasfiye ve tathîr olunub ahere yaʿnî yabâncı meʾmûre verilmedikçe matlûb vechile taht-ı zabtiyeye girmeyeceği emri aşikârdır …" Ibid.

crucial. Most of the correspondence mentions that for two or three hundred years, Diyarbekir could not be properly controlled and that notables of the region had become accustomed to doing whatever they wanted without any surveillance. Therefore, the issue could not be handled with the execution of a few, or the summoning of some others to Istanbul. It was claimed, for instance, that the removal of the beys of Zırkî, the former allies of Emin Pasha, had not ended the trouble; rather, there were plenty of similar "insects" (*haşerats*). In line with this belief of central and provincial authorities, a series of operations in the Ottoman East[73] – from Garzan to Revanduz – took place in the second half of 1830s, first under the command of Reşid Pasha and then of Hafız Pasha. And Emin Pasha was among the other Kurdish notables who fought against the Kurds of Garzan with irregular troops in 1835.[74]

3.5 Muş in the Course of Centralization Efforts: The First Phase of the Abolition of Yurtluk-Ocaklıks

Emin Pasha not only took part in operations against the Kurdish powerholders and tribes in Diyarbekir but was also involved in military reforms of the era. The new reforms brought together administrative transformations that affected Muş and therefore the power of Emin Pasha and his family. As an extension of the military reforms of the era of Mahmud II, a *redif* (reserve) army was to be established in 1834. Emin Pasha, as the mütesellim of Muş, prepared a report detailing the potential of Muş for the constitution of the Redif. It was a policy affected all the empire. As Erik J. Zürcher states, ten to twelve battalions of the Redif were established per province. The recruits were between twenty-three and thirty-two years of age and trained twice a year. They joined the regular army during times of war. Moreover, the main task of the Redif in the early nineteenth century was to maintain order in the countryside.[75]

---

73 The term "Ottoman East" was formulated by Cora et al. to refer to a geography, "roughly south of the Black Sea Cost, north of the Levant and east of the centre of the Antolian plateau, extending to the Ottoman borderline with Russia and Iran." Yaşar Tolga Cora, Dzovaniar Derderian, and Ali Sipahi, "Introduction: Ottoman Historiography's Black Hole," in *The Ottoman East in the Nineteenth Century: Societies, Identities and Politics*, eds. Yaşar Tolga Cora, Dzovaniar Derderian, and Ali Sipahi (London: I.B. Tauris, 2016), 1. When the term used in this study, it used in accordance with this definition.

74 BOA. HAT. 451/22359, 1 Cemaziyelahir 1251 (24 September 1835).

75 Erik Jan Zürcher, "The Ottoman Conscription System, 1844–1914," *International Review of Social History*, no. 43 (1998): 438.

Although recruitment was regarded as beneficial, collecting *iane* (supplementary taxes collected during extraordinary times) in Muş, as in many other places, was also necessary. Musa Çadırcı argues that beyond a budget for the expenses of the Redif (*Redif Mansure Hazinesi*) that covered costs like salaries and clothes, expenses during training, like food and other necessities, were collected from the people of the sanjaks where the training of recruits was being carried out.[76]

The issue of funding the Redif organization resulted in many administrative reforms in Muş concerning both its tribes and landholding practices. First, a population census needed to be carried out, and second, besides those tribes, the status of which was still contested with the Iranian state, other tribes of Muş should be settled.[77] However, both those matters could only be tackled in the long term. More importantly, as the following quotation from a report of Reşid Mehmed Pasha shows, the land tenure system in Muş was the main obstacle in the funding of the Redif:

> Both Muş and some other places in its environs have been contracted out as yurtluk-ocaklık since time immemorial to groups known as local dynasties. Their allies and relatives seized some villages and places, treated them as their private property, and devoured their revenues and appropriations as they wanted. The central treasury did not benefit one piaster from those places until then. [Moreover] allying with them or co-opting them through decorations and promotions is not possible due to the character of these people, so they cannot so far serve a purpose. It is not the proper time to take back the places that they have been treating as their own properties and govern them otherwise. It is a requirement for state affairs to expel some of them and to remove the ones who deserve it, [but] instead of an outsider, if need be, the available ones can be used as they are already local. Briefly, the sanjak of Muş has also been governed with the old system mentioned. Some have argued that if its revenues are collected properly, the annual income for the treasury would be four thousand purses. Based on my investigation, I can ensure that the central treasury would benefit from an amount of two thousand kese. I do not have any information about the revenues of the sanjak except for the

---

76   Musa Çadırcı, "Anadolu'da Redif Askeri Teşkilatının Kuruluşu," DTCF Tarih Araştırmaları Dergisi VII–XII, no. 14–23 (1975): 69–70.
77   BOA. HAT. 329/19070, 18 Cemaziyelahir 1251 (11 October 1835).

cizye (poll tax). Nevertheless, it is apparent that the revenues can be collected properly if the necessary steps are taken thanks to His Majesty.[78]

Although the abolition of yurtluk-ocaklıks in Erzurum would only be carried out some ten years after his report, the words of Reşid Mehmed Pasha drew attention to the loss to the treasury from the yurtluk-ocaklık type of land ownership. Like many Ottoman pashas, he was also dissatisfied with the freehold status of such types of lands in practice. More dramatically, unlike the potential revenue from the sanjak of Muş, Reşid Pasha argues that if the donation were to be collected from Muş for the expenses of the Redif organization, just a little amount of money could be collected, and this would be a burden on the shoulders of the poor.[79] This point turned out to be true to a great extent. Çadırcı argues that mütesellims and military officers started demanding double and threefold taxes in the name of the redif, benefiting from the situation as much as possible.[80] However, Reşid Pasha believed that in the course of time the Redif organization, the recruits, would be helpful in the control of those revenues by the imperial treasury.[81]

When new regulations regarding the functioning of the Redif organization were determined in September 1834, it entailed transformations to the administrative situation of Muş. According to the new decision, the sanjaks in which the redif were already established would be unified in appropriate administrative units, which were in turn called "*müşirlik*" (military governorship). One of the müşirliks was that of Erzurum, which consisted of Bayezid, Van, and Erzurum. And Esad Pasha became the müşir.[82] Therefore, after a while, despite the objections of Reşid Pasha who claimed that Muş should remain under his control as reforms had not yet been achieved there, the sanjak of Muş was granted to Esad Pasha.[83] The reason for this change of post was the fact that the revenue from Muş was allocated directly to the Mansure Treasury, the treasury of the imperial army.[84]

This was a milestone in the history of yurtluk-ocaklıks in the sanjak of Muş. The attachment of Muş to the müşirlik of Erzurum in 1836 officially ended the yurtluk ocaklık status of Muş as a sanjak. The debate on the yurtluk-ocaklık

---

78   BOA. HAT. 533/26254 A, 15 Ramazan 1251 (4 January 1836).
79   Ibid.
80   Çadırcı, "Anadolu'da Redif" 70.
81   BOA. HAT. 533/26254 A, 15 Ramazan 1251 (4 January 1836).
82   Çadırcı, "Anadolu'da Redif" 70–71.
83   BOA. HAT. 637/31417, 24 Cemaziyelahir 1252 (6 October 1836).
84   BOA. HAT. 314/18497 D, 19 Ramazan 1252 (28 December 1836). Çadırcı argues that many sanjaks around the empire were allocated to the Mansure Treasury in 1832. Çadırcı, "II Mahmut Döneminde," 288.

status of Muş, as well as many other places in Ottoman Kurdistan, had already started before 1839, that is before the Tanzimat reforms. Esad Pasha also explained that when the sanjak of Muş was granted to him in 1836, the confiscation of the yurtluk-ocaklıks of Muş and of the Bitlis khanate had been decided.[85] The confiscation of yurtluk-ocaklık lands was gradual and in the case of Muş, first its yurtluk-ocaklık status as a sanjak was abolished in 1836 and then, as will be discussed in the following chapters, the yurtluk-ocaklık villages of Emin Pasha and his brothers were totally confiscated in 1849, after the Tanzimat.

After being granted Muş, Esad Pasha emphasized that the revenue of the sanjak, the annual amount of which would hopefully be high, would be transferred to the treasury of the Mansure Army. Another issue was the matter of the mütesellimlik of Muş. Having no intention of losing power, Emin Pasha bargained with Esad Pasha, to whom he had already sent his brother Murad Bey as signs of respect and regret for his previous, unpleasant acts.[86] Then Esad Pasha called for Emin Pasha to obtain information about the revenues (temettuat) of Muş and to determine its annual revenue. At this meeting, Emin Pasha expressed sorrow for his previous acts, emphasizing that he would put his heart and soul into state affairs.[87] Furthermore, because of the significant tribal population of Muş (*aşiret yatağı*), he wanted to recruit redifs, yet as the winter was severe he could not begin. Finally, with the promise of submitting a record book for the revenues of Muş and regarding the formation of the three squads (*bölük*) of redif from Muş, Emin Pasha remained as mütesellim of the sanjak.[88] Except for the tithe and some other ancient taxes, Emin Pasha was allowed to keep the kışlak tax as well as some other taxes as the mütesellim of Muş. However, Emin Pasha and his family were still held responsible for the collection and tax farming of the tithe and other taxes. In return for them, Murad Bey ensured that they would pay six hundred purses

---

85   BOA. HAT. 1242/48291 E 29 Zilhicce 1254 (15 March 1839).
86   BOA. HAT. 314/18497 D, 19 Ramazan 1252 (28 December 1836).
87   However, a few years later Emin Pasha brought a bribery case against Esad Pasha and told a different story. Emin Pasha accused Esad Pasha of taking forcefully nineteen hundred purses akçe from him in a year. Two pashas were interrogated in Dâr-ı Şûrâ-yı Bâb-ı Âli (Consultative Assembly of Sublime Porte). On the course of time, Emin Pasha withdrew his accusations against Esad Pasha. BOA. HAT. 1242/4891, 29 Zilhicce 1254 (15 March 1839). For details, see Gülseren Duman Koç, "Provincial Governors and Yurtluk-Ocaklık Holders on the Eve of the Tanzimat Reforms: The Embezzlement Case of Mehmed Esad Muhlis Pasha," *Archiv Orientální* 91 no. 1 (2023): 69–88.
88   "… livâ-i mezkûr 'aşair ve kabail yâtâğı yerler olduğu münâsebetiyle livâ-i mezkûrde dâhi birâz redif 'asker-i mansure tahrîr itmek gibi hidmetlere ezhâr-ı hevâhiş eylemiş …" BOA. HAT. 314/18497 E, 19 Ramazan 1252 (28 December 1836), BOA. HAT. 314/18497, 29 Zilhicce 1252 (6 April 1837).

to the imperial treasury and two hundred purses to the governor-general of Erzurum himself, yearly, starting from March 1252 (March 1837). Moreover, the voivodeship of Malazgirt and Hınıs was contracted out to Murad Bey.[89] All of this new arrangement shows that the Alaaddin Pashazades lost their monopoly over the most significant revenue of an agrarian society, the tithe. They were no longer the mutasarrıfs of Muş – which refers to the governing Muş as a yurtluk-ocaklık sanjak – but they were still kept ruling positions in Muş, Bitlis, Malazgird, and Hınıs. In addition, by allocating the collection of the kışlakiye to Emin Pasha, Esad Pasha recognized the power of Emin Pasha in taxing semi-nomadic tribes.

Even if the sanjak of Muş was administered by the governor of Erzurum, as a part of a powerful local dynasty and as a provincial notable, Emin Pasha could guarantee his position as mütesellim. Esad Pasha had no choice but to collaborate with a local power holder to get information about the revenues of Muş, to manage the settlement of tribes, and to make them part of the regular army and to rule the region. Alliances were changing in the course of the time, bringing former rivals together. In this new coalition between Emin and Esad Pashas, the müşir of Sivas, Reşid Pasha was excluded. Having been asked about the mütesellimlik of Emin Pasha, Reşid Pasha stated in a report that Emin Pasha's being mütesellim was neither desirable and nor essential (*matlûb ve mültezem*), therefore it did not matter if he remained in his post or not. He further added that everyone knew that his mütesellimlik was a necessity (*hasbe'l-icâb*) and it was simple as this.[90] Like Esad Pasha, Reşid Pasha also knew that they could not rule the region without the collaboration of hereditary leaders.

Nevertheless, the letter of Reşid Pasha is important as it shows the situation of Muş in the 1830s. Order had not been yet restored in Muş, where taxes could not be collected properly. In line with this, the settlement of tribes like the Haydaran and Sıpkî that continued to be a matter of debate between the Ottoman and Iranian states, and of the Cibran had not been resolved. The escape of settled tribes could not be prevented. Furthermore, there was trouble in the vicinity of Muş, too. For instance, problems related to the beys of Van and the issue of Garzan could not be handled because all the forces were deployed for the suppression of the revolt in Revanduz. According to Reşid Pasha, once said problems were straightened out, it would not matter who

---

89   BOA. HAT. 1242/48291 E 29 Zilhicce 1254 (15 March 1839).
90   BOA. HAT. 637/31417 A, 29 Zilhicce 1252 (6 April 1837). This document is probably misdated, as Reşid Pasha passed away in Diyarbekir in October–November 1836. Mehmet Süreyya Bey, *Sicill-i Osmanî*, 6 vols., vol. 5 (Istanbul: Tarih Vakfı Yurt Yayınları, 1996), 1381.

governed Muş.⁹¹ However, all of these problems would be taken over by his successor, Hafız Pasha.

After the death of Reşid Pasha, Hafız Pasha replaced him as the müşir of Sivas. At the time, Esad Pasha was also dismissed from the governorship of Erzurum.⁹² During Hafız Pasha's mission in Sivas, Muş was again annexed to Sivas. He was charged with continuing reforms where his predecessor had left off. With the new müşir, the position of Emin Pasha was also about to change. Hafız Pasha in a report stated that compared with Emin Pasha, Hüseyin Pasha, his cousin, was more loyal. The latter promised to uncover the revenues of Muş, which was said to be four to five thousand purses. In addition, Hüseyin Pasha had also intended to help Hafız Pasha with four or five thousand soldiers in his aim to restore order from Garzan to Muş. Hafız Pasha, therefore, suggested sending Emin Pasha away to Istanbul and that necessary steps should be taken to prevent any kind of trouble in the region. Here again a rivalry arose between two members of the Muş dynasty over power in the region. However, Hafız Pasha warned Osman Pasha, the new governor of Erzurum, not to publicize the idea of replacing Emin Pasha with Hüseyin Pasha until he started to carry it out. As a part of his plan, Hafız Pasha called Emin Pasha to Istanbul.⁹³

At this point, Emin Pasha sought to guarantee twenty-four villages in Muş for himself and his brothers. As both members of the family and provincial authorities previously emphasized, the sanjak of Muş, including about four hundred villages, had been under the control of the mutasarrıfs of Muş as yurtluk-ocaklıks. The family of Emin Pasha had been in power for generations (*eba'an ced*). However, with the operations against local Kurdish families, the sanjak of Muş was first granted to Reşid Pasha and then, because of the redif organization, to the müşir of Erzurum, Esad Pasha, and lastly to Hafız Pasha, who replaced Reşid Pasha. Having lost his exclusive control over the resources of Muş, and being aware of the future of the yurtluk-ocaklık system, Emin Pasha appealed to secure his twenty-four villages in Muş for him or his three brothers.⁹⁴

---

91 BOA. HAT. 637/31417 A, 29 Zilhicce 1252 (6 April 1837).
92 BOA. HAT. 1322/51635 B, 1 Şaban 1253 (31 October 1837).
93 "... kimesneye ifşâ olunmamak üzere mektûm tutulmuş olub ..." BOA. HAT. 1248/48350 C, 26 Cemaziyelevvel 1254 (17 August 1838). In Istanbul, Emin Pasha came into the presence of Sultan Mahmut II and decorated by him. BOA. HAT. 1618/71, 29 Zilhicce 1254 (15 March 1839).
94 Hafız Pasha emphasizes how Muş was an extensive sanjak consisting of four hundred villages, yet it remained under the exclusive control of its mutasarrıfs as yurtluk ocaklık. His choice of the term "seizure" for such a type of land tenure is also important. Hafız Pasha, like many Ottoman pashas was opponent of yurtluk-ocaklık system as it curtailed their material and political power. "... Muş sancâğı dört yüz kadar kurâya müştemil bir cesim

In order to realize this aim, Emin Pasha left his brother as his deputy and launched forth to Istanbul to talk to Hafız Pasha.[95] Having argued that Emin Pasha should be moderately rewarded (*ne pek aşûri iltifât ve ne de derûn taltifât*), Hafız Pasha was of the opinion that the request of Emin Pasha be satisfied. Although Hafız Pasha did not favor Emin Pasha, claiming such men were notorious for being liars, he accepted the fact that Emin Pasha could serve up significant numbers of soldiers to carry out the reforms for which Hafız Pasha was responsible.[96] In the end, the villages were granted to Emin Pasha and some members of his family as yurtluk-ocaklıks.[97] Emin Pasha was no longer the mutasarrıf of Muş – a title which he and his ancestors were used to be granted with the imperial decrees – which was allegedly composed of four hundred villages. Yet, he and his family managed to keep twenty-four fruitful villages in the plain of Muş as yurtluk-ocaklıks with the title of mütesellim of Muş. The boundaries and revenues of the villages would be a matter of discussion in the following years when the yurtluk-ocaklık lands were finally confiscated after 1845. The nephews of Emin Pasha would keep bringing the revenue of those villages onto the agenda even in the 1870s.

The decision ending the yurtluk-ocaklık status of Muş brought an end to the control of the mîrs of Muş over the whole sanjak as a yurtluk-ocaklık. The case of Muş clarifies the difference between the yurtluk-ocaklık sanjaks and yurtluk-ocaklık villages. Despite the loss of the sanjak of Muş, Emin Pasha and his brothers kept certain villages as yurtluk-ocaklık. Emin Pasha and Şerif Bey kept the mütesellimlik of Muş and Bitlis respectively. Murad Bey held the voivodeship of Hınıs and Malazgirt, as well.[98] In addition, as will be elaborated in chapter 4, those who were tax farming the villages of Muş and Bitlis were relatives and men of the family. The steward of Emin Pasha, İbrahim Efendi, would become the target of the Tanzimat state because of his misdeeds while purchasing tax farm contracts of the villages of the sanjak, like over taxing.

The power of the family was only curtailed when they were totally uprooted from the region towards the middle of the century. This also sheds light on the gradual transformation of yurtluk-ocaklık lands. In fact, the status of the sanjak of Muş as a yurtluk-ocaklık had been fluctuating since the sixteenth century, yet the family of Alaaddin Pasha managed to assert control during the first half of the eighteenth century. The struggle of Emin Pasha was to keep

---

sancâk olarak şimdiye kadar sâye-i zılliyyet-vâye-i hazret-i tâcdârîde yûrtluk ve ocâklık vechile Muş mutasarrıfı bulunanlar taraflarından zabt ve idâre altına gelmiş ..." BOA. HAT. 634/31307 A, 3 Cemaziyelahir 1254 (24 August 1838).

95   BOA. HAT. 634/313307 C, 27 Cemaziyelahir 1254 (17 September 1838).
96   BOA. HAT. 634/31307B, 29 Cemaziyelahir 1254 (19 September 1838).
97   BOA. HAT. 381/20579, 29 Zilhicce 1254 (15 March 1839).
98   BOA. HAT. 1242/48291 E, 29 Zilhicce 1254 (15 Mart 1839).

the sanjak of Muş intact as a yurtluk-ocaklık through holding its mutasarrıflık, which his ancestors had enjoyed. Thus, he strived to hold the mutasarrıflık of Muş for the entirety of his career, for approximately fifteen years.

3.5.1 *The Exile of Emin Pasha to Vidin*

According to a report of the Dâr-ı Şûrâ-yı Bâb-ı Âli (Consultative Assembly of the Sublime Porte), because of the attitudes and characters of both Emin and Hüseyin Pashas, it was decreed to take them out of Muş. However, at that point, the governor of Sivas, Hafız Pasha requested the same as what his predecessor Reşid Pasha had demanded: to employ Emin Pasha with a great number of soldiers under his command. Although Hafız Pasha was of the belief that Emin Pasha's "criminal past" was not "as clean as" desired,[99] he demanded Emin's stay and also granted him the twenty-four villages for which he had asked before.[100] From the beginning of their collaboration, Hafız Pasha was actually not very positive about Emin Pasha, and when the time came, he was the one who demanded that the pasha be tried. In short, Hafız Pasha aimed to bypass Emin Pasha after having benefited from his influence, just as his predecessor Reşid Pasha had done.

The involvement of Hafız Pasha only delayed the exile of Emin Pasha for a few months. Two important events that took place in 1838 and 1839 were the most probable reasons for postponing Emin Pasha's dismissal. The first was the revolt of Han Mahmud of Müküs in 1838,[101] and the second was the "issue of Egypt," namely the troubles the Ottoman Empire suffered because of the powerful governor of the Egypt, Mehmet Ali Pasha, and most importantly the defeat in Nizip in 1839.

Han Mahmud benefited from his strategic location on the frontier with Iran. Having taken control of the castle of Hoşap, Han Mahmud was governing Müküs, Westan (Gevaş). Not only Mir Bedirhan of Cizre and Nurullah Bey of Hakkari but also the beys of Muş were unhappy and suspicious of Han Mahmud's rise to power (which would result in the failure of his revolt). Therefore, it was Emin Pasha who was called to the Sublime Porte to present

---

99 "... pâşâ-yı mûmâileyhüma her ne kadar te'mîn ve iltifât olunsalar bunların öteden berû mücerreb olan mizâçlarına göre işe yarar adamlar olmadıkları derkâr ..." BOA. HAT. 1248/48350 A, 29 Zilhicce 1254 (15 March 1839), BOA. HAT. 1248/48350 B, 29 Zilhicce 1254 (15 March 1839).

100 BOA. HAT. 381/20579 A, 29 Zilhicce 1254 (15 March 1839).

101 In the same year, İsmail Pasha of İmadiye (Bahdinan) in the south also revolted. See Sinan Hakan, *Osmanlı Arşiv Belgelerinde Kürtler ve Kürt Direnişleri (1817–1867)* (Istanbul: Doz 2007), 88.

information about the limits of Han Mahmud's power.[102] This collaboration would result in the surrender of Han Mahmud and his exile to Istanbul.[103]

The developments regarding Mehmet Ali Pasha of Egypt altered the situation. The first phase of Mehmet Ali Pasha's revolt (1831–33) resulted in the defeat of the Ottoman Empire in Konya and the Kütahya Agreement in 1833.[104] Mahmud II, in order to overcome the effects of the previous defeat and to reclaim Syria, relied on military reforms and prepared an army to enter Syria. This army was constituted from the Asakir-i Mansure, as well as Kurdish and Turkish tribesmen. As Consul Brant stated, Emin Pasha together with his brother Şerif Bey and 2,500 cavalrymen from Kurdish tribes joined the army. Moreover, his other brother, Murad Bey also joined with 600 cavalrymen from Hınıs, and 300 more were about to join.[105] However, the army of Egypt under the commandership of Ibrahim Pasha, the son of Mehmet Ali Pasha, once again defeated Ottoman troops in June 1839 in Nizip.[106] The battle with Mehmet Ali Pasha required collaboration with Kurdish beys. This not only delayed the removal of Emin Pasha from Muş, but also led to the return of Han Mahmud to the region.[107]

However, these developments delayed the exile of Emin Pasha only up to the end of the battle of Nizip. At the end of war, Emin Pasha and his brothers were arrested and accused of "treachery."[108] Hafız Pasha demanded the prosecution of Emin Pasha and his brothers, Miralay Murad Bey and Kaimakam Şerif Bey, who had been under his command during the battle. Upon being accused of playing a role in the defeat, at the battle of Nizip, and treachery by Hafız Pasha, their trials were handed over to the *Dâr-ı Şûra-yı Askeri* (Deliberative Council of the Army) and were handled in the framework of the code of *Divan-ı Harb* (Military Court). However, Emin Pasha managed to defend himself against the accusations; their treachery could not be proved and so, they could not be punished under the relevant articles of criminal law. As discussed above, Hafız Pasha had already reached a decision to replace Emin Pasha with his cousin Hüseyin Pasha as the mütesellim of Muş. The defeat in Nizip gave him the opportunity to realize this aim and the accusation of treachery was a pretext.

102 Ibid., 100.
103 This would be his first exile – as will be elaborated upon in the next chapter, the power of Han Mahmud would be eradicated to a great extent in 1847.
104 Shaw and Shaw, *History of the Ottoman Empire*, 2, 33–4.
105 FO. 78/366, No: 9, Brant to Palmerston, Erzurum, May 13, 1839.
106 Shaw and Shaw, History of the Ottoman Empire, 2, 50.
107 Hakan, *Osmanlı Arşiv Belgelerinde Kürtler*, 115.
108 FO. 78/366, No: 20, Brant to Palmerston, Erzurum, July 20, 1839,

Nevertheless, it was not deemed appropriate to send them back to their hometowns, so due to their "inappropriate behaviors" (*harekât-ı nâmarziye*) they were settled in a different place, Vidin, for a while. Their families were allowed to go with them, and for the duration, their properties and goods in their hometowns along with some other places were not to be attacked or damaged.[109] Therefore, Emin Pasha and his brothers, having been deprived of their medals and swords, were sent to Vidin directly from Birecik together with their twenty-two subjects.[110] As they could not afford it, the expense of the journey from Istanbul to Vidin which was eleven thousand and four hundred forty five guruş, was covered by the treasury.[111]

After a year of stay in Vidin, Emin Pasha wrote a petition explaining how he and his brothers were immiserated and in poverty, and demanded to live in Istanbul. Although his immiseration and poverty had been noted, his coming to Istanbul was not deemed appropriate, though he might be transferred to Edirne.[112]

3.5.1.1 Struggle for Power to the End

Around two years after his demand that his place of exile be changed, Emin Pasha submitted a report both explaining his situation and coming up with new suggestions. In this report, Emin Pasha explained how he, together with his three brothers had acted in the imperial army with two thousand regular and irregular soldiers. He sacrificed life and property in service of the state – almost fifteen hundred soldiers were killed and his property was destroyed during the battle of Nizip against the forces of Ibrahim Pasha of Egypt. Despite this, they were exiled in Vidin. Finally, after two years and despite the earlier decision regarding their resettlement in Edirne, they were forgiven and allowed to come to Istanbul.[113]

---

109   BOA. HAT. 1648/15, 29 Zilhicce 1278 (27 June 1862). This document is misdated as the event occured in late 1839.
110   BOA. C. AS. 469/19549, 29 Ramazan 1255 (6 December 1839). Meanwhile, some people from Muş were talking about the exile of Emin Pasha in the coffeehouses of Istanbul. Certain Musa Agha from Muş and Kadri from Erzincan were blaiming Hafız Pasha for the exile of Emin Pasha. Apparently, the local people of Muş did not believe in the accusations against Emin Pasha and his brothers, and emphasized the role of Hafız Pasha in their exile. Cengiz Kırlı, *Sultan ve Kamuoyu: Osmanlı Modernleşme Sürecinde "Havadis Jurnalleri" (1840–1844)* (Istanbul: Türkiye İş Bankası Kültür Yayınları, 2008), 123.
111   BOA. HAT. 1623/33, 10 Şevval 1255 (17 December 1839), BOA. C. DH. 279/13922, 15 Zilkade 1255 (20 January 1840), BOA. İ. DH. 7/298, 5 Zilhicce 1255 (9 February 1840), BOA. C. ZB. 27/1344, 29 Zilhicce 1255 (4 March 1840).
112   BOA. İ. DH. 27/1305, 18 Şevval 1256 (13 December 1840).
113   BOA. İ. DH. 51/2557, 29 Zilhicce 1257 (11 February 1842).

Emin Pasha's report includes not only crucial details about the gradual transformation of the yurtluk-ocaklık lands in Muş, but also about the accommodation of a local actor to this transformation. The pasha starts with the statements recalling his dynasty's status in Ottoman administrative practice: the sanjak of Muş, consisting of around four hundred villages, had been granted to the family of Emin Pasha generations before (*bâ berât-ı âlişân ebâ-'an-cedd fâmilyamıza rahmen 'inâyet ve ihsân*). However, in time, twenty-four of the said villages were separated out and granted to the pasha, his family, and their subjects as a salary, while the revenues of the others, no matter the amount, were allocated to the Mansure Army. Besides, Emin Pasha had been asked about the revenues of Muş and recruitment. However, at the same time he was appointed to the army and during the confusion, the remaining villages were granted to forty–fifty people, some local and some from outside. To put it differently, it had been determined that they should be granted to cavalrymen as fiefs (*ya'ni süvâri-i 'askeriye tevcîh gibi*). However, Emin Pasha argued, as these cavalrymen were generally living in Istanbul, that they were keeping the said revenues undeservedly.[114]

After having explained the situation, Emin Pasha emphasized that the revenues of the twenty-four villages granted to him together with those of the said fiefs, that is the other villages given to cavalrymen, was enough to constitute a regiment. Furthermore, if the fiefs in Kars and Bayezid were ascertained and united with those of Muş, if these were contracted out to Emin Pasha and his brothers, and if they were honored with the appropriate ranks and if there was no intervention by the governors of neighboring provinces, a battalion of cavalrymen could be recruited from Van, Bayezid, Hınıs, and Malazgirt. Day by day, it would grow. In other words, Emin Pasha was meticulously reclaiming for the yurtluk-ocaklık lands of his family which had been confiscated. By claiming that the real revenues of Van and Bayezid had not been properly determined, Emin Pasha was asking to be made responsible for determining the value and revenue of those districts. In this way, the re'âyâ of the region, who had been in poverty until that time, could be brought together and the revenue of the region would no longer be concealed. Moreover, the inhabitants of those regions could be saved from poverty and suffering, and security could also be maintained.[115]

Another point in Emin Pasha's report was with regard to the conditions of the frontier tribes. He argued that a few thousand common people from Muş and its environs had crossed the frontier and become the subjects of Iran.

---

114 Ibid.
115 Ibid.

Moreover, Kurdish tribes had also dispersed, and the security of the region was damaged. However, they wanted to come back to their hometowns (*vatan-ı asliye*) and hoped to get fields, properties, vineyards, and orchards. Emin Pasha implied that he had influence over the Kurdish tribes and the common people of Muş. In addition, appropriating the concepts of the Tanzimat, the pasha argued that, if those people came back and tribes were settled, the taxes could be allocated justly, according to everyone's capacity. Furthermore, with population growth, more people could be engaged in agriculture and husbandry, which would result in development and an increase in regular soldiers (*i'mar-ı mülk farizası ve tezâyüd-i 'asâkir-i muntazamma*). Emin Pasha also referred to the previous efforts of himself and his brothers to prevent the assault of Kurdish tribes on the settled population. Moreover, redif soldiers, whom they had also previously used, had dispersed, and if they were called up it would be possible to bring them together in the course of time.[116]

Emin Pasha, who was now in Istanbul, demanded to be transferred to Erzurum along with his brothers. The new governor, Halil Kamili Pasha, argued that since his official post in Erzurum began, he was receiving many reports about Emin Pasha's virtues.[117] Therefore, argued Kamili Pasha, given Emin Pasha's regret and his having been pardoned, he would not object to his return to Erzurum. Rather, Emin Pasha would be helpful in dealing with the "evil conditions" (*ahvâl-i şeytaniyet*) of the Kurdish tribes in the region.[118]

As the points Emin Pasha had introduced in his report were considered important, he was called to Erzurum with his brothers to discuss the situation thoroughly. As stated in his report, Emin Pasha wanted to be awarded Van, Kars, Muş, and Bayezid, but also emphasized that the reforms he had promised would take time. Furthermore, the governor of Erzurum thought there could be some drawbacks to placing the responsibility for all of these places on the pasha. For instance, while Emin Pasha was respected and liked in Bitlis and Muş, Ishak Pasha was respected in Van. As for Kars, it was far from Muş and also situated in a delicate place in the borderlands with Russia. Furthermore, Halil Kamili Pasha had the impression from Emin Pasha and his brothers that although they made promises about Muş, Van, Kars, and Bayezid, their real aim was to be granted the mutasarrıflık of Muş. He suggested that instead of separating Muş from Erzurum and granting it to Emin Pasha, it would be more proper to appoint the pasha as mütesellim of Muş. It can be argued that

---

116   Ibid.
117   "... hüsn-i hâlini söyleyenler sû-i hâlini ifâde idenlerden mütecâviz bulunmakdan nâşi ..." Ibid.
118   Ibid.

Emin Pasha reformulated his old wishes with the vocabulary of the Tanzimat. Indeed, as the governor of Erzurum emphasized, Emin Pasha was seeking for the channels to maintain power in Muş as the way it used to be during the era when he and his family members were granted the sanjak as yurtluk-ocaklık. In the end, although Emin Pasha had aimed to expand his power, or at least to be the mutasarrıf of Muş again, he was only appointed as mütesellim of Muş after three years of exile.[119] The yurtluk-ocaklık system was on its way to being abolished completely, thus neither provincial nor central authorities considered to restore the yurtluk-ocaklık status of Muş again.

Although Emin Pasha struggled hard to regain power, he did not enjoy it for long as he passed away within two years. Upon his death, his brother Şerif Bey became mütesellim of Muş. Emin Pasha's yurtluk-ocaklık villages were confiscated by the treasury, as he had passed away without any children. Şerif Bey, who inherited his elder brother's struggle for the negotiation of power, objected harshly to their confiscation claiming that they should remain within the family.[120] Furthermore, the term of office of Şerif Bey in Muş corresponded to a time when the sanjak of Muş was included in the Tanzimat package.

3.6 Conclusion

Emin Pasha's motivations and reasons for revolt and his coalitions and maneuvers reveal significant points about both the region and the rebellion itself. The revolt mainly stemmed from problems related to the cross migration of the disputed tribes between the Ottoman and Qajar empires and taxation. In addition, behind the scenes, it is possible to observe the opposition of Emin and Esad Pashas to each other. In the course of their careers, they never got along with each other. It was obviously a clash of interests: Emin Pasha sought to be exempt from the intervention of the governor while the governor reasserted his control at every opportunity. Nevertheless, the peculiarities of the region required the employment of Emin Pasha. Similarly, Emin Pasha's intentions did not seem to challenge the central authorities. He claimed his status, negotiated it and revolted for it when necessary, yet he never intended to break ties with the Ottoman state. Therefore, Emin Pasha revolted with the same motivations as his counterparts – to reclaim or enhance his authority.

In the same vein, both coalitions, the one of Emin Pasha and the one against him, were constituted of tribes of the region. Emin Pasha sought trans-border

---

119   BOA. İ. DH. 59/2950, 13 Rebiülahir 1258 (24 May 1842).
120   BOA. C. ML. 585/24051, 4 Cemaziyelahir 1260 (21 June 1844).

allies, as well. Besides, the governor, Esad Pasha made use of intrafamilial rivalry, appointing Hüseyin Pasha, the cousin of Emin Pasha, as the new mutasarrıf of Muş. Therefore, the dissolution of Emin Pasha's front took place thanks to the efforts of Esad and Hüseyin Pashas who had secretly contacted tribal leaders. Nevertheless, Emin Pasha never declined to negotiate. In this way, the reforms and military operations of Reşid and then Hafız Pasha led to his pardon and reappointment to Muş. After pacifying the notables of Rumelia and Anatolia, Reşid Pasha headed towards Ottoman Kurdistan. Muş was no exception.

Although the pacifying of the beys of Muş would take time and was realized towards the middle of the century, their economic power diminished slowly. Military reforms and operations changed the status of the sanjak, as well. With the reforms and military operations under Reşid Pasha, the governor of Sivas, Muş was granted to him. Then, after the constitution of müşirliks, the sanjak was annexed to the müşirlik of Erzurum, and its revenues were spared for the Mansure Army in 1836. With this, the yurtluk-ocaklık status of the whole sanjak changed. Emin Pasha, who had sought to keep the inherited lands, his ancestors had enjoyed, intact over the entirety of his career tried to guarantee the rights to twenty-four villages in the sanjak of Muş for him, his brothers, and his relatives. Here, the difference between yurtluk-ocaklık sanjaks held through mutasarrıflık and yurtluk-ocaklık villages is clarified. That is why Emin Pasha's career hovered between mütesellimlik and mutasarrıflık throughout the first half of the nineteenth century. Nevertheless, the annexation of Muş by Reşid and then Hafız Pasha prompted Emin Pasha to separate some productive villages for his family.

The family's joining forces against İbrahim Pasha of Egypt delayed their prolonged punishment only for a short while. In the aftermath of the defeat of Nizip, Emin Pasha and his brothers were tried and exiled to Vidin. However, circumstances, ranging from the family's knowledge of the region, influence over the tribes, and relations with notables in its environs led to the rise of the family to power once again. Şerif Bey became mutasarrıf of Muş after his elder brother's death. However, his term of office was shaped by transformations taking place in the name of the Tanzimat.

CHAPTER 4

The Tanzimat State in Muş: Collaboration with and Punishment of Local Actors

> The province of Erzurum is situated in a delicate location, as most parts of it border Russia and Iran. Besides, its population is partially composed of Kurds and tribes that have already migrated to their summer-quarters. At present, on the one hand, the auspicious reforms of the Beneficent Tanzimat are gradually being implemented, [and] on the other hand, in accordance with the imperial order, the surveys of real estate and incomes are being carried out. Besides, apart from the expenses of the region between November 1260 and March 1261, it has become successively necessary to collect more than two thousand purses from the sanjaks and districts of the province. Therefore, it would be difficult to carry out a census properly and according to the imperial order. Moreover, as mentioned, the tribes have gone to their summer pastures and the census cannot be carried out at present. Therefore, it would be proper to delay the census of the province of Erzurum for a few months.[1]

This quotation is from a decision of the *Meclis-i Vâlâ-yı Ahkâm-Adliye* (Supreme Council of Judicial Ordinances, hereafter Meclis-i Vâlâ). Established in March 1838, the Meclis-i Vâlâ was the most critical institution of the Tanzimat era as it was responsible for the legislation, execution, and supervision of the reforms of the era.[2] The Meclis-i Vala penned this report in 1845, a few months after the inclusion of the province of Erzurum together with Diyarbakır, Maden-i Hümâyûn, and Sivas under the Tanzimat.[3] The peculiarities behind the delay of the census of Erzurum explained in this report have shaped

---

1 BOA. MVL. 2/18, 3 Cemaziyelahir 1261 (9 June 1845).
2 The Meclis-i Vâlâ, which occupies an important place in the reforms of Mahmud II, was acting as a legislative and judiciary body, yet experienced a division of labor in the course of time. In 1854, it was divided into two – the Meclis-i Tanzimat and the Meclis-i Vâlâ – and the former took up the legislative duties of the institution. Then, in 1861, the two organs were reunited. In 1868, it was again divided into two under the names Şurâ-yı Devlet and Divân-ı Ahkâm-i Adliye. For more detail about the historical development of the institution, see Mehmet Seyitdanlıoğlu, *Tanzimat Devrinde Meclis-i Vâlâ, 1838–1868* (Ankara: Türk Tarih Kurumu Basımevi, 1994).
3 BOA. İ. DH. 97/4852, 14 Muharrem 1261 (23 January 1845).

this chapter, which introduces an account of the gradual implementation of Tanzimat reforms in the province of Erzurum in general, and in the sanjak of Muş in particular. The chapter tries to show how the local notables of Muş accommodate themselves to this new organization planned with the Tanzimat and how they took part in the implementation of the reforms. Together with the following chapter 5, this chapter will focus on the transformations of provincial administration, taxation, and land tenure politics that the Tanzimat state envisaged. The main concern of the chapter is to shed light on the agency of the Muş's notables in the reform process and on the dynamics which necessitated their exile in 1849.

With the promulgation of the Gülhane Rescript in 1839, the application of Tanzimat reforms was the harbinger of a set of reorganizations in the administrative, fiscal, military and judicial spheres of the Ottoman Empire.[4] However, these reforms were not implemented throughout the empire simultaneously; first pilot regions were chosen, and then reforms were expanded gradually. In addition, the application of the reforms did not prescribe a formula that was valid throughout the empire; rather, it was determined by the peculiarities of the region, as clearly explained in the decision of the Meclis-i Vâlâ, which approved the postponement of the census in Erzurum and suggested the Tanzimat reforms be applied gradually (*refte refte*). Two preliminary features of the province of Erzurum determined this decision: its location on the eastern borderlands of the Ottoman Empire and its tribal landscape.

The delicacy of Erzurum stemmed from its being on the Ottoman-Russian and Ottoman-Iranian borders, which meant that any turmoil on the Ottoman side of the border could lead to cross-border chaos. Moreover, tribal and frontier issues with Iran were not yet resolved. The modus vivendi of the same Kurdish tribes also created great difficulties for carrying out a census. Finally, government authorities on one hand were carrying out tax-surveys, and on the other, were in need of financial support to cover their costs, and so they levied a cash tax. As the central government was deprived of the necessary mechanisms to realize all these aims at once, it became necessary to take gradual, cautious steps. In fact, it was the main motivation of the Tanzimat state to establish those mechanisms by carrying out income surveys and a census, settling the tribes, and breaking the power of the local notables and administrative elites.

---

4   For a brief discussion of the context in which the Tanzimat emerged and its peculiarities, see Halil İnalcık, "Tanzimat Nedir?," in *Tanzimat: Değişim Sürecinde Osmanlı İmparatorluğu*, eds. Halil İnalcık and Mehmet Seyitdanlıoğlu (Istanbul: Türkiye İş Bankası Kültür Yayınları, 2012), 29–56; Findley, "The Tanzimat," 11–38.

During the Tanzimat era, a set of reforms were inaugurated to increase the infrastructural power of the central government. However, the issues of taxation and conscription were the main tasks of this era. Thus, "the Gülhane Rescript"[5] centered on a just tax-collection system by evoking the ills of a tax farming system, on one side, and a new tax based on the incomes and property of subjects, on the other side.[6] Similarly, the duration of military service fixed at five years, became compulsory for all male subjects, and conscripts were chosen by lottery.[7] The preliminary step for applying the reforms was to make a population and income survey (*tahrir ve temettu*) which would enable the Tanzimat state to collect taxes and recruit men for the army. In order to realize this aim, tax collectors (called *muhassıl*) were centrally appointed to the regions included in the Tanzimat program. Second, muhassıls established councils at the provincial, sub-provincial (called *büyük meclis,* large council), and district levels (called *küçük meclis*, small council). These councils were composed of local administrative, religious, fiscal, and security authorities, community representatives, and members chosen from among inhabitants. With these councils, the authority of governors was curtailed; they became responsible for just administrative duties.[8] Local councils not only enabled

---

5 The Rescript also promised equality between Muslim and other communities and the security of life, property and honor for all subjects. For an analysis of the Tanzimat Rescript, Yavuz Abadan, "Tanzimat Fermanı'nın Tahlili," in *Tanzimat: Değişim Sürecinde Osmanlı İmparatorluğu*, eds. Halil İnalcık and Mehmet Seyitdanlıoğlu (İstanbul: Türkiye İş Bankası Kültür Yayınları, 2012), 57–88; Ibid.; Şerif Mardin, "Tanzimat Fermanı'nın Manâsı: Yeni Bir İzah Denemesi," Ibid., eds. Halil İnalcık and Mehmet Seyitdanlıoğlu, 145–65.

6 Upon a decision in 1840, the treasuries of Mansure, Redif and Amire were annihilated, and the Finance Treasury, under the Ministry of Finance, became the only institution administrating the revenues and expenditures of the empire. Tevfik Güran, *Tanzimat Döneminde Osmanlı Maliyesi: Bütçeler ve Hazine Hesapları (1841–1861)* (Ankara: Türk Tarih Kurumu Basımevi, 1989), 7. For the fiscal reforms of the Tanzimat, see among others, the studies of Şener, Tanzimat Dönemi Osmanlı; Özbek, *İmparatorluğun Bedeli*; Çakır, "Tanzimat Dönemi Vergi Uygulamalarında."

7 The military reforms were announced in 1843 and implemented starting in 1844. Meanwhile, the army was renamed "Asâkir-i Nizâmiye" (the regular army). Musa Çadırcı, *Tanzimat Döneminde Türkiye: Askerlik* (İstanbul: İmge Kitabevi, 2008), 66–67. Nevertheless, the non-Muslim male population was not conscripted under the Tanzimat and continued to pay a cizye (poll tax). With the Islahat Fermanı of 1856, the cizye was abolished and the military duties of non-Muslim males were clarified. Nevertheless, they could be exempted from military service by paying a tax called *bedel-i askeri* which was a reformulation of the cizye. Shaw and Shaw, *History of the Ottoman Empire*, 2, 100.

8 However, with a regulation issued in 1842, the authority of the governor increased. Shaw, "Local Administrations," 36.

local notables to continue their intermediary role through such institutions, but also left a legacy of election and participatory politics.⁹

In addition to these permanent councils established by muhassıls, temporary councils were established in places where the implementation of reforms required further supervision. These councils called *İmâr Meclisleri* (Councils of Public Works) were established in 1845 and were composed of officials directly sent from the Meclis-i Vâlâ accompanied by Muslim and non-Muslim representatives from each region.¹⁰ Administrative reforms were gradual, and with the Provincial Law of 1864, provincial administration was reshaped to be more hierarchical and to define and determine the responsibilities of each official, preventing "overlapping and conflicting authority." Similarly, the Provincial Law restituted the authority of the governor.¹¹

When the province of Erzurum was brought under Tanzimat, the local dynasty of Muş was still occupying crucial roles in the administration of the sanjak, yet they were working harder to keep their position intact. In effect, during the first phase of the implementation of the reforms those local families were employed. Despite the pacification of the mîrs of Soran, Baban, and Rewanduz and partially of Diyarbekir in the 1820s–30s, Han Mahmud in Van, Bedirhan Bey in Cizre-Bohtan, Nurullah Bey in Hakkari, and Şerif Bey, the brother of Emin Pasha, in Muş were still in power. They first negotiated and then challenged the implementation of Tanzimat reforms, which would eventually bring about their end. This chapter will focus on the elimination of those mîrs, putting the local dynasty of Muş at the center.

The socioeconomic situation on the eve of the Tanzimat reforms is crucial to understand the postponement of reforms and the employment of local notables in their execution. In effect, depicting the socioeconomic situation of Muş immediately before the Tanzimat also casts light on the local actors whose power stemmed from their exploitation of the rural population in myriad ways. In this discussion, the case of the steward (*kethüda*) İbrahim Efendi is prominent as he established a long-standing relationship with the governors of Muş mainly based on the exploitation of the inhabitants. Second, İbrahim

---

9   To name a few pioneering studies on local councils: Ortaylı, Tanzimat Devrinde Osmanlı; Akiba, "The Local Councils," 176–204; Shaw, "Local Administrations," 33–49; Musa Çadırcı, Tanzimat Döneminde Anadolu Kentlerini'nin Sosyal ve Ekonomik Yapısı, 2 ed. (Ankara: Türk Tarih Kurumu, 1997); Elizabeth Thompson, "Ottoman Political Reform in the Provinces: The Damascus Advisory Council in 1844–45," *International Journal of Middle East Studies* 25, no. 3 (1993): 457–75.
10 Mehmet Seyitdanlıoğlu, "Tanzimat Dönemi İmâr Meclisleri," OTAM, no. 3 (Ocak 1992): 325–26.
11 Shaw, "Local Administrations," 42–45.

Efendi would be punished first upon application of Tanzimat reforms in Muş. Third, the case of the steward is also significant to demonstrate how the inhabitants of Muş were not passive receivers of the reforms; rather, they used the channels of the Tanzimat state to make their voices heard, utilizing the language and vocabulary of the Tanzimat.

Thus, in the following lines, the case of İbrahim Efendi will first be introduced as a means of illustrating the political and economic networks in the region. Then, the employment of Şerif Bey in the implementation of the reforms in Muş will be discussed, pointing out how the mediation of local notables was required for the fulfillment of the reforms. Finally, the role of the mîrs of Muş in the revolt of Bedirhan Bey, which attracts the most attention in the literature on Kurdish notables, will be discussed. Together with his family and brothers Şerif Bey, despite his defection from the coalition of Bedirhan Bey, was exiled, which was certainly the determining factor in the eradication of the dynasty's political and economic power in the region.

4.1   On the Eve of the Application of Tanzimat Reforms: A Network of Exploitation

The British Consul of Erzurum, James Brant wrote down a memorandum on the situation of Muş in 1844, a few months before Muş was included in the Tanzimat program. In one of the passages Consul Brant writes that:

> Hussein Pasha is paid a salary, but has no direction of affairs in Moosh, all being managed by İbrahim Effendy. The Cadi, a thorough bigot, is the intimate ally of the Effendy's, and acts in concert with him. Zachariah Vartabet, the head of the Armenian portion of the population, assisted by Ussep, the Millet bashee, or head of the nation. The Vartabet (Bishop) takes care to enrich his Convent, and Ussep, himself.
>
> Thus, the poor inhabitants of Moosh are completely enthralled: the Mohamedans by İbrahim Effendy and the Cadi, and the Armenians by Zachariah Vartabet and Ussep, and they are perfectly understood among themselves. If these persons wish to get up a petition in favor of, or against, any Governor, they pen it themselves; the Mohamedans are made to sign it by the Cadi and the Armenians, by the Bishop; but neither know to what they are affixing their seals. Memorials of the most contrary nature are continually coming from Moosh. They have come, both in favor, and against Sheriff Beg, as also in favor of Hussein Pasha, as well as against

him. In short, these papers mean nothing more than that the four rulers have some temporary purpose to answer, by bringing them forward.¹²

The passage is important first because it sheds light on the system of exploitation led by İbrahim Efendi, the steward of the administrators of Muş, second because it shows how both Muslim and non-Muslim inhabitants of Muş were oppressed by their representatives, and third because it highlights how the present mutasarrıf, Hüseyin Pasha was not competent enough to eliminate the oppression and to govern the region properly.

As discussed in the previous chapters, the local dynasty of Muş, whose power stemmed from its lineage, its large land holdings, called yurtluk-ocaklık, and its influence in the network of the region, had long been involved in the government of the region. This situation continued, as in other peripheral regions of the empire, until these powerful local actors were deprived of their sources of power with the introduction of new tax and land tenure politics. After the passing of Emin Pasha, his brother Şerif Bey struggled to be the mutasarrıf of Muş. He had a few rivals except for his cousin, Hüseyin Pasha, who had been also a rival of his brother. The government authorities replaced one with the other one on many occasions, before both were eventually exiled.

In 1844, Şerif Bey had trouble with the governor of Erzurum, Halil Kamili Pasha, concerning the yurtluk-ocaklık villages of his deceased brother Emin Pasha. As the latter had died without a child, his yurtluk-ocaklık villages were legally passed to the Imperial Treasury. However, Şerif Bey demanded that the villages be granted to his own sons. Upon being rejected, he tried to resist and sought the assistance of his followers; however, he did not succeed and was dismissed from the mütesellimlik of Muş.¹³ Although Emin Pasha's villages were confiscated by the treasury based on the absence of any descendant, the interpretation of "heir" was not the same for all yurtluk-ocaklıks. In the Mahcil district of Lazistan sanjak, a certain Osman Bey appealed for the salary paid for the confiscated yurtluk-ocaklık villages of his deceased brother who died without a child. The Meclis-i Vâlâ accepted his appeal claiming that "descendant" also included brothers.¹⁴ Thus, the treatment of yurtluk-ocaklık holders changed from region to region, and in the case of Şerif Bey, the rejection of his

---

12 FO. 195/227, No:21, "Memorandum regarding the state of Moosh" Brant to Canning, Erzurum, December 9, 1844.
13 BOA. C. DH. 117/5810, 20 Rebiülahir 1260 (9 May 1844).
14 Ömer Toraman, "Trabzon Eyaletinde Yurtluk-Ocaklık Suretiyle Arazi Tasarrufuna Son Verilmesi (1847–1864)," *Uluslararası Karadeniz İncelemeleri Dergisi*, no. 8 (2010): 65.

claim to his brother's villages was the result of anxiety and designed to prevent further strengthening of the family.

Therefore, when Hüseyin Pasha was appointed as mütesellim, Şerif Bey tried to obstruct his entry to Muş but failed. Then, as Consul Brant reported, he took shelter in the house of Han Mahmud in Müküs (contemporary Bahçesaray) with his brother Murad Bey.[15] Whereas, Hüseyin Pasha was regarded as the lesser of two evils, a few years earlier the people of Muş had complained about him alleging that he had collected money from the people on various grounds and besides, he had no talent for governing the sanjak.[16] Having heard that Hüseyin Pasha would be the new governor of Muş, some inhabitants of Muş went all the way to Erzurum to show their dissatisfaction about his appointment before Kamili Pasha, the governor of Erzurum. The reason for this complaint was that the people viewed Hüseyin Pasha as an oppressive governor. Moreover, he was deeply in debt, so they were afraid of being overtaxed because of his debts. Therefore, the common people wanted Şerif Bey to remain, even though, according to Kamili Pasha, he was also cruel towards the inhabitants.[17] Both the provincial authorities including European agencies occasionally referred to the 'cruelty' of hereditary Kurdish rulers. Blaming local notables for cruelty was a means for these actors to legitimize the Tanzimat reforms and their own rule.

It is possible that the people who oppose the nomination of Hüseyin Pasha were the supporters of Şerif Bey and did not represent the common view of the inhabitants of Muş. Indeed, after a short while, another petition signed by both Muslim and non-Muslim populations of Muş was submitted to the governor of Erzurum. This new petition, that might have been initiated by Hüseyin Pasha, rejected the previous one, which favored Şerif Bey, and claimed that the people had signed it under duress. Having expressed their satisfaction with the discharge of Şerif Bey, whom they accused of "extortion" and "treachery," the people claimed that if he had remained in his post all the reʿâyâ would have left Muş.[18] Nevertheless, this also did not reflect everyone's views. After a short while, when the cruelty of İbrahim Efendi, the steward, increased and when

---

15   FO. 195/227, No: 7, Brant to Canning, Erzurum, July, 15, 1844. The French Consul of Trabzon also reports that Şerif Bey sought the support of Bedirhan Bey at the same time. MAE. 69CCP, vol. II, Clairamboult to Guizot, Trabzon, June 24, 1844.
16   BOA. İ. MVL. 10/154, 8 Şaban 1256 (5 October 1840).
17   FO. 195/227, No: 6, Brant to Canning, Erzurum, May 29, 1844.
18   Ibid. No: 7, 10 June 1844. However, both cousins continued to claim the administration of Muş and accused each other of being unjust. BOA. MVL. 11/4, 29 Safer 1263 (16 February 1847).

Hüseyin Pasha could no longer wield power, even Kamili Pasha claimed that Şerif Bey would have been less oppressive.[19]

The preference for Şerif Bey over Hüseyin Pasha was not simply a matter of "who was less cruel." If the way the petitions were written is taken into consideration, the matter was who was more skillful at controlling other power groups – like the steward and tribal leaders – and conciliate their interests. Şerif Bey would be nominated to execute Tanzimat reforms in Muş, not because he was less cruel but because he could manipulate every opportunity to negotiate the range of his power. He would benefit from the alliance with the surrounding beys of Van and Hakkari and from his influence over the Kurdish tribes, as well.

Despite uncertainty regarding the issue of whether the peasants of Muş would have preferred Hüseyin Pasha or Şerif Bey, it is undeniable that these peasants were dissatisfied and immiserated before the region was brought under the Tanzimat. The primary reason for this miserable situation was over taxation, as can be understood from the main accusations against the two governors of Muş. The main problem was the common people's inability to pay regular taxes due to a decrease in the population. Consular reports point out that the population of Muş had diminished by almost a third compared to six years earlier, due to famine and plague.[20] Yet the Ottoman government demanded that the people pay the same total of taxes despite the population decrease.[21] In the same vein, the French Consul of Erzurum, Thedore Goepp, reports that districts of Muş and Bitlis were suffering from unrest; people were refusing to pay taxes, and men were objecting to conscription, as well. The inhabitants of both districts claimed that plague and famine had decimated them and it was not fair they had to pay the same amount of taxes regardless of the population decrease.[22] This issue of overtaxation points out that when the provincial authorities were accusing local notables of Muş of being cruel, they were also the same when it comes to the extracting of surplus from the peasants.

Although it is difficult to obtain sound data regarding the amount of regular taxes levied on the inhabitants of Muş in the pre-Tanzimat period, Consul Brant presented some information about regular and irregular taxes in Muş. According to his report, regular taxes levied on the population included *sâlyâne* (annual tax), *öşr* (tithe), and *haraç* (*cizye*, poll tax). The most demanding

---

19   FO. 78/572, No: 10, Brant to Aberdeen, Erzurum, 9 December 1844.
20   As stated by Donal Quataert, the plague remained a significant event in Ottoman society until the second quarter of the nineteenth century. Donald Quataert, *The Ottoman Empire, 1700–1922* (Cambridge: Cambridge University Press, 2005), 114.
21   FO. 195/227, No: 6, Brant to Canning, Erzurum, May 29, 1844.
22   MAE. 69CPC, Vol. II, Goepp to Guizot, May 24, 1844.

one was sâlyâne, which had doubled in a year, from 500 to 1100–1200 guruş. The same amount was levied on villages as a poll tax. The main problem was the decrease of the population while the same or increased amount of the taxes was levied.[23]

However, the worst were irregular taxes, which brought forth the exploitative politics of local actors. On top of their inability to recover even regular taxes, local authorities forced peasants to pay taxes both in cash and in kind. Here, local representatives played crucial roles, as they levied these irregular taxes as much as they wished. For instance, the taxes that İbrahim Efendi took each month from each village point to how local power-holders enriched themselves at the expense of the dispossession, indebtedness, and suffering of the peasants.

The inhabitants of every village were bound to supply İbrahim Efendi monthly with one somar of barley (equivalent to nineteen imperial bushels, lbs), two to three batmans of butter (equivalent to 31,4 to 47 lbs), three to five cart-loads of straw, twenty to thirty trusses of hay, and two sheep supposedly to be delivered to Hüseyin Pasha. According to Brant, probably a small amount of these products was sent to the palace of Hüseyin Pasha. İbrahim Efendi and the kadı, his collaborator consumed the largest portions or even sold them for profit.[24]

Beyond over taxation, İbrahim Efendi was also indirectly worsening the living conditions of the inhabitants. First, he forced bakeries in Muş to buy wheat from him at an above-market price. In return, he allowed the bakeries to sell their bread at higher prices. Similarly, the village headmen (*muhtar*) were replaced for trivial reasons every three or four months. Actually, the main reason was the requirement that every new headman present an amount of money to İbrahim Efendi. This amount was added to the annual taxes of the village. By these means, a few people were becoming rich and powerful at the expense of the labor of the majority.[25]

In order to understand this system of exploitation led by İbrahim Efendi, it is necessary to analyze the components of his power. The power of İbrahim Efendi for the most part stemmed from the network he had established over the years. That network was composed of local actors who had direct control over resources. He was the steward (kethüda/kahya) of the mutasarrıfs and

---

23 FO. 195/227, No: 21, Brant to Canning, December 9, Erzurum, 1844.
24 Ibid. 1 somar = 307.966 kg; 1 batman= 7.694 kg in Asia Minor, 19th. Certainly, there are regional differences, for details see Halil İnalcık and Donald Quataert, eds., *An Economic and Social History of the Ottoman Empire*, 1300–1600, 2 vols., vol. 1 (Cambridge: Cambridge University Press, 1997), xxxviii–xLii.
25 Ibid.

mütesellims of Muş since the time of Emin Pasha. Besides, he could obtain the assistance of influential local actors, like the kadı, the bishop, and the *milletbaşı* (the representative of the non-Muslim community) in the exploitation of the inhabitants. When the specificities of the population of Muş are taken into consideration, it can be noticed that a significant part of the alliance of İbrahim Efendi was composed of Kurdish tribes. Tribal members or chiefs who showed loyalty to İbrahim Efendi could also take products ranging from barley to cheese from villagers either on behalf of İbrahim Efendi or just for themselves. Besides as a part of the corvée, when the Kurdish chiefs arrived in Muş, İbrahim Efendi sent their servants and horses to the houses of Armenians who would host them. In the same way, Brant claimed, winter-quartering (*kışlakiye*), which means the requirement for the villagers to cover the needs of Kurdish tribes – that spent winters in their villages – like shelter and food was abolished by the Porte (as a result of the Tanzimat). However, it was still in effect in Muş, as well as in many other places.[26]

İbrahim Efendi used various forms of exploitation both to enhance his network and to enrich himself. The disgruntlement of the people was barely alleviated by the local governors. When the people could not reach the Porte, the best option remained to emigrate. Nevertheless, the Ottoman government only responded to the complaints about İbrahim Efendi after the Tanzimat reforms were scheduled to be applied in the region, as will be discussed in the following paragraphs.

If the cruel application of taxation was the main source of the complaints and suffering of the Armenian population of Muş, for the Muslim portion of the population, an equally significant problem was conscription. Although it only concerned Muslims, the inhabitants claimed that conscription dreadfully affected the harvest.[27] Indeed, when Hüseyin Pasha was required to collect two thousand men for the army, he only managed to recruit thirty men. To avoid service, Brant argued, male Muslim commoners applied a set of strategies ranging from emigration to Iran or Russia to deliberately mutilating themselves. Another option was to take refuge among Kurdish tribes that were not easily accessible.[28] Although it is necessary to take the numbers stated by Consul Brant with a grain of salt, it is significant that the inhabitants of Muş took advantage not only of it being situated in a frontier region, but also its tribal social structure in order to resist over taxation and hard conscription policies. Moreover, the insufficiency in the imperial infrastructural power to supervise

---

26 Ibid.
27 FO. 195/227, No: 6, Brant to Canning, Erzurum, May 29, 1844.
28 Ibid. No: 9, 25 July 1844.

conscription as well as lack of security in the region led to tribalization; if not in large scale, male population were joining tribes to avoid conscription.

The common people of Muş suffered from the struggle of different actors over usurping their income. The only solution for them was to leave their homes, which in return diminished the population and so left the sanjak's fertile lands uncultivated.[29] In such circumstances, when the imperial edict of the Tanzimat was read publicly in a village of Muş, it was engraved in the mind of a local peasant as the introduction of a new tax and the annihilation of the corvée labor (*angarya*).[30] Thus, the villagers of Muş perceived the Tanzimat as the abolition of over taxation and forced labor, most probably similar to the way peasants perceived it throughout the empire. Many scholars share the argument that the focus of the Tanzimat was tax reform.[31] It first appeared as "agricultural reform" in consular reports of the era.[32] However, the Tanzimat was also the precursor of a new era in which reformers were determined to apply a new way of governing by eliminating local power holders which they held responsible for the poverty and dissatisfaction of the inhabitants.

Accordingly, the first step once Muş was brought into the Tanzimat program was to take precautions against Şerif Bey and his brothers together with their rival and cousin, Hüseyin Pasha and the notorious steward, İbrahim Efendi. A Meclis-i Vâlâ report was paying a special attention to their cruel and extortionist ways of governing and emphasizing that it would be eliminated with the "Auspicious Tanzimat." The report emphasized that the inhabitants were scared of them. The ongoing dispute between Şerif Bey and Hüseyin Pasha influenced their relatives in Muş, and this resulted in divisions and conflict

---

29 For further discussion of the decrease of the population of Muş in the nineteenth century, see chapter 6 of this book.

30 Ibid. No: 23, 17 December 1844. In the same vein, Halil İnalcık emphasized that the issue of angarya was important as even before the promulgation of Tanzimat, in August 1838, imperial orders were sent to the governors of Rumelia about the angarya, causing the revolts of the re'âyâ. Halil İnalcık, "Tanzimatın Uygulanması ve Sosyal Tepkiler," in *Osmanlı İmparatorluğu: Toplum ve Ekonomi*, ed. Halil İnalcık (İstanbul: Eren, 1993), 367. Uğur Bayraktar also argues that in the Ottoman Balkans, the abolishment of angarya did not actually take place despite continuous warnings from the Sublime Porte. Uğur Bayraktar, "The Political Economy of Çiftliks: The Redistribution of Land and Land Tenure Relations in the Nineteenth Century Provinces of Ioannia and Trikala" (master's thesis, Boğaziçi University, 2009), 111–12. In addition, see chapter 6 of this book for the continuance of forced labor and the implementation of winter-quarters in the plain of Muş.

31 See İnalcık, "Tanzimatın Uygulanması;" Özbek, İmparatorluğun Bedeli; Şener, Tanzimat Dönemi Osmanlı.

32 FO. 78/614, "Report on the Trade of Erzeroom, and the State of the Pashalık for the Year 1844," Brant to Aberdeen, Erzurum, January 28, 1845.

among inhabitants, too. Therefore, according to Tanzimat bureaucrats, in order to maintain order and safety and enhance the welfare of the inhabitants, those local elites should no longer be employed in Muş.[33] This struggle between the allies of Şerif Bey and those of Hüseyin Pasha continued for a while after their exile. Yet, this new language of Tanzimat drawing attention to cruel administration of local notables was for legitimizing the administrative and fiscal transformation which was deemed to be implemented throughout the empire.

Breaking the power of local notables was definitely a result of the aim to govern the periphery with centrally appointed officials, which had actually been discussed for a few decades. Nonetheless, it might also be the result of a reflection that the Tanzimat was the harbinger of a new era and that those notables were reminders of the old system that the people associate with heavy tax burdens and the assaults of Kurdish tribes who were encouraged and protected by local notables. However, the elimination of the relics of the "old system" was a tough, challenging process; indeed, the implementation of reforms became impossible without their cooperation. As will be discussed in the following lines, although some local actors like Şerif Bey maintained and negotiated their positions in the new system, the ones like İbrahim Efendi, were easily punished.

4.2   The Tanzimat State in Muş

Immediately after the promulgation of the Gülhane Edict, the tax farming system was reorganized in the places included in the Tanzimat, and muhassıls were dispatched instead with duties ranging from tax collection to the establishment of local councils.[34] The Tanzimat also heralded the abolition of forced labor and planned a single tax (*virgü, vergi*) according to the income, agricultural land, and livestock of the taxpayer. Therefore, in order to put this into practice, the first duty of the muhassıls together with scribes (kâtib) was to begin an income (*temettuat*) survey. The appointment of muhassıls was

---

33   "... kâffe-i sekenesinin mûmâileyhden gözleri korkmuş olmasıyla mücerred-i âsâyiş ve refâh-i hâl-i reʿâyâ zımnında mûmâileyhümanın fîmâbaʿd livâ-i mezbûr imârâtında istihdâm olunmamakla ve bunların beynlerinde derkâr olunan mübâyenet Muş'da bulunan akrabâ ve müteallikatına dâhi sirâyet iderek memleket ahâlisi dâhi birkaç taraf olduklarından ..." BOA. MVL. 2/26, 26 Cemaziyelahir 1261 (2 July 1845).

34   Özbek, İmparatorluğun Bedeli, 46. Except for Bosnia, Albania, Erzurum, Trabzon, Van, Kars, Diyarbekir, and Baghdad, it was decided to implement the system of muhassıllık in 1840. Ibid. For a discussion of muhassıllık, also see Ayla Efe, "Muhassıllık Teşkilatı" (PhD diss., Eskişehir Anadolu Üniversitesi, 2002).

abolished in 1842, and afterwards, reforms were carried out by the existing administrative elites in provinces included in the Tanzimat.[35] Therefore, the inclusion of the province of Erzurum in the Tanzimat system started with some innovations: nomination of a "proper agent" to introduce the new tax, the determination and dispatch of representatives from Erzurum to Istanbul to specify the problems of the province, and the nomination of a new kaimakam, Ahmed Kaşif Agha to Muş to replace the local dynasty.[36]

The new, "proper agent" was a *defterdar* (provincial treasurer). His reception by the inhabitants was noteworthy. As Consul Brant narrated, the inhabitants of Erzurum were hopeful about the arrival of the defterdar, yet the consul worried about the fact that the official would reside near the building of the governor of Erzurum, Halil Kamili Paşa, which meant that their dialogue could lead them to pursue their own interests at the expense of the people's immiseration.[37] In the same series of events, soon after the defterdar embarked on the income survey, rumors spread that a new sheep tax (*ağnam*) and a new annual tax would be imposed. Moreover, the mineral springs which the people used freely would be auctioned off and tax-farmed, so that they could not use them without paying a fee.[38] Despite this initial report by the consul, he would later note that all of this news turned out to be false. Neither a new cattle tax nor a new annual tax was imposed. All the defterdar did was to register the livestock in the possession of subjects and collect arrears for the previous six months. The tax farming of mineral springs was not even a matter of discussion. According to the defterdar, Muslims were not content with the new tax regime, and spread the news, as mentioned above.[39] This was not specific to the province of Erzurum; rather, it was commonly observed in all the places where Tanzimat reforms were applied.[40]

Although it is questionable to what extent the defterdar succeeded in instituting the income registration (*temettuat sayımı*) in the province of Erzurum, it is important to understand the anxiety of Muslims regarding the new tax rates mentioned by Consul Brant. Nevertheless, it is apparent that the income

---

35   Güran, "19. Yüzyıl Temettüat," 76.
36   FO. 195/227, No: 34, Brant to Canning, Erzurum, October 8, 1845.
37   Ibid. No:1, "Report on the Trade of Erzurum and the Situation of the Pashalık for the year 1844," January 16, 1845. Consul Brant added that Kamil Pasha was uncomfortable with the centrally-appointed official even if he did not let it be known. Yet soon after Kamil Pasha was replaced with Bekir Sami Pasha. Ibid., No: 5, February 20, 1845.
38   Ibid. No: 10, April 9, 1845.
39   Ibid. No: 11, April 19, 1845.
40   For seminal studies on the implementation of Tanzimat reforms in Balkan provinces, see Uzun, *Tanzimat ve Sosyal Direnişler*; İnalcık, "Tanzimatın Uygulanması."

registration was carried out in some parts of Erzurum, even if not in all the sanjaks and villages of the province. As Consul Brant explained, in the town of Erzurum, the properties of the inhabitants were recorded three or four times, yet inhabitants rejected the results each time, arguing that they were unfair. The problem was resolved by asking both Muslims and Christians what they could "bear."[41] This case of Erzurum is in line with the main tenet of the new tax regime, which was that taxes were supposed to be collected according to the economic ability of the taxpayer, expressed as *komşuca* (literally 'neighborly' referring to its fairness) or *hoşnud-i umûmî* (to the contentment of all).[42]

Despite the fact that income registers, which would determine the amount of the tax each house was able to pay, were only partially successful in the province of Erzurum, as will be discussed thoroughly in the following pages, equality regarding taxation had been heralded with the Tanzimat at the beginning. As Nadir Özbek argued, Tanzimat reformers did not schedule a detailed program to frame a just taxation regime, but it created expectations among a large part of the population.[43] As described above, villagers in the plain of Muş perceived the Tanzimat primarily as the abolition of forced labor.[44] Second, it meant for the Armenian peasantry the prohibition of the burden of quartering Kurdish tribes in winter on peasants, who had been obliged to provide them with hay, straw, and shelter. Complaints about forced labor and winter quarters would continue in the years to come, but the reflection of Tanzimat reformers on their abolition was still significant. As a third factor, the equal taxation of Muslims and non-Muslims also became an issue.[45] The taxes collected on agricultural produce – in other words tithe (*a'şâr*) – was fixed at one-tenth of production by the Tanzimat.[46] According to Brant, previously, non-Muslims

---

41   FO. 195/227, No: 7, Brant to Canning, February 11, 1846. The difficulty in collection of information about taxable properties was not specific neither to the province of Erzurum nor to the Ottoman Empire in general. Alp Yücel Kaya discusses similar tendencies in French countryside in the 1850s. Both the landowners and farmers sought to understate their products and exaggerate their production costs. Alp Yücel Kaya, "Politique de L'enregistrement de la richesse economique: Les Enquetes Fiscales and Agricoles de L'empire Ottoman and de La France au Milieu du XIXe Siecle," (PhD diss., École des Hautes Études en Sciences Sociales, 2005), 152–157.
42   Özbek, *İmparatorluğun Bedeli*, 41; Şener, *Tanzimat Dönemi Osmanlı*, 95.
43   Özbek, *İmparatorluğun Bedeli*, 40.
44   For a discussion of similar expectations of provincial Armenians from Tanzimat reforms, see Masayuki Ueno, "'For the Fatherland and the State': Armenians Negotiate the Tanzimat Reforms," International Journal of Middle East Studies, no. 45 (2013).
45   FO. 195/227, No: 7, Brant to Canning, Erzurum, February 11, 1846 "Report on the Trade of Erzurum and the Situation of the Pashalık for the year 1845."
46   Şener, *Tanzimat Dönemi Osmanlı*, 129. However, during financial crises it was raised as high as fifteen percent. Şevket Pamuk, *Türkiye'nin 200 Yıllık İktisadi Tarihi* (Istanbul:

had generally been paying twenty percent and Muslims not more than five in the province of Erzurum.[47] In fact, the numbers given by the consul can be misleading, yet the distribution of the tithe was largely unequal. The emphasis on equality under the Tanzimat mainly derived from this reality.[48]

With the inclusion of the province of Erzurum in the Tanzimat program, two methods of tax allocation were followed. In places where income surveys were accomplished, which were few in the beginning, taxes were determined according to those surveys. In other places, where the income surveys had not yet been completed, taxes were allocated according to previous amounts (*ale'lhesâb*). Muş was among the latter.[49] Accordingly, the amount of taxes the inhabitants of Muş had been paying in total before the Tanzimat was two thousand two hundred purses, twenty-eight guruş. However, on the eve of the Tanzimat, the peasants had dispersed because of the immiseration they went through for the variety of reasons discussed above. On the request of Governor Esad Pasha, the amount was reduced to fifteen hundred purses starting in 1261 (1845).[50] With the Tanzimat, the dispersed inhabitants of Muş gradually returned to their homes, and seminomadic tribes were settled there. In this way, starting in 1265 (1849), the total tax of Muş was increased to two thousand purses. However, the tax was still some three hundred purses less than the amount before the Tanzimat. The Meclis-i Vâlâ emphasized that the reforms would be fully succeed in the course time; the tribes would be settled and the people would be prosperous, then, taxes would be raised according to the incomes of taxpayers.[51]

The second task upon which Tanzimat bureaucrats embarked was the dispatching of "competent" persons from the provinces to the capital of the empire to determine both the necessities and problems of their regions.[52] As Tanzimat reforms had not yielded major successes by 1845, the Meclis-i Vâlâ decided to summon two representatives from each province to obtain better

---

Türkiye İş Bankası Kültür Yayınları, 2012), 130. For details concerning the tithe, its collection and relationship between tax farmers and peasants in the Tanzimat and post-Tanzimat contexts, see Özbek, İmparatorluğun Bedeli, 39–112.

47   FO. 195/227, No: 48, Brant to Canning, Erzurum, December 12, 1845.
48   Cevdet Küçük also notes that before the Tanzimat, a one-fifth tithe was collected from the peasants in the province of Erzurum. Cevdet Küçük, "Tanzimât Devrinde Erzurum" (PhD diss., İstanbul Üniversitesi, 1975), 251. Nevertheless, regional variations were certainly inevitable.
49   BOA. C. ML. 299/14949, 15 Rebiülâhir 1261 (23 April 1845).
50   BOA. C. ML. 654/26778, 29 Cemâziyelâhir 1266 (12 May 1850).
51   BOA. İ. MVL. 162/4718, 10 Rebiülevvel 1266 (24 January 1850).
52   FO. 195/227, No: 8, Brant to Canning, Erzurum, March 7, 1845.

regional knowledge.⁵³ Those representatives, whose travel expenses were covered by the local treasury, were welcomed in the imperial capital city.⁵⁴ After providing information about the peculiarities and problems of their regions, those representatives returned to their provinces along with delegations to establish İmâr Meclisleri, which were constituted temporarily to inspect and solve problems regarding implementation of the reforms.⁵⁵

Along the same lines, after the province of Erzurum was brought under the Tanzimat, one of the first tasks the imperial bureaucrats embarked upon was to dispatch representatives to the capital of the empire.⁵⁶ Taking demographic specificities of the province into consideration, Cennetzade Abdullah Efendi and Mustafa Agha as representatives of Muslims and Köseoğlu Kivork and Muradoğlu Mattos, as representatives of Armenians were nominated and sent to Istanbul. After providing information about the province of Erzurum and the reforms it needed, these four representatives returned with three delegations appointed by the Meclis-i Vâlâ to establish İmâr Meclisi in Erzurum.⁵⁷

As Consul Brant discussed, it was an advantage that all four men were capable of giving correct information regarding the revenues, problems, and the necessities of the population. Yet the matter was whether giving correct information would be in line with their interests. In spite of being accurate sources for better comprehension of the region, these men were also part of the very system from which the common people suffered.⁵⁸ For instance, the

---

53   Tevfik Güran, "Temettuat Registers as a Resource about Ottoman Economic and Social Life," in *The Ottoman State and Societies in Change: A Study of the Nineteenth Century Temettuat Registers*, eds. Hayashi Kayoko and Mahir Aydın, Islamic Area Studies (London: Kegan Paul, 2004), 5. Also "19. Yüzyıl Temettüat," 76.
54   Ortaylı, *Tanzimat Devrinde Osmanlı*, 44.
55   Seyitdanlıoğlu, "Tanzimat Dönemi İmâr," 327.
56   Cevdet Küçük also notes that, in 1839, after the promulgation of the Tanzimat, Istanbul ordered the dispatch of representatives from the provinces to the capital city. The müşir of Erzurum, Hafız Pasha, delegated this responsibility to a notable of Erzurum, Hacı Abdullah Bey, the bey of Kığı, Mehmed Bey, and a notable from Kars, Hacı Ahmet Bey. Despite the absence of documents detailing the mission of those delegates, Küçük argues that based on the views of the representatives dispatched from each province, it was decided to implement the Tanzimat first in the provinces proximate to Istanbul. Küçük, "Tanzimât Devrinde," 160–61.
57   BOA. A. MKT. 25/5, 17 Cemâziyelâhir 1261 (23 June 1845). As stated by Cevdet Küçük, the inspection of the Council of İmâr lasted seven to eight months, and they prepared reports that were examined in the Meclis-i Vâlâ. One of the main issues was the repair of the road between Erzurum and Trabzon for which engineers were employed. Ibid., 220–21.
58   FO. 195/227, No: 9, Brant to Canning, Erzurum, April 8, 1845. This point is parallel with the argument of Phillou who emphasizes that Muslims and non-Muslims were part of the same "overlapping" social networks at the turn of the nineteenth century. And, both "were using the same operational logic to augment their wealth and their share in

Cennetzades were influential actors in Erzurum who controlled revenues of the region through tax farming and became members of the council under the Tanzimat.[59] In addition, Ortaylı emphasizes that the people dispatched to Istanbul were actually representatives of influential actors in the region, so they could not provide satisfying information about the problems of the provinces.[60]

As stated at the beginning of this chapter, one of the first duties of the muhassıl was to establish muhassıllık councils (Muhassıllık Meclisleri and then Memleket Meclisleri) as soon as he arrived in a region. These councils would assist the muhassıls in the execution of reforms. The determination of the revenues of inhabitants and the allocation and collection of taxes were carried out through those councils. In that sense, the muhassıllık council was the first example of the local administrative institution in the strict sense.[61] As Jun Akiba reflects, although the muhassıllık system was abolished in 1842, local councils were established in places where the Tanzimat reforms were later applied.[62] However, it was inevitable that local notables took part in those councils, as the election procedures clearly stated that the members of the councils should be chosen from among sensible, distinguished, wealthy inhabitants.[63] Indeed, these councils became platforms for local actors to increase their power. These councils would play a key role not only as an "intermediary between the central governments and local residents,"[64] but also as channels for local people to submit their complaints.

The third part of novelty with the application of the Tanzimat in Erzurum specifically concerned Muş. A new kaimakam other than Şerif Bey and Hüseyin Pasha was appointed to Muş – as Consul Brant described him, an outsider with no connections in the region.[65] The central state legitimized the appointment of a new kaimakam, shortly after the application of the Tanzimat in the region to limit some of the disorder in Muş stemming from the rivalry between Hüseyin Pasha and Şerif Bey. After the appointment of Ahmed Kaşif Agha to

---

sovereignty." Philliou, "The Ottoman Empire's Absent Nineteenth Century," 145. Similarly, Cora demonstrates that Armenian notables were not different from their counterpart Muslim notables in the mid-nineteenth century. Cora, "Transforming Erzurum/Karin," 47.

59   Küçük, "Tanzimât Devrinde," 325.
60   Ortaylı, Tanzimat Devrinde Osmanlı, 44.
61   Ibid., 33.
62   Akiba, "The Local Councils," 178–79. Similarly, Şener states that after the annihilation of the muhasıllık, the councils continued to exist. Şener, *Tanzimat Dönemi Osmanlı*, 98.
63   For more details about the election system, see Ortaylı, *Tanzimat Devrinde Osmanlı*, 35–37.
64   Akiba, "The Local Councils," 176.
65   FO. 195/227, No: 34, Brant to Canning, Erzurum, October 8, 1845.

Muş, the exile of both Şerif and Hüseyin pashas along with İbrahim Efendi, the steward of Hüseyin Pasha, was discussed. The cruelty of İbrahim Efendi, was revealed regarding his tax farming in the villages and sub-districts of Bitlis in 1844.[66] However, it was only İbrahim efendi who was punished in the end and Şerif Bey became the administrator of Muş once again. In what follows, the debate over the oppressive acts of İbrahim Efendi during his tax farming will first be briefly explained, and then the circumstances that allowed Şerif Bey to govern Muş for the last time will be discussed.

The commoners of Muş had been exposed to great extortion and oppression from İbrahim Efendi, and his allies, on the eve of the application of the Tanzimat reforms in the district.[67] With the promulgation of the Tanzimat, the newly established provincial and district councils, as new apparatuses of the Tanzimat state, became a recourse for the problems of local people. The petitions of the people, although initially sent to the Meclis-i Vâlâ, started to be discussed first in the Provincial Council of Erzurum. Similarly, the petitions of the Muslim and non-Muslim commoners of Muş submitted through Armenian Patriarchate regarding the embezzlement practices of İbrahim Efendi and Hüseyin Pasha was handled in the Erzurum Provincial Council, and the related records were submitted to Istanbul.[68]

The allegations against İbrahim Efendi and his allies, the milletbaşı of Bitlis, Oseb, two Armenians Hacı Manok and Simon, and Hamparsum from Köseoğulları and Kivork, culminated in the allegations of abuse regarding tax farming in 1844. It was reported that İbrahim Efendi tax farmed the sanjak of Muş together with district of Bitlis (with its sub-districts and villages) for a lump sum (*maktuan*) of three thousand purses. However, together with his allies, he arbitrarily levied taxes amounting to more than seven thousand purses (in some later documents, the amount indicated is six thousand) on the inhabitants. Upon the submission of the issue to the Meclis-i Vâlâ, it was decided the matter would be investigated, and the opinions of Kamil and Bekir Sami Pashas, the former and current governors of Erzurum, were to be ascertained.[69]

In his report, Kamil Pasha explained the allegations against İbrahim Efendi and his allies, which he had heard from certain peasants of Muş. Accordingly, İbrahim Efendi and his collaborators used every method of extortion on peasants who could not pay the demanded amount, from making people sell their

---

66   BOA. MVL. 2/26, 26 Cemaziyelahir 1261 (2 July 1845).
67   BOA. A. MKT. 28/84, 6 Şevval 1261 (8 October 1845).
68   BOA. A. DVN. 17/62, 23 Şaban 1262 (16 August 1846).
69   BOA. A. MKT. 30/13, 6 Zilkade 1261 (6 November 1845).

houses to threatening to injure their children and wives. In some cases, they physically tortured people; even by hanging pregnant women upside down and exposing them to smoke that also injured unborn children. The suggestion of Kamil Pasha was that an official be appointed to investigate both the cruel acts and the amount of money extorted.[70] Accordingly, their debt to the peasants of Muş turned out to be six thousand purses; however, Hüseyin Pasha and İbrahim Efendi admitted to only half of the debt and denied the other half. The petitioners were certain of the amount in spite of the denial.[71]

Besides excessive taxation, according to the petition of the peasants, the former mutasarrıf of Muş and the steward caused further trouble for the people by provoking their network of allies in the province. The *sarraf* (money lender) Köseoğulları of Erzurum were supporting some houses among the Kurdish tribes, known as Hacı Mahmud, Beyzadelu, İsâlu, Süvar and Bölükbaşı, in their attack on the villages of Muş during which they plundered products and houses and killed and injured the people. Even worse, peasants were paying those Kurds four times more than the annual regular tax as they were afraid of their cruelty.[72] The inhabitants claimed that the Kurdish tribes were patronized by Ferik Bahri Pasha, the lieutenant general of the regular army in Erzurum, who rejected all their complaints instead of protecting them against those kinds of encroachments. Thus, it was not only tax farmers, moneylenders, administrators, and tribes but also higher military authorities who took part in the usurpation of common people's revenues and assaults on them. With an emphasis on the requirements of the Tanzimat-ı Hayriyye, the peasants demanded that their disgruntlement be resolved so that they can be occupied with their work and pay annual taxes according to their possessions and incomes without fear for security of their lives and property.[73]

The preliminary effect of the Tanzimat on the inhabitants of Muş was that they used its terminology and utilized newly established mechanisms like provincial councils to make their voices heard. Similarly, the volume on the case of İbrahim Efendi, in the Ottoman archives, suggests that the Tanzimat reformers were wary regarding the resolution of the problems of the inhabitants. For instance, they were worried that although most of the signatories of the petition were Muslim, the people preferred to send them through the patriarchate.[74] Emphasizing that Muş was located on the frontier with Iran

---

70   Ibid.
71   BOA. A. DVN. 17/62, 23 Şaban 1262 (16 August 1846).
72   Ibid.
73   Ibid.
74   "… mahâzır-ı mezbûrde olan yüz kırk dokuz 'aded mührün seksân bir 'adedi ahâlî-i islâm ismine iken mahâzırın patrik tarafına gönderilmesi emr-i müstagreb görülmüş …" Ibid.

and Russia, the central authorities were eager to resolve the complaints of the people "against friends and foes."[75] The problems of the inhabitants of Muş needed to be solved not only because of delicate border issues, but also because of the urgent situation of the welfare of the region. The British Consul in Erzurum perfectly depicted the situation in the first half of the nineteenth century as follows:

> The soil and climate are excellent, and the province ought to be rich and to yield a great revenue, but it is verging to the state of an uncultivated waste, frequented by a scanty population of wandering tribes, uniting the characters of shepherds and robbers. The continuing in power of any native whatever, will only involve the province in irrecoverable anarchy and ruin. It requires a disinterested, intelligent and courageous Governor, who will sacrifice his comfort and interest to its improvement.[76]

It was not just consular reports, but also central and provincial ones that largely acknowledged the necessity of the region being governed by someone other than the local gentry. However, the nomination of Ahmed Kaşif Agha to Muş did not ameliorate conditions. In this way, Şerif Bey became the kaimakam of Muş for the last time until his ultimate exile. As is discussed in detail below, two factors paved the way for Şerif Bey to again be the kaimakam of Muş. On one hand, there was the difficulty of applying Tanzimat reforms in Muş with a governor who did not have knowledge about the specificities of the region; on the other, there was turmoil in Van, which was grounded in reactions to the Tanzimat reforms.

4.3 Old Actors and the New Regime

In spring 1845, when the defterdar (provincial treasurer) of Erzurum, Ali Tevfik Efendi, reported the difficulties in carrying out income and population surveys in Muş together with Kars, Çıldır, and Erzurum, the kaimakam of Muş was Kaşif Agha, a stranger to the region. Muş was just one of the places where they could not carry out an income survey. As the region was close to Van, turmoil there could easily affect Muş, which was mostly inhabited by tribes

---

75 "... her nasıl ise livâ-i mezbûr Erzurum eyâleti dâhilinde bulunmuş olduğundan ve oraların İranlu ve Rusyalu hudûduna karâbeti cihetiyle re'âyânın müteâ'kıben vâki' olan sızıldılarının yâr ve agyâra karşu ber-taraf edilmesi ..." Ibid.
76 FO. 195/227, No: 17, Brant to Canning, Erzurum, March 24, 1846.

and clans (*aşair ve kabail taifesi*). Although, the official in question, Kaşif Ağa promised that Tanzimat would be applied soon in Muş, the central authorities needed to find someone who was accustomed to the region, had influence over the tribes, and could be a mediator vis-à-vis the chaos in Van.[77] Therefore, although his exile was discussed previously, together with those of Hüseyin Pasha and İbrahim Efendi, Şerif Bey was appointed as kaimakam of Muş. In the same way, Hüseyin Pasha was nominated as district governor (*müdir*) of Ispir and Bayburd. The incorporation of Kurdish notables in the administrative system after the Tanzimat was not specific to Muş. By this means, central authorities tried to diminish, if not prevent, the anxiety of the provincial gentry regarding reforms. This precaution was also in line with the gradual (*refte refte*) implementation of the reforms.

The initial anxiety of Kurdish notables stemmed from the transformation of the land regime under the Tanzimat reforms. When the matter of the abrogation of yurtluk-ocaklık lands was discussed as a means of increasing the share of the central treasury in the struggle over revenues, softening the reactions of the holders of this kind of inherited land became crucial. Hence, putting them on salary and appointing them as district governors were two means of incorporating these unreliable notables. Similarly, after the provinces of Erzurum and Diyarbakır together with the district of Maden-i Hümâyûn were brought under the Tanzimat, the abrogation of yurtluk-ocaklık lands in the districts of Palu and Eğil was added to the agenda. The motivation was to triple the revenues of the central treasury. In return, proper salaries would be assigned to the possessors of these lands and some, if thought to be appropriate, would be nominated as district governors.[78] However, the problem was that most of the yurtluk-ocaklıks were in the province of Erzurum, which was exempted from this decision due to its location on the frontier. The problem was that when other yurtluk-ocaklık holders heard about the enforcement of this decision in the districts of Diyarbakır, the rumors would spread which in turn would lead to general disorder and an insurrection.[79]

These fears were not groundless. The eastern borderland of the empire was in turmoil. The reason for Van's rebellion was opposition to the implementation of the Tanzimat. The revolt in Van influenced its neighbors, especially in Çıldır, Kars, Erzurum, and Muş. Nevertheless, the logic of the uprisings was

---

77 BOA. C. DH. 299/14949, 15 Rebiülahir 1261 (23 April 1845).
78 BOA. MVL. 2/24, 11 Cemaziyelahir 1261 (17 June 1845).
79 "… bu misillû vâridâtın çoğu Erzurum eyâletinde bulunmuş ve eyâlet-i merkûme ser-haddân-ı hakânîyeden olmak mülâbesesiyle müstesnâ tutulduğu hâlde zikr olunan kazâlar ahâlîsinin mesmû'ları olarak kîl û kali mûceb olacağı zâhir görünmüş olduğundan …" Ibid.

simple and obvious to both Tanzimat reformers and foreign observers: it was not common people but notables whose interests clashed with the new taxation and land politics that were causing the unrest. The local notables whose power alliances were deeply rooted in the region could manipulate news and spread rumors.[80]

In the province of Çıldır in 1845, as a part of the Tanzimat, the tithes of all fiefs, yurtluk-ocaklıks, and mâlikânes (life term tax-farms) were to be collected by the central treasury. However, this was only to ascertain the worth of those lands; the revenues would be returned to their holders. Nevertheless, this led to anxiety among the notables. Some even went to Sublime Porte. Fearing that all of their lands would be confiscated by the central treasury, they asked how they could maintain their families' survival. In regard to this, the former governor of Çıldır was blamed for his inability to properly explain the aims and benefits of the Tanzimat-ı Hayriyye.[81]

Therefore, the Tanzimat state required capable agents to convey the objectives of the reforms to the people. In Muş, the appointment of Şerif Bey can be analyzed in this context. Kamil Pasha – who was appointed to supervise the implementation of reforms in Ottoman Kurdistan – depicted Ahmed Kaşif Agha, the previous governor of Muş, as a person who pursued only his interests and who, as a "foreigner" could not carry out the tasks of the region.[82] Similarly, the British Consul of Erzurum argued that the agha had neither friends nor connections in the region and trusted in Oseb, the milletbaşı for every matter.[83] This was the first example of a centrally-appointed administrator relying on provincial leaders to carry out business in Muş. In the same vein, the peasants complained that given the power vacuum, oppression and extortion by Kurdish tribes had increased.[84]

In this conjuncture, despite his unpunished crimes, Şerif Bey was appointed first due to his familiarity with the region and his network of allies. He had influence not only over the tribes of Muş, but was also kin to Han Mahmud of Van and Nurullah Bey of Hakkari. He had mediated between Han Mahmud and the central authorities before, and could encourage him to pay the required taxes

---

80 As discussed above, in Muş, when the newly appointed defterdar was carrying out his duties, rumors spread that a new cattle tax was to be imposed and that the mineral springs that the people were using in common were to be put up for auction and given to tax-farmers. All turned out to be false. FO 195/227, No: 10, Brant to Canning, Erzurum, April 9, 1845.
81 BOA. İ. MSM. 49/1233, 17 Ramazan 1261 (19 September 1845).
82 Ibid.
83 FO. 195/227, No:34, Brant to Canning, Erzurum, October 8, 1845.
84 BOA. İ. MSM. 49/1233, 17 Ramazan 1261 (19 September 1845).

as well as obeying the orders of the Ottoman government. Moreover, to justify the appointment of Şerif Bey, reference was made to his previous services for the Imperial Army, during the eras of Reşid and Hafız Pashas.[85]

Moreover, the Ottoman government noted that the rebellion in Van had already created troubles on the frontier; the central and provincial authorities came to a consensus on the idea that the discipline and removal of local notables should be delayed until the Tanzimat reforms were implemented, in order to prevent further turmoil in the region. On this basis, Şerif Bey was appointed to help implement the Tanzimat reforms, but, his nomination was temporary.[86] As clearly stated in official documents, once the revolt of Van was suppressed the region would again be governed by centrally-appointed kaimakams and müdirs who "proved" themselves.[87] The removal of Kurdish notables was gradual as was the implementation of the reforms.

While declaring the appointment of Şerif Bey to Muş, Erzurum's governor, Esad Pasha, warned Şerif Bey about giving or receiving presents while in his official post. Due to the Tanzimat, he did not need to submit presents to anyone. Rather, it would be contrary to the consent of the sultan if he accepted any presents.[88] The governor also stressed that the system had changed. The only thing Şerif Bey should do to keep his position and be promoted was to perform his duties decently.[89] Halil Kamili Pasha, the former governor of Erzurum who was then entrusted with the implementation of the Tanzimat in Ottoman Kurdistan, warned Şerif Bey himself concerning the issue of presents.[90] These warnings point to changes in administrative practices, in which present exchange from that point was to be deemed as corruption and therefore forbidden.[91] For instance, Consul Brant heard speculation about Şerif Bey

---

85 Ibid.
86 "… Van ihtilâli henüz bitişmemiş ve nizâmât-ı cedîde icrâ ve te'sîs olunmamış olduğu hâlde bu misillû erkân-ı eyâletin tard ve teb'îdleri sâir vücûh ve mu'teberân-ı eyâletin tevhîşiyle izâle-i emniyetini istilzâm iderek tahrîkât ve ifsâdâtın vuku'una sebeb vireceği …" Ibid.
87 "… ihtilâl-i mezkûrun indifâ'ından sonra oralara bendegân-ı saltanat-ı seniyyeden mucerreb kâimakâm ve müdirler nasb ve ta'yîni tasavvurâtına göre bunların me'mûriyyetleri muvakkat hükmünde bulunacağına mebnî …" Ibid.
88 Ibid.
89 FO. 195/227, No: 47, Brant to Canning, Erzurum, December 12, 1845. As paraphrased in a report of Consul Brant, the words of the Pasha were as following: "The pasha told the Bey he had been very foolish in feeing so many people who would do him no good, but as the system was now changed, he need not give a single piastre to anybody, but he was required to act uprightly and fairly, which would do more to keep him in his post than the largest bribes." Ibid.
90 FO. 195/227, No: 32, Brant to Canning, Erzurum, September 9, 1845.
91 Cengiz Kırlı, "Yolsuzluğun İcadı: 1840 Ceza Kanunu, İktidar ve Bürokrasi," *Tarih ve Toplum Yeni Yaklaşımlar* 4 (2006): 52.

giving money to Sami Bekir Pasha and Enveri Efendi, who were Ottoman representatives in frontier negotiations with Iran, to be nominated to Muş. The consul stressed how deeply the system of bribery was rooted in that region.[92] These warnings indicated how the Kurdish nobility was paying provincial authorities to maintain rule over their yurtluk-ocaklık lands before the Tanzimat.

When Şerif Bey became kaimakam of Muş, two urgent topics were on the agenda, the revolt of Van and the disobedience of Kurdish tribes in Muş; the settled groups constantly complained of their cruelty. As mentioned before, the predecessor of Şerif Bey, Ahmed Kaşif Agha, had not effectively dealt with the tribal attacks, which in turn increased both the suffering and complaints of the people. The network that Şerif Bey's family had established with the Hesenan, Cibran, Haydaran and Zilan was detailed in the chapters 2 and 3. Therefore, the belief that Şerif Bey could be influential in controlling the Kurdish tribes – and bring about their settlement, taxation and conscription in the context of the Tanzimat – was one of the factors that enabled him to become kaimakam of Muş.

Although the Tanzimat reforms in respect to the tribal population of Muş will be thoroughly discussed in chapter 7, it is necessary to briefly describe the Tanzimat reforms regarding tribes to comprehend both the role of Şerif Bey and to grasp the situation of a neighbor sanjak, of Van, where the people were rising up against the Tanzimat. As Esad Pasha, the governor of Erzurum, described in summer most Kurdish tribes dwelled in tents in the pastures of Muş, and they spent winters in some of its villages where they terrorized villagers, attacked them, and plundered their property.[93] Şerif Bey was employed for almost a year to settle some of these tribal families in empty houses, prevent their attacks on the livelihood of the villagers, and tax them. He was partially successful. However, the governor was certain that the settled population could be definitely relieved by the settlement of the tribes, which could only be carried out slowly. The most urgent issue was to deal with five houses of the tribes of Hesenan and Cibran, namely Hacı Mahmud, Beyzadelu, İsâlu, Süvar and Bölükbaşı about which both the Muslim and Armenian populations of Muş complained. Şerif Bey was authorized to send these families to Erzurum on the pretext of determining the amount of taxes they could pay. Therefore, they would be settled in appropriate districts in Erzurum. If they did not depart willingly, Şerif Bey was given the authority to dispatch them forcefully.[94] Şerif

---

92   FO. 195/227, No: 32, Brant to Canning, Erzurum, September 9, 1845.
93   BOA. MVL. 8/38, 15 Ramazan 1262 (6 September 1846). This 'plunder economy' is discussed in chapters 7 and 8 in detail.
94   Ibid.

Bey was also charged with capturing tribesmen involved in murder and theft and sending them to the governor of Erzurum.[95]

One of the famous tribal leaders for the capture of whom Şerif Bey was responsible was Rıdvan Agha of Hesenan, whose story will be elaborated in chapter 8.[96] Having plundered the *nahiye* (sub-district) Bulanık of Muş, Rıdvan Agha first fled to the Castle of Malazgird, then sheltered in the house of Han Mahmud and later became part of the coalition of Han Mahmud and Bedirhan Bey.[97] The sheltering of Rıdvan Agha by Han Mahmud exemplified the fears of both central and provincial authorities, regarding the possibility of joining of neighboring Kurdish tribes in the turmoil in Van. In his report, Bahri Pasha specifically stressed that until the problems in Van were solved, Şerif Bey was fully authorized to deal with disaffected tribes.[98]

4.3.1   *The Settlement of Accounts*

Şerif Bey had his own agenda when he was employed to supervise the implementation of Tanzimat reforms. Consul Brant also emphasizes how Şerif Bey implemented reforms only if they were in line with his interests:

> The Government of Sheriff Bey is one of terror, he shows not the least intention of fulfilling the promises given to Essat Pasha. He enforces the Tanzimat, where it is favorable to his interest, and where it is not, he disregards it. He lives by supplying every want from the villages without payment, and, in short, the country was never more oppressed than at the present moment, the people are reduced to the lowest state of misery, and there is neither commerce, nor personal security.[99]

While carrying out (or not) government directives Şerif Bey also used his authority to settle old scores with his rivals in the region. One was with the famous Hüseyin Pasha, his cousin. The other one was with the new milletbaşı of Muş and Bitlis, Simon. These cases are important in depicting the networks and conflicts of interest of local power holders in Muş and their struggle over its revenues. The competition between Emin Pasha (and later Şerif Bey) and Hüseyin Pasha affected local power holders and tribal leaders in Muş and its vicinity. Hüseyin Pasha argued that Şerif Bey was determined to take revenge

---

95   BOA. MVL. 9/38, 4 Zilhicce 1262 (23 November 1846).
96   BOA. A. MKT. 59/80, 7 Muharrem 1263 (26 December 1846).
97   Ahmet Kardam, *Cizre – Bohtan Beyi Bedirhan: Direniş ve İsyan Yılları* (Ankara: Dipnot Yayınları, 2011), 322.
98   BOA. MVL. 9/38, 4 Zilhicce 1262 (23 November 1846).
99   FO. 195/227 No: 17, Brant to Canning, Erzurum, March 24, 1846.

on people and tribes who had previously crossed his family. Those people consisted of almost five thousand houses, among which were those of Şerafeddin Bey of Hizan, Halil Bey of Huyud, Süleyman Agha of the Cibran, and Rıdvan Agha of the Hesenan.[100] Hüseyin Pasha appealed for justice by using the language of the Tanzimat, emphasizing that Şerif Bey's behavior was contrary to the Tanzimat (*mugayr-ı usûl-i Tanzimat*).[101]

As reflected on the archival documents, his rivals accused Şerif Bey of seeking to deprive them of their material wealth benefiting from the strength, which stemmed from his official duties in the provincial administration of Muş. A certain Salih, the treasurer (haznedar) of Hüseyin Pasha and former administrator of Bulanık, claimed that he was the guarantor of the Hüseyin Pasha's debt to a merchant called Ayvazoğlu Mıgırdıç. To pay his debts, Hüseyin Pasha mortgaged his house in Muş and the properties around it.[102] However, Şerif Bey intervened, evacuating the tenants of Hüseyin Pasha, forcefully seizing and destroying their properties. On top of this, he usurped three thousand guruş, the revenue from Hüseyin Pasha's landed property. Referring to the rule of Tanzimat-ı Hayriyye, Salih asked for an imperial decree for investigating the case and securing justice. Şerif Bey legitimized his acts by saying that this land was needed for the settlement of troops of the Imperial Army. Moreover, Esad Pasha defended Şerif Bey, arguing that the land and the house of Hüseyin Pasha were held as a place for troops upon a decision of the council of Muş, and its rent was being paid, contrary to the claims of Hüseyin Pasha and Salih.[103]

A similar case in which Şerif Bey was cleared of blame took place with the representative of the Armenian inhabitants of Muş, Simon. As reported by the governor of Kurdistan, Esad Pasha, in a petition dated 22 December 1847, the milletbaşı of Bitlis and Muş, Simon, accused the kaimakam of Muş, Şerif Bey, and his brother Hurşid of usurping his property, valued at two hundred thousand gurus, selling it for forty-seven thousand guruş and taking the money. Allegedly, Şerif and Hurşid beys threatened to execute him, and he had

---

100   As reported by Osman Pasha, the müşir of the Anatolian Army, Şerif Bey also dismissed Şerafeddin Bey from Hizan, which his family had been holding as hükûmet with a berat-ı alişan (imperial certificate). Instead, he allegedly appointed his brother. The müşir confirmed that Şerafeddin Bey had the right and following correspondence with Istanbul, Osman Pasha was authorized to decide. Accordingly, Şerafeddin Bey was reappointed. BOA. İ. MSM. 50/1278, 8 Ramazan 1263 (20 August 1847).
101   BOA. MVL. 11/4, 29 Safer 1263 (16 February 1847).
102   BOA. MVL. 29/29, 26 Zilkade 1264 (24 October 1848).
103   BOA. A. MKT. 168/35, 15 Safer 1265 (10 January 1849). Nonetheless, Consul Brant also reported that Şerif Bey took all the property in the house of Hüseyin Pasha, where his wife – the sister of Şerif – was living, claiming that her husband had debts. FO. 195/227 No: 23, Brant to Canning, Erzurum, April 24, 1846.

to flee Muş, come to Istanbul, and ask for justice [*ihkâk-ı hak*]. In response, the governor of Erzurum was ordered to investigate the details of the accusation. He interrogated both openly, and confidentially, the members of both the Muş and Bitlis councils as well as the representatives of both the Muslim and non-Muslim communities. At the end of the investigation, it was reported that Simon was imprisoned by Şerif Bey, because he had embezzled taxes collected from peasants, to the amount of nine thousand guruş. After a while, having guaranteed that he would repay the money, he was released. Yet he escaped without paying his debt. Adding that they had no information about whether Şerif Bey took anything from Simon, witnesses from the councils of Muş and Bitlis explained that Simon was not the kind of person who would have property valued at two hundred thousand guruş. Thus, their testimonies were in line with the statements of Şerif Bey. Emphasizing the bill of debt and acts of Simon, Esad Pasha argued that it was hard to say that Simon had not been involved in embezzlement. The Pasha was of the opinion that Simon's words were most probably the results of his grudge against Şerif Bey, so they were just lies [*tezvîrât*]. Therefore, the governor demanded that Simon pay the debt and also be punished for his lies. Esad Pasha also pointed out that although Şerif Bey was not the kind of kaimakam who governed justly and who could be trusted, in this case, based on witness' testimonies, he was innocent.[104]

Whether the testimonies of the council members from Muş and Bitlis were under the influence or fear of, Şerif Bey or not, this interrogation showed the relations of kaimakam of Muş with tax collectors and local Armenian actors. Şerif Bey had also had a symbiotic relationship with the previous milletbaşı of Muş and Bitlis, Oseb. Consul Brant reported that Şerif Bey was even suspected of killing Oseb when their interests clashed.[105] Moreover, Şerif Bey obviously had a deep-rooted network in the newly established council. Regardless of Şerif Bey's role with regard to the allegations, not only the local councils but also the provincial governors clearly took his side. It was possible that fear that the turmoil in Van could spread to Muş and the role of Şerif Bey in the suppression of

---

104 "... mîr-i mûmâileyh kâimakâmlık umûrunu usûl-ı muaʿdelet şumûle tatbîken tesviye ve rüʾyet ve iltizâm-ı hüsn-i hareket ider takımından olmıyarak ..." BOA. MVL. 24/56, 11 Cemaziyelahir 1264 (15 May 1848).

105 FO. 195/227 No: 38, Brant to Canning, Erzurum, October 31, 1845. Oseb was found dead in prison due to apoplexy. The doctor of quarantine in Muş suspected either poisoning or torture. Yet as he could not do an autopsy on the body, he could not assert it with certainty. Meanwhile, the inhabitants of Muş believed that Şerif Bey was behind the death of Oseb, but could not say it out loud. Ibid. Istanbul decided to investigate the case, yet the doctor did not dare declare his opinion. In addition, Brant states that two hundred people, none of whom ever saw the body of the deceased, attested that Oseb died of natural causes. Ibid., No: 17, March 24, 1846.

Bedirhan Bey's revolt – or in the words of Sabri Ateş, his leaving the "league of notables"[106] – were key factors for ignoring his part in the described offenses.

4.4 Şerif Bey as Mediator: The Beginning of the End

As Ahmet Kardam put it, tensions in Van started when the province of Erzurum was brought under the Tanzimat at the beginning of 1845, turned into an open rebellion towards spring, and ended in July 1847 with the suppression of Bedirhan Bey's revolt.[107] The documents and reports concerning turmoil in Van were copious in both Ottoman and British Consulate records. Accordingly, the inhabitants of Van sought to prevent the implementation of the Tanzimat there by not letting the newly appointed kaimakam, Sırrı Pasha, and a battalion of soldiers enter the city. Consul Brant stressed that the reason for the people's resistance to the Tanzimat was that they were not aware of its content; or more correctly, those whose interests clashed with the reforms were misleading the common people.[108] Although this perception regards the common people as passive receptors, opposition to the Tanzimat was indeed strong among the privileged – the holders of mâlikânes and yurtluk-ocaklıks. As mentioned in the foregoing paragraphs, the anxiety of those elites was strongly felt in the Kurdish periphery of the empire.

In Van, the inhabitants were determined to prevent the implementation of the Tanzimat. Reportedly, instead of Sırrı Pasha, the officially appointed kaimakam who was not allowed to enter in the city, Timur Pashazade Mustafa Bey, a person from the local dynasty, was chosen by local power holders as the kaimakam of Van. Upon that, the governor of Erzurum dispatched two officials to Van to investigate the issue and advise the rebels. However, the inhabitants of Van sent a petition sealed by ten persons to be submitted to governor himself. They demanded the approval of the nomination of Mustafa Bey as kaimakam of Van and insisted they would not accept the Tanzimat.[109] This back and forth exchange of petitions and discussion of agreements continued for some time.

The significance of the Van issue stemmed from its being part of the alliance of Bedirhan Bey, which would be broken apart in summer 1847. The motivations

---

106   Ateş, *The Ottoman-Iranian Borderlands*, 87–89.
107   Kardam, *Cizre – Bohtan Beyi Bedirhan*, 219.
108   FO 195/227, No: 13, Brant to Canning, Erzurum, May 16 1845. Ibid., No: 15, June 6, 1845.
109   Kardam, *Cizre – Bohtan Beyi Bedirhan*, 219.

and objects of Bedirhan Bey are beyond the scope of this study.[110] Bedirhan Bey became the mir of the Bohtan emirate in 1821 and established a powerful rule afterwards by subduing many rulers under his authority. By 1845, controlling a large area from Diyarbekir-Mosul to Persian border, he had expanded his sphere of influence beyond Cizre, the seat of his emirate.[111] The main cause behind Bedirhan Bey's revolt lies in the administrative transformations of the nineteenth century. The decision to attach Cizre to Mosul, with the governor of which, Mehmed Pasha, Bedirhan Bey was not getting along, triggered Bedirhan Bey's revolt.[112]

As Bedirhan Bey's sphere of influence also included Muş, the attitude of the beys of Muş will be briefly discussed here. The consular reports emphasized that the Porte suspected a "plot" had taken place between Han Mahmud and Bedirhan Bey even before the revolt of Van began. They were also aware that Şerif Bey was part of it.[113] Şerif Bey was appointed as kaimakam once again to mediate in the Van revolt and to implement Tanzimat reforms in Muş, yet his appointment can be thought of as a precautionary measure to nullify the coalition of Bedirhan Bey.

Aware that his position in Muş is weak, Şerif Bey complied with the rules, trying to garner the approval and appreciation of the governors of Erzurum. The governors of Erzurum sent him to Van to convince the rebels to give up their opposition.[114] Here, his efforts brought about results. In a report, the late governor of Erzurum, Süleyman Bahri Pasha, spoke highly of him. Stressing his influence in the pacification of Kurdish tribes in Muş, Bahri Pasha claimed that Şerif Bey worked hard to apply Tanzimat reforms, and until then, he had not acted against orders.[115]

It appears that both in the Van Revolt and in his relations with Bedirhan Bey, Şerif Bey played both sides. Although he sent men to suppress the Van revolt, both central and provincial authorities knew that he would join Han Mahmud

---

110 For Bedirhan Bey, see Hakan, *Osmanlı Arşiv Belgelerinde Kürtler*; Kardam, *Cizre – Bohtan Beyi Bedirhan*; Mehmet Alagöz, "Old Habits Die Hard, A Reaction to the Application of Tanzimat: Bedirhan Bey's Revolt" (master's thesis, Boğaziçi University, 2003); Yener Koç, "Bedirxan Pashazades: Power Relations and Nationalism (1876–1914)" (master's thesis, Boğaziçi University, 2012).
111 Van Bruinessen, *Agha, Shaikh, and State*, 178–180.
112 Hakan Özoğlu, *Kurdish Notables and the Ottoman State: Evolving Identities, Compating Loyalties, and Shifting Boundaries*, (Albany: State University of New York Press), 59–60.
113 FO. 195/227, No: 21, Brant to Canning, Erzurum, December 9, 1844.
114 Ibid. No: 60, November 27, 1846.
115 BOA. MVL. 9/38, 4 Zilhicce 1262 (23 November 1846).

and Bedirhan if it became certain that the rebels would be successful.[116] In other words, although neither central nor provincial authorities completely trusted Şerif Bey on this issue, his alliance was vital for the suppression of the revolt as the main strategy was to break the coalition that Bedirhan and Han Mahmud had established.

Şerif Bey refrained from openly supporting Han Mahmud or Bedirhan Bey and was praised and rewarded by the central government, due to the support of local actors like the defterdar of Erzurum and the Ottoman representative in the border negotiations with Iran, Enveri Efendi.[117] In the course of preparing military operations to subdue Bedirhan Bey and his alliance, Şerif Bey, like many other beys and aghas in the Ottoman East, clarified his alliance with the government. For this, central authorities applied to myriad means to convince and win back the Kurdish notables and tribal and religious leaders around Bedirhan Bey.[118]

With the aim of guaranteeing Şerif Bey's support of the Imperial Army in the planned operation against Bedirhan Bey, Osman Pasha, the *müşir* (marshal) of the Anatolian Army, granted him the rank of *Istabl-ı Amire* (Imperial Stables).[119] Osman Pasha, in a letter addressed to Şerif Bey, clearly expressed first the determination of central authorities to eliminate Bedirhan Bey, who insisted on opposition and rebellion. Osman Pasha charges Şerif Bey and his brothers, who were awarded with ceremonial daggers and swords, to act in accordance with the demands of Ahmet Pasha who would command the troops from Muş and Bitlis against Bedirhan Bey. Moreover, the müşir ordered Şerif Bey to inform him about people who were being forced to support Bedirhan Bey out of fear, as well as about those who thought it was too late to be forgiven. Thus, the main scheme in the dissolution of Bedirhan Bey's revolt was to isolate him, and Şerif Bey played a crucial part.[120]

---

116   In the same vein, Consul Brant noted in February 1846 that in the case of any mistake in the suppression of the Van revolt, both Bedirhan and Şerif Beys would declare their support with for rebels. FO. 195/227 No: 23, Brant to Canning, Erzurum, July 1, 1845.
117   BOA. A. MKT. 64/72, 15 Safer 1263 (2 February 1847).
118   For a detailed account of Bedirhan Bey's pacification and the dispelling of his alliance, see Kardam, *Cizre – Bohtan Beyi Bedirhan*, 299–366.
119   "…'arz ve beyân olduğu vechile lüzûm ve icâbına mebnî ıstabl-ı 'amire pâye-i refi'esine mahsûs bir kıta' nişân Muş kâimakâmı Şerif beğ bendelerine virilmiş …" BOA. A. MKT. 79/82, 16 Cemaziyelevvel 1263 (28 April 1847). Meanwhile, Hurşid Bey was ranked as *dergâh-ı âli kapucubaşı*. BOA. A. MKT. NZD 93/37, 29 Zilhicce 1267 (25 October 1851). And Murad Bey had already been a *Miralay*. BOA. HAT. 634/313307 C, 27 Cemaziyelahir 1254 (17 September 1838).
120   BOA. A. MKT. MHM. 2/103, 27 Cemaziyelevvel 1263 (13 May 1847).

Şerif Bey's promotion to a higher rank was a sign of his submission to the Sublime Porte and the Ottoman pashas used his example to encourage other beys to leave the alliance led by Bedirhan Bey. The rank of Istabl-ı Amire is a manifestation of Ottoman government's intention to take the support of Kurdish notables against Bedirhan Bey by incorporating them into the court dignity. In spring 1847, Osman Pasha dispatched numerous letters to Nurullah Bey and Han Mahmud through Şerif Bey. Many letters extended the rewards for Şerif Bey, with imperial gifts in return for his loyalty. His case was thus depicted as an example that needs to be imitated by those grandees. For instance, Osman Pasha asked both Nurullah Bey and Han Mahmud to trust in Şerif Bey and ordered them to immediately submit to the central authority. The pasha emphasized that it was in their best interest to benefit from this opportunity.[121]

Han Mahmud maintained his relationship with Bedirhan Bey, but because of these persuasive messages, Nurullah Bey of Hakkari left the coalition, as Şerif Bey had done. His son-in-law Yezdanşer (İzzeddin Şîr), who was also the nephew of Bedirhan Bey, was influential in the defection of Nurullah Bey. Yezdanşer also departed Cizre and took shelter with Esad Pasha in Mosul. Thereupon, he became effective in the dissolution of Bedirhan Bey's alliance.[122] In the same vein, Han Mahmud's allies were also dispersing. His brother Han Abdal, promising to surrender the castle of Hoşap, also submitted to the governor of Erzurum.[123] Losing control of such a strategic castle tremendously affected the result of the revolt.

The alliance of Bedirhan Bey was thus broken quickly, within a month.[124] Kardam emphasized that the period between the call to surrender and the surrender of Bedirhan Bey and Han Mahmud was sixty-seventy days. Combat between the Ottoman Army and the forces of Bedirhan and Han Mahmud continued at intervals, for thirty-seven days.[125] Hence, the crucial point was to negotiate with and win over the components of Bedirhan Bey's alliance, among whom Şerif Bey and his brothers' roles were critical. Hereafter, the revolt was easily and quickly suppressed.

Bedirhan Bey and Han Mahmud surrendered in July 1847. The former in the Castle of Evreh and the latter in Tatvan. Soon thereafter, together with their families and some of their allies they left for Samsun where they took a ship

---

121 "... mûmâileyh Şerif beyin ifâdesine itimâden hiç kimesnenin sözlerine aldanmıyarak hakkında olacak ni'met ve taltîfâtı beyhude elden çıkarmıyarak hemân tarafımıza muvâsalat eylemeniz ..." Ibid.
122 Kardam, *Cizre – Bohtan Beyi Bedirhan*, 329.
123 Ibid., 333.
124 Ibid., 370.
125 Ibid., 342.

to Istanbul.[126] Thereafter, neither Bedirhan Bey nor Han Mahmud was allowed to return to their homelands. Furthermore, by eliminating power holders like Bedirhan Bey and Han Mahmud who were influential among the Kurds, the major source of resistance against the Tanzimat reforms was removed. Hence, through transforming the administrative units and most importantly depriving notables of their sources of power – both from their hereditary lands and network of allies – by exiling them, central and provincial authorities considered that the implementation of the reforms were smoothly realized.

After the pacification of Bedirhan Bey and Han Mahmud, which Ottoman authorities referred to as the "conquest of Kurdistan", the first administrative reorganization undertaken at the end of 1847 was to constitute the province of Kurdistan which included Diyarbakır, Van, Muş, Hakkari, Cizre, Bohtan, and Mardin. Reportedly, this decision stemmed from the necessity of providing for the prosperity and security of the inhabitants of Ottoman Kurdistan by governing it properly and bringing it under control.[127] Therefore, the governor was to be an experienced, well-known official in the region, that is Mehmed Esad Muhlis Pasha, who had long been at the governorship of Erzurum Province.[128]

Although with the elimination of Bedirhan Bey and Han Mahmud a significant part of the Kurdish coalition was pacified, central and provincial authorities had to incorporate those who had left Bedirhan Bey's league for a while. Among them was Yezdanşer, the nephew of Bedirhan, who became the mütesellim of Cizre upon the exile of Bedirhan Bey. Nurullah Bey became the administrator of Hakkari. In addition, Abdal Bey, the nephew of Han Mahmud (not Han Abdal, his brother, who was exiled together with Han Mahmud), was appointed to Müküs.[129] Similarly, Şerif Bey and his brothers kept their positions. Nevertheless, the situations of Şerif, Nurullah, and Abdal Beys and Yezdanşer were temporary. Although they had coordinated with Ottoman authorities against the coalition of Bedirhan Bey, they were also regarded as potential obstacles to the implementation of the new regime in the current context. The blueprint for the new land tenure politics targeted the abrogation of their yurtluk-ocaklıks, which had been taking place gradually since the 1830s.

---

126 Ibid., 360.
127 "Havâlî-i Kürdistânın bir idâre-i muntazama ve zâbıta-i hüsn-i tahtına konularak tesîs-i nizâmât-ı dâimiyesiyle ahâlînin husûl-i sa'âdet ve âsâyiş-i hâlleri lâzımeden olmasıyla ..." BOA. İ. MVL. 122/3116, 27 Receb 1264 (29 July 1848).
128 Esad Pasha remained as the governor of Kurdistan Province until his death in March 1851. Mehmet Süreyya Bey, *Sicill-i Osmanî*, 6 vols., vol. 2 (Istanbul: Tarih Vakfı Yurt Yayınları, 1996), 495.
129 Kardam, *Cizre – Bohtan Beyi Bedirhan*, 379–81.

4.5 Exile of Alaaddin Pashazades from Muş

Soon after Bedirhan and Han Mahmud's exile, in October 1847, the governor and defterdar of Erzurum emphasized in a joint report that as long as Şerif Bey and his relatives remained in the region, it would be impossible to bring the revenue of the region into view. However, conditions were not yet suitable, as the pacification of the tribes of Dersim continued.[130] These remarks importantly show that the time for the exile of Şerif Bey and his family was arriving and that his collaboration for the suppression of revolts in Cizre and Van had only delayed this process. Almost a year later, after preliminary steps like the constitution of a new province of Kurdistan were taken, the disciplining of Şerif Bey was again put on the agenda. Esad Pasha, the governor of Kurdistan, wrote an evaluation of Şerif Bey's situation about which he had been asked. Having established order to some extent by eliminating resistance in Van and Cizre-Bohtan, central authorities were questioning the necessity of keeping Kurdish notables with whom they had previously collaborated. Since order had been established there (*elhâletü hazihi bu havâlî usûlüne girmiş*) and since Şerif Bey was a native (*yerlûsundan*), his attitude toward the new regime and his rule was questioned in order to determine whether it was necessary to keep or punish him. Recalling his experience during his governorship in Erzurum, Esad Pasha felt certain that Şerif Bey and his brothers should be dismissed. Therefore, he asked to keep Şerif Bey in custody in Diyarbekir, or that he be sent to Istanbul for a reckoning (*ihkâk-ı hak*) with his complainants.[131] The reasons for the position of Esad Pasha are important both in order to grasp the details of the implementation of reforms in Muş, and to shed light on local actors in the context of the Tanzimat.

The main obstacle to the application of Tanzimat reforms in Muş was the deeply rooted power networks in the region. The political economy of the region – land tenure system and the right to levy taxes – was the main platform on which this network consolidated itself. As Esad Pasha stated, the tithe and some other taxes in the region were mostly undertaken by relatives of Şerif Bey. Additionally, it was discovered by the property clerk (*mal kâtibi*) in Muş, Mustafa Efendi, that in addition to taxes determined by the center, many other taxes were collected arbitrarily on various pretexts. On the top of that, it was reported that Şerif Bey, as kaimakam of Muş, was collecting taxes (*virgü*)

---

130 BOA. A. MKT. 100/13, 19 Zilkade 1263 (29 October 1847).
131 BOA. İ. MVL. 122/3116, 27 Şaban 1264 (29 July 1848). Among them was his cousin Hüseyin Pasha.

higher than the authorized rate (*biraz zammiyeluce*).¹³² However, it could not be proved, as all administrators of the sub-districts of Muş were relatives of Şerif Bey.¹³³

Not only the governors and tax farmers of the sanjak but also community leaders were involved in over taxation. For instance, the *karabaşı* (bishop) of Çanlı Church in Muş, Zakarya, was accused of pursuing his own interests in collection of the *emval-i miri* (imperial taxes) and the *cizye-i şerri* (poll-tax) from some parts of the re'âyâ of Garzan who were dwelling in Muş.¹³⁴ These remarks depict the implementation of tax reforms, in regions where the networks of interest groups were deeply rooted. Although the Gülhane Edict promised the abolition of taxes other than those determined according to one's possessions and income, this case exemplifies how local actors still had great authority in practical fulfillment of this reform. As will be discussed in chapter 6 of this study, even after the exile of influential Kurdish families far from their hometowns, the implementation of just taxation did not immediately take place.

Apart from taxation issues, as official documents point out Christian inhabitants of the region were especially disgruntled with regard to Şerif Bey, because of the tribes that were settled in Armenian villages. During the time of Kaşif Ömer Efendi, the previous administrator of the sanjak of Muş, a group of Kurds referred to as Rizko,¹³⁵ consisting of a thousand houses, had petitioned to settle and engage in agriculture in specific places called Göksu and Patnos. Halil Kamili Pasha and the Provincial Council of Erzurum jointly accepted the request of the tribe. Then, Şerif Bey became responsible for tribal settlement upon his appointment to the post. Afterwards, as stated in the archival documents, "with provocation and encouragement" (*tahrik ve teşvikleriyle*) from Şerif Bey and his brothers, stemming from their ambition (*nefsaniyet*) – and with the approval of Esad Pasha – the said tribe was divided among and settled in Armenian villages, and they were allowed to engage in agriculture on the villagers' lands.¹³⁶ The settlement of tribes was among the Tanzimat reforms and Şerif Bey was nominated, by the Ottoman authorities, to carry out the

---

132 With the Tanzimat, all the customary duties (*tekâlif-i örfiye*) were combined into just one tax, which was called the special tax (*vergi-i mahsûsa*) or simply *vergi* (tax). See Özbek, *İmparatorluğun Bedeli*, 40.

133 BOA. İ. MVL. 122/3116, 27 Receb 1264 (29 July 1848).

134 BOA. A. MKT. MVL. 6/63, 19 Muharrem 1264 (27 Aralık 1847).

135 I have not come across a tribe section called Rizko that was settled in Muş. It is possible that the said Kurds were the tribal households under the leadership of Rıdvan Agha of the Hesenan, as the agha himself was referred to as "Rizko" from time to time.

136 BOA. İ. MSM.52/1343, 12 Şevval 1264 (11 September 1848).

semi-nomadic tribes' settlement in Muş. However, when the settlement of the tribes led to disgruntlement among the settled groups, they were local notables who were to be blamed. If the settlement project had been succeeded, it would have been the government which to be acclaimed.

This decision was mainly justified despite the fact that the seminomadic groups' oppression of the peasants of Muş was known to provincial authorities. This tribe was settled in small groups, just three to five houses in each Armenian village. And it was believed that as villagers would outnumber tribe members, they would not be oppressed. However, Armenian villagers complained that the tribe members insulted and tyrannized them, taking their churches and using them as barns. In addition, the suffering peasants were so exhausted that they could not cope with the attacks about which they had long been resentful. All of this exhaustion maybe resulted in a reaction against Şerif Bey. In response, provincial and central councils discussed settling the Rizko Kurds in Muslim villages or sparing some other places for their resettlement.[137]

With such allegations and in line with the opinion of Esad Pasha, the Meclis-i Vâlâ decided and the sultan approved the dismissal of Şerif Bey. Accordingly, Şerif Bey was kept in Diyarbekir, the center of the province of Kurdistan, and Esad Pasha would nominate a new kaimakam to Muş who would be able and competent and work for the previous salary of the kaimakamlık, which was four thousand five hundred guruş, or less. The kaimakam could have been appointed from the center, yet it would have resulted in a delay in the arrangement of the affairs of the region, especially in the auction of tax farms, which had been already held in Diyarbekir and Muş was the next place to carry out the auction.[138]

Whether the complaints of the Armenian peasants of Muş were the real reasons for Şerif Bey's dismissal or just pretexts are debatable. As the governor of the newly established Province of Kurdistan and because of his long experience with the notables of Muş, Esad Pasha's opinion played a key role in their dismissal.[139] However, relations between local notables and provincial authorities had been volatile and included both conflict and collaboration. Thus, as emphasized before, provincial authorities also pursued their own interests; they were also "locals" in the struggle over resources. One of the fundamentals of nineteenth century reform was to maintain a direct role in provincial

---

137 Ibid.
138 BOA. İ. MVL.122/3116, 27 Receb 1264 (29 July 1848).
139 "… Şerif beğ ve birâderlerinin mukaddemâ Erzurumda sebkât iden me'mûriyyet-i çâkeride meşhûd olân mişvâr ve girdârlarına nazaren bunlardan hüsn-i hidmet me'mûl olmıyacağına ve ahâlî ve fukarâ dâhî kendülerinden hoşnûd olmadıklarına binâen bunların fâmilyâca burâdan kaldırılmaları …" BOA. İ. MSM. 52/1346, 4 Zilkade 1264 (2 October 1848).

administration. In line with this aim, from the beginning, the elimination of local yurtluk-ocaklık holders was crucial to the achieving of such rule in the Kurdish periphery. Nevertheless, it was a gradual process; the same local actors were also essential for the implementation of the reforms. Similarly, even after the uprooting of the most influential figures from their areas of economic and political power, their relatives and allies, in addition to less powerful local actors, took part in provincial administration, as council members or tax collectors. In the same vein, members of the dynasty of Muş would be reincorporated into the administration of the sanjak in the course of time.

Despite Şerif Bey's dismissal, his sons and brothers still held posts in the sanjak of Muş.[140] The elimination of Şerif Bey and his family and relatives took approximately a year and half. Following the elimination of Bedirhan Bey and Han Mahmud, the exile of Şerif Bey's family and local actors in Van and Hakkari was the second phase in the elimination of Kurdish notables.

Following the suggestions of Esad Pasha, the removal of Şerif Bey from the governorship of Muş became definite with a decree of the Sultan dated 13 Ramadan 1264 (13 August 1848). He was ordered to settle in Diyarbekir, as a precaution against the possibility that he would create turmoil in Muş. Şerif Bey was circumspectly informed of his dismissal from the post, on the pretext that the constitution of the Province of Kurdistan required a change in the kaimakamlık of Muş. Nevertheless, due to their agreeable (*rızacuyane*) behaviors and with a concern for not alarming Nurullah Bey of Hakkari, Esad Pasha kept Şerif's son Mehmed Bey as the administrator of the district of Muş, and Murad Bey as the administrator of Bitlis, as well as Hurşid Bey as the administrator of Hınıs, Malazgird, and Bulanık. Şerif Bey also began from time to time to reside in Bitlis (contrary to the initial decision to keep him in Diyarbekir). Moreover, Murad and Hurşid Beys accompanied officials who were charged with the settlement of Kurdish tribes in Muş. Therefore, although neither Şerif Bey's nor his sons and brothers' employment in the region was considered desirable, Esad Pasha, who was charged with nominating a proper kaimakam in Muş, suggested keeping those beys for a while until the trouble in Hakkari ended, contrary to his previous proposition.[141] The Ottoman authorities were careful in the gradual replacement of Şerif Bey and his family, in order to prevent unrest from spreading from Hakkari to Muş. Meanwhile, Şerif Bey and his brothers were busy with the settlement of the tribes. The settlement of tribes was at the top of the agenda, as can be understood from the willingness of Esad Pasha to keep Şerif and his brothers on for a while longer.

---

140   BOA. A. MKT. 143/66, 11 Ramazan 1264 (11 August 1848).
141   BOA. İ. MSM. 52/1346, 4 Zilkade 1264 (2 October 1848).

If settlement of tribes was one side of the coin in the postponement of Şerif Bey's dismissal, the other side concerned disturbances in Hakkari and Van where problems with Nurullah Bey and Abdal Bey respectively coincided with tribal and frontier issues with Iran. Both those beys, together with Şerif Bey, had left the alliance of Bedirhan Bey and were therefore rewarded with posts in the administration of their hometowns in return for their services. However, this situation was not permanent. Although, the local notables, like Şerif Bey and Nurullah Bey, defected to the coalition of Bedirhan Bey upon negotiations with the imperial authorities to keep their positions intact, the latter broke their promises. The Ottoman authorities regarded traditional Kurdish nobility as the kind of people who would disrupt the continuity of security and order in Ottoman Kurdistan. In order not to destroy the results obtained in the region and in order to implement the Tanzimat, these notables needed to be expelled from the region together with their families.[142]

After benefiting from inter-frontier and tribal issues to delay his surrender,[143] Nurullah Bey surrendered to Reşid Pasha, the *müşir* (army field marshall) of Anatolian Army in April 1849, and he was sent to Istanbul through Trabzon.[144] Meanwhile, Şerif Bey and his brothers were arrested by Esad Pasha, as their exile had been delayed until the end of the trouble in Hakkari.[145] When the order demanding their arresting was reached, Şerif and Hurşid were in Van with Esad Pasha, and Murad Bey was in Muş. Having heard the news, Murad Bey surrendered to Esad Pasha, as well.[146] The order at first was to send them to Istanbul along with Nurullah Bey, yet later this decision was postponed. After they were allowed to settle their matters in Muş for seven or eight days, the three brothers went to Istanbul accompanied by a proper official.[147]

Not being sent with Nurullah Bey, meant that Şerif Bey and his brothers would be handled differently. Indeed Reşid and Esad Pashas, in a joint report, emphasized that as Şerif Bey and his brothers had not been involved in an open revolt, as Nurullah and Bedirhan had been, it was not necessary to send them far away (*mahal-i ba'îde*), yet it was not also acceptable to keep them

---

142 Ibid.
143 As stated in a British consular report, by February 1849 Nurullah Bey had taken refuge in Iran, which led to a great diplomatic problem between the two states. However, Nurullah Bey was so cautious that he claimed that as snow had closed the roads, he could not leave Berdasor, a castle in Iran. FO. 78/797, No: 5, Brant to Palmerston, Erzurum, February 16, 1849 and ibid. No: 13, Brant to Canning, Erzurum, March 13, 1849.
144 Ibid. No: 15, Brant to Palmerston, April 16, 1849.
145 Ibid. No: 14, Brant to Palmerston, April 12, 1849, BOA. HR. TO. 212/11 (14 April 1849).
146 BOA. MVL. 226/61, 17 Şaban 1265 (8 July 1849).
147 BOA. İ. DH. 197/11181, 12 Şaban 1265 (3 July 1849).

nearby (*bu havâlîye takrîbleri*), as they had been involved in a series of atrocities in the region. Both the governor and the müşir emphasized that Şerif Bey and his brothers were not so different from Bedirhan and the others as their previous acts, disposition, and manners proved.[148] They were not alone in their perception of Kurdish notables; another imperial agent, consul Brant, wrote the following lines upon their exile:

> The measure is a prudent one, for, while they remained in the country neither tranquility nor security could be hoped for: I do not believe that in any country with the slightest pretensions to civilisation, such criminals were left unpunished; they have been guilty of more numerous and more heinous crimes than can be easily imagined. Some other Koordish beys have also been seized and will be sent out of the country, and I hope this long ill-governed province will now begin to flourish.[149]

Eventually, Şerif, Murad, and Hurşid Beys were dispatched to Istanbul from where they would be sent to settle in Damascus.[150] For their remaining relatives and friends, who were numerous (*kesirü'l müteaʿlikât*), Esad and Reşid Pashas emphasized that although they can no longer dare to create trouble and disturb the region, an order was required to catch and exile them immediately in case of their improper behavior.[151] Thus, not all of the Alaaddin Pashazades, but the most senior ones like Emin Pasha's brothers and their immediate families were sent to exile and their exile used as a threat for the remaining ones. Breaking the Kurdish beys' connection to their areas of influence eliminated the basis of their political power, which stemmed from their yurtluk-ocaklıks.

It was initially decided to send Şerif Bey, his brothers, and all of their relatives (*taallukat*) to settle permanently in Damascus in order to cut all their relationship with their former home districts.[152] In Damascus, according to Brant, there was a Kurdish quarter called Salahiyeh (Salihiye), so Şerif Bey and his family would feel at home.[153] All three brothers and their families, except

---

148 Ibid.
149 FO. 78/797, No: 14, Brant to Palmerston, Erzurum, April 12, 1849.
150 BOA. MVL. 226/61, 17 Şaban 1265 (8 July 1849). Meanwhile, their other brother, Hacı Ahmed Bey, who had long been dwelling in Ahlat and had no relation with his brothers and was not involved in any of their actions, was allowed to continue his life in Ahlat on the condition that he never go to Muş. Ibid.
151 BOA. İ. DH. 197/11181, 12 Şaban 1265 (3 July 1849).
152 "... eski vatanlarında bi'l-külliye katʿ-ı ʿalâyık ile dâimi sûretle Şam-i Şerifde iskân olunmaları ..." BOA. A. MKT. 213/51, 24 Şaban 1265 (15 July 1849).
153 FO. 78/797, No: 30, Brant to Palmerston, Erzurum, August 9, 1849.

one of Murad Bey's three wives, and the wife of his son, Selim Bey's wife, who were ill, were exiled. Those already in Istanbul would take a biweekly ship to Izmir where they would transfer to the ship to Beirut. From there, they would continue on their journey with the help of the governor of Sayda.[154] Those still in Muş would be sent directly to Damascus. In the reports of both the Grand Vizierate and the governor of Kurdistan, it was clear that orders had been sent to the müşir of Zaptieh, to the governor of Damascus, and the officials who would accompany the family from Kurdistan to Damascus, to pay special attention to their safety and comfort on the journey.[155]

Meanwhile, Şerif Bey and his brothers were writing petitions to be allowed to settle in Istanbul, and in the end this request was accepted with the justification that they could be more easily guarded (*daha ziyâde dâire-i mahfûziyette bulunacakları*) in the capital city.[156] However, the part of the family in Muş had been compelled to sell their immovable properties and had been expelled from Muş (*ihrâc kılınmış*). According to Esad Pasha, by the time the order about the change to the place of their exile was received by messenger, they would have already arrived in Halep or traveled even further. Thus, the pasha suggested either sending them to Istanbul from Beirut or settling them there. The details of the sale of their properties were and would be a matter of discussion. The family mainly complained about the sale of their properties for less than their value and in some cases without their consent.[157] This matter together with the fate of the family's yurtluk-ocaklık villages will be the focus of the next chapter.

4.6 Conclusion

On the eve of inclusion of the sanjak of Muş into the Tanzimat program, its inhabitants were burdened by over taxation, forced labor, and indebtedness due to the exploitative rule of local administrators, tax farmers, Armenian notables, and provincial authorities. Therefore, when the Tanzimat was declared in Muş, villagers understood it as tax reform. Notably, both the common people and the notables of Muş applied the language of the new regime to fulfill their

---

154 BOA. A. MKT. 213/51, 24 Şaban 1265 (15 July 1849).
155 "… esnâ-yı râhde bir güna sefâlet ve meşakkate düçâr olmayacak sûretle yanlarına kazâ be kazâ mücerreb ve muʿtemed adamlar terfîkiyle … " BOA. A. MKT. 225/82, 3 Zilkade 1265 (20 September 1849), BOA. A. MKT. 236/69, 29 Zilhicce 1265 (15 November 1849).
156 BOA. A. MKT. 229/50, 24 Zilkade 1265 (11 October 1849), BOA. İ. DH. 202/11557, 18 Zilkade 1265 (5 October 1849).
157 BOA. MVL. 229/37, 27 Zilhicce 1265 (13 November 1849).

requests. Nonetheless, the rest of the reforms were difficult to implement, as the frontier situation and tribal landscape of the region required first a suspension of the reforms and then their gradual execution.

As a harbinger of a set of transformations in the fiscal, administrative, and judicial spheres, Tanzimat reforms aimed to establish direct rule in peripheral provinces. Thanks to their rights over large tracts of lands called yurtluk-ocaklıks, their control over nomadic and seminomadic tribes, and their deep knowledge of the region, Kurdish notables enjoyed a great autonomy that began to be challenged in the early nineteenth century and more determinedly with the Tanzimat. The reforms aimed to take control over the agricultural surplus of the region, which had remained up to then at the disposal of notables. Such an aim also entailed the administration of the region through officials other than local notables. Thus, the struggle over the revenues of the region again reframed the terms of negotiation.

The socioeconomic peculiarities of Muş in particular shaped the fate of its local dynasty. Both developments in its vicinity and its tribal landscape required the employment of Şerif Bey to carry out the reforms. Resistance to reform in the city of Van, the revolt of Bedirhan Bey, and the settlement of the Kurdish tribes were the main factors that delayed the family's exile. Having been incorporated into the new regime with the posts and promotion, Şerif Bey left the alliance of Bedirhan Bey and mediated for the dissolution of the rebellion. Nevertheless, the existence of Şerif Bey and his brothers in the region was regarded as contrary to the implementation of Tanzimat reforms by certain provincial authorities. However, their exile resulted in an ongoing debate over their yurtluk-ocaklık lands. Moreover, with their exile, an idealized form of rule could still not be established. The following two chapters will focus on the story of Muş after the exile of the Kurdish notables and abolition of a land tenure system that had persisted for centuries.

CHAPTER 5

Aftermath of the Exile of the Yurtluk-Ocaklık Holders

The defection of Şerif Bey from the coalition of Bedirhan Bey, and his incorporation into the Ottoman army by being promoted through several ranks did not prevent him from suffering the same fate as the other Kurdish notables. The mediation of Şerif Bey was temporary, not constant. He was initially employed to implement Tanzimat reforms, yet the opportunity created by the suppression of Bedirhan Bey and Han Mahmud made it possible to eliminate remaining local power holders like him. Several Ottoman bureaucrats had advocated breaking the power of the notables in the Ottoman East, since the beginning of the nineteenth century. Their main motivation was direct control over provincial revenues. The reflections on the implementation of this long-desired direct rule will be elaborated upon in chapter 6, but the present chapter will focus on the establishment of a new land policy by completely abolishing the yurtluk-ocaklık system.

Before investigating the details of the debate that started with the confiscation of the yurtluk-ocaklık lands of Şerif Bey and his family immediately after their exile, two points argued in the previous chapter should be recapitulated. First, the abrogation of such types of land ownership in Ottoman Kurdistan had occupied the minds of some Ottoman bureaucrats since the beginning of the nineteenth century. Emphasizing the yurtluk-ocaklık status of the sanjak of Muş, the governor of Diyarbekir and Ma'den-i Hümayun complained as early as 1836 that taxes other than the poll tax were not being transferred from the sanjak to the central treasury. As argued, although the best option was to confiscate lands that were being treated like private property (*mülk ittihaz itdikleri*), the conditions were not suitable.[1] Deprived of the necessary infrastructural power to establish a direct rule in its Kurdish periphery, the Ottoman state required the collaboration of local notables in wars with Russia and Iran, as well as with tribal and border issues with the latter. These dynamics had provided Emin Pasha, the eldest brother of Şerif Bey, with the necessary channels to increase his power in the 1820s.

Second, the abolishment of yurtluk-ocaklık and hükûmet lands was a gradual process. The Muş Beys of the nineteenth century probably exerted

---

1 BOA. HAT. 533/ 26254 A, 15 Ramazan 1251 (4 January 1836).

themselves much more than their ancestors had to keep their political and economic power. The account of Emin Pasha confirms this. Although the sanjak of Muş was granted to its mutasarrıfs who were from the lineage of Alaaddin Pasha, as a yurtluk-ocaklık, the sanjak started to be governed consecutively by Reşid Mehmed and Hafız Pashas during the operations against Kurdish notables in the 1830s. Then in 1836, it was attached to the müşirlik of Erzurum and its revenues were allocated to the Mansure Treasury. In other words, Muş was no longer a yurtluk-ocaklık sanjak, yet this did not preclude the existence of yurtluk-ocaklık villages and mâlikânes. As the mütesellim of Muş whose brothers, relatives, and men were appointed as administrators and tax farmers in the sanjak during that period, Emin Pasha bargained with central authorities to keep twenty-four villages along with his brothers. In a report dated to 1842, Emin Pasha argues that:

> around four hundred villages of the sanjak of Muş were granted to our family from generation to generation with *berât-ı 'alişân*. However, as a requirement of servitude and as a sign of service and loyalty, it was suggested by your humble servant that of the four hundred villages twenty-four ones be separated out and granted to us as a salary, and the rest would remain and their revenues would be allocated for the expenses of the cavalry.[2]

In addition to the petition of Emin Pasha, the subsequent petitions of his brothers emphasized that it was "their own" decision and a sign of loyalty that they gave up the sanjak of Muş. The confiscation of their yurtluk-ocaklık villages became a platform of struggle. To improve their conditions, the lineage of Alaaddin Pasha consistently resorted to reminding the Ottoman state of the former yurtluk-ocaklık status of the sanjak of Muş, and emphasized how they had left it voluntarily to the treasury as a service to the state.

In 1849, the family was at first to be exiled to Damascus, but that idea was rescinded and they were allowed to remain in Istanbul. This decision was justified by arguing that their custody would be easier.[3] Nevertheless, the exile of

---

2 "… Muş sancâğında vâki' dört yüz kadar kurâhâ bâ berât-ı âlişân ebâ-'an-cedd fâmilyâ-mıza rahmen 'inâyet ve ihsân buyrulmuşken vâcibe-i zimmet-i 'ubûdiyyet olacağı üzere mücerred-i ibrâz-ı hüsn-i hidmet ve sadâkat emel-i hayriyyesiyle fakat yirmi dört pâresi kurâhâ-i mezkûreden bi'l ifrâz medâr-ı ma'âş olarak çâkerlerine 'inâyet ve ihsân ve mütebâki kalan kurâları terk ile hâsılât-ı vâki'aları ne mikdâra bâliğ olur ise de idâre olunacak mikdârı süvâri 'askerinin tahrîr buyrulmak hususuna taraf-ı çâkerânemden istidâ'a olunmuş …" BOA. İ. DH. 51/2557, 29 Zilhicce 1257 (11 February 1842).
3 BOA. A. MKT. 229/50, 24 Zilkade 1265 (11 October 1849).

the Kurdish notables of Muş brought about new dynamics in the negotiation of their power. Being far from their homelands the family members resorted to petitioning much more than before. Family members petitioned to reclaim their yurtluk-ocaklık villages, for an imperial pardon, and for more privileges in the Ottoman bureaucracy. While the discussion over yurtluk-ocaklık lands and the sale and situation of their immovable properties, at least for a while, became a field of struggle, they were also seeking positions in the bureaucratic system of the empire.

The position of central and provincial authorities was not always affirmative with respect to those petitions. Despite their determination regarding the boundaries, revenues, and restitution of yurtluk-ocaklık villages and the prohibition of the family's return to Muş, demands for posts in the capital city were more appreciated. For instance, the son of Şerif Bey, Mehmed asked to be employed in one of the government offices soon after their resettlement in Istanbul. It was decided to employ him in the *Hariciye Mektubi Kalemi* (Foreign Correspondence Office) with the assumption that the more family members were occupied in Istanbul, the more they would break off material and moral relations with their homelands.[4] Such employment was in fact an important part of the imperial strategy to incorporate notables and was not specific to Muş.[5]

On the other hand, family members were gradually allowed to return to Erzurum, if not Muş. During their time in Istanbul, they continuously petitioned to return. Hurşid Bey was among the first who managed to do so, albeit by distancing himself from his brothers. He was allowed to return on the condition that he did not get in contact with Muş, and he was appointed to the administration of certain districts in the province of Erzurum. Then Murad Bey together with the women and the children of his family were allowed to settle in Erzurum. Left alone in Istanbul, Şerif Bey was pardoned last and allowed to return in the 1860s. Despite not being allowed to be involved in the affairs of the sanjak of Muş, family members waited for an opportunity to reclaim power in their homelands.

Accordingly, in the following passage, the debate over the yurtluk-ocaklık villages, assets, and immovables of Şerif, Hurşid, and Murad beys will be introduced. Second, the imperial pardon of family members after a long process of repeated petitioning and the effect on the administration of Muş will be

---

4 "… bunların bu tarafca revâbıtı çoğalması memleketlerinde olan ʿalâik-i mâddiye ve maʿneviyyelerinin azalmasını istilzâm ideceği …" BOA. İ. DH. 211/12262, 10 Cemaziyelevvel 1266 (24 March 1850).

5 For instance, the sons and grandsons of Bedirhan Bey were educated in the Tanzimat schools and were employed in the bureaucracy, even if not in higher ranks. Koç, "Bedirxan Pashazades," 51–52.

discussed. Then, in the 1870s, when the effects of the Land Code of 1858 were finally felt in the region, the debate over the confiscated villages of Emin Pasha will be elucidated. The chapter will end with discussion of the future, for the salaries assigned, in return of confiscated yurtluk-ocaklık villages.

5.1 Confiscation of the Yurtluk-Ocaklık Villages of Şerif Bey and His Brothers and Its Implications

From the moment they were dispatched to Istanbul, family members initiated debate not only over their yurtluk-ocaklık villages but also landed property and assets. Family members complained about the process of the sale of their properties in Muş just before their displacement. By the same token, Hurşid Bey, the youngest brother of Şerif Bey, submitted a petition shortly afterward about this problem. Hurşid Bey started by referring to his services to the empire, emphasizing that since he was fifteen he had worked and fought wholeheartedly and with loyalty for "His Excellency." Emphasizing his role in the suppression of various rebels like Han Mahmud, Hurşid Bey argued if governors and officials in Erzurum and Diyarbakır were to be asked, it would come out that he had been ready to work day and night and even give his life for the empire. Yet he was exiled.[6] He then continued by complaining about Esad Pasha, who, he claimed, had sent his family to the Arabian desert without his knowledge. Then, he claimed that the governor had sold his properties for well under their values (*yüz gurûşluk eşyâmı on guruşa firoht itdirmiş*). Similarly, he accused Esad Pasha, who was then carrying out the process of tithe collection in his yurtluk-ocaklık villages, pointing out that he had not the slightest idea who was keeping the revenues of his villages. On top of it, he was uninformed about properties like mansions, mills, and vineyards that, in his opinion, were unprotected and could be ruined in his absence.[7]

---

6 "... On beş yaşımdan bu ana kadar cânsiperâne ve sadâkatrâne hidmet-i şâhânede bulunduğum ve nice defaʿ Han Mahmud ve gibi tuğyân-ı devlet olan kimesne ile ve gerek sâir tuğyânlar ile uğûr-ı şâhânede cenk ve cidâl ve bezl-i vücûd ve cevr itdiğimi isbât iderim ve çâkerlerinden iʿtimâd olunmaz ise Erzurum ve Diyarbekir ve ol havâlîde bütün vâlîler ve meʾmûrlardan istiʿlâm buyrulsun ol vaktde maʿlûm olur ve şeb û rûz iktizâ ider ise cânımı hizmet-i şâhânede bezl ve fedâ itmek hülyasında iken Kürdistân eyâleti vâlîsi devletlû Esad pâşâ hazretleri kullarınızı ihzâren Dersaʿâdete gönderûb ..." BOA. A. MKT. UM. 7/39, 16 Rebiülevvel 1266 (30 January 1850).

7 "... yûrtluk taht-ı tasarruf-ı çâkerânemde bulunan kurâlarımı müşârünileyh hazretleri taʿşîr itdirub yaʿni yüz kile taʿşîrinden on kile husûle getürülmiyerek ve husûle gelan mikdârı dâhi kimler yeddinden kaldığını bilemiyerek ve konaklarım ve değirmen ve bağ misillû emlâklarım dâhi bilâ sâhib kaldığını ve onlar dâhi bu sene bütün bütün virâne olacakları derkâr ... " Ibid.

The petition of Hurşid Bey provides crucial information about the confiscation process of yurtluk-ocaklık lands. Although Hurşid Bey clearly stated his concerns regarding his property in his homeland, with their exile it was also decided that the tithes of the villages that the family had been holding as yurtluk-ocaklıks would be granted to them as salaries.[8] In other words, landed property (*emlâk*) under their exclusive authority as yurtluk-ocaklıks would be confiscated by the treasury and the annual revenues would be granted to them as monthly salaries.[9] Although the salaries would be equivalent to the annual income of their villages, it was sometimes described as an imperial gift (*ihsân*).[10] Whether the salary was the value of their landed properties, or it was a question of the sultan's beneficence was a matter of discussion.[11]

In addition, Hurşid Bey's emphasis on the decrease of his family's revenues importantly shows the economic privileges the family had been enjoying under the yurtluk-ocaklık system. The family had been entitled to collect the taxes, including the ones paid by tribes in return for winter quarters, and they had been exempt from taxation themselves. Now, the holders of the yurtluk-ocaklıks of Muş had to be content with the tithe from those lands, which was paid to them as salaries. Similarly, Hurşid Bey made a distinction between yurtluk-ocaklık villages and properties like vineyards, orchards, mills, and mansions. The bey was aware of the distinction between mîrî and mülk lands. The distinction stemmed from the fact that while the yurtluk-ocaklıks were confiscated by the treasury, the remaining lands were not. As in the empire's classical land classification, lands on which houses were built and trees planted were considered private property.[12]

The mîrî/mülk status of yurtluk-ocaklık lands are the subject of many studies. As emphasized throughout this study, ideological biases and acceptance of the clear-cut definitions in the law books have veiled not only practical

---

8   "... yûrtluk ve ocâklık vechile 'uhdelerinde bulunân karyeler bedel-i 'aşârı kendülerine virilmek üzere ..." BOA. İ. DH. 197/11181, 12 Şaban 1265 (3 July 1849).

9   "... yûrtluk ve ocâklık vechile 'uhdelerinde bulunan emlâkın dâhi hazîne-i celîleden zabtıyla bedelât-ı seneviyyesinin kendülerine ma'âş sûretiyle tahsîs ..." BOA. İ. DH. 202/11557, 18 Zilkade 1265 (5 October 1849).

10 BOA. A. MKT. 225/82, 3 Zilkade 1265 (20 September 1849).

11 In fact, putting Kurdish notables on salary was common after uprooting them from their areas of influence. For instance, 19 thousand guruş was paid per month to the family members of Bedirxan Pasha. Yener Koç argues that the salary became a matter of discussion between the state and the family members. The question was whether the salary was aid from the sultan or if it was compensation for confiscated land. See Koç, "Bedirxan Pashazades," 50–51.

12 Halil Cin, *Mirî Arazi ve Bu Arazinin Mülk Haline Dönüşümü* (Ankara: Sevinç Matbaası, 1969), 22.

outcomes, but also regional and temporal differences. For instance, Mehmet Ali Ünal, in his piece on the hükûmet of Palu, claims that the hükûmet was granted as property, yet what was meant by property was not the land itself, but the right to collect taxes. This is an over interpretation of the distinction between "rakabe" (state ownership) and "usufruct" (*tasarruf*) rights in the Ottoman land tenure system.[13] Recent microstudies have unearthed peculiarities of yurtluk-ocaklık lands in Ottoman Kurdistan. Based on her study of the hükûmet of Palu, which was still designated as a yurtluk-ocaklık in the nineteenth century, Özok-Gündoğan emphasizes the reality that the yurtluk-ocaklıks in Palu had mülk status. "Palu Beys were granted not only the revenues but also the ownership of these lands."[14] She further asserts that the confiscation of yurtluk-ocaklık lands in the second half of the nineteenth century was a way of granting mîrî status to those lands. That is, the confiscation of yurtluk-ocaklık lands signifies the mülk status of that type of hereditary land ownership.[15] Focusing on the yurtluk-ocaklık lands of the Zirki Beys in Hazro and Mihrani, Uğur Bayraktar describes such lands as something between mîrî and mülk, yet more akin to the latter.[16]

When it comes to Muş, or more specifically to the yurtluk-ocaklık lands of the Alaaddin Pashazades, it is necessary to clarify a few points. First, the family members used terms "yurtluk-ocaklık," "hükûmet," and even "mâlikâne" interchangeably to define the lands they held. In correspondence, Ottoman bureaucrats used the term "mülk" to define the lands of yurtluk-ocaklık holders, as well. However, it is necessary to recall that in the official documents unlike for hükûmets, the yurtluk-ocaklıks was not defined as "possessed as private ownership" (*mülkiyet vechile uhdelerinde*). Hence, it is possible to argue that the mutasarrıfs of Muş, who had been granted the sanjak, had almost exclusive rights over the tax-revenues of their yurtluk-ocaklık lands, which together with

13   Ünal, "XVI. Yüzyılda Palu," 251. On the other hand, Huricihan İslamoğlu asserts that raqaba "does not represent a title of ownership in the modern sense but an ability on the part of the ruler, or the central government, to distribute rights to revenues from land." Huri İslamoğlu, "Property as a Contested Domain: A Reevaluation of the Ottoman Land Code of 1858," in *New Perspectives on Property and Land in the Middle East*, ed. Roger Owen (Cambridge, Massachusetts: Harvard University Press, 2000), 17. Similarly, Özok-Gündoğan challenges Ünal's proposition regarding the hükûmet of Palu by arguing that he did not look at what was really happening in Palu territory, how the beys controlled agriculture, and to what extent and with what means the state regulated these rights of the Palu Beys. Özok-Gündoğan, "The Making of the Ottoman Modern State in the Kurdish Periphery," 167.
14   "The Making of the Ottoman Modern State in the Kurdish Periphery," 169.
15   Ibid., 171.
16   Bayraktar, "Yurtluk-Ocaklıks," 241.

their control and influence over tribes of the region enabled them to maintain partial autonomy. Moreover, in the reports of the provincial officials of the era, it was often complained that the yurtluk-ocaklık holders were treating these lands/villages as private property. Thus, it is possible to argue that regardless of the official mirî status of these lands, they were used like private property in practice. Likewise, there were fluctuations in the status of these lands in the course of time, as observed in the case of Muş.

Moreover, neither the exact boundaries nor revenues of the yurtluk-ocaklık villages were known when the central treasury confiscated them. This fact shows how the central government's knowledge regarding the region was limited as late as the 1850s, and underscores the exemptions and privileges yurtluk-ocaklık holders enjoyed. On the other hand, the vagueness about the legal status established a platform upon which the exiled beys of Muş could negotiate the revenues of their lands through the new institutions of the era, the most popular among which was the Supreme Council. In addition, the berats, which were last renewed after the enthronement (*cülus*) of Abdülmecid I would be used as proof in the discussion regarding the limits (where their lands start and where they end) and revenues of their villages.

5.1.1 Debate on the Revenue and Boundaries of the Yurtluk-Ocaklık Villages of the Alaaddin Pashazades

When the governor of the province of Kurdistan sent the beys of Muş to Istanbul in spring 1849, two deputies were appointed, one by the governor and the other by Şerif Bey, to carry out an investigation regarding the revenues of their yurtluk-ocaklık villages. Accordingly, the villages would thereupon be governed by the treasury through *emanet* (through appointed officials called *emin*, trustee).[17] This reinforces the fact that until the confiscation of these hereditary lands, the central government had not known their real value. In addition, appointing deputies from both sides also points to the fact that the beys of Muş still had enough leverage to claim rights over their hereditary lands.

Having prepared and submitted a register showing his family's villages, properties, along with their value and revenues, Şerif Bey asked for the members of his family to be provided with salaries according to this register. However, the governor of province of Kurdistan, Esad Pasha, argued that the registers were arranged from the vantage point of the beys (*kendi kavl-i hodlarıyla*) and that

---

17 "... yûrtluk ve ocâklık vechile 'uhdelerinde bulunân emlâkın cânib-i mîrîyeden zabt sûretiyle emâneten idâre olunmak üzere taraf-ı çâkeriden ve kendü taraflarında birer nefer me'mûr ta'yîn olunarak hâsılât ve vâridâtı meydâna çıkârılmakda bulunmuş olduğu ..." BOA. A. MKT. 225/82, 3 Zilkade 1265 (20 September 1849).

they should not be respected. Instead, the limits, annual revenues, and forms of possession of their villages and properties should be investigated in detail. Accordingly, the registers, bills (sened) and imperial orders (*evâmir-i aliyye*) should be sent from the sanjak. Then a sound result could be achieved.[18]

Consequently, under the supervision of Ahmed Naim Efendi, the interim kaimakam of Muş, the tithes from their yurtluk-ocaklık villages for the year of 1265 (1849) were collected and grain was taken from the village stores carefully, without concealing anything (*asla ketm ve ihfâ sûretleri vukû'a getürülmeyerek*). Then, the grain was auctioned through the local council, according to the local rate (*mahalli râyicine*). According to the report prepared by the council and submitted to the governor of the province of Kurdistan, the amount came out as 52,299 guruş and two para which was kept and guarded in the local treasury (*mal sandığı*).[19]

Esad Pasha's report about the issue details the administration of confiscated yurtluk-ocaklık villages, which in the end would be the basis for determining the salaries to be paid to Şerif Bey's family. However, the limits and the forms of possession of those villages and properties were not determined contrary to Esad Pasha's first order. Therefore, the pasha wrote to Ahmed Naim Efendi about the issue. Moreover, he asked for copies of related documents (*seneds, evâmir-i aliyyes*) that Şerif Bey and his relatives had taken with them, when they moved out of Muş.[20]

In spite of the absence of bills and registers concerning the boundaries and revenues of the yurtluk-ocaklık villages, with the help of delegates from both sides, and probably by means of witnesses, the revenues of the villages were auctioned and the amount was calculated. However, at this point, Esad Pasha brought up the debts of the family, which were twofold. First, the families of Şerif, Murad, and Hurşid Beys had borrowed money from the local governments of Muş and Diyarbakır to cover the expense of their journey from Muş to Damascus in return for bills of debt. The second debt was taxes collected by the family members, which highlights the political and economic power of the beys of Muş before their exile. The governor of Kurdistan argued that taxes imposed upon certain tribes in the sanjak of Muş in the year 1262 (1846) had been collected, but not delivered to the local treasury. As the kaimakam of Muş at the time, Şerif Bey was accused of the embezzlement of these taxes imposed on the tribes. In the end, the total debt of the family was determined to be 50,454 guruş and twenty-seven para. As Şerif Bey and his brothers had

---

18   BOA. MVL. 231/57, 6 Cemaziyelevvel 1266 (20 March 1850).
19   Ibid.
20   Ibid.

settled in Istanbul and were not allowed to return, collection of the debt would be difficult. Therefore, Esad Pasha asked that the debt be covered by the money – the monetary equivalent of the revenues of the yurtluk-ocaklık villages, that is 52.299 guruş – that was kept in Muş's local treasury. It would be easier for brothers to then settle their accounts among themselves. According to this calculation, the money remaining for their salaries was 1,844 guruş and four para.[21]

Informed of the registers showing the worth of their yurtluk-ocaklık villages, Şerif Bey and his brothers objected by means of a joint petition both to the calculations and partially to their debt. Accepting some parts of the debts, Şerif Bey objected to the charge of embezzlement regarding taxes collected from the Hesenan, and some other tribes, during his governorship in Muş.[22] He claimed that the amount of the tax imposed upon the tribe was fifty thousand guruş and he had collected around thirty-four thousand, which he had delivered to the local treasury. The details concerning the remaining amount were recorded in registers left behind in the sanjak.[23]

This discussion over the debt indicates two important issues. First, it reinforces the point argued throughout this book that the right to collect taxes was an important part of the power that the beys of Muş had enjoyed. Therefore, upon being exiled they lost their political and economic authority over the tribes, together with their loss of exclusive control over revenues and the land itself. Secondly, the debate on embezzlement can be read within a pre-modern framework, discussed by Cengiz Kırlı, in which the distinction between the personal revenues of administrative elites and the revenues of the region or institution over which they governed had been blurred in the politics of early modern period. Along with changes to the administrative mentality that started in the nineteenth century, with the Tanzimat reforms and that continued with the Penal Code of 1840, the demarcation between personal income and the revenues of the administrative region was crystallized.[24] This was probably the first time Şerif Bey was questioned about the embezzlement of tribal taxes. Tribal taxes had once been part of the revenues of the mutasarrıfs of Muş, and only with the judicial transformations in the middle of the nineteenth century did they become an issue, for which the yurtluk-ocaklık holders

---

21 Ibid.
22 BOA. A. MKT.M VL. 33/4, 26 Zilkade 1266 (3 October 1850), BOA. C. ML. 410/16784, 19 Rebiülevvel 1269 (31 December 1852).
23 BOA. İ. MVL. 181/5442, 8 Zilkade 1266 (15 September 1850).
24 Kırlı, "Yolsuzluğun İcadı," 50–51.

had to account. This change provides a clear transformation in the rights of the yurtluk-ocaklık holders.

Apart from the issue of debt, family members objected to the calculated revenues of their yurtluk-ocaklık villages. Emphasizing that they had submitted registers concerning the tithes and revenues of their villages for the year 1848 about five months previously, they contested the accounting of the year 1849 which had been carried out by the order of Esad Pasha.

> The total revenue [stated in the register] can only be the revenue of a single village. Just as Esad Pasha first moved us and then our families from Muş and appointed an official [*mübaşir*] to sell our properties and assets at very low prices, like plunder, he also appointed an official to collect the tithes from our villages, and although the local rate is twelve and a half guruş per *şinik*,[25] in that register it is recorded as nine and a half guruş.[26]

Therefore, the family members demanded the register that they had submitted previously be taken into consideration, while calculating the salaries to be paid to them, not the register sent by Esad Pasha. In the meantime, they continued filing numerous petitions claiming rights to their confiscated lands and their surplus. Because of their restricted influence over the determination of the salaries and their belief that the process was negotiable, the brothers reclaimed their yurtluk-ocaklık villages. Emphasizing that they were part of an ancient dynasty (*şu kadar yüz senelik hânedan*) and that their ancestors had given their lives in service to the empire, Şerif, Hurşid, and Murad Beys once again pointed out how their lands had been much vaster than the villages in question. They emphasized that all of the mâlikânes granted to their ancestors as rewards (*mükâfaten*) in return for their services, which had been under the family's control for generations, had been bequeathed to the imperial treasury, and in return the brothers had been granted the villages in question as a beneficence and an imperial gift.[27] Here they were referring to how their family had been

---

25 A unit of measurement for grain. It is equivalent to 0.5 or 0.25 kile. A kile is 24, 215 kilograms, yet with many regional variations. In Diyarbakır, a kile was equivalent to 12, 829 kg. İnalcık and Quataert, An Economic and Social History, xl–xlii.

26 " ... hâsılât-ı mezkûr ancak bir karyenin hâsılâtı çünki sene-i mezkûrede müşârünileyh Es'ad pâşâ evvelen kullarını sonra fâmilyâlarımızı ne vechile hitâb ile memleketden ihrâç idub emvâl ve eşyâmızı yağmâ ider misillû mübâşir ta'yîn idub dûn bahâ ile firoht itdirmiş olduğu gibi karyelerimize mahsûs mübâşir ta'yîn iderek ta'şîr itdirmiş ve râyic-i belde hıntanın şiniki on iki biçuk guruş iken defter-i mezkûrda dokuz biçuk guruşa kayd olmuş ... " BOA. MVL. 87/41, 17 Cemaziyelevvel 1266 (31 March 1850).

27 BOA. MVL. 88/98, 20 Cemaziyelevvel 1266 (3 May 1850).

controlling the sanjak of Muş as yurtluk-ocaklık. As emphasized, the strategy of the family in this debate was to remind the state that the abolition of the yurtluk-ocaklık status of the sanjak of Muş had been their own decision and a sign of loyalty to the state.

With these claims, the brothers demanded to keep their hereditary villages. If their demands were accepted, they would send delegates to collect the tithes of the villages, and they would be satisfied with the remaining revenue. To put it differently, instead of salaries determined without their control, the brothers asked to maintain exclusive control over the revenues of their villages. In the same way, they demanded repayment to their deputies of the tithes on production from the year 1265 (1849), and for the properties that had been sold at allegedly low prices. They were also ready to repay the money to whomever their properties were sold.[28] Thus, they rejected both the sale of their properties immediately after their exile and the calculation of the value of their landed properties. In objecting to the revenues for the year 1849, their argument was actually based on reports that had been sent from the region, according to which the total revenues of their lands were upwards of 103 thousand guruş.[29] Despite their exile, the family members still had relatives and followers in the region who could inform them about the developments there.

Concern about losing control over their hereditary lands informed this demand. In the determination of salaries, the debate was around revenues, not their other rights that were inherent to the yurtluk-ocaklık system. As yurtluk-ocaklık holders, they had enjoyed enormous political and economic power in Muş and its vicinity including political alliances with semi-/nomadic tribes and regional powerholders. In addition, their economic power was far beyond the tithes of several villages. The family members had control over the taxes of the sanjak of Muş, Hınıs and Tekman to a great extent. The tax collected in return for winter-quarters of tribes was also an important revenue for the notables of Muş. Thus, the power of the family would be curtailed no matter how high the salary was set. Exiled far from their lands, Şerif Bey and his brothers were aware that not only would they be put on salaries below the actual worth of their villages, but they would also be deprived of the tools to make claims about the boundaries of their lands. This concern was obvious in their argument that the *raiyyet* (commoners) of the villages had started to farm their lands and use meadows and fields that had once belonged to them. In doing so, these villagers were claiming that that land and those fields and meadows were part of their villages. Therefore, the brothers claimed that it

---

28 Ibid.
29 BOA. MVL. 87/40, 11 Şaban 1266 (22 June 1850).

was probable that the limits of the villages had been incorrectly calculated and that there were parcels that were not included among their landed properties. In order to accelerate the determination of the limits and revenues of their yurtluk-ocaklık lands, Şerif Bey and his brothers asked that Esad Pasha be given orders about the issue again and that an official be dispatched to Muş together with their own delegates, the travel expenses of which they proposed to cover. They also wanted to send Selim Bey, the son of Murad Bey, to accompany the officials with the pretext of moving his family from Muş – but also to take care of these issues.[30]

Despite their efforts in sending a family member to Muş to carry out their businesses, the family members already had agents in the region. For instance, a certain Süleyman Agha had been appointed to supervise the yurtluk-ocaklık villages of Şerif Bey, and he was paid fifteen hundred guruş per month from the revenues of the villages themselves.[31] In the same vein, the fields and vegetable gardens of Hurşid Bey in the village of Mekrak and his clover field in the village of Çiriş were the responsibility of his man, Ceylan Agha. Upon a complaint of Hurşid Bey about an encroachment in his fields in Çiriş, the imperial center questioned the kaimakam of Muş, Habib Efendi.[32] As mentioned before, yurtluk-ocaklık villages were differentiated from orchards and vineyards. Despite the confiscation of the former, the latter remained untouched.

Despite the Şerif Bey's and his brothers' insistence, delivery of the imperial orders, berats, bills, and receipts proving both the limits of the yurtluk-ocaklık villages and also the debts of the family took a long time. Thus, the salaries to be paid to family members could not be determined. Besides, since their departure from Muş, members of the family survived on daily wages, that, after a while, were also cut. Having argued that they were numbered about seventy, the brothers asked to be paid enough to live on and to cover the expenses of their families' journey from Damascus to Istanbul. They ensured that the amount could be deduced from salaries when they were determined.[33] The back and forth negotiations over the limits and revenues of the villages continued for years, but the one over the amount of the salary ended – for a while – at the beginning of 1851.

---

30 "... kurâhâ-yı mezkûreler 'uhde-i 'acizânemizlerimizde ihâle olunmazdan mukaddem mezkûr kurâlar sekenesi bulunân raiyyet mahalli karyemizin sinûr ve hudûdur diyerek zirâ'at itmişler ve tarla ve çayırımızdır deyu tasarruf itmişler ..." BOA. A. MKT. NZD. 7/39, 3 Şaban 1266 (14 June 1850).

31 BOA. MVL. 81/37, 15 Şaban 1266 (26 June 1850).

32 BOA. A. MKT. UM. 85/46, 25 Muharrem 1268 (20 November 1851).

33 BOA. MVL. 81/37, 15 Şaban 1266 (26 June 1850); BOA. A. MKT. MHM. 22/42, 9 Şaban 1266 (20 June 1850).

5.2 Limits of the Villages and the Determination of Salaries

Şerif Bey and his brothers explored every avenue to increase their power vis-à-vis provincial and central authorities who were ever more determined to keep them away from the region. Their main strategy was to keep on filing petitions. The petitions of the three brothers shed light on the fate of their confiscated yurtluk-ocaklık villages, which were tax-farmed in later years.[34] These villages were mostly in the plain of Muş and Bulanık and were mainly inhabited by Armenians. The beys of Muş accused these commoners of violating their rights by claiming rights to land and meadows that were once part of their yurtluk-ocaklık villages. In addition, after their exile, as will be discussed in chapter 6, it was the inhabitants of those villages who complained about over taxation, corvée, indebtedness, and the cruelty of local actors including governors, tax farmers, council members, moneylenders, and community leaders.

Despite their repeated petitions Şerif Bey and his brothers' demand to re-examine the revenues and limits of the villages was declined. Based on the investigation and auction carried out by the governor of the Kurdistan Province, the total revenue of the yurtluk-ocaklık lands of the brothers minus the expense of collecting the tithe (*gayr-ı ez-i masârif-i ta'şîriyye*) was determined as around 52 thousand guruş for the year 1265 (1849). Upon the appeal of the brothers, the Meclis-i Vâlâ, in consultation with the governor of the province of Kurdistan, decided that given that the price of grains had been low that year that even if a new official was appointed to conduct a reinvestigation, the result would not change. Moreover, the demand that Selim Bey be sent to Muş to accompany some parts of the families was not seen as appropriate.[35] Probably, this was because the central government wanted to cut their connections with their homeland. In the end, the salaries were based on the amount determined on the initiative of the governor, Esad Pasha. However, a year passed after this discussion and a new harvest season came. Accordingly, the villages of the brothers were auctioned at an amount of 100 thousand guruş and the tax farmer made a profit.[36] The three brothers complained that although the prices increased in a year's time and the tax farmer made profit,

---

34   Some of the yurtluk-ocaklık villages of Emin Pasha, despite the initial decision to confiscate them, were held by certain zawiyahs in Bulanık.
35   BOA. İ. MVL. 198/6184, 25 Rebiülevvel 1267 (28 January 1851).
36   "… yûrtluk ve ocâklık nâmıyla mutasarrıf oldukları karyeleri giçen altmış beş senesinde elli iki bin ve altmış altı senesinde yüz bu kadar bin guruşa firoht olunmuş ve mültezimleri dâhi kırk elli bin guruş ticâret itmiş …" BOA. MVL. 93/62, 29 Şevval 1266 (7 September 1850); BOA. A. MKT. UM. 30/89, 2 Zilkade 1266 (9 September 1850).

they had not been paid yet. This also highlights the economic loss of the family with the confiscation of their yurtluk-ocaklık lands. Having been put on fixed salaries, the family members could not even benefit from a good harvest.

Although the villages were contracted out by the means of emanet in 1849 (1265),[37] in ensuing years they were contracted out to tax-farmers on a lump sum basis (*maktuan*).[38] The revenues of the villages of Şerif Bey and his brothers for the year 1850 were as follows:

TABLE 1   The values of yurtluk-ocaklik villages of the three brothers in 1850

	Amount (guruş)
Şerif Bey	43,145
Murad Bey	25,870
Hurşid Bey[a]	31,010
Total	100,025

a   In the document, the name of Hurşid Bey was confused, stated as "the other brother Şerif," yet the name of Şerif Bey, as seen, was already stated at the beginning. BOA. İ. MVL 198/6184, 25 Rebülevvel, 1267 (28 January 1851).
SOURCE: BOA. İ. MVL 198/6184, 25 REBİÜLEVVEL 1267 (28 JANUARY 1851)

In the determination of the salaries, the Meclis-i Vâlâ argued that the revenues of the villages changed from year to year and the tithes of the villages were sometimes collected by the means of emanet. Therefore, the revenues for two years were combined and compared, and the salaries were determined accordingly.[39] Apart from pragmatic reasons, this methodology was a precaution against future claims by Şerif Bey and his brothers over the boundaries and revenues of the lands. The names and revenues of the villages of three brothers and the method used to determine the salaries were as follows:

---

37   BOA. A. MKT. 225/82, 3 Zilkade 1265 (20 September 1849).
38   For the development of the methods of tithe-collection during the Tanzimat (1839–1876) and Hamidian (1876–1908) periods, see Özbek, İmparatorluğun Bedeli, 45–91.
39   "… bu makûle bedelât-ı a'şârının senesi senesine uymıyarak ba'zen noksân tutacağı cihetle hasbe'l usûl iki seneliğin mukâyesesi icâb-ı maslahatdan bulunduğuna …" Ibid.

TABLE 2   Two-year revenues of the yurtluk-ocaklik villages of Şerif Bey

Name of the village	The revenue of the year 1265 (1849)	The revenue of the year 1266 (1850)
Hars [Güneyik][40]	7,632.20	12,055.00
Zinyaret [Ziyaret]	5,267.20	9,400.00
Salorik [Dilimli]	6,501.00	10,610.00
Tebavenk [Güzelsu]	4,534.20	7,100.00
Alizurum [Tandoğan]	1,814.20	3,980.00
Total	25,750.00	43,145.00
Cost of collecting the tithe	2,575.00	4,314.20
Net amount	23,175.00	38,830.20

SOURCE: BOA. ŞD. 374/27, 14 ŞABAN 1315 (9 DECEMBER 1897)

The total for two years was 62,005 guruş twenty para and the mean (*bi'l münasafa-i seneviyesi*) was 31,002 guruş thirty para, which amounted to 2,583 guruş per month.[41]

TABLE 3   Two-year revenues of the yurtluk-ocaklik villages of Murad Bey

Name of the village	The revenue of the year 1265	The revenue of the year 1266
Orginos (Çukurbağ)	6,081	8,060
'Arus, aka, Kiravi [Şenoba]	5,053	7,000
Ardonk [Konakdüzü]	4,621	5,100
Oşnam, aka, Üçdam [Yukarı Üçdam-aşağı Üçdam]	2,805	5,710
Total	18,560	25,870
Cost of collecting the tithe	1,856	2,587
Net amount	16,704	23,283

SOURCE: BOA. ŞD. 374/27, 14 ŞABAN 1315 (9 DECEMBER 1897)

---

40 The names in parentheses are modern Turkified names. According to Mayevsky Hars was one of the richest villages in Muş. Besides, in Zinyaret there were vast gardens and pastures. Bayraktar, *20. Yüzyılın Dönemecinde Rus General Mayevsky'nin Türkiye Gözlemleri*, 404–07.

41 BOA. ŞD. 374/27, 14 Şaban 1315 (9 December 1897).

The total for the two years was 39,987 guruş and the mean was 19,993 guruş twenty para, which amounted to 1,666 guruş per month.

TABLE 4   Two-year revenues of the yurtluk-ocaklik villages of Hurşid Bey

Name of the village	The revenue of the year 1265	The revenue of the year 1266
Uruk, aka, Arak [Sarıbahçe]	6,689.20	15,010.00
Argevank [Umurca]	2,625.20	6,000.00
Salbak ?	4,483.00	10,000.00
Total	13,798.00	31,010.00
Cost of collecting the tithe	1,379.00	3,101.00
Net amount	12,419.00	27,909.00

SOURCE: BOA. ŞD. 374/27, 14 ŞABAN 1315 (9 DECEMBER 1897)

The total for the two years was 40,328 guruş. The mean for the two years was 20,164 guruş, which amounted to 1,680 guruş per month.

According to the numbers, the imperial treasury had to pay around six thousand guruş per month to the three brothers in return for their confiscated yurtluk-ocaklık villages in Muş. However, in their earlier petitions, the brothers mentioned "twenty-four villages" that had been granted to them. Yet if the five villages of Emin Pasha – Yoncalı, Liz [Erentepe], Bostangend [Bostankent], Kömüs/Goms [Bozbulut] and Norşen [Sungu] – are added to the total, the villages number only seventeen. Perhaps that is why in a report dated 1837, the number of villages granted to Emin Pasha and his brothers were stated as seventeen or eighteen.[42] Some other villages had also been granted to the subjects (tebaa) of Emin Pasha. In addition, the archival documents refer to three disputed villages.

The villages of Vartinis [Altınova], Tevnig [Durugöze], and Erişter [Eşmepınar] which included the fiefs of Makrak and Gebre had been initially granted to the brothers together with twenty-one other villages as yurtluk-ocaklıks. However, a certain Tahir Agha, Abdullah, and Edhem among the cavalrymen in Erzurum claimed that said villages were among their fiefs. The case could not be resolved in the local councils, so it was transferred to the Meclis-i Vâlâ. According to the investigation of the Meclis-i Vâlâ, two of the above-mentioned three villages were among the escheated property of Şerif Bey's father, and the third was also granted to the brothers. When twenty-four villages

---

42 BOA. HAT. 637/31417 A, 29 Zilhicce 1252 (6 April 1837).

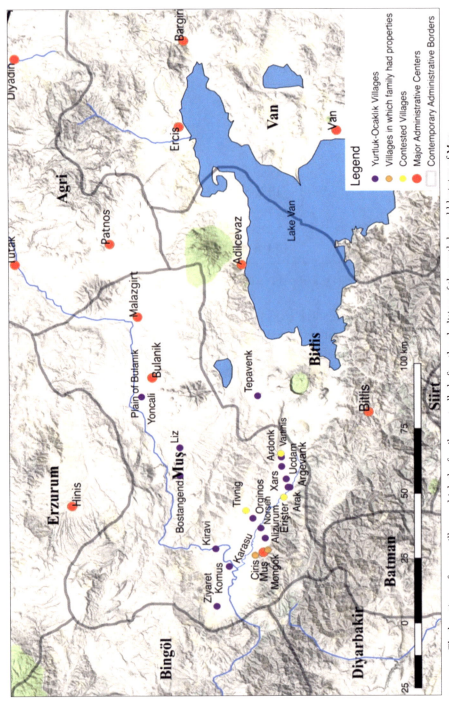

MAP 2   The locations of some villages which the family controlled after the abolition of the yurtluk-ocaklık status of Muş
MADE WITH QGIS

were granted to the family members, the berats for these three villages which Tahir et al. claimed were not prepared properly. Although berats had not been provided for the villages of Vartinis, Tevnig, and Erişter, they were granted to Emin Pasha's family.[43] Şerif and Hurşid Beys benefited from these three villages until said members of the cavalry objected. The Meclis-i Vâlâ gave a preference to the claims of the cavalrymen and an order was prepared to grant control of the villages to Tahir Agha and the others.[44] Thus, the family members turned out to be indebted to these cavalrymen. For four years Hurşid Bey had collected the revenues of the harabe of Makrak, one of the above-mentioned three villages, without a berat, so he was obliged to compensate the amount. Hurşid Bey claimed that Makrak was within the boundaries of his villages, but the treasury refuted this claim emphasizing the absence of any registry.[45] The registry confirmed that these villages were among the ancestral lands of the family, yet most probably during the family's exile in Vidin after the defeat at the battle of Nizip, those villages were granted as fief. Accepting the claims of cavalrymen over the villages of the family, the Tanzimat state once again showed its insistence in eradicating the local notables' power in Muş.

In the same vein, after the investigation in the registries, the brothers continued to negotiate the limits and number of their yurtluk-ocaklık villages for a while. For instance, Murad Bey held up the berat that was renewed during the reign of Abdülmecit I, as proof to claim his rights over a village called Oşnam. Stating that the village consisted of two quarters, one Muslim the other non-Muslim, Murad Bey argued that the Muslim part had been separated out and auctioned separately and was not included in the revenues that ought to have been granted as his salary. He claimed that if the registers of the Imperial Registry (*Defterhâne-i Amire*) were checked, it could be find out that there is only one village – not two – called Oşnam in the district of Muş. Therefore, he asked for the revenues of the quarter that had been separated out.[46]

Moreover, the brothers claimed that the hamlets (mezra) of the villages had also been separated out. Şerif Bey and his brothers had previously objected to the revenue calculation for the year 1849 claiming that the limits of the villages

---

43   The lineage of Alaaddin Pasha has lands in contemporary Tevnig (Durugöze). This fact may reinforce the claim that Tevnig was the family's ancestral lands.
44   "... mukaddemâ yûrtluk ve ocâklık vechile mîr-i mûmâileyhüma yirmi dört 'adet karyenin tevcîhi esnâda mûmâileyh Tâhir ağâ ve 'Abdullah ve Edhemin iddiâsında olduğu kurâ-i sâlise-i merkûmenin berâtları mâliye hazînesinden tanzîm olunarak usûlı vechile tahvîl kalemine tahvîlât vürûd itmemiş olduğundan kayıdları açık kalarak bu cihetle tevcîhâtı tekerrür eylemiş idüğü ..." BOA. İ. MVL. 27/430, 4 Receb 1257 (21 September 1841).
45   BOA. C. ML. 410/16784, 19 Rebiülevvel 1269 (31 December 1852).
46   "... hâlbuki karye-i mezbûr Oşnâm nâmıyla bir olub yedd-i 'âcizânemizde olan berevât-ı şerîfe münderiç olduğu ..." BOA. İ. MVL.198/6184, 25 Rebiülevvel 1267 (28 January 1851).

had not been carefully determined. They also argued that peasants of their yurtluk-ocaklık villages had claimed rights over their villages. With these claims, they repeatedly asked for the dispatch of special officials, their delegates, and someone from among their families to investigate and determine the limits of their lands. In the end, Esad Pasha put an end to debate by asserting that the beys had gradually appropriated and started taking tithes from fields that were state property, like those of both the cultivated and the unused lands in the vicinity of their yurtluk-ocaklık villages. Since this was revealed during the investigation, these lands that the brothers had annexed to their yurtluk villages in the course of time were separated out and returned to the Treasury.[47] Similarly, the above-mentioned case of the harabe of Makrak also consolidated Esad Pasha's argument. The absence of Muş Beys in the region hindered them in asserting control during the investigation, albeit.

Finally, although the demands and objections of Şerif Bey and his brothers would continue, the salary granted to them for life (*kayd-ı hayat*) was based on an amount determined by combining the revenues of the years of 1849 and 1850. Minus the expense of collecting the tithe (*masârîf-i ta'şîriyesi*), the amount came out to be seventy-one thousand piasters each year. Accordingly, the salaries to be paid per month to Şerif Bey and his brothers starting in March 1851 was as follows: 2,583.50 piasters to Şerif Bey, 1,666.00 to Murad Bey, and 1,680.00 piasters to Hurşid Bey.[48] Now given salaries for life as compensation, the family as a whole lost the hereditary rights to their lands and titles.

Similar examples provide for a better understanding of the method followed in the confiscation of the yurtluk-ocaklık villages of Şerif Bey and his brothers. Beginning in 1857, Hüseyin Pasha, their cousin and rival, petitioned that the district of Bulanık (in Muş) was his yurtluk-ocaklık, but with the Tanzimat, it had been confiscated and nothing had been paid in return.[49] Moreover, the district of Hizan in the sanjak of Muş, consisting of around sixty prosperous villages, was under the exclusive control of Şerafeddin Bey and his two brothers as a yurtluk-ocaklık. The governor of Erzurum, Bekir Sami Pasha and defterdar Selim Efendi in a joint report complained that despite the prosperity of the district nothing other than poll tax could be collected there. The Tanzimat could not be applied there due to the intimacy between Şerafeddin Bey and Bedirhan Bey.[50] Finally, the yurtluk-ocaklıks of Şerafeddin Bey were

---

47 "... Muşda bulundukları avânda 'uhdelerinde bulunân yûrtluk ve ocâklık karyelerine hemcivâr bulunân birtakım arâzî-i mîrîden olan harâbe ve mezârî'yi dâhi karyeleri arâzîsine 'ilâveten zabt ve ta'şîr idegeldiklerinden (...)" Ibid.
48 BOA. İ. MMS. 14/600, 8 Şaban 1275 (13 March 1859).
49 BOA. A. MKT. NZD. 230/65, 5 Zilhicce 1273 (27 July 1857).
50 BOA. İ. MVL. 66/1254, 26 Cemaziyelahir 1261 (2 Temmuz 1845).

confiscated together with those of Şerif Bey and his brothers. Şerafeddin Bey was paid 2,000 guruş and his other brothers 750, based on the revenues of their villages.[51] Furthermore, despite the initial order that Şerafeddin Bey be settled in Erzurum, his request to live in Muş was later accepted.[52] Similarly, the Zirki Beys of Diyarbekir had also been assigned monthly salaries since 1836, as recompense for their confiscated lands.[53] However, in Palu, a different practice was in place. The beys and aghas of Palu kept one-third and one-fifth of their lands, respectively, on the condition that they paid the tithe and other taxes. The rest of the land was confiscated and offered for sale.[54]

Emphasizing that they were from a well-established family with an eight-hundred-year legacy, the family members did not cease sending petitions claiming that their salaries did not accurately reflect the income of the villages, the ownership of which they enjoyed for generations. For instance, Şerif Bey claimed that his revenue should have been around three hundred purses.[55] Therefore, in the end, the salaries were raised according to revenues from the year 1857.[56] Their insistence concerning the salaries was an outcome of their loss of financial privileges. In the case of Şerif Bey, he was not only paid a salary of around five thousand piasters as the kaimakam of Muş in the 1840s but he also had control over both the land and the revenues of the yurtluk-ocaklık villages.[57] Moreover, enjoying long-established agreements with the central state and the power of negotiation as yurtluk-ocaklık holders, the beys of Muş dominated the surplus of the region and even enlarged their landed property holdings by seizing neighboring lands.

Despite the fact that being far from their homelands limited their capacity to negotiate, they still had the ability to make use of any chance to improve their situations. On one hand, they constantly appealed for an imperial pardon to go back to their homelands until their demands were accepted. On the other, their demands regarding the yurtluk-ocaklık lands took on a different dimension in the 1870s after the respective deceases of Murad and Şerif Beys. Hurşid Bey together with his son, who was employed in the Şûrâ-yı Devlet, began to reclaim the yurtluk-ocaklık villages of Emin Pasha. Thus, the

---

51 BOA. MVL. 90/65, 22 Receb 1266 (3 June 1850).
52 BOA. İ. MVL. 219/7325, 29 Şevval 1267 (27 August 1851).
53 Bayraktar, "Yurtluk-Ocaklıks," 142.
54 Özok-Gündoğan, "The Making of the Ottoman Modern State in the Kurdish Periphery," 196.
55 BOA. MVL. 180/9, 27 Cemaziyelevvel 1273 (23 January 1857).
56 BOA. İ. MMS. 14/ 600, 8 Şaban 1275 (13 March 1859).
57 In 1853, the salary of the kaimakam of Muş was registered as four thousand and five hundred guruş. BOA. İ. MVL. 277/10796, 10 Şevval 1269 (17 July 1853).

following pages first explain the process by which Şerif Bey and his brothers reestablished relations with the region. Then, the debate over the late Emin Pasha's yurtluk-ocaklık lands, which again became an issue in 1876, will be introduced.

5.3 Struggle for Forgiveness

Immediately after settling in Istanbul, Şerif Bey and his brothers wrote petitions to be allowed to return at least to Erzurum, if not to Muş.[58] Especially after the determination of the yurtluk-ocaklık salaries, the family complained about the difficulties surviving not only in the expensive circumstances of Istanbul but also in its climate. Not only the men but also the women of the family engaged in petitioning. After a while, petitioning by the family yielded the results. Upon a petition by Hurşid Bey's wife, their family except for Hurşid Bey himself and their eldest son, was allowed to settle in Erzurum together with her younger children at the end of the year 1851.[59]

Nevertheless, after his family's departure, Hurşid Bey asked to go to Muş temporarily himself to sell properties that had been allegedly seized by strangers in order to purchase a house for his family in Erzurum. In this way, he claimed, he would completely cut his relations in Muş, which was also a discursive strategy.[60] Permission depended on the consent of the governor of the Kurdistan Province, who could determine whether such permission could be harmful or not.[61] Following a report of the Council of Erzurum, which clarified that Hurşid Bey was different from his brothers and that settling in Erzurum was appropriate, the Meclis-i Vâlâ decided to permit Hurşid Bey to settle in Erzurum on the condition that he would never go to Muş. However, after it was submitted for his approval, the Sultan rescinded the decision (*sarf-ı nazar*).[62]

Hurşid Bey was not alone in his request. Having argued that some members of his family had passed away, as they could not adjust themselves to the climatic conditions of Istanbul (*buraların âb ve havâsıyla 'adem-i imtizâcları*), Şerif Bey proposed sending his family to Muş while he, his eldest son Mehmed Bey, and his brother Murad Bey remained in Istanbul.[63] Meanwhile, Hurşid

---

58 BOA. A. MKT. NZD. 93/37, 29 Zilhicce 1267 (25 October 1851).
59 BOA. İ. MVL. 225/7675, 9 Safer 1268 (4 December 1851); BOA. A. MKT. MVL. 48/46, 23 Safer 1268 (18 December 1851).
60 BOA. A. MKT. UM. 113/25, 1 Safer 1269 (14 November 1852).
61 BOA. A. MKT. UM. 113/69, 4 Safer 1269 (17 November 1852).
62 BOA. İ. MVL. 277/10774, 6 Şevval 1269 (13 July 1853).
63 BOA. MVL. 121/ 24, 28 Zilkade 1268 (13 September 1852).

Bey – believing that his request to settle in Erzurum was rejected because of the same demand from Şerif Bey – wrote a petition discrediting his brother. Interestingly, he argued that unlike himself, Şerif Bey had not complied with the orders of the state, had oppressed the people, extorted and plundered their properties, and pursued his own interests.[64] In other words, Hurşid Bey differentiated himself from his brother in order to be allowed to live with his family in Erzurum. Around the beginning of 1854, Hurşid Bey achieved his objective and was allowed to reside in Erzurum.[65]

Şerif Bey increased the frequency of his petitions to settle in Erzurum together with his family upon the permission given to Hurşid Bey. According to a report of the Meclis-i Vâlâ, Şerif Bey and his brothers had been exiled because of the administrative necessities of the time during the governorship of Esad Pasha. However, those regions were currently under control and their security was relatively ensured, as well. The report continued to emphasize that the family members could not create trouble even if they wished to do, pointing out the fact that since Hurşid Bey's arrival in Erzurum, he had not been involved in any trouble. Therefore, the Meclis-i Vâlâ decided to allow Şerif Bey to settle in Erzurum like his brother, but without any contact with Muş. However, this decision did not get imperial approval.[66]

After a long period of negotiation, except for Şerif Bey, the rest of his family and Murad Bey together with his family were allowed to settle in Erzurum.[67] Alone in Istanbul, Şerif Bey continued to complain about the difficulties of subsisting on the salary paid to him in return for his confiscated yurtluk-ocaklık villages, as he also had to support his family in Erzurum. Therefore, he asked either to be allowed to settle in Erzurum or that his family be returned to Istanbul.[68] It was a part of the politics of notables that no matter the decrease of their economic and political power upon the confiscation of their hereditary lands, they did not give up the bargain with the state. In this case, requesting permission for women and children to return to their homelands was a tactic to gain the eventual forgiveness of the notables. Besides, the permission

---

64 "... evâmir-i ʿaliyye-i cenâb-ı mülkdârilerine ʿadem-i itâʿatle birâber dâima fukarâyı tecrim ve herkesin emvâl ve eşyâsını gasb ve garât itmekde ve zâten dâhi hevâ ve hevesine tâbîʿiyyet ider takımdan bulunduğu ..." BOA. İ. DH. 283/17817, 7 Safer 1270 (9 November 1853).
65 BOA. A. MKT. MHM 757/67, 14 Safer 1271 (6 November 1854).
66 BOA. İ. MVL. 318/13462, 16 Safer 1271 (8 November 1854).
67 BOA. A. MKT. NZD. 132/22, 23 Cemaziyelevvel 1271 (11 February 1855), BOA. A. MKT. UM. 183/20, 3 Cemaziyelahir 1271 (21 February 1855).
68 BOA. A. MKT. NZD. 206/80, 29 Rebiülahir 1273 (27 December 1856).

given to Hurşid Bey encouraged the rest of the family to pursue forgiveness in the same way.

In their petitions, the brothers asked for permission to settle in Erzurum where they would be occupied with sharecropping (*ortakçılık*). This request can be interpreted that the family would not claim their traditional rights. It is also possible to trace the situation of Hurşid and Murad beys after their settlement in Erzurum. Hurşid Bey was appointed as administrator in the districts of the province of Erzurum, and Murad Bey requested a similar post, as well.[69] The murahhasa (bishop) of the Catholic Community in Erzurum filed a petition that the district of Hınıs be administered by Murad Bey, who, he believed, was capable and equipped with the necessary qualities to govern that district, which was inhabited by forty-fifty Christian families and surrounded by Kurdish tribes. Moreover, the inhabitants of Hınıs emphasized in their petitions that they would be pleased by the administration of Murad Bey.[70] Before his exile, Murad Bey had been ruling Hınıs, so the local population was demanding their traditional ruler.

The request of the inhabitants of Hınıs is understandable, the commoners of Muş demanded a capable governor to control in particular the deeds of Kurdish tribes. Similarly, upon the continual requests of Şerif Bey, the governor of Erzurum Arif Pasha was asked whether it would be appropriate to send Şerif Bey to Erzurum.[71] The response of the governor points to the reception of the return of Hurşid and Murad Beys to the region and sheds light on their actions. Since their arrival, both beys had been appointed to posts in the administration of certain districts. He added that they had joined in the Imperial Army "in the latest issue" (*mesele-i zâile esnasında*) – referring most probably to the Crimean War. Moreover, Hurşid Bey took part, along with his Kurdish cavalrymen, in the capturing of the fugitives who became involved in highway robbery on the Trabzon-Bayezid road.[72] As the governor of Erzurum, Arif Pasha explains that Hurşid Bey was capable of finding and capturing such fugitives, it is possible to conclude that the bey performed similar services in the region. Arif Pasha was even in the opinion that Hurşid Bey should be granted an imperial gift in return for his services and expenses that he had incurred during his looking for the fugitives.[73] As a result, the governor of Erzurum did not object to the return of Şerif Bey.[74]

69　BOA. A. MKT. UM. 330/1, 13 Rebiülevvel 1275 (21 Ekim 1858).
70　BOA. MVL. 577/47, 15 Rebiülevvel 1275 (23 Ekim 1858).
71　"… Erzurumda ortâkçılık usûlüyle zirâa't ve hırâset itmek üzere …" BOA. A. MKT. UM. 326/3, 8 Safer 1275 (17 September 1858).
72　Özkan, "A Road in Rebellion, A History on the Move," 351–52.
73　BOA. MVL. 568/83, 16 Ramazan 1274 (30 Nisan 1858).
74　BOA. MVL. 577/55, 26 Rebiülevvel 1275 (3 November 1858).

Despite the report of Arif Pasha about the virtues of Hurşid and Murad beys, the return of Murad Bey and the family of Şerif Bey to Erzurum created suspicion in the beginning. When they arrived, it was in the middle of the Crimean War. After a while, it was reported that Murad Bey had provoked his supporters in Muş to delay the transfer of the grain to the army. Even the former kaimakam of Muş, Ömer Pasha, argued that as long as the brothers of Şerif Bey were there, he could not perform his job properly. After that, it was again asked whether the residence of Murad Bey and the family of Şerif Bey in Muş was appropriate or not.[75] Given the report of Arif Pasha praising Hurşid and Murad Beys, the complaint of Ömer Pasha was not effective in discrediting them. Regardless of whether Murad Bey was involved in any trouble, those employed in the administration of Muş upon the exile of the local dynasty would not welcome the return of these exiled notables.

It is true that Hurşid and Murad brothers watched for opportunities to become influential in Muş. Thus, Ömer Pasha is partially right in his accusations against Murad Bey, who was involved in the politics of Muş. Similarly, some documents also point out that Hurşid Bey together with his followers disturbed the tax farming of the villages in the plain of Muş. Although the contract with local tax farmers for the villages of Muş was renewed in 1856, Hurşid Bey and his followers offered a higher bid in the province of Erzurum and so the right to tax farm was contracted out to them. However, local tax farmers had already collected the harvest and contention arose between the two groups. To solve the conflict, the case was taken up in Erzurum. Local tax farmers in Muş delegated a certain Yakub and Halil Aghas and signed empty sheets to fully authorize them. However, Hurşid Bey allegedly bargained with those agents and filled the empty sheets with accusations against the kaimakam of Muş, Emin Pasha. Upon a complaint by the local council of Muş, the case was transferred to the Meclis-i Vâlâ.[76] Unfortunately, it is not certain how the case ended. However, as will be seen in the next chapter, the beys of Muş were suspected to have had a hand in the petitions filed against the kaimakams of Muş.

A few years after settling in Erzurum, Murad Bey passed away. Emphasizing that his family in Erzurum was in a miserable condition, Şerif Bey asked either to settle in Erzurum, where he could be occupied with agriculture, or be granted the revenues of his villages as before. According to reports from Muş, the revenues of his villages were 103,920 guruş and that of his late brother Murad's were 54,599 guruş in 1856.[77] However, both options were rejected.

---

75   BOA. A. MKT. UM. 229/68, 16 Şaban 1272 (23 March 1856), BOA. A. MKT. MHM 86/75, 19 Şaban 1272 (25 April 1856).
76   BOA. A. MKT. UM. 287/24, 16 Zilkade 1273 (8 July 1857).
77   BOA. İ. MMS. 14/600, 8 Şaban 1275 (13 March 1859).

Rather, as his main problem was financing both himself and his family, it was decided to send his family back to Istanbul[78] and increase his salary in relation to any increase in revenues from villages.[79]

Two years later, in November 1861, permission to settle Şerif Bey together with his family in Erzurum was approved by the sultan.[80] However, there are no details about the deeds of Şerif Bey in Erzurum. Whether he was appointed to an official post like his brothers is unclear. However, his rank was increased from *Istabl-ı Amire* to *Mîr-i Miran* in 1863, for which he had been waiting for a long time.[81] Hereafter, he was a "pasha." Nevertheless, he never gave up struggling for his landed property until his passing in September 1868.

While his elder brother Emin Pasha had been ruling Muş, Şerif Pasha had been the mütesellim of Bitlis. J. Shiel had described his mansion in 1836 as following: *"We were lodged in the Governor's house, a large stone square building inclosing a wide court, and placed on top of a high hill, where it stood alone, overhanging a part of the city."*[82] In January 1864, Şerif Pasha aired grievances about his *kargir* (stone) mansion in Bitlis of more than fifty rooms. He argued that during the time of Reşid Pasha there was a demand to rent his mansion to the Imperial Army for fifteen hundred purses, yet its value had been five thousand. He claimed that if it had been necessary, he would have granted access to the mansion for free as a sign of his family's four-hundred-year loyalty to the state. Yet, the demand was not realized, and after his exile he could not take care of his mansion. In the course of time, he claimed, his mansion was destroyed and its grounds used as fields by the people who thought that nobody would question them. Thus, he asked for identification of the perpetrators and compensation for damages.[83]

Besides the mansion, Şerif Pasha argued that shops that had been part of the mosque's waqf, which he had built, had also been damaged according to the information given by the waqf's trustee.[84] Following on from this petition, an investigation was carried out by the councils of Muş and Bitlis. After questioning Muslim and non-Muslim population of the region, both councils reported that the mansion was destroyed, but not because of the intentional

---

78   BOA. A. MKT. MVL. 106/ 25 23 Şaban 1275 (28 March 1859).
79   BOA. A. MKT. MHM. 155/9, 23 Şaban 1275 (28 March 1859).
80   BOA. İ. MVL. 458/20546, 26 Cemaziyelevvel 1278 (29 November 1861), BOA. A. MKT. UM. 523/9, 7 Cemaziyelahir 1278 (10 December 1861).
81   BOA. İ. DH. 514/34990, 2 Rebiülahir 1280 (16 September 1863).
82   J. Shiel, "Notes on a Journey from Tabriz, through Kurdistan," 71.
83   BOA. MVL. 435/12, 10 Şaban 1280 (20 January 1864).
84   BOA. MVL. 681/8, 18 Rebiülevvel 1281 (21 August 1864).

acts of the inhabitants. Rather, as it was located on the top of a hill and had not been used for a long time, the house was ruined as a result of seasonal changes – rain, snow, and wind.[85] Nevertheless, Şerif Pasha continued to claim that his mansion was not outside the city and that it was not destroyed in the way described.

At the end of an investigation in which officials from the Erzurum and Muş Councils were sent to Bitlis, the decision regarding the destruction of the mansion did not change. It was accepted that timbers and some other equipment in the mansion had been stolen, but due to the location of the mansion it was difficult to ascertain the thieves. Moreover, the council of Bitlis reported that in the case of the shops, leaseholders had not evacuated the shops because someone had annoyed them. Upon the petition of the waqf's trustee, the leaseholders had been summoned to the government office and kept in custody. The investigation showed that because it was not a well frequented part of the city the shops became unprofitable and the merchants moved away to other shops.[86]

Regardless of the result of the debate over Şerif Pasha's mansion and waqf shops, this debate provides a better comprehension about how notables, who mainly took their power from their lineages and hereditary lands were also deeply involved in the market economy of the city-centers through endowments.[87] Thus, it enables us to imagine more clearly the power they wielded and the loss they incurred after being uprooted from their spheres of influence. Therefore, they struggled for change by which they could reach their previous statues.

In the same vein, the reclaim of Şerif Bey's mansion and pious foundation can also be regarded as a reflection of the Land Code of 1858. Although the code did not stipulate directly about waqf and mülk lands, Şerif Bey regarded it as an opportunity to restore his property. Similarly, Hurşid Bey, having lost his elder brothers Murad and Şerif, struggled for the confiscated villages of his eldest brother Emin Pasha in the 1870s. He was not alone in this pursuit; his son Süleyman Bahri Pasha, a part of Şûra-yı Devlet, helped him. The incorporation of family members in the Ottoman bureaucracy provided them with new channels to claim their hereditary lands even decades after their confiscation.

---

85   Ibid.
86   BOA. MVL. 694/48, 16 Şaban1281 (14 January 1865).
87   For further details about the pious foundations in Muş, including those of Alaaddin Pasha, see Bilal Yılmaz, "Muş Vakıfları" (master's thesis, Yüzüncü Yıl Üniversitesi, 2009).

5.4 Debate over the Yurtluk-Ocaklık Villages of Emin Pasha

In 1876, the heirs of the pious foundation of Sheikh Abdülmelik, who was entombed in a village of Bulanık called Abri, asked the Ministry of Pious Foundations (Evkâf-ı Humâyun Nezâreti) for the renewal of their berats for two villages of Muş called Liz and Bostangend. However, Süleyman Bahri Pasha, the son of Hurşid Bey, objected claiming that said villages were among the yurtluk-ocaklık villages of his deceased uncle Emin Pasha. Therefore, he asked for a delay in the renewal of the berats of those villages until after the arrival of the necessary documents from the Imperial Registry, the Finance Ministry and the Erzurum Provincial Council.[88]

In fact, Liz and Bostangend – together with Norşen, Yoncalı, and Kömüs – had been granted as yurtluk-ocaklıks to Emin Pasha in 1254 (1838) after the abolition of the yurtluk-ocaklık status of sanjak of Muş. Upon Emin Pasha's death without an heir, these villages were confiscated by the central treasury, yet it would turn out that some of them were not. For a while Şerif Bey also struggled to have those villages granted to his son Mehmed Bey and his nephew Selim Bey.[89] However, this demand was rejected on the pretext that when yurtluk-ocaklık holders died without a child, their lands would be confiscated by the central treasury. By the nineteenth century, as discussed before, the abrogation of such hereditary land ownership was a significant part of the fiscal and administrative reforms. The death of Emin Pasha without an heir presented the necessary excuse to confiscate his lands. As narrated before, Şerif Bey led to a small uprising upon the rejection of his demand and was thus discharged and replaced by Hüseyin Pasha.[90]

The subject of the yurtluk-ocaklık villages of Emin Pasha came up again approximately thirty years later because of conflicting claims by the heirs of the Sheikh of Abri's foundation and the relatives of Emin Pasha. In order to clarify the multiple claims to the villages, the berats, waqf charters and official registers were investigated by the Provincial Council of Erzurum, the Imperial Registry and the Ministry of Finance. The results were important not only for verifying or nullifying the claims. They also reveal the means through which the beys of Muş consolidated their material power.

In the report of the *Divan-ı Muhasebat* (Court of Exchequer), a disparity between the claims of the heirs of the sheikh and the original documents was highlighted. Accordingly, the village of Liz was named in a berat, dated 1733,

---

88 BOA. ŞD. 261/16, 2 Rebiülevvel 1293 (28 March 1876).
89 BOA. ŞD. 2881/40, 5 Cemaziyelahir 1293 (28 June 1876).
90 BOA. C. DH. 117/ 5810, 20 Rebiülahir 1260 (9 May 1844).

of the zawiyah-keepers (Islamic convent) of Sheikh Abdülmelik. In the same vein, Bostangend was among the villages in the berat of the heirs of Sheikh Burhaneddin. However, it also noted that the revenues of those villages had been taken by these religious endowments only since 1262 (1845), immediately after the death of Emin Pasha. If they were granted the revenues of these two villages only after 1845, how could they possess berats dating to 1733 at the same time? Therefore, a detailed investigation through the early registers was carried out.[91]

These documents allow us to understand how the villages of Emin Pasha were handed down since the eighteenth century. While the villages of Yoncalı and Liz were at the disposal of tribal beys called Abdi and Mustafa, the villages were annexed to Erzurum Customs Office in 1238 (1822). Similarly, while the village of Norşen was part of Bitlis, it had been granted to Maksud Pashazade Murad Bey (the uncle of Emin Pasha) as a yurtluk-ocaklık in 1213 (1798) when Muş became a separate sanjak. Moreover, Bostangend had been granted as a fief to Süleyman and Kömüs to Ali in 1129 (1716) and 1171 (1757), respectively. However, it was emphasized that as time passed, those villages began to be controlled by Emin Pasha, and finally, in 1254 he was granted them as yurtluk-ocaklıks.[92]

This point is important in showing that the power yurtluk-ocaklık holders exercised was expansionist. No matter how many villages they were granted as yurtluk-ocaklıks, they could easily dominate nearby villages as they held the mutasarrıflık of Muş. In the case of Emin Pasha, his yurtluk-ocaklık villages were confiscated upon his death, which means that after 1260 (1844), the governorship of Erzurum was supposed to take the control of those villages. However, it failed to do so and trustees of certain pious endowments enjoyed the revenues of some of these villages in the meantime. Therefore, after a detailed investigation, it was revealed that Liz and Bostangend were not originally among the waqf villages of Sheikh Burhaneddin and Sheikh Abdülmelik and that the beneficiaries of the waqf had forged the berats.[93]

This case also indicates that the notables of Muş were capable of using the new legal transformations on the land. Hurşid Bey's choice of language enables us to speculate about the influence of the Land Code of 1858 in the reopening of the case of the yurtluk-ocaklık villages of Emin Pasha.[94] Hopeful about

---

91 BOA. ŞD. 2881/40, 5 Cemaziyelahir 1293 (28 June 1876).
92 Ibid.
93 Ibid.
94 The effects of Land Code of 1858 were more drastically felt after the 1870s in the sanjak of Muş. Thus, discussion of the Land Code is limited in the present study, as the period under study does not warrant a full-fledged discussion. Nevertheless, for the historiography on the

getting rights to those lands, Hurşid Bey travelled from Erzurum to Istanbul. He argued that the sheikh of Abri had seized the villages of Liz and Bostangend and for fifteen years had collected revenues worth seventy-eight thousand annually by means of counterfeited berats. Therefore, having specified his role in uncovering the facts regarding the villages of Liz and Bostangend, Hurşid Bey argued that those villages were his hereditary right, as both Murad and Şerif Bey had already passed away and Emin Pasha had left no child behind.[95] Besides, he wanted to be rewarded in return for whistle-blowing (*ihbariyye*) – that is, thanks for his help uncovering the reality about the villages of Liz and Bostangend. In a report of the Şûra-yı Devlet it was emphasized that Hurşid Bey had neither the right to these villages and nor an award for whistle-blowing. Nevertheless, Şûra-yı Devlet decided it would be appropriate to appoint him to a mutasarrıflık.[96]

Regardless of the fact that Hurşid Bey's claim to his late brother's villages bore no results, his use of a new terminology brought a new dimension to negotiations with the central government. Hurşid Bey and his son expected to benefit from new codifications concerning state lands. Besides, villages that were supposed to have been confiscated by the treasury were being controlled by pious foundations and unnoticed for fifteen years. Thus, the process confiscating yurtluk-ocaklık lands and their control by the treasury were far from perfect. Local actors, in this case religious leaders, benefited from the power lacuna created by the exile of yurtluk-ocaklık holders and annexed the some yurtluk-ocaklık villages in their waqf lands. How the power of the religious leaders increased after the exile of Kurdish mîrs has long been discussed.[97] This case also confirms the rise of the sheikhs in the Muş's locality after the exile of Kurdish notables.

After this fruitless fight over the yurtluk-ocaklık villages of the late Emin Pasha, for the beys of Muş, the only thing that remained of their yurtluk-ocaklık lands was the salaries paid to them in return. Because of this, the

---

Land Code of 1858 in the Ottoman Empire and particularly in the Middle East, see, Owen, *New Perspectives on Property*; Martha Mundy and Richard Saumarez Smith, *Governing Property, Making the Modern State: Law Administration and Production in Ottoman Syria* (London: I.B. Tauris, 2007); Haim Gerber, The Social Origins of the Modern Middle East (Boulder: Lynne Rienner Publishers, 1994). For literature review E. Attila Aytekin, "Hukuk, Tarih ve Tarihyazımı: 1858 Osmanlı Arazi Kanunnamesi'ne Yönelik Yaklaşımlar," *Türkiye Araştırmaları Literatür Dergisi* 3, no. 5 (2005): 723–44.

95 "... ırsen hak-ı 'ubeydânem olduğu hâlde âhere i'tâsı gadri mûcib olunduğu ..." BOA. ŞD. 2886/54, 5 Cemaziyelahir 1293 (28 June 1876).

96 Ibid.

97 Van Bruinessen, *Agha, Shaikh, and State*.

continuation of yurtluk-ocaklık salaries from parents to children was also an object of struggle.

5.5 Future of the Yurtluk-Ocaklık Salaries

The base of yurtluk-ocaklık salaries granted to Şerif Pasha and his brothers were initially calculated by combining the revenues of the years 1265 (1849) and 1266 (1850) and then halving the result. In other words, as the revenues of the two years were different, they were equalized. Later, this amount was paid to them as a lifelong (*kayd-ı hayat*) monthly salary beginning in March 1267 (March 1851).[98] However, upon the passing of Murad Bey in early 1859, Şerif Bey asked if Murad's salary was assigned to his family as a charity of the sultan (*sadaka-i seniye*).[99] It was decided and approved by the sultan that these salaries would be passed to his children according to law (*nizamî vechile*).[100] Thus, with a four hundred guruş increase, the salary of Murad Bey was allocated among his sons Yusuf, Selim, Abdülkerim, Nuri, and Said.[101]

Although what is meant with "nizamî" is vague, later on it was specified as the Land Code.[102] As specified, such salaries should be distributed equally among the daughters and sons of the deceased. However, daughters were not regarded equal to sons in the allocation of inheritance because of their marriages. Yet daughters could not be deprived of such salaries altogether, so it was decided by the Şûrâ-yı Devlet to apply the method of partition of inheritance.[103] Accordingly, sons received two shares while the daughters received only

---

98 BOA. ŞD. 374/27, 14 Şaban 1315 (9 December 1897).
99 BOA. İ. MMS. 14/600, 8 Şaban 1275 (13 March 1859).
100 Ibid.
101 BOA. A. MKT. MHM. 155/9, 23 Şaban 1275 (28 March 1859).
102 As those salaries were initially compensation for confiscated lands, it was decided to be evaluated within the Land Code. The related article was number 54: "When the owners of Arazi-i Miriye and mevkufe die, their lands are freely inherited by their sons and daughters without price regardless if they are in the place where the land is." "Kanunnâme-i Arazi" in Mustafa Budak, Önder Bayır, and Mümin Yıldıztaş, eds., *Tanzimat Sonrası Arazi ve Tapu* (İstanbul: Osmanlı Arşivi Daire Başkanlığı, 2014), 113.
103 "… bu makûle ma'âşların arâzî-i kanunnâme-i humâyun ahkâmına tatbîken evlâd ve zükûr ve inâsa müsâveten tahsîsi evvelce karârlaştırılmış ise de evlâd-ı inâs izdivâcda bulunarak evlâd-ı zükûrun anlara kıyâsı olamıyacağı gibi evlâd-ı inâsın bu ma'âşlarında külliyen mahrûmiyeti dâhi tecvîz olunamıyacağından ba'dezîn hâl-i vukû'ında a'del-i usûl olân taksîm-i mirâs kâi'desine tevfîken tahsîs olunmasının …" BOA. ŞD. 308/26, 29 Zilkade 1302 (9 September 1885).

one.¹⁰⁴ Thereupon, it is possible to trace the transition of the yurtluk-ocaklık salaries to the granddaughters and grandsons of Şerif Pasha and of his brothers in particular, and the possessors of such salaries in general.¹⁰⁵

In later years, two important developments concerning yurtluk-ocaklık salaries were observed. The first is a deduction in the salaries. In a petition, Hurşid Bey claimed that in September 1879 and March 1880, his salary, which was two thousand guruş, had been reduced by one-tenth and one-fifth respectively. Arguing that this salary was not of the kind being paid to officials and retirees, but rather compensation for his confiscated property, Hurşid Bey reclaimed the amount that was deducted.¹⁰⁶ The opinions of the family members concerning their salaries changed according to their demands. Sometimes they regarded them as a "gift" and, at other times, as in this case, as compensation for their hereditary lands. Nevertheless, after correspondence between the Ministry of Finance and the Şûra-yı Devlet, it was decided to repay the deduction, as these were salaries paid as compensation for confiscated property, like the yurtluk-ocaklık villages, and they could not be deducted even if the owners were also officials – so they were put on two separate salaries.¹⁰⁷

However, in the course of time, as yurtluk-ocaklık salaries were divided among heirs, it became a matter of complaint. The children of Şerif Pasha and his brothers complained that their shares had become insufficient for their living costs. In a joint petition by the cousins, they emphasized that the yurtluk-ocaklık lands of their ancestors had been passed from generation to generation; to consolidate their claims to those lands they referred to the *Sharafnama*, which accounted for the collaboration between the Kurdish Beys and Sultan Selim I after the Çaldıran War.¹⁰⁸

---

104 "... müteveffânın evlâdlarına a'del-i usûl olân taksîm-i mirâs kâ'idesine tevfîken evlâd-ı zükûra iki ve inâsa bir olarak tahsîsi ..." BOA. ŞD. 301/28, 24 Ramazan 1301 (18 July 1884).

105 Those salaries became so important that upon her father's passing, the daughter of Şerif Pasha, Nigar Hanım complained about her uncle, Hurşid Bey, who wanted to forcefully marry her to his son, Süleyman Bahri. BOA. ŞD. 2855/2, 3 Şaban 1286 (9 October 1869). As an example of the transition of yurtluk-ocaklık salaries to children: when Hurşid Bey passed away in December 1883, his salary was apportioned among his sons İbrahim Ahid, Hasro, and İzzet Beys, and Bahri Pasha, and his daughters Naile and Gülbeyaz. BOA. ŞD. 301/28, 24 Ramazan 1301 (18 July 1884); In the same line, when Şerif Pasha's son Mustafa Fazıl died, his salary passed on to his only heir, Mehmed Emin Bey. BOA. ŞD. 316/27, 7 Zilkade 1304 (28 July 1887); Similarly, after her passing, the salary of Nigar Hanım passed to her children. BOA. ŞD. 358/16, 20 Cemaziyelahir 1312 (19 December 1894).

106 BOA. ŞD. 295/35, 7 Rebiülevvel 1300 (15 February 1883).

107 BOA. İ. ŞD. 64/3763, 20 Şaban 1300 (26 June 1883).

108 "... Bi'l-umûm tevârih-i saltanat-ı seniyye ve kuyûdât-ı hakânîyede ve husûsen ünvân'ül-Şeref nâm tarih-i kadîm Farsi'ül ibâre mufassal ve sarâhatle mebsût olduğu üzere cennet-mekân Sultan Selim hân-ı evvel hazretlerinin Çâldırân sefer-i zafer rehber-i hümâyunları

The family members kept getting the salaries until 1908. Then with the Second Constitutional Period, beginning in September 1908, the payment schedule of yurtluk-ocaklık salaries became a matter of discussion in the Meclis-i Vükela (Council of Ministers). Emphasizing that the recipients of yurtluk-ocaklık salaries had already been employed in official posts they were being paid twice and because the monthly cost was thirty-forty thousand guruş, it was discussed to pay the yurtluk-ocaklık salaries for the next ten years in advance and thus to remove them from the budget.[109] The yurtluk-ocaklık salaries became a burden on the budget in the course of time, yet payment of yurtluk-ocaklık salaries continued to as late as 1913.[110] Based on interviews with family members, those salaries were paid up until the First World War. During the war and the occupation of eastern provinces by Russian forces, it is difficult to imagine that the salaries were paid regularly.[111]

5.6 Conclusion

Although the yurtluk-ocaklık status of the sanjak of Muş was annulled in the mid-1830s due to administrative changes required by the establishment of the Redif Army along with the respective military operations of Reşid and Hafız Pashas, the final blow to such hereditary land-holdings was accomplished with the exile of Alaaddin Pasha's lineage from the region. The struggle over the boundaries and revenues of yurtluk-ocaklık villages and over the landed property, vineyards, and orchards of the family continued for a long time, albeit. To determine the revenues and limits of the family's yurtluk-ocaklık villages, an official, together with an agent appointed by the family were employed. The beys were already in a disadvantaged position as they were far from the stage of this struggle. However, they tried to benefit from the lack of detailed surveys and records about their yurtluk-ocaklık lands. Nevertheless, Esad Pasha, the governor of the province of Kurdistan, was determined to refute the claims of the exiled beys over their yurtluk-ocaklık lands. Thus, by claiming that Şerif Bey and his brothers had commandeered lands near their real yurtluk-ocaklık villages in the course of time, Esad Pasha rejected the registries that the beys provided. Thus, the salaries paid for the compensation of their yurtluk-ocaklık

esnâsında bi'lcümle ümerâyı ekrâd devlet-i ebed müddet-i 'aliyyeye arz-ı etba ve inkıyâd ile ..." BOA. ŞD. 374/27, 14 Şaban 1315 (9 December 1897).
109   BOA. MV. 120/74, 23 Şaban 1326 (20 September 1908).
110   BOA. BEO. 4232/317336, 4 Zilhicce 1331 (4 November 1913).
111   Interview with Abddurrahman Yıldırım, Muş, July 23, 2014.

villages were determined by averaging the revenues from two years, based on an investigation carried out by the governor.

The investigation process revealed important points about the peculiarities and the aftermath of the yurtluk-ocaklık lands. By exercising the right of mutasarrıflık of the sanjak of Muş as a yurtluk-ocaklık, the line of beys of Muş had maintained exclusive control over the revenues of the sanjak. However, after being granted just certain villages as yurtluk-ocaklıks upon the abrogation of the yurtluk-ocaklık status of Muş as a whole, family members extended the boundaries of their villages. Then, upon their exile and the confiscation of these yurtluk-ocaklık villages, the commoners of those villages reclaimed those lands. Their confiscated villages were supposed to be controlled and tax farmed by the treasury. Yet as uncovered in the 1870s, other local notables of the region, like religious leaders, benefitted from the exile of the Muş dynasty and took control of the revenues of some of their yurtluk-ocaklık villages for years.

However, negotiation did not end with the exile of the Kurdish notables. Şerif Bey and his brothers did not renounce their claims with regard to the boundaries and revenues of the yurtluk-ocaklık villages and their properties. Similarly, family members continued to file petitions for forgiveness and permission to return to Muş. In the course of time, they reformulated their demands. First, women and children were allowed to return, and then, Hurşid, Murad, and Şerif beys were allowed to return to Erzurum in the 1850s and 1860s, in turn, as long as they did not get involved in the affairs of Muş.

Hurşid and Murad Beys were appointed as administrators in certain districts in the province of Erzurum upon their pardon and Hurşid Bey served the Imperial Army during the Crimean War. Despite limited information about the repercussions of the return of the exiled beys, there are some clues. As will be elaborated in the following chapter, the inhabitants of Muş often petitioned for the reappointment of the exiled Kurdish beys to the region. Thus, the inhabitants of Hınıs, who were forty–fifty families of Armenian and surrounded by Kurdish tribes, requested the appointment of Murad Bey as their administrator after hearing of his return. Similarly, despite the prohibition on becoming involved in the politics of Muş, Hurşid Bey became involved in the tax farming auction for the revenues of the villages of Muş.

Family members seized every opportunity to improve their conditions. The struggle of Şerif Bey in the middle of 1860s concerning his ruined mansion and pious foundation in Bitlis, and that of Hurşid Bey for the confiscated yurtluk-ocaklık villages of his deceased brother Emin Pasha, can be interpreted within the framework of the Land Code of 1858. Although they failed in regaining the ownership of these lands, it is certain that they continued receiving their salaries and handed the right down to their descendants until the outbreak of the First World War. In addition, they were incorporated into provincial administrations, though for small districts. Their sons were employed in the bureaucracy in the imperial center, as well. Moreover, although it is uncertain when and by what means they returned to Muş, later generations of the family still live in some of the villages that were once among their yurtluk-ocaklık lands.

With the exile of the Kurdish notables of Muş, the implementation of administrative and financial reforms that the nineteenth century bureaucrats envisaged, and that peaked with the promulgation of the Tanzimat Edict, entered a new phase. The most important tenet of this reform program was to increase state revenues by annihilating the centuries-old land tenure system in Ottoman Kurdistan. The establishment of the province of Kurdistan after the suppression of the revolts of Bedirhan and Han Mahmud finally heralded the implementation of Tanzimat reforms that had been delayed several times. In the case of Muş, like in other places of the empire, central and provincial authorities initially had to rely on local notables to implement the reforms, but in the end, the regional governors' opinion was especially to eliminate these local power holders. Therefore, despite their defection from the coalition being led by Bedirhan Bey, Şerif Bey and his brothers were exiled and eliminated from the administration of the region. However, as will be discussed in the next chapter, the pacification of local notables also brought about a range of difficulties and proved that they were required for the implementation of reforms.

CHAPTER 6

The Post Tanzimat Era: Evaluation of the Reforms through the Petitions of Ordinary People

The sanjak of Muş, consisting of twenty-eight districts and more than eight hundred villages[1] is surrounded by eighty Kurdish tribes, each of which consists of one to two thousand families, so they are huge in number. The previous kaimakams had thoroughly understood the peculiarities of these tribes and locations of those Kurds, so in the case of plunder of the properties, goods, and livestock of the poor inhabitants, they embarked on their recovery. Thus, during the governance of Şerif Bey of Muş, we were well-off thanks to His Majesty. [However] the present kaimakam of Muş, Habib Efendi, is not capable of governing the sanjak, and so the Kurdish tribes always attack us, take our property, kill [our] people, and up to now they have stolen more than seven hundred sheep. As they are involved in such acts, there is no safety of life and property. Thus, as the region is on the frontier, a few thousand people migrate to Russia annually, so the inhabitants are dispersing. This time around, thirty people from the region have come especially to explain the situation. Şerif Bey, who has been in Istanbul a few years, is well-informed [about the region] and knows the peculiarities of these tribes, and has been employed in our region since time immemorial, and should be sent back to Muş and granted its mutasarrıflık. As the bey is from Muş, he knows about all those bandits, who would not dare to commit such acts as they are afraid of him. Thus, undoubtfully, our safety of life, honor, and property would be maintained, and we would be spared from all of these attacks.[2]

This excerpt is from among the dozens of the petitions penned by both Muslim and Armenian inhabitants of Muş, submitted to the central government, and

1 The numbers were exaggerated to some extent. According to the yearbooks of the vilayet of Erzurum in 1871, 1872, and 1873 the villages of the sancâk of Muş were given as 574, 615, and 618, respectively. *Salnâme-i Vilâyet-i Erzurum* 1288, 145, ibid., 1289, 145, ibid., 1290, 146. The petitions of the Alaaddin Pashazades and also the official correspondences mostly stated that the sanjak of Muş consisted of four hundred villages in the 1830s.
2 BOA. İ. MVL. 227/7731, 22 Safer 1268 (17 December 1851). This file consisted of four different petitions on the same issue.

discussed in the Meclis-i Vâlâ throughout the 1850s and 60s. In this petition, signed by "the poor inhabitants of Muş," two important points emerge. First is the oppression and extortion undertaken by the Kurdish tribes. Second, the complaints about the incapacity of the existing kaimakams of Muş which was the formulation of a demand for the restoration of the exiled beys of Muş, who were described as accustomed to the region, possessing good knowledge of its aspects and having great influence and control over the Kurdish tribes. The petitioning of the common people of Muş was certainly a plea for administrators who knew the local customs and who knew how to settle disputes. As a result, local inhabitants were migrating and dispersing, a situation that would continue and even aggravate in upcoming decades. In the ensuing years, despite the fact that the call for the return of the local beys did not materialize, the people continued to submit petitions with complaints about the administrators of Muş who were alien to the people and the region. The deprivation of producers of their surplus through over taxation, extortion, and corvée as well as their dispossession through indebtedness in the post-Tanzimat context will be discussed in this chapter via an analysis of the petitions of the ordinary people of Muş.

Petitions (*istidʿa, ʿarz-ı hâl*) are particular and indispensable documents that shed light not only on the demands and grievances of ordinary people but also their negotiation and discursive strategies. The literature on petitioning agrees that petition-writing includes important nuances about the relationship between the ruler and the ruled. According to Eyal Ginio, "one of the main legitimate devices that was at the disposal of people from all strata of society, including commoners, was the submission of a petition to the sultan asking for a redress of grievances."[3] By the same token, petitioning served to maintain the notion of "justice," the underlying legitimacy tool of monarchies. Lex Heerma van Voss argues that "as the distribution of justice and largesse are important parts of ruling, rulers can hardly deny their subjects the right to approach them to implore them to exercise justice, or to grant a favor."[4] In the same vein, Halil İnalcık argues that the notion of justice (*adâlet*) is an important principle in the ruling system of Middle Eastern states, and petitions enable rulers to identify

---

[3] Eyal Ginio, "Coping With the State's Agents 'from below': Petitions, Legal Appeal, and the Sultan's Justice in Ottoman Legal Practice," in *Popular Protest and Political Participation in the Ottoman Empire: Studies in Honor of* Suraiya Faroqhi, eds. Eleni Gara, Christoph K. Neumann, and M. Erdem Kabadayı (Istanbul: İstanbul Bilgi University Press, 2011), 41.

[4] Lex Heerma Van Voss, "Introduction," in *Petitions in Social History*, ed. Lex Heerma Van Voss (Cambridge: Cambridge University Press, 2002), 1.

and alleviate the grievances of their subjects.[5] Likewise, Michael Ursinus also points out the functioning of the *Divân-ı Hümâyun* (Imperial Council) as a "court of appeal," to provide "a link between the ruler and the ruled" without the need for intermediaries.[6]

Nevertheless, as Eleni Gara argues the "useful myth" that "a good person heading the state" is the ultimate authority to whom one must apply for justice has limitations.[7] Although this "paternalistic image" of a "just and benevolent ruler" fomented a "protest culture" in the Ottoman Empire by providing an opportunity "for all kinds of popular protest," the success or failure of each such protest did not depend on the benevolence of the ruler so much as "on the constellation of power relations and on the leverage of protesters." To put it differently, if officials who were considered to be fully authorized to implement the justice of the sultan failed to respond to the expectations of the people, not only the notion of "justice" but "the legitimacy of Ottoman rule" would be harmed.[8] Taking these points into consideration the chapter examines how the peasants of Muş appealed to the "justice" of the sultan while drawing attention to how his agencies were failing to realize it.

Petitions provide detailed, vivid images about the social and economic conditions of Muş region.[9] The petitions of the ordinary people of Muş allows us to move beyond the interpretations of local power holders, administrative authorities, central governments, and higher councils. Providing us with a view from below, petitions enable us not only to elaborate upon the tribal landscape, the struggle over resources, power relations, and the negotiations and tensions among different power holders in a region at the periphery of the Ottoman Empire, but they also depict the post-Tanzimat era and trace the fate of the yurtluk-ocaklık villages once held by Emin Pasha and his brothers.

Highlighting the demands of petitioners, this chapter examines the effects and reception of Tanzimat reforms in Muş by utilizing the petitions

---

5 Halil İnalcık, "Şikayet Hakkı: 'Arz-ı Hâl ve 'Arz-ı Mahzar'lar" Osmanlı Araştırmaları Dergisi 7–8 (1988): 33.
6 Michael Ursinus, Grievance Administration (Şikâyet) in an Ottoman Province: The Kaymakam of Rumelia's 'Record Book of Complaints' of 1781–1783 (London: Routledge, 2005), 3. About the role of Divân-ı Hümâyun, see also İnalcık, "Şikayet Hakkı," 33–51.
7 Van Voss, "Introduction."
8 Eleni Gara, "Popular Protest and the Limitations of Sultanic Justice," in *Popular Protest and Political Participation in the Ottoman Empire: Studies in Honor of Suraiya Faroqhi*, eds. Eleni Gara, Christoph K. Neumann, and M. Erdem Kabadayı (Istanbul: İstanbul Bilgi University Press, 2011), 102–04.
9 As an example of a study scrutinizing nineteenth-century developments in a locality through an analysis of petitions, see Yuval Ben-Bassat, *Petitoning the Sultan: Protests and Justice in Late Ottoman Palestine* (London: I.B. Tauris, 2013).

of inhabitants, the reports of local authorities, and documents related to the cases of the kaimakams of the sanjak who were questioned about corruption and tyranny. From the 1850s onwards, state archives were filled with documents that reflect the new tax regime, the role of local councils and coalitions, and tensions with local authorities. Although petitioning was a practice among the ordinary people of the empire long before the Tanzimat,[10] this chapter will demonstrate how the commoners of Muş conspicuously adopted the language of the Tanzimat, and sought their rights within the terms of its fundamental tenets and through its newly established institutions. Milen Petrov, writing on the case of legal reforms in the province of Danube, conceptualizes the attitudes of the ordinary people in the face of reforms as "compliance": "the willingness to modify discourse and behavior in accordance with what political power expected (or assumed) an individual to say and do in order to demonstrate his or her *bona fide* status as trustworthy suspect, witness and 'subject' in general."[11]

By the same token, John Chalcraft challenges the arguments that considered the state and the peasantry to be two opposite, mutually-exclusive entities. Instead, based on his study of the petitions of the Egyptian peasantry during the 1860s and 1870s, he points out "the possibility of more complex, differentiated and mutually constitutive political relationship between peasants and the state".[12] In this relationship, he further argues, peasants "evoke not passivity, silent subversion, or outright revolution, but surprisingly, sophisticated engagement and negotiation with state practice and discourse."[13]

In the same vein, in everyday practices of the peasantry or the people in general, neither the state nor the peasantry was a "homogenous" entity.[14] While everyone from a tax-collector to the provincial governor was officially a representative of the state, or rather of the central government, they did not necessarily reflect the state's agenda, and they pursued their own interests. As emphasized by Chalcraft, "peasants did not relate to these often heterogeneous agencies in the same way, and these relations cannot always be characterized as those of violent opposition on the one side or quiet avoidance

---

10   İnalcık points to archival collections like *şikâyât defterleri*, *'arz-ı mahzarlar*, and *ma'ruz* to emphasize the tradition of submitting of petitions and their importance in a system of rule based on the notion of "justice." İnalcık, "Şikayet Hakkı," 34.
11   Milen V. Petrov, "Everyday Forms of Compliance: Subaltern Commentaries on Ottoman Reform, 1864–1868," *Comparative Studies in Society and History* 46, no. 4 (2004): 758–59.
12   John Chalcraft, "Engaging the State: Peasants and Petitions in Egypt on the Eve of Colonial Rule," *International Journal of Middle East Studies* 37, no. 3 (2005): 303.
13   Ibid., 304.
14   Ibid., 305.

on the other."[15] Referring to the Tanzimat-ı Hayriyye, the commoners of Muş appealed to the sultan as the "benevolent ruler" who guaranteed their rights and well-being on the one hand. On the other they negotiated for the amelioration of their conditions by presenting complaints about other agencies of the sultan, like the kaimakam or council members, and pointed out possible outcomes in the event that necessary steps were not taken – like decreases in revenues or in the population.[16]

Recalling the quotation at the beginning of this chapter, the grievances of the commoners of Muş largely stemmed from the novelty of the Tanzimat reforms and governance of the region with a rotating of administrators alien to the region and its people other than local dynasties. In what follows, the comparison the people made between their former and current governors, the reasons for their dissatisfaction, and also the clues it provides to assess the limits of Tanzimat reforms will be discussed. In the absence of hereditary local rulers, the Ottoman government was unable to penetrate into the local society. Such an introduction is helpful not only to comprehend in which ways centrally-appointed administrators were unable to redress the grievances of the inhabitants but also to include the characteristics of one of the Tanzimat's new institutions – the local councils – in the discussion.

The second part of the chapter will deal with the case of a kaimakam of Muş, Ömer Pasha, who governed the sanjak during some of the turbulent years of the Crimean War. The complaint of the people about the Pasha led to a trial in which he was accused of being involved in corruption together with district council members and of exploiting the state of emergency during the war by embezzling money intended to pay for grain, supplied by the peasantry for the army. The Crimean War resulted in the promulgation of the *Islahat Fermanı* (Reform Edict) which aimed further to consolidate equality between Muslim and other communities all over the Ottoman Empire. However, in the middle of the 1860s the peasants of Muş were still seeking the money embezzled by a network of moneylenders, kaimakams, community leaders, and council members. Likewise, as the complaints about Ömer Pasha mostly came from Armenians in the villages on the Muş plain, which were once the yurtluk-ocaklık villages of Emin Pasha and his brothers, it is possible to draw a

---

15 Ibid., 306.
16 Analyzing the role of the petitions of the peasants of the Vladimir region, Andrew Verner also regards petitions "as integral parts of complex negotiations among as well as between the peasants and outside (…)". Andrew Verner, "Discursive Strategies in the 1905 Revolution: Peasant Petitions from Vladimir Province," *The Russian Review* 54, no. 1 (1995): 67.

picture of those villages of the beys of Muş following their confiscation by the central treasury through an analysis of peasants' petitions.

The last part of the chapter deals with the issue of "migration." On one hand, it will focus on how both central and local authorities responded to the decrease in the population of Muş and also the connotations of both migration and forced evacuation. On the other hand, it emphasizes how the province of Erzurum and the sanjak of Muş became places for the settlement of Crimean and Circassian immigrants.

6.1 Conflicting Viewpoints Regarding Governors

One of the main topics of the previous chapters was the inclusion of Muş in the Tanzimat reform program, along with the end and the exile of the Kurdish notables in the summer of 1849. Hereafter, the hereditary governance of Muş by the line of Alaaddin Pasha came to an end. The necessity of centrally-appointed governors other than local dynasties had been talked about in Istanbul since the beginning of the nineteenth century.[17] However, this became possible only after the inclusion of the province of Erzurum in the Tanzimat program and after the exile of local notables. It can be argued that this ideal of the provincial authorities conflicted with the demands of the local people, in other words, the kaimakams – appointed after the exile of local notables – had little knowledge and experience with regard to the peculiarities of the region, leading to a multifaceted problem.

Such a stance was neither nostalgia for the old days nor a eulogy for the governance by the local notables – the oppressiveness of and complaints about Şerif Bey's rule have already been discussed in the previous chapter. Rather, such a stance lays the groundwork to analyze not only how the conditions were aggravated for the inhabitants of Muş since the exile of local beys, but also the effects and reception of Tanzimat reforms that preluded to a "new organization." As Sabri Ateş argues, the peasantry might have benefitted from the exile of Kurdish nobility, as they had also been overtaxed, forced into corvée and indebtedness during their rule. However, "they had direct access to their rulers" and with the exile of traditional Kurdish rulers, the peasantry had to face with "non-familiar Ottoman administrators and tax collectors." These new administrators began to impose enormous new taxes not for the state but for

---

17   BOA. HAT. 1087/ 44245, 1 Zilkade 1243 (15 May 1828).

their own pockets.[18] The preference of the ordinary people of Muş for local rulers over centrally-appointed kaimakams also parallels Martin van Bruinessen's argument pointing out how the influence and power of Kurdish rulers over the tribes enabled them to solve conflicts among them.[19] Thus, the rule of the local notables can be defined as the best of the worst.

Complaints of the people of Muş about their kaimakam had been already brought to the local and central authorities' attention by the beginning of 1851. Emphasizing the protection of its subjects from any kind of cruelty by officials, the Tanzimat state placed importance on the investigation of the matters in the petitions.[20] In the beginning, the main demand of the collective petitions was the reinstatement of Şerif Bey. Having emphasized that Şerif Bey was from a well-established family, the petitioners argued that he had guarded their agriculture (*hıfz-ı haraset*) and have been respectful of their rights (*hakkımıza hürmet*). They pointed out how he was exiled with his family during the revolts in the region (that is, the turmoil during Bedirhan Bey's revolt). The petitioners' statement importantly sheds light on local relations, as they argued that the priest (*karabaş*) in Çanlı Monastery, Zakarya, had played a role in Şerif Bey's exile. Having collaborated with members of the district council of Muş, Zakarya allegedly filed a petition via the patriarchate in Istanbul, without the consent of the inhabitants of Muş, claiming that Şerif Bey was tyrannizing the people. The petitioners stated that they became upset and worried having heard such news and immediately dispatched their delegates to Istanbul. Having judged the priest and the delegates a few times, the patriarchate acknowledged that the inhabitants' accusations were right and decided to exile Zakarya.[21]

---

18 Sabri Ateş, "The End of Kurdish Autonomy: The Destruction of the Kurdish Emirates in the Ottoman Empire" in *The Cambridge History of the Kurds*, eds. Hamit Bozarslan, Cengiz Güneş, and Veli Yadırgı, (Cambridge: Cambridge University Press, 2021), 95–96.
19 Van Bruinessen, *Agha, Shaikh, and State*, 69.
20 BOA. A. MKT. UM. 50/64, 1 Cemaziyelevvel 1267 (4 March 1851).
21 BOA. MVL. 108/25, 13 Muharrem 1268 (8 November 1851). Despite insufficient clues into the conflict between Zakarya and Şerif Bey, a few years previous, there were some complaints about both of them because of the collection of taxes and the poll-tax on non-Muslims at Garzan, most of whom were regularly participating in the activies of Çanlı Monastery in Muş. Allegedly, both of them were seeking their own benefit and manipulating the tax-collection process. BOA. A. MKT. MVL 6/63, 19 Muharrem 1263 (7 January 1847). This particular anecdote points out the relations between the Kurdish notables and Armenian clergy in Muş. In a similar vein, Richard E. Antaramian shows the relations between the Armenian clergy of Aghtamar and Khan Mahmud and his lineage. The family had involved in the debates over election of catholicos. Even, in the 1860s, a grandson of Khan Mahmud assassinated the catholicos, Bedros Bülbül. Richard E. Antaramian *Brokers of Faith, Brokers of Empire: Armenians and the Politics of Reform in the Ottoman Empire*, (Stanford: Stanford University Press, 2020), 77–82.

More importantly, contrary to the priest's allegations, a common petition of the Muslim and non-Muslim inhabitants argued that, after the uprooting of Şerif Bey and his relatives, tyranny increased. Having become tired of the theft and murder committed by the Kurdish tribes, the over taxation and extortion by council members, and the forced conversions to Islam, they claimed that they had no more strength to stand. Besides, they were stonewalled by members of the district council while trying to petition the Sublime Porte. As a consequence, more than a thousand households had no choice but to emigrate to Russia and Iran. Thus, the petitioners concluded with a strong opinion that their emancipation depended on the return of Şerif Bey to Muş.[22]

Hereafter, successive petitions were filed and delegates were dispatched to the Sublime Porte, to complain that their previous petitions had not been taken into consideration. Signed as "the Muslim and non-Muslim inhabitants of Muş and Bitlis," the following excerpt will exemplify on one hand how the inhabitants of Muş were suffering from extortion, over taxation, and corvée, and on the other hand how they sought justice by utilizing the language of the Tanzimat:

> Twenty-four Kurdish tribes of the region have been attacking our districts, plundering and ruining our properties and goods, and (...). In a few months' time, they injured and ravaged twenty to thirty poor people and in the summer quarters they also mutilated cows by cutting their feet, as well. They also set fire to the fodder and stole seven to eight thousand sheep. On top of this, when we informed the council about our situation, as they had also set fire to our harvest of grain, the governor employed an amount of three to four thousand soldiers and officials whom we had to host in our houses without payment together with their livestock for a month. Although we want the restitution of our stolen property thanks to His Just Majesty, when those officials returned, each of the officials of the council seized a large amount of money and mule carts from us. Thus, this council of officials did not supervise and just looked after their own interests. Every year they add two hundred thousand piasters on top of our regular tax and allocated and collected it forcefully. [In the same vein] they employ special officials to search those who are dispatched to the imperial center, and if they are carrying petitions or similar documents they are sent back and jailed, tortured, and oppressed. Thus, we [the representatives of Muş's commoners] who have already been in the Sublime Porte together with the ones have already dared to explain our condition. As we have been told, around two thousand families emigrate

---

22 BOA. MVL. 108/25, 13 Muharrem 1268 (8 November 1851).

to foreign lands annually. [Thus] as mercy and as a requirement of the Auspicious Tanzimat, the poor inhabitants shall be saved, and it would be the kindness, grace, and favor of His Majesty if Şerif Bey, who is from a local dynasty, acquainted with the region, and competent to govern, is appointed and authorized.[23]

Although the number of households that had emigrated, livestock usurped, and people killed changed from one petition to the other, the main point – the incapacity of the existing kaimakam, Habib Efendi – was invariable. The petitioners argued that Şerif Bey and his elder brother Emin Pasha had often governed Muş; understood state business; protected the properties, lives, and honors of the people; and were ready to sacrifice their lives if required. On the other hand, the new kaimakam was not familiar with the region and not well informed about the peculiarities of the Kurdish tribes. He failed to manage the tribes, protect the inhabitants, and govern the region.[24] The members of the local council which was established to oversee the local affairs were as cruel – if not more – as Kurdish tribes towards the peasantry. Therefore, the petitioners argued that since the displacement of Şerif Bey, three years since, banditry had gotten out of control.[25]

In these petitions, Şerif Bey and his ancestors, who had governed Muş for a few centuries, were depicted as capable unlike newly appointed administrators who were outsiders and could not protect the inhabitants. Although such local notables were not blameless, based on the many petitions submitted from Muş, the conditions of inhabitants had become worse after their exile.[26] As will be clarified with the case of Ömer Pasha, petitioners were mostly from villages on the plain of Muş which had once been in the possession of Şerif Bey's family as yurtluk-ocaklıks. Besides, as discussed thoroughly in chapter 2, the ability to negotiate with the tribes was an integral part of the notables' influence and leverage. As will be discussed partially in this chapter and thoroughly in chapters 7 & 8, the striking result of the power vacuum that emerged after their exile was the lack of control over the nomadic and seminomadic groups.

The assaults, or the banditry of semi-nomadic and nomadic Kurdish tribes described in the petitions were not given. "[E]ach case of violence and banditry and each large-scale raid [of the nomadic and semi-nomadic tribes] should be contextualized and treated as the product of certain historical

---

23   BOA. İ. MVL. 227/7731, 22 Safer 1268 (17 December 1851).
24   BOA. MVL. 108/52, 18 Muharrem 1268 (13 November 1851).
25   BOA. MVL. 108/82, 29 Safer 1268 (24 December 1851). They praised Şerif Bey's rule like that: " ... mîr Şerif ehl-i dirâyet ve müdebbir ve fukarâ-i zuafâ hakkında mutasarrıf ve mütedebbir olub ..." BOA. İ. MVL 227.7731/ 22 Safer 1268 (17 December 1851).
26   BOA. MVL. 119/58, 15 Şevval 1268 (2 August 1852).

economic and political conditions."²⁷ Tribal banditry could be a manifestation of inter-imperial, inter-dynastic or inter-tribal conflicts. It could be used not only as way of reaping profits but also punishing rival tribes, dynasties or empires.²⁸ In this case of Muş, semi-nomadic tribes' plundering of the properties of Muş's peasants could not be analyzed in a nomadic/settled dichotomy.²⁹ Rather, it showcases the insufficiency of a tribal economy and its dependency on a settled economy.

Notwithstanding the demand of the commoners of Muş, Tanzimat bureaucrats were determined to establish a new regime curtailing the power of local notables. Therefore, although central authorities paid great attention to the petitions of the inhabitants of Muş – sending orders to kaimakams to alleviate the grievances, appointing officials to investigate the allegations, and hearing out the petitioners in the Meclis-i Vâlâ, the demand for Şerif Bey's return was not approved. Questioning that such petitions might be written down regardless of the grievances of the people and with the incitement of Şerif Bey, the Meclis-i Vâlâ decided that it was not appropriate to restore such officials as they had been discharged and exiled for their abuses.

Despite the Tanzimat high bureaucrats' firmness and caution with respect to not reappointing members of local dynasties, this decision was not straightforwardly implemented. This firmness could not be maintained for smaller administrative units like districts (*kazâ*). For instance, in 1861, in a correspondence between the central state and the governor of Erzurum, it was stated that there were lots of complaints about the müdirs (district administrators) of the sub-districts (*nahiye*) of Erzurum Province and the central government emphasized the necessity of replacing them with centrally-appointed ones.³⁰ Thus, the insistence of the inhabitants of Muş on the return of Şerif Bey does not mean that the inhabitants were content with local notables everywhere. Yet, the inhabitants still preferred them to the "outsiders." In a petition dated 1852, inhabitants argued that although müdirs in some districts were locals, they did not protect them as if they were outsiders.³¹ This points to how commoners identified officials other than local notables as "outsiders" who did not

---

27 Yener Koç, "Nomadic Pastoral Tribes at the Intersection of …," 125.
28 For a detailed account of historicizing the tribal banditry of nomadic and semi-nomadic tribes at the northeastern frontier of the Ottoman Empire, see Koç, "Nomadic Pastoral Tribes at the Intersection of …," 125–136.
29 In an article, Yonca Köksal and Mehmed Polatel present the important economic functions that the nomadic tribes performed during the nineteenth century focusing on the case of meat provisioning of the tribe of Cihanbeyli. This case shows that how tribes played crucial roles in economy rather than disrupting it. Yonca Köksal and Mehmet Polatel, "A tribe as an economic actor: The Cihanbeyli tribe and the meat provisioning of İstanbul in the early Tanzimat era." *New Perspectives on Turkey*, no. 61 (2019), 97–123.
30 BOA. A. MKT. UM. 509/74, 18 Rebiülahir 1278 (23 October 1861).
31 BOA. MVL. 119/58, 15 Şevval 1268 (2 August 1852).

have any interest in the protection of the people. This complaint also shows that although yurtluk-ocaklık holders were exiled to implement fiscal transformations, the implementers of the reforms were nonetheless local notables who had been incorporated into provincial administration.

The inhabitants of Muş continued filing petitions, yet the central government's initial responses did not go beyond replacing the kaimakam. Noting that Habib Efendi, the present kaimakam of Muş, did not contradict the imperial commands, yet as he was indifferent (*gevşekliğinden*), the Meclis-i Vâlâ decided not to punish but to discharge him. Drawing attention to the Kurdish and tribal population of Muş, the Meclis-i Vâlâ concluded that an experienced governor was required. Therefore, the previous kaimakam of Van, İshak Pasha, was appointed as the new kaimakam of Muş with a salary of four thousand five hundred guruş.[32]

6.2   New Administrators, Old Habits

Soon after the appointment of Ishak Pasha, contradictory correspondence arrived from Muş. On one hand, the council of Muş was busy praising Ishak Pasha, emphasizing his insight into the proceedings of the Tanzimat, his industriousness, his ability to collect taxes, and his coordination with the council itself.[33] On the other hand, in a petition in the name of "all the inhabitants of Muş," it was stressed that Ishak Pasha was failing to control the region and protect people due to his old age, his skills notwithstanding. They further emphasized that if the Sublime Porte was forsaking the people of Muş by turning a deaf ear to their grievances, they preferred to be thrown into the sea.[34] Pointing out grievances and their results if they were not ended was a discursive strategy often used in the petitions.[35] However, the council decided that the Kurdish tribes' misdemeanors had increased, not because of the inability of the pasha but because of turmoil in Mutki and Sason. As the Council of Muş reported, the inhabitants of both districts refused to pay their taxes and enlist

---

32 BOA. İ. MVL. 227/7731, 22 Safer 1268 (17 December 1851), BOA. A. AMD. 34/38, 17 Safer 1268 (12 December 1851).

33 "... Tanzîmât-ı Hayriyye-i usûl-i mehâsin-şumûlune ..." BOA. MVL. 251/64, 1 Zilkade 1268 (17 August 1852), BOA. MVL. 252/87, 25 Zilkade 1268 (10 September 1852).

34 BOA. MVL. 121/63, 28 Zilkade 1268 (13 September 1852).

35 Eyal Ginio points to Suraiya Faroqhi's remarks about this strategy: "Faroqhi brings ample evidence of the ability of commoners to successfully challenge local officials and to put an end to what they subjected as injustice and misdemeanors to which they were unfairly subjected." Ginio, "Coping With the State's Agents 'from below'," 41.

in the army.³⁶ Opposition to taxation and conscription in Mutki and Sason troubled central and local authorities in ensuing years, as well.

The petitioners drew a conspicuous analogy between the rule of the previous kaimakam of Muş, Hüseyin Pasha – the account of whom was elaborated in chapter 4 – and the current one. İshak Pasha was performing the state affairs with the notorious kethüda of Hüseyin Pasha, İbrahim Efendi. The efendi was feathering İshak Pasha's and his own nests. Furthermore, they released people who had been jailed by Esad Pasha, the deceased governor of the province of Kurdistan. These people in turn were troubling, injuring, and devastating poor inhabitants of the region. The petitioners pointed out that although their ruler was concerned for the safety and welfare of his subjects, officials were oppressing them believing that this situation would not be heard in remote regions like Muş.³⁷ Such language shows that the subaltern classes were aware to use the discourse of power and hierarchy to their advantage. They differentiated "just ruler" from "unfair," and "corrupt".³⁸

The charges against İshak Pasha and İbrahim Efendi also included nuances regarding the implementation of Tanzimat reforms. Keeping his hands out of state affairs, İshak Pasha employed İbrahim Efendi who in turn administered these affairs in the way to which he was accustomed. Therefore, the people complained that cruelty and extortion had increased to a level even more than in the previous era. Receiving bribes while hearing and settling the cases, and employing Kurdish tribes for tax collection were among the many accusations against İbrahim Efendi. Especially the complaint about taxation is noteworthy, as it points out the difficulty of maintaining the rate of the tithe, which had been set as ten percent by the Tanzimat. Tribal members, taking courage from İbrahim Efendi, threatened to burn villager's grain and fodder if they did not pay an additional three percent on top of the tithe. For instance, they burned grain and grasses in the village of Argevanik, which was once among the yurtluk-ocaklık villages of Hurşid Bey. Although burning grain and straw used to occur in Muş, they were happening tenfold often than before, the petitioners claimed.³⁹ Consul Brant stated that Armenian peasants were in a great distress as most of their stocks of hay that had been stored for winter had been set alight. Besides, their grievances about plunder and ill-treatment had not

---

36 BOA. MVL. 252/87, 25 Zilkade 1268 (10 September 1852).
37 BOA. A. DVN. 82/99, 13 Safer 1269 (26 November 1852).
38 Emphasizing that states are constituted of heterogeneous agencies, Chalcraft points out that the peasantry relates to these agencies in different ways. Chalcraft, "Engaging the State," 306.
39 BOA. A. MKT. UM. 42/94, 17 Zilhicce 1267 (13 October 1851).

been redressed. The consul emphasized that Kurdish tribes ignored the orders of İshak Pasha, whose old age led to his inability to administer the region.[40]

İshak Pasha was mainly charged with employing İbrahim Efendi, who was the actual center of the complaints. The extortionist governance of Hüseyin Pasha along with his steward, İbrahim Efendi in the pre-Tanzimat period was discussed in chapter 4. As a harbinger of the Tanzimat, they had been punished and exiled when the complaints about them reached a peak. Although it is not certain by which means and by whom İbrahim Efendi was released, it is noteworthy that he was entrusted by İshak Pasha to carry out state affairs. In the absence of local notables, İshak Pasha had to rely on a 'local' who had experience in Muş to run the affairs of the sanjak. The inhabitants of Muş identified İbrahim Efendi with the arbitrary taxation, corvée, bribery, and tyranny of the previous era that the Tanzimat proclaimed to eradicate. As a consequence, the people appealed to the Sublime Porte using the language of Tanzimat to remind it of the principles of security of life, property, and honor.

Having complained about the rule of İshak Pasha, the inhabitants of Muş asked for the return of Şerif Pasha. Emphasizing that the sanjak of Muş included more than five hundred villages inhabited by two hundred-fifty thousand people, the Muslim and non-Muslim populations of Muş argued in one petition that they would soon leave their lands, as they could no longer bear the assaults of the semi-nomadic Kurdish tribes. Accordingly, given the absence of Şerif Bey, the tribes had taken the opportunity to increase their oppression, they were stealing and spoiling people's property, and were attacking, violating and murdering them. More importantly, five or six kaimakams had been appointed since the exile of Şerif Bey, yet none could govern the Kurdish tribes as they were not accustomed to them.[41] On the top of this, they underlined that – ganging up with the tribes – İbrahim Efendi had seized their seals and filed petitions praising İshak Pasha's rule. As he was deluding the central government with misinformation, he impeded the security and welfare of the region.[42] Therefore, the milletbaşı of Muş, Simon, argued that the whole population was ready to vouch for Şerif Bey as they had suffered considerably.[43]

Consul Brant also drew attention to the results of the rule of İshak Pasha and İbrahim Efendi. He emphasized that some part of the population had already left for Kars and Georgia, and if the situation continued, "not a single family of the agricultural population," would remain. Not only Christians but

---

40 FO. 708/906, No: 45, Brant to Hugh Rose, Erzurum, December 6, 1852.
41 BOA. MVL. 131/116, 29 Rebiülahir 1269 (9 February 1853).
42 BOA. MVL. 134/49, 28 Cemaziyelevvel 1269 (9 March 1853).
43 BOA. MVL. 133/55, 15 Cemaziyelevvel 1269 (24 February 1853).

also Muslims would emigrate, leaving the area to become the Kurdish tribes' pasturelands. However, the consul also was skeptical about the reappointment of Şerif Bey:

> Were he to be restored, as the people asked, the present part in power would flee; but the Beg would then take their place, and oppress and despoil the people, as he always has done, and thus, the existing evils would be perpetrated. It would be a fatal step to restore Sheriff Beg, but İbrahim Effendy, Leshgo,[44] and the Koordish Chiefs should be exiled, and then with a vigorous and independent Pasha, or even a good Caimakam under Erzeroom, tranquility and confidence would be restored, but nothing short of this will be of any avail. I formerly stated that Ibrahim Effendy had got up the memorial in favor of Sheriff Beg. I knew he was his Kiahia, and his strenuous supporter, but I did not know that they afterwards quarreled and are now sworn enemies. The Memorial was really the petition of the population, urged on by Sheriff Beg's friends. There people, are, however, very short-sighted, and do not know their own interest. They forget, under their present intolerable sufferings, what they bore under Sheriff Beg.[45]

The remarks of Brant are important: the sufferings of the commoners of Muş were so great that they ignored what they had suffered under the rule of local beys. Although both provincial and central authorities were determined to break the influence of local notables, the new kaimakams of Muş were obliged to collaborate with some of its remnants to govern the sanjak. For instance, one reason for the employment of İbrahim Efendi by İshak Pasha was his acquaintance with the region. Apparently, coalitions quickly changed in the region, in spite of their previous amity, Şerif Bey and kethüda İbrahim Efendi became enemies. All of these petitions in favor of Şerif Bey also indicates that despite their exile along with their families, Şerif Bey and his brothers maintained their power in the region – and more importantly in the district council – to some extent.

The extension of the influence of Şerif Bey to the local council was clear in accusations that he was provoking Kurds and tribes of the region in order

---

44   I have not come across an influential Kurdish chief called "Lesgho" or "Lezgo." It is most probably "Rızko," an abbreviation for Rıdvan Agha of the Hesenan tribe.
45   FO. 78/955, No: 1, Brant to Hugh Rose, Erzurum, January 5, 1853.

to again become kaimakam of Muş.⁴⁶ İshak Pasha emphasized the role of the followers of Şerif Bey, some of whom were local council members, in petitions submitted in the name of the inhabitants of Muş. The former registrar, Çerko, Hasan, and Ahmed, who had been dispelled from the council because of their offenses during the conscription lottery (*kurr'a-i şerri*), were the supporters of Şerif Bey.⁴⁷ They collaborated with Sheikh Abdullah, an ally of Şerif Bey, to influence and provoke people to have Şerif Bey appointed as kaimakam. Accordingly, they prepared petitions and had them signed by circulating them in the marketplace.⁴⁸ They gathered in the house of the sheikh and used his influence to send for each council member and get the petitions they had prepared sealed.⁴⁹

İshak Pasha further argued that as the turmoil in Mutki and Sason was disturbing, such behavior created further troubles, preventing the collection of taxes and maintenance of control in the region. Emphasizing that the sheikh was being paid from Muş's local treasury (*mal sandığı*) and that he should not intervene in government affairs, İshak Pasha was of the opinion that the sheikh had been involved in filing petitions and leading the way for insurrection in the region since the time of Habib Efendi, his predecessor.⁵⁰ The emphasis on the role of a local sheikh in local affairs corroborates van Bruinessen's argument regarding the rise in both the number and political weight of sheikhs in Ottoman Kurdistan between 1820 and 1860.⁵¹

According to İshak Pasha, partisanship (*meyyal ve tarafdârlık*) played a crucial role in Muş and that people were accustomed to the nomination and removal of kaimakams by filing petitions. Having emphasized the necessity of breaking this pattern, he argued that as long as the sheikh, together with the council members, was not punished and exiled, provocations would not cease in the sanjak and it would not be properly governed.⁵²

İshak Pasha also claimed a role on behalf of the Armenian population of Muş in petitions favoring Şerif Bey. He argued that although they resented Şerif Bey – as they had neither security of life and property nor the protection of their honor during his rule – Armenian peasants were now asking for

46   BOA. A. MKT. UM. 114/77, 11 Safer 1269 (14 November 1852), BOA. A. MKT. UM. 42/94, 17 Zilhicce 1267 (13 October 1851).
47   Çerko along with Bayram and the *müftü* (religious jurisprudent) of Muş, Fethullah Efendi was accused of assaults against the Armenian peasants of Muş like extortion, burning down the monastery with certain tribal members in a report by the Armenian Patriarchate. BOA. HR.SYS 80/28, 5 Muharrem 1268 (31 October 1851).
48   BOA. İ. MVL. 263/9985, 24 Cemaziyelevvel 1269 (5 March 1853).
49   Ibid.
50   Ibid.
51   Van Bruinessen, Agha, Shaikh, and State, 69.
52   BOA. İ. MVL. 263/9985, 24 Cemaziyelevvel 1269 (5 March 1853).

his return. They convinced priests sent from the Armenian Patriarchate in Istanbul to Çanlı Monastery in Muş to certify their petitions, by offering money if Şerif Bey was allowed to return.[53]

As the new administrator of Muş, İshak Pasha was certainly biased towards the hereditary rulers of Muş. The legitimacy of his own rule was based on the disrepute of Şerif Bey. Nonetheless, these remarks of the pasha imply two important points about the petitions from commoners. On the one hand, petitions signed "poor Muslim and non-Muslim inhabitants of Muş" are not clear of the suspicion that they were counterfeited by local notables. They might be forged, especially when petitions favoring or disfavoring existing and previous administrators of Muş were taken into consideration. Nevertheless, even if influential people were manipulating the peasantry's discontent, as Chalcraft argues, the claims of peasants were regarded as "politically relevant; otherwise there would be no need to mobilize them."[54] On this basis, petitions show the influence and discursive strategies of the peasantry in local politics as they were negotiating the terms of the appointment and discharge of kaimakams. It is noteworthy that petitioners often emphasized that unless their grievances were redressed, the population would decrease and tax collection would be interrupted. They were conscious of the fact that the extraction of their surplus, taxation, was at the heart of Ottoman rule. As Chalcraft emphasizes that "there was no surer way to attract government intervention than to note that cultivation was in danger of being disrupted."[55] Furthermore, that petitions only show elite interests cannot be generalized, as most of them were delivered in person to the imperial capital by agents whom the peasants of Muş had chosen from among themselves.[56]

As for İshak Pasha, in a nutshell he denied all the accusations against him and underscored Şerif Bey's and his supporters' provocations in the petitions disfavoring him. Similarly, Şerif Bey, who was interrogated in Istanbul, rejected his role in these petitions by swearing an oath.[57] In those days Şerif Bey and his brothers were also directly petitioning to be pardoned and to be allowed to return. They even negotiated a deal that the women and children be allowed to return, on the condition that Şerif Bey and his elder son remained in Istanbul.

---

53 Ibid.
54 Chalcraft, "Engaging the State," 308.
55 Ibid., 310. In the same vein, Cengiz Kırlı points out that the tone of the common people of Ivranya in their petitions became reproachful and threatening when complaints about the governor, Hüseyin Pasha, were not redressed. Cengiz Kırlı, "İvranyalılar, Hüseyin Paşa ve Tasvir-i Zulüm," Toplumsal Tarih, no. 195 (2010): 9.
56 Chalcraft also emphasizes that "these petitions were more than simply the bogus products of powerful notable schemes." Chalcraft, "Engaging the State," 308.
57 BOA. A. MKT. UM. 42/94, 17 Zilhicce 1267 (13 October 1851).

Besides, Hurşid Bey was asking for a temporary permit to carry out businesses in Muş. Whether Şerif Bey really mobilized his followers in Muş and had them forge such petitions did not come to light. Nevertheless, this possibility damaged their demands to return to their homeland.

Consequently, neither the petitions of peasants insisting on the reappointment of Şerif Bey as kaimakam of Muş, nor those of the family claiming their rights to lands were recognized. Far from again appointing Şerif Bey as kaimakam of Muş, the central authorities did not even give temporary permission to family members to return. The reason for this caution was the possibility of further trouble in the region for the authorities, given that the family's supporters had played principal roles in filing the petitions. Nevertheless, grumbling among the commoners of Muş about practices against "the soul of the Tanzimat" was heard. It was decided to punish İbrahim Efendi and never employ him in the affairs of the country again due to complaints about his tyranny and extortion.[58]

The governor of Kurdistan, Mehmed Ragıb Pasha[59], also noted that as İshak Pasha did not get along with the inhabitants and that they bore grudges against each other, his rule in Muş had become controversial. In addition to the petitions of locals, the Armenian Patriarchate and the director of the quarantine in Van also reported that İshak Pasha was failing to control the sanjak and provide security. Thus, it was obvious that as long as the pasha maintained his post, the inhabitants would keep on petitioning. Therefore, İshak Pasha was replaced by Mesrur Bey, the *müderris* (professor of religious education) of Lofça.[60] Yet, again, a foreigner who was alien to the region and its people.

The kaimakams of Muş changed several times after the exile of the dynasty of Muş. However, reactions against the inability of appointed kaimakams to control Kurdish tribes, prevent over taxation, and keep order and security resulted in the necessity of further solutions. In a report, the murahhasa of the Armenians drew attention to difficulties and problems stemming from the distance between Muş and the center of the province of Kurdistan, Diyarbekir, which was sixty hours away. Such remoteness not only encouraged Kurdish tribes to increase their oppressiveness – stealing and burning goods, killing people, and violating honor – but it also prevented the carrying out of

---

58 BOA. İ. MVL. 263/9985, 24 Cemaziyelevvel 1269 (5 March 1853).
59 After the death of Esad Pasha in 1851, Abdi Pasha governed the province of Kurdistan for a year. Hakan Özoğlu, *Kurdish Notables and the Ottoman State: Evolving Identities, Compating Loyalties, and Shifting Boundaries*, (Albany: State University of New York Press), 62. Then, Mehmed Ragıb Pasha was appointed as the governor of Kurdistan in September, 1852. BOA. A. MKT. MHM 49/101, 27 Zilkade 1268 (September 12, 1852).
60 Ibid., BOA. A. MKT. UM. 131/19, 29 Cemaziyelahir 1269 (April 9, 1853).

government affairs. Therefore, he suggested Muş, as it was previously, should be attached to the province of Erzurum, which was only twenty hours away. Thereby, he emphasized, the security of life and property and the protection of honor along with the principles of the Tanzimat-ı Hayriyye would become a reality for the inhabitants of Muş.[61] This demand was found reasonable as the sanjak of Muş was detached from Kurdistan Province and attached to Erzurum effective March 1269 (March 1853).[62]

The governance of İshak Pasha importantly shows the limits of centrally-appointed governors in a region situated on the frontier and inhabited by nomadic and semi-nomadic groups. İshak Pasha, in spite of being an experienced bureaucrat, failed to ameliorate the relations between the peasantry and the tribes to a great extent. More importantly, as a statesman nominated to implement Tanzimat reforms, he collaborated with individuals like İbrahim Efendi who continued the regime of over taxation, corvée, extortion, and oppression that had been banned by the Tanzimat. Therefore, it is possible to imagine the desperation of the inhabitants of Muş while filing petitions, dispatching delegates to the imperial center, and asking for the return of exiled local notables. It is possible that some petitions were penned with the encouragement of the allies of Şerif Bey. It was also not extraordinary to file petitions favoring or disfavoring an official. Yet the contents of these documents significantly show the oppression, over taxation, extortion, and corvée that the inhabitants suffered. In the same vein, desperately requesting the return of their traditional leaders does not mean that they had lived in harmony free of any abuse under their earlier rule; rather, it implies that the conditions had become aggravated in their absence.

Although Istanbul recognized the local people of Muş's demands, punished İbrahim Efendi and discharged İshak Pasha, and attached Muş to Erzurum, the grievances did not dissipate. The newly appointed governor, Mesrur Bey, soon passed away and was replaced with Veli Agha.[63] Paying attention to the tension (*galeyan*) between the Kurdish tribes and Armenian peasants in Muş, the Meclis-i Vâlâ discussed that despite his knowledge about the locality, Veli Agha was not a pasha. Rank as such was important to be influential over the

---

61 "... Tanzîmât-ı Hayriyye usûl-i mu'adelet-şümûlunun es-i esâsı olan mâl û cân ve 'ırzlarından tamâmen husûl-i emniyyet ve maslahatca dâhi ..." BOA. İ. MVL. 263/9985, 24 Cemaziyelevvel 1269 (5 March 1853).

62 Ibid., BOA. A. MKT. UM. 136/65, 23 Şaban 1269 (1 Haziran 1853). Similarly, it was reported that following petitions of its Muslim and non-Muslim inhabitants, Hınıs was separated from the province of Kurdistan and attached to Erzurum, as it had formerly been. BOA. A. MKT. MVL. 60/33, 16 Rebiülevvel 1269 (27 January 1853).

63 BOA. MVL. d. 2, 26 Ramazan 1269 (3 July 1853), p. 59.

inhabitants of the region – so it was necessary to appoint a higher-ranking person to Muş. Thus, Kenan Pasha, the son-in-law of the late Esad Pasha, was seen as fitting to be the kaimakam of Muş.[64]

Nonetheless, the grievances of the people reached to another phase soon afterward. With the outbreak of the Crimean War, Muş became one of the main suppliers for the army assembled in Kars.[65] Muş's geographical peculiarity greatly shaped the policies of both central and local authorities. This peculiarity affected the negotiation terms of local notables. The petitions of the inhabitants of Muş shed light on the effects of the Crimean War on the locality of Muş more broadly. Especially the accusations against Ömer Pasha, the kaimakam of Muş during part of the war, depict the suffering of the people which doubled with the requirement that they supply provisions for the army.

6.3   Socio-Economic Results of the Crimean War for Muş's Locality

Ottoman society was informed of the empire's declaration of war against Russia in an article of news published in *Takvim-i Vekayi*, the official newspaper, on 4 October 1853.[66] The main reason for the declaration was Russia's invasion of the Danubian Principalities under the command of General Gorchakov in July 1853 and its rejection of an ultimatum to evacuate presented by Ömer Pasha, the commander-in-chief of the Rumelian Army. The war started on one hand in Rumelia, where troops had crossed the Danube, and on the other in Erzurum and Kars where provincial troops were transferred to the southern Caucasus. At the same time, the Ottoman fleet sailed along the Black Sea and anchored in Sinop. Thus, the war continued along Danube, in Black Sea and in the Caucasus. France and Britain allied with the Ottoman Empire, declared war against Russia in March 1854.[67]

The battles on the Caucasian Front are significant for this study as its socio-economic results determined the politics of the province of Erzurum. Especially, financing the war laid a burden on poor inhabitants of the region.

---

64   BOA. MVL. d. 2, 21 Şevval 1269 (19 July 1853), p. 90. However, soon after, with the breaking out of the Crimean War, Kenan Pasha was asked to return to Siirt, and Osman Pasha, the former governor of Kars, was appointed to Muş with an increase in salary amounting to ten thousand guruş. BOA. MVL. 265/36, 5 Rebiülevvel 1270 (5 January 1854).

65   BOA. MVL. 265/36, 5 Rebiülevvel 1270 (5 January 1854).

66   Candan Badem, *The Ottoman Crimean War, 1853–1856* (Leiden: Brill, 2010), 99; Fuat Andıç and Süphan Andıç, Kırım Savaşı Ali Paşa ve Paris Antlaşması (Istanbul: Eren Yayıncılık, 2002), 13.

67   Shaw and Shaw, History of the Ottoman Empire, 2, 138.

Consul Brant describes the situation of the villages near army headquarters as miserable and deserted. Grain and agricultural equipment was collected for the army. If any peasants were left behind in these villages, they had few oxens to plough their lands or seed to sow them. Agents who were sent to the villages to collect grain demanded double the amount required by the government from the peasants. The villages who bribed the agents could be exempted from providing their share in the contribution of grain.[68] Candan Badem argues that the burden of the war was shouldered by poor villagers rather than the well-off. Accordingly, in Erzurum, soldiers were quartered in poor villages as the rich offered bribes to be exempted from this obligation.[69] By the same token, the conditions of soldiers themselves were dreadful as described by Badem.

The Ottoman armies in Kars, Erzurum and Batum spent the winter of 1853–1854 in very unhealthy conditions. They were scarcely fed and badly clothed, quartered in poorly heated, unventilated, filthy, crowded inns (khans) or houses in conditions ripe for the spread of contagious diseases like typhus. 18,000 to 20,000 soldiers died from disease and malnutrition.[70]

6.3.1 The Case of Ömer Pasha

Gevranlızâde Ömer Pasha was appointed as the kaimakam of Muş during the Crimean War. His maladministration during the war later led to an investigation. His story serves as an example of the socio-economic effects of the war on inhabitants on the eastern periphery of the empire. Ömer Pasha was from one of the local families of Diyarbekir. As kaimakam of Dersim when the Crimean War broke out, Ömer Pasha was called to serve in the Imperial Army.[71] After two years, he was charged with imposing discipline on Kurdish tribes in Muş, the assaults and tyranny of which local people suffered heavily. His efforts during the suppression of the turmoil created by Mirza Agha of Huyud were greatly appreciated. Mirza Agha (the father of the notorious Musa Bey)[72] assaulted certain villages of Huyud, killing people and seizing property. Ömer Pasha

---

68 FO 78/1115, "No: 20, "Report on the Pashalık of Erzurum for 1854" Erzurum, April 22, 1855.
69 Badem, The Ottoman Crimean War, 292.
70 Ibid., 190.
71 BOA. MVL. 304/49, 3 Cemaziyelevvel 1273 (30 December 1856).
72 Musa Bey of Huyud was infamous with his atrocities against the Armenian peasants of Muş in the 1880s and especially with kidnapping an Armenian girl from Bulanık/Muş named Gülizar. For the details, see Musa Şaşmaz, *Kürt Musa Bey Olayı, 1883–1890* (İstanbul: Kitabevi, 2004); Arménouhie Kévonian, *Gülizar'ın Kara Düğünü*, trans. Aslı Türker and Ece Erbay, (Istanbul: Aras Yayıncılık, 2015).

successfully captured and sent him and his men to Istanbul. In return, as a reward, he was appointed as the new kaimakam of Muş.⁷³

Not surprisingly, the nomination of Ömer Pasha to Muş was at first appreciated in a petition signed in the name of all the *ulema* (Muslim scholars), *meşayih* (sheikhs) and "poor inhabitants" of Muş. It was argued that he successfully undertook and implemented all the requirements of the Tanzimat, tax collection, and the transport of provisions demanded by the army fairly and without oppressing people. Another major aspect of his administration was his ability to control the region and discipline the Kurdish tribes.⁷⁴

In fact, such a report praising the rule of Ömer Pasha was the same as ones penned for previous kaimakams of Muş. In the same vein, news of discontent would arrive immediately afterward. The Consul of Erzurum, Mr. Brant, defined Ömer Pasha – who bribed the governor of Kars, İsmail Pasha, in order to be appointed as the kaimakam of Muş – as "rapacious." Besides, the consul described the pasha as someone able to make use of every opportunity to extort, so the inhabitants were disgruntled in reaction to him.⁷⁵ It did not take long for the pasha to be summoned to Erzurum to be questioned by the *Meclis-i Kebir* (Grand Council) about the complaints of local people. Meanwhile, Ziya Bey sat in for him to continue the supply of provisions to the army, as the war was continuing.⁷⁶

According to a register prepared and submitted by nine informants (*muhbir*), Ömer Pasha was accused of not paying for supplies and other commodities the inhabitants of Muş had provided. The pasha denied the allegations arguing that he had paid for some, and for the arrears he had provided owners with bills of debt. However, the informants rejected Ömer Pasha's defense, arguing that he had not distributed any bills at all. Therefore, it was decided to confront the parties and examine the issue in detail through local councils. Nevertheless, in Muş, more immediate duties remained like supervising the transportation of provisions to the army and dealing with cavalry regiments that had already arrived in Muş. Ömer Pasha was not allowed to return to carry out such duties as he was on trial, so İsmail Pasha, the mutasarrıf of Kars, was employed both to temporarily govern Muş and carry out a fair investigation of the case of Ömer Pasha.⁷⁷ Needless to say, the inhabitants of Muş, meanwhile,

---

73 BOA. A. MKT. UM. 240/98, 21 Şevval 1272 (25 June 1856), BOA. A. MKT. MVL. 72/36, 8 Şaban 1271 (26 April 1855).
74 BOA. A. MKT. UM. 200/26, 19 Şevval 1271 (5 July 1855).
75 FO 78/1115, No: 20, "Report on the Pashalık of Erzurum for 1854" Erzurum, April 22, 1855.
76 BOA. MVL. 294/75, 16 Rebiülevvel 1272 (26 November 1855).
77 BOA. A. MKT. MVL. 78/70, 3 Receb 1272 (9 April 1856).

were demanding the replacement of Ömer Pasha with Şerif Bey.[78] As will be discussed, the impact of the local beys of Muş on the case would be an important part of Ömer Pasha's defense.

The ad interim kaimakam of Muş İsmail Pasha had two main tasks to carry out: continuation of the flow of the supplies to the army and the thorough investigation of the accusations against Ömer Pasha. The pasha was also entrusted with the discipline of Kurdish tribes, especially that of the Hesenan. However, the foremost task of İsmail Pasha was to finish the investigation of Ömer Pasha before he returned to Kars.[79] Therefore the pasha assembled a special council (*meclis-i mahsus*) to examine the allegations against Ömer Pasha and his collaborators.

As İsmail Pasha reported, the poor, and oppressed inhabitants of Muş who had suffered from the extortion of Ömer Pasha appeared before him to demand justice. The claims against Ömer Pasha ranged from his forcibly taking food and beverage for his own house, without paying, to embezzlement of money while settling debts between individuals. Moreover, İsmail Pasha argued that mismanagement and wrongdoings of Ömer Pasha lead to deterioration in the conditions in which the people of Muş were living in as he left the ground to the leaders of Kurdish tribes and administrators of some sub-districts.[80]

Notwithstanding, Ömer Pasha filed petitions arguing that the sanjak of Muş was close to the army barracks, was the first store (*birinci anbarı*) of the army, and that the money (namely *iane-i cihadiye*, supplementary tax for the war) collected from inhabitants was substantial. He emphasized that he paid utmost attention in order not to harass people while carrying out government tasks. All the complaints were from the people who held grudges against him (*ashâb-ı ağrâz*), so colonel Salih Zeki Bey, who was in the second regiment of the regular cavalry in Muş should be consulted to get sound information about his deeds.[81]

After İsmail Pasha's return to Kars, the governor of Erzurum continued to carry out and conclude the investigation of Ömer Pasha.[82] Then, Ömer Pasha and his complainants were confronted and examined in the presence of İsmail Pasha; consequently, a report was submitted by the Council of Muş consisting

---

78 "... pâşâ-yı mûmâileyhin 'azliyle yerine Muşlu Şerif beğin kâimakâm ta'yîn olunması ahâli-i merkûme tarafından bi'l-i'lâm ve mahâzır inhâ ve istida' kılınmış olmasıyla ..." BOA. A. MKT. 231/15, 24 Receb 1272 (30 April 1856).
79 BOA. A. MKT. UM. 241/25, 23 Şevval 1272 (27 June 1856).
80 BOA. A. MKT. UM. 236/24, 2 Ramazan 1272 (7 May 1856).
81 BOA. A. MKT. UM. 240/98, 21 Şevval 1272 (25 June 1856).
82 BOA. A. MKT. UM. 241/25, 23 Şevval 1272 (27 June 1856).

of twenty-five clauses describing Ömer Pasha's offences and listing the items he had unjustly received or embezzled.[83]

Examining the allegations against Ömer Pasha, enables us to generally depict the peculiarities of embezzlement or corruption in which administrators could become involved in the nineteenth century. In the register attached to the report, the grain and other items Ömer Pasha had taken, the amount he had paid, and the arrears were shown village by village. His total debt was sixty-three thousand one hundred five guruş. Moreover, registers based on claimants' accounts were compared with the register submitted by the pasha himself. Most of the debt was from grain and other goods taken, either for the army, or for his own house. Actually, the main accusation against him was extortion. It was argued that unlike all of other kaimakams of Muş who had bought their supplies in the market where all kinds of goods were available, Ömer Pasha bought nothing from the market and sent *zaptiehs* to the villages to take his supplies from the inhabitants.[84] Similarly, bills of debt villagers were provided with by Ömer Pasha were falsified; either the numbers of the villages or the amounts of the supplies were registered below their real number or value. As the claimants alleged, zaptiehs typically delivered the bills to the pasha instead of giving them to the suppliers. The Council of Muş reported that the testimonies of zaptiehs, during their interrogation, proved the claims of the inhabitants despite Ömer Pasha's denial.[85]

Furthermore, Ömer Pasha employed the Ilıcanlu tribe from his homeland to transport provisions from the villages to army headquarters, despite the sufficient number of zaptiehs. On top of that, the pasha together with zaptiehs and armed tribal members in his company spent nights in the houses of the villagers of Muş and provided the households with bills that were far below the real costs of their stay.[86] Apart from pointing out Ömer Pasha's corruption, such accounts emphasized the continuation of forced labor that was supposed to have been abolished with the Tanzimat and showed the extent of the reach of the reforms. However, complaints like forced labor and the involvement of

---

83 BOA. İ. MVL. 433/19083, 15 Şevval 1272 (19 June 1856).
84 For the collection of the taxes with the aid of military forces and its results, see Nadir Özbek, "Policing the Countryside: Gendarmes of the Late-Nineteenth-Century Ottoman Empire (1876–1908)" *International Journal of Middle East Studies*, no. 40 (2008): 47–67; Nadir Özbek, "'Anadolu Islahatı,' 'Ermeni Sorunu,' ve Vergi Tahsildarlığı," Tarih ve Toplum Yeni Yaklaşımlar, no. 9 (2009): 59–85.
85 "… lede'l suâl merkûm zabtiyeleri dâhi ahâlî merkûmenin ifâdât-ı vâki'sini ba'dehâ (…) tasdîk ve temhîr …" BOA. İ. MVL. 433/19083, 15 Şevval 1272 (19 June 1856).
86 Ibid.

Kurdish tribes in tax collection were not specific to Ömer Pasha; the previous kaimakams of Muş were accused of similar acts.

In addition to forced labor, Ömer Pasha continued to collect extra taxes in murder and pecuniary cases with the title of the kaimakam of the sanjak. The commoners of Muş complained that he extorted them at every possible opportunity. Moreover, he appointed his men or relatives as administrators of sub-districts or registered them as zaptieh, as he did for his son. Consequently, due to his atrocities, the peasants of twenty-three villages had dispersed and the decrease in the population in turn led to a reduction in tax revenues. According to the report of the council, however, some villagers were persuaded to return to their lands under the influence of İsmail Pasha.[87]

The interrogation of Ömer Pasha and his confrontation with the claimants against him were carried out by a special council constituted and led by İsmail Pasha, along with the members of Muş's local council, who were also among the witnesses. The report and attached register were prepared and submitted to the Sublime Porte demanding a decision that Ömer Pasha pay his debts to the inhabitants of Muş.[88] Although it was reported that Ömer Pasha, who was held in Erzurum during the investigation of the case, remained silent when the accusations were read to him during the interrogation or denied them, immediately afterwards he filed many petitions nullifying the report and the register of the local council, and justifying himself.

Ömer Pasha argued that the allegations were arranged by members of the Muş Council who nursed grudges against him. More importantly, he claimed the notables of Muş, that is the family of Şerif Bey from among the Alaaddin Pashazades, played a role in accusations against him. Emphasizing that his duty was hard as Muş was inhabited by tribes and that he had been careful while collecting provisions for the Imperial Army, without pressuring the common people, Ömer Pasha asserted that his success bothered the notables of Muş and those notables were of the opinion that their existence in the region was indispensable – that without them the sanjak could not be governed.[89]

---

87 "… pâşâ-yı mûmâileyhin mugâyir-i mu'adelet-i seniyye olarak vâki' olan envâ'i zulm ve ta'addîsine mebnî Muş kazâsına tâbi' yirmi üç pâre kârye ahâli-i meskûnesi kadertâb olamıyarak ahâli-i merkûme herbiri bir tarafa nakl ve firâr iderek kurâ-i ahâli-i muharrere hâli ve emvâl-i matlûbe-i seniyye mua'ttal kâlmış olduğu …" BOA. İ. MVL. 433/19083, 15 Şevval 1272 (19 June 1856).

88 Ibid.

89 "… aşâir ve kabâilden 'ibâret olan mahalin bu vechile hüsn-i idâresine muvaffakıyet-i bendegânem livâ-i mezbûrun idâresi birâz vaktden berû ellerinden nez' olunmuş ve dâimen oraca kendülerinin lüzûm-ı vücûd-ı me'mûriyyetleri esbâbının taharrîsinde bulunmış olan Muş ümerâsının efkâr-ı zâtiyelerine mugâyır …" BOA. MVL. 301/93, 28 Muharrem 1273 (28 September 1856).

Murad Bey had been allowed to settle in Erzurum with his family in the early months of 1855,[90] and Ömer Pasha drew attention to the reality that the return of Murad Bey encouraged the family's networks which had already reached the local council. Those local members, Ömer Pasha argued, were hateful towards him, as they could not find opportunities to be involved in extortion during his term of office, as they were accustomed to.[91]

Therefore, Ömer Pasha accused council members, namely, İbrahim Efendi, the registrar, and Bayram, Cergü, Hasan, Selim, and Halid Aghas of plotting against him. Having collaborated with some village headmen (*muhtar*) said council members arranged informants from villages, as they had wanted to avoid suspicion, and sent those informants to İsmail Pasha immediately after his arrival in Muş to complain about Ömer Pasha. Thus, the report and register sent by the Council of Muş were not the outcome of a trial, but rather just the testimonies of said informants, claimed Ömer Pasha. Therefore, the pasha urgently requested that the case be reheard by the Erzurum Provincial Council (*Meclis-i Kebir-i Eyâlet*) and the Temporary Military Council (*Meclis-i Muvakkat-i Askeri*).[92]

As to the allegations, Ömer Pasha emphasized that the market of Muş did not always store sufficient goods, contrary to statements in the report, and that therefore he had to purchase some goods from the villages. He also added that as he had been in a financial difficulty because of the war, he had paid for some goods through moneylenders and provided suppliers with bills of debt for the arrears. However, the pasha stressed that the values of the items in the register were recorded as four times higher than they really were. Moreover, the goods were bought in the harvest season and when such goods were abundant the prices were lower. His debt had been fixed according to current market rate (*rayiç-i belde*) at that time. However, his debt in the register had been based on calculations, when the goods were rare and the prices were higher.[93]

Along the same lines, Ömer Pasha complained that goods that the zaptiehs had taken for themselves were also charged to him. The pasha argued that if anyone had complained about such abuse by the zaptiehs, he could have prevented it. He also added that he had warned officials several times not to take goods without payment (*meccânen*), so he could not be held responsible for the debts of the zaptiehs. Thus, rather than the sixty thousand guruş registered

90 BOA. A. MKT. NZD. 132/22, 23 Cemaziyelevvel 1271 (11 February 1855), BOA. A. MKT. UM. 183/20, 3 Cemaziyelahir 1271 (21 February 1855).
91 BOA. MVL. 304/10, 18 Rebiülahir 1273 (16 December 1856), BOA. MVL. 306/44, 12 Cemaziyelahir 1273 (7 February 1857).
92 BOA. MVL. 302/21, 15 Safer 1273 (15 October 1856).
93 BOA. MVL. 302/29, 16 Safer 1273 (16 October 1856).

to him as arrears, Ömer Pasha argued that his total debt was just four thousand guruş.⁹⁴

Ömer Pasha also consolidated his arguments by attaching the documents provided by the revenue officer (*serkâtib-i mal*), Hasan, and moneylenders of Muş (*sarraf-ı sandık*), Ovannes and Bedros, indicating that he had no debt. However, Ömer Pasha also needed the affirmation of the Council of Muş that he had no debt in order to submit his case to the central treasury and prove his innocence. Because council members were supposedly the advocates of the notables of Muş, he could not get the affirmation he needed.⁹⁵

Claiming that he was aggrieved and insulted, Ömer Pasha asserted that what he was going through had happened to all the other kaimakams of Muş for many years. Council members, upon the provocation of Muş's notables, had been striven to create the impression that no one other than those notables could govern Muş. However, the pasha argued, if said council members did not stir up trouble, the sanjak could be governed properly. Therefore, Ömer Pasha concluded with the warning that the region would get out of control if those council members were not disciplined.⁹⁶

Ömer Pasha's insistence resulted in another hearing of the case within a short time. The previous report and register, prepared during the time of İsmail Pasha, were sent to Arif Pasha, the current governor of Erzurum, to be reinvestigated. For the reexamination, claimants were summoned to Erzurum. However, reports indicate that the claimants were reluctant to show up. In the end, their deputies, the deputy-murahhasa of Çanlı Monastery, Agob, and the informants for certain villages – the *kahya* (stewards) of the villages of Norşen, Kömes, Argevanik, and Ziyaret – arrived in Erzurum where Saroyan, the murahhasa of Catholic community, joined them. According to the report of Provincial Council of Erzurum, the deputies could provide no proof when the content of the previous report was read to them clause by clause. Instead, after negotiation, these deputies declared that they would give up their claims if Ömer Pasha would not file a complaint of honor and expenditure against them,⁹⁷ (the pasha had been arguing that he had incurred costs as he had been in Erzurum for many years, in vain, and that he was also insulted because of accusations, as well).⁹⁸

---

94   Ibid.
95   Ibid.
96   Ibid.
97   Ibid.
98   BOA. MVL. 314/42, 23 Muharrem 1274 (13 September 1857).

Consequently, both parties were reconciled and their representatives certified that the villagers were withdrawing all their claims about Ömer Pasha.[99] Both the Provincial Council of Erzurum and the Temporary Military Council underscored that not all among the Muslim and non-Muslim populations of Muş had complained about Ömer Pasha. Rather, it had mostly been Armenian villagers in the Muş Plain, who were exhausted from supplying provisions to the Imperial Army during the Crimean War.[100] In line with this, Ömer Pasha had been very strict about supply and transportation of the provisions, so the villagers had become aggrieved and offended, and complained about the Pasha.[101] Therefore, as reported, the claimants' allegations were groundless. They had acted upon the provocation and persuasion of persons who nursed grudges against the pasha.[102] In a nutshell, the Provincial Council of Erzurum decided that all of the complaints stemmed from the exhaustion and hatred of the villagers of the plain, which council members turned into an opportunity to dismiss Ömer Pasha and ensure the return of Muş's notables.

The case of Ömer Pasha continued for almost two years, and in the end he was cleared of all accusations. The exculpation of the pasha was controversial. It is possible to believe that the Pasha was cleared partly because people withdrew their claims against him, as they probably feared that the pasha would file complaints against them. Furthermore, the bills taken from the moneylenders of Muş proving that he owed no debt to the local treasury did not mean that he had not taken goods from the peasants, without payment or by the force of zaptiehs. His spending nights in the villages with his men and horses was a burden, showing the continuation of corvée. Thus, while his opponents on the Council of Muş were influential in distorting the facts, not all of the accusations were groundless.

However, this case has further implications for the post-Tanzimat conditions in Muş. The prominence of provincial and district councils in the frame of the Tanzimat reform program has already been discussed in the previous chapters. As highlighted previously, the collaborators of exiled traditional rulers served

---

99 BOA. MVL. 313/40, 14 Muharrem 1274 (4 September 1857). "… 'umûm de'âvîden birbirlerinin zimmetlerini ibrâ-i 'âmm ile ibrâ ve iskât itmiş olduklarını …" BOA. MVL. 314/72, 14 Safer 1274 (4 October 1857).

100 BOA. MVL. 315/46, 7 Rebiülevvel 1274 (26 October 1857). "… da'va-yı mezbûrenin mücerred tarafeynin yekdiğere incinmesinden neş'et itmiş bir şey olduğu livâ-i mezbûrun sâir kazâsı ve kurâsı ahâlî-i İslâm ve re'âyâsı taraflarından ednâ bir iddiâ' vâki' olmıyarak yalnız mezkûr ova kurâsında mutavattın olan Hristiyân taraflarından vuku' bulmasıyla dâhi bedîhî ve meczûm bulunmuşdur …" BOA. A. MKT. UM. 254/2, 21 Muharrem 1273 (21 September 1856).

101 BOA. MVL. 313/40, 14 Muharrem 1274 (4 September 1857).

102 BOA. MVL. 315/46, 7 Rebiülevvel 1274 (26 October 1857).

on the district councils which were the principal institutions "in charge of local administration including supervision of taxation, maintenance of public order, conscription, land survey, waqf administration, and public works."[103] Furthermore, local councils worked as the places of "dispute resolution" where both the abuses of the local officials were resolved – until the establishment of *Nizamiye Mahkemeleri* ('secular' courts) – and criminal cases were heard.[104] Therefore, with their exclusion from local politics, the power of the Kurdish beys was curtailed to a great extent, others among the local notables – that is, less influential aghas, some of whom were the relatives of the exiled beys, took part in the Tanzimat's institutions.

Likewise, the case points to peculiarities regarding the social landscape of Muş. It is a fact that the villages in the plain were more productive also because of their location in the fertile plain. Not only were they the principal source of supplies during extraordinary circumstances like war, but they also suffered from extortion. It is noteworthy that the deputies sent to Erzurum to testify were from the villages that Muş's notables had held as yurtluk-ocaklık. This shows the material power of the exiled beys, as these were the most fertile lands in Muş. But the fact that these villages were mostly inhabited by Armenians also provides clues about tensions between the Armenian peasantry and the Kurdish aghas in Muş, which would become more contentious in the following years. In fact, reports from the region dated in the 1850s drew attention to the fact that the inhabitants of Muş – especially the Christian population – were being oppressed to a great extent.[105] Although in the beginning the local authorities intended to calm the Sublime Porte by emphasizing that they had received no complaints about oppression from non-Muslim subjects, district administrators, council members, and Muslim and non-Muslim notables would be at the top of the agenda in ensuing years due to their assaults on the Armenian peasantry.[106]

Although Ömer Pasha was cleared of the accusations against him, he could not be reappointed to Muş. Having heard that a new kaimakam had been appointed, the local council, the *meşayih* and the *ulema*, and the Muslim and Christian notables of Muş filed a petition to extend the term of İsmail Pasha in lieu of a new kaimakam. Depicting a picture of Muş of post-Tanzimat, the petitioners argued that the sanjak had not been yet been brought under control

---

103   Akiba, "The Local Councils," 179.
104   Ibid.
105   BOA. MVL. 300/89, 29 Şevval 1272 (3 July 1856).
106   For instance, the general-in-chief of the Anatolian army argued that despite news that non-Muslim populations in Muş and Bitlis were being oppressed, he had heard no complaint about the issue. BOA. A. MKT. UM. 157/38, 21 Şaban 1270 (19 May 1854).

and that it was a part of Kurdistan (emphasizing its sensitive geography). On top of that, the tribes living there were numerous and scattered, so it was impossible to successfully govern the sanjak through the kaimakamlık, as the cases of previous kaimakams, including Ömer Pasha, demonstrated. Besides, this petition is significant in showing how the situation in Muş resembled the pre-Tanzimat period.

> Honorable people, poor inhabitants, and commoners have been tormented and have suffered extreme troubles for a long time. Before the Tanzimat, they were exposed to all kinds of atrocity and torture, [yet] in 1266, the late Esad Pasha also dropped by here and, in fact, carried out many reforms in the sanjak of Muş. And the vicious tribes were restrained and thanks to His Majesty our well-being was largely provided for. Nevertheless, the pasha did not stay long and as soon as he departed, whether because of the incapability of the kaimakams or not, matters reverted to their previous course. Thus, due to the trials and judgments carried out during the governance of Esad Pasha, certain tribal leaders and bandits [were offended] and bore grudges and wanted to take revenge, so much more mischief occurred than before. In the end, the kaimakams also could not discipline them and so the kaimakams have been changed several times and this situation resulted in the increase of the torture and banditry. Everyone is tired of life and all the sanjak is in a tumultuous situation.[107]

The rest of this chapter will focus on two interrelated issues. On one hand, the financial matters of the Crimean War continued, and on the other, oppression by a coalition of council members, kaimakams, müdirs, moneylenders, and tax-farmers of the peasants of Muş increased day by day, which in turn resulted in depopulation especially among Armenian peasants. Meanwhile, being at the end of the Crimean War, the imperial capital was busy with the promulgation of a new reform edict, the Islahat Fermanı, which heralded an important phase in the reform era of the Ottoman Empire, targeting the equality of the Muslim and non-Muslim populations.

6.3.1.1 The Edict of Reform and Its Results for the Armenian Population

The concern of European powers regarding the situation of non-Muslim communities of the empire had partially determined Ottoman bureaucrats' reform efforts for the amelioration of the conditions of the empire's subjects. Therefore, the issue of reform occupied Ottoman bureaucrats both before and

---

107 BOA. MVL. 300/89, 29 Şevval 1272 (3 July 1856).

during the Crimean War. Although it was the Islahat Fermanı that formulated Muslim and non-Muslim equality in the empire, the issue of the rights and privileges of the non-Muslim population was already among the four articles discussed at the Vienna Conference, which had been held in March 1855 to discuss the peace protocol.[108] The Ottoman Empire declared The Edict of Reform on 18 February 1856, and the issue of reform also constituted the ninth article of the Treaty of Paris ratified on 30 March 1856. Even though the Ottoman delegate Ali Pasha was reluctant to do so.[109] This article emphasized that the signatories would support and be respectful of the Islahat Fermanı that had been promulgated by the Ottoman bureaucrats immediately before the peace negotiations.[110]

Promising Muslim and non-Muslim equality, the Edict of Reform was one of the milestones of the long nineteenth century reform program. In particular, amendments about the poll-tax (*cizye*), abrogating the zımmî status of non-Muslims and their conscription in the army were noteworthy. However, as Frederick F. Anscombe rightly argues, the Ottoman governments after 1858 had little intention of ruling the empire in a manner "blind to religion."[111] The replacement of poll-tax with *bedel-i askeriyye* (the money paid for exemption from military service) might be an example of this fact. The poll-tax was abolished, yet anyone who could not serve in the army would pay a tax called the *iane-i askeriyye* or *bedel-i askeriyye*. As it was the non-Muslims rather than the Muslims who paid bedel-i askeriyye, it was a reformulation of the poll-tax. The problems regarding the recruitment of non-Muslims would continue until the downfall of the empire. Similarly, the admission of non-Muslims to civil and military schools was a novelty of the edict. The abolition of the use of insulting titles for non-Muslims was equally important.[112] The repair and construction of churches, schools, and hospitals

---

108 Badem, *The Ottoman Crimean War*, 335.
109 Andıç and Andıç, Kırım Savaşı Ali Paşa, 80. The Sublime Porte concerned that including the reform in the peace agreement was that the non-Muslim population might think that it was included as a result of the efforts of European powers, so they would be grateful to them, not to the Porte. Badem, *The Ottoman Crimean War*, 337.
110 Shaw and Shaw, *History of the Ottoman Empire*, 2, 140; Murat Bebiroğlu, *Tanzimat'tan II. Meşrutiyet'e Ermeni Nizamnameleri* (Istanbul: Ohan Matbaacılık, 2003), 40.
111 Frederick F. Anscombe, *State, Faith and Nation in Ottoman and Post-Ottoman Lands*, (Cambridge: Cambridge University Press, 2014), 94. Similarly, as Anscombe states, although European powers push Ottoman governments for secular law and way of governing, they did not press Ottoman Christian subjects to put a distance to their religious identity. Ibid.
112 In fact, preliminary steps concerning this issue were taken with the Tanzimat Fermanı. Candan Badem states how the name of *Gavur Dağı* in Maraş had been already changed to *Bereket Dağı* by an irade dated to February 1854. Badem, The Ottoman Crimean War, 343.

were facilitated. Previously, construction or repair required the permission of the sultan; with the edict, churches, and cemeteries could be repaired without permission, permission was still necessary for new construction.[113] Besides, the representation of non-Muslims in provincial and district councils was strengthened through amendments to the regulations. The most important among them was the Provincial Law of 1864, which as underscored by Roderic Davison improved the "representative quality" of local councils.[114]

The Edict of Reform was generally undertaken as a result of a combination of the pressure of the European powers for the amelioration of the rights of the Christian subjects of the empire and the imperial center's decision to reform. However, Tolga Cora rightly notes that these reforms, like admission of non-Muslims to provincial councils, were not parts of a top-down decision by the Ottoman "center" to promote equality between its subjects. Rather, it was an acknowledgement of the rights and power of local Armenian notables and the need the Ottoman government for them in the provinces.[115] Similarly, the articles of the edict concerning building and repair of churches can also be regarded as "concessions" to the non-Muslim subjects as a reward for their services and assistance during the Crimean War.[116]

In line with the aforementioned novelties, the Islahat Fermanı laid the groundwork for amendments to the administrative functioning of the communities (*millet*).[117] The transformation of the millet system first started with the Armenians and was followed by Greeks and Jews. Shaw and Kural define this process as an increase in the secularization of the Ottoman society, as this movement framed the authority of the clergy.[118] A combination of internal conflicts and external factors led to the transformation in the Armenian community's political structure.[119] On one hand, the power of religious institutions and

---

113 Shaw and Shaw, *History of the Ottoman Empire*, 2, 124–25; Bebiroğlu, *Tanzimat'tan II. Meşrutiyet'e*, 36–37.

114 Roderic H. Davison, *Reform in the Ottoman Empire, 1856–1876* (New Jersey: Princeton University Press, 1963), 142. In the same vein, the regulation changed the names of the councils first as known "Muhasıllık Meclisleri." Accordingly, in the provinces, Vilayet İdare Meclisi; in the sanjaks, Liva İdare Meclisi; and in districts Kazâ İdare Meclisleri were established. Çadırcı, *Tanzimat Döneminde Anadolu Kentlerini'nin*, 252.

115 Cora, "Transforming Erzurum/Karin," 11.

116 Ibid., 222.

117 For an evaluation of the Islahat Fermani and its reception, see chapter 2 in Davison, Reform in the Ottoman Empire.

118 Shaw and Shaw, History of the Ottoman Empire, 2, 124. They argue that the preliminary signs of secularization of Muslims began with the promulgation of the Tanzimat when the power of the religious authorities was controlled and they were assigned salaries instead of foundation revenues. Ibid.

119 Hagop Barsoumian, "The Eastern Question and The Tanzimat Era," in *Armenian People from Ancient to Modern Times*, ed. Richard G. Hovanissian (New York: St. Martin's Press, 1997).

Armenian notables called *amiras* was challenged in the nineteenth century by middle class, like artisans and young Armenian intellectuals who demanded more participation of the laity in the administration of the community.[120] On the other hand, both the Tanzimat and Islahat edicts contributed to limiting in the power of ecclesiastical-feudal authorities in Armenian community.[121] The process, especially after the separation of two councils for civil and spiritual administration of the community, respectively, in 1847 culminated with a National Constitution, *nizâmname* in 1860 (which was finalized in 1863 followed the amendments demanded by the Porte), and the Armenian National Assembly.[122]

One could question whether the transformations presented above affected the daily lives of inhabitants in the provinces. This would not undervalue the constitutionalizing and democratization of the Armenian community, yet would highlight the daily experience of the peasantry in eastern provinces in the early decades of the nineteenth century. As Lillian Etmekjian states in 1869 the Armenian National Assembly "for the first time decided to push for a solution" to the problems of provincial Armenians, and the newly elected patriarch Bishop Khrimian met with Grand Vizier Ali Pasha to discuss conditions of not only Armenians but also Muslims in the provinces.[123] As will be discussed in the following lines, in an era when the Armenian National Constitution was being promulgated and when consular reports were pointing out that central rule was increasing in the eastern provinces,[124] the Armenians in Muş were still claiming their right to be reimbursed for financing the corps during the Crimean War through petitions.[125]

---

120 Amira was an honorary title used in Armenian community which first emerged in the sixteenth century, yet it was mostly used in the eighteenth century. Amiras were mostly moneylenders. Thus, with their financial capability stemming from their profession, they were influential in the Ottoman bureaucracy and could play an intermediary role between the Armenian community and Ottoman bureaucracy. Aylin Koçunyan, "Nizâmnâme-i Millet-i Ermeniyân Anayasa mıydı?," Toplumsal Tarih, no. 216 (Aralık 2011): 47.

121 Vartan Artinian, *The Armenian Constitutional System in the Ottoman Empire 1839–1863: A Study of Historical Development* (Istanbul 1988), 52–53.

122 For a detailed discussion of the Armenian National Constitution, see Ibid.; Barsoumian, "The Eastern Question"; Bebiroğlu, *Tanzimat'tan II. Meşrutiyet'e*.

123 Lillian Etmekjian, "The Armenian National Assembly of Turkey and Reform," *The Armenian Review*, no. Spring 29 (1976): 38. Accordingly, the Armenian National Assembly prepared two reports concerning the oppressions in the provinces in 1872 and 1877, successively. Ibid., 38–52.

124 FO. 78/1669, No: 9, Consul Robert Dalyell, "Report on Eyalet of Erzurum," February 28, 1862.

125 Dzonivar Derderian demonstrates how the editor of journal *Artzvik Taronoy*, Garegin Srvandztiants encouraged the Armenians of the Ottoman East to forward their complaints to the Sublime Porte as a way of improving their conditions in the early 1860s. Dzovaniar Derderian, "Shaping Subjectivities and Contesting Power through the Image

6.4 Council Members, Tax Farmers, Moneylenders and Peasants

In a petition dated August 1863 certain Haci Ohan, Kirkor, and Parsih stated that the peasants of Muş and Bitlis had provided the Anatolian Corps with cereal worth 3,700,000 (thirty-seven yük) guruş during the previous event (*mesele-i maziye*), that is the Crimean War. Although the central treasury had granted money for the suppliers, the members of Muş's council appropriated money, resulting in the misery of the people.[126] In subsequent petitions, it appeared that together with the embezzlement of their money paid for provisions during the Crimean War, the people of Muş suffered from the cruelty of not only Kurdish tribes but also moneylenders, tax farmers, council members, and the kaimakam of Muş.

It is noteworthy that the petitions did not single out Kurdish tribes or notables alone, but a good number of Armenian notables as well. The inhabitants of Muş were vacating their houses (*nakl-i hâne*) due to atrocities by Kurdish tribes, the tax farmer Hacı Esad Agha (who had also been a member of Muş's council), Kürkçübaşı Agob, his son-in law Manas, the former treasurer Ohannes, and the çorbacı (non-Muslim notable) Vartan and the council members.[127] It can be understood that the Crimean War aggravated situations of Muş. For instance, Kürkçübaşı Agop, who provisioned the army during the war, hoarded a huge amount of grain before and during the war in Erzurum.[128] Similarly, he purchased grain from the Armenians of Muş during the war and he did not pay in return.[129] The representatives of the inhabitants claimed that the population of Muş had previously been eighty thousand and it had decreased to twenty-five thousand.[130] In the same vein, migration became an integral part

of Kurds, 1860s," in *The Ottoman East in the Nineteenth Century: Societies, Identities and Politics*, eds. Yaşar Tolga Cora, Dzovaniar Derderian, and Ali Sipahi (London: I.B. Tauris, 2016), 99.

126   BOA. MVL. 425/136, 3 Rebiülevvel 1280 (18 Ağustos 1863). The petitioners also demanded that the center of the *kaimakamlık* of Muş remain in Bitlis to which it had been transferred a few years earlier. The issue of the center of the kaimakamlık was a matter of dispute between the districts of Muş and Bitlis.

127   BOA. MVL. 694/7, 21 Receb 1281 (19 January 1865), BOA. MVL. 707/57, 6 Muharrem 1282 (1 June 1865). Cora notes that Kürkçübaşı Agob emerged as a notable in Erzurum in 1850s by taking advantage of tax farming and army provisioning during the Crimean War. Cora, "Transforming Erzurum/Karin," 155–227.

128   Yaşar Tolga Cora, "The Crimean War and the Armenian Elite in the Ottoman Empire" *Archiv Orientální* 87 (2019): 428.

129   Ibid., 202.

130   BOA. MVL. 462/55, 16 Şaban 1281 (14 January 1865). "Muş sancâğının giçen altmış dört senesinde seksan bin nüfûsı mevcûd iken mahal-i meclis a'zâsıyla eşkiyâ-yı ekrâdın ve Kürkçübaşı, Ohannes ve Manas nâm kimesnelerinin mezâlim ve ta'addiyâtı

of the daily lives of the peasants of Muş during the nineteenth century. The reasons and patterns of migration were intrinsic to the system of exploitation by tax farmers, moneylenders, council members, and Armenian notables.

In the middle of the 1860s, the peasants of Muş continued to file similar petitions, sending them in person through representatives. It is noteworthy to emphasize that these petitions and the complaints they included were cross-sectarian as they had been in the 1850s. For instance, representatives Hüdaverdi and Halil Aghas submitted a common petition signed by more than one hundred fifty inhabitants of Muş to the Meclis-i Vâlâ itemizing the offenses of the tax farmers, moneylenders, non-Muslim notables and council members. Consequently, the governor of Erzurum decided to appoint a certain Yusuf Bey from Erzurum's provincial council to examine the basis for the grievances.[131]

However, as reported by Halil, Hüdaverdi as well as Mıgırdıç, the representatives of the people of Muş who were still in Istanbul, Yusuf Bey aligned himself with the council members instead of pursuing the rights of the claimants or investigating their allegations. On this basis, they reported, the people were filing a petition with two thousand fifty signatures to be submitted to Istanbul through their representatives, Hacı Tayyib Efendi (from the Nakşibendi dervish community), Osman Efendi,[132] Hafız Abdülaziz Efendi (from the Kadiri dervish community), Eyyüb Agha and the deputy-murahhasa of Çanlı Monastery, Kocabaşı Mahitar. These representatives informed Halil, Hüdaverdi and Mıgırdıç by a telegraph that they had appeared before the governor of Erzurum to take permission for their leave for Istanbul, yet he said nothing. However, when they left to deliver the petition to Istanbul, the governor sent four zaptiehs to take them back to Erzurum.[133] Despite the governor's efforts, Hacı Tayyib and the other representatives arrived in Istanbul to deliver the petition in the end. It is important to note that how the governor of Erzurum sought to prevent the delivering of the petitions to Istanbul and how the people of Muş managed to reach Istanbul and to make their complaints be heard. This account also exemplifies how the spread of telegraph lines throughout the Ottoman Empire from 1860s onwards contributed not only to

---

cihetiyle dâğılûb şimdi yirmi beş bin nüfûs kalmış olduğu ..." BOA. MVL. 694/7, 21 Receb 1281 (19 January 1865).
131   BOA. MVL. 706/1, 5 Zilhicce 1281 (1 May 1865).
132   The name of Osman Efendi was absent from other petitions.
133   "Halil ve Hudaverdiye: Bâ mahzar-ı 'umûmi oltarafa gelur iken Bayburddan vâlî Erzuruma aldırdı bizi oltarafa telgrafla matlûb itdiresiniz." BOA. MVL. 469/64, 29 Zilkade 1281 (25 April 1865).

the infrastructural power of Ottoman government but also facilitated the filing of petitions by commoners.[134]

While the representatives were in Istanbul, the council of Muş submitted a report to the Meclis-i Vâlâ at the same time informing it about the process of the investigation. This report did not mention the wrongdoings of Yusuf Bey, the official appointed to conduct the investigation; rather, it brought the claimants into disrepute. The council pointed out the difficulty of the case as the claimants were large in number, the accused numbered five, and the subjects of the complaints were manifold. Therefore, the council invited petitioners to specify whom they were accusing and for what they were accusing them of in individual petitions. Allegedly, despite the fact that petitioners agreed to this in the beginning, the following night (as it was the holy month, the council was carrying out business in the evenings) at around half past two o'clock, four to five hundred people gathered before the council, leading to an uproar (*arbede*). The crowd demanded to be questioned collectively although the council had previously required them to specify the accused and to clarify the alleged points (*ta'yîn hasm ve tasrîh-i müdde'a*).[135]

The kaimakam of Muş Abdi Pasha and the council emphasized that even if the people were right in their accusations, such gatherings and associations (*hey'et-i cumhûriyyet ve tarz-ı cem'iyyet*) were dangerous. Moreover, according to the council of Muş, people's appeal to the language of banditry (*lisân-ı şekâvet*) was the result of provocation and sedition on the part of the people who signed the petition against the council members and some other local actors. These remarks by the kaimakam importantly show the limits of popular protest from the viewpoint of provincial authorities. As Eleni Gara argues, "the legitimacy [of] contentious forms of popular protest" on the part of the empire's subjects was questionable to a great extent in the eyes of Ottoman government.[136] In this case the gathering of the inhabitants of Muş offended local authorities. On the other hand, local authorities tried to draw the attention of

---

134   From the documents, it can be determined that the telegraph lines between Erzurum-Muş, Muş-Bitlis, and Van-Bayezid were completed after 1865. BOA. A. MKT. MHM. 367/96, 6 Receb 1283 (14 November 1866), BOA. A. MKT. MHM. 391/8, 11 Cemaziyelevvel 1284 (10 September 1867). Yuval Ben-Basat also points out that the advent of the telegraph both reduced costs and shortened the distances. Also "payment per word" on the telegraph led to discursive changes in the petitions; namely, they became shorter and "normative blessings and embellishments" were excluded. Ben-Bassat, *Petitioning the Sultan*, 181–82.
135   BOA. MVL. 705/62, 29 Zilkade 1281 (25 April 1865).
136   Gara, "Popular Protest and the Limitations," 91. Gara further argues that the Ottoman state's attitude toward popular protests was "ambivalent" and "pragmatic." The punishment of protesters depended on various factors from the political situation to local power relations. Ibid., 93.

the central government to the questionability and legitimacy of this act, so as to cast a shadow on the righteousness of the petitioners.

Persuaded that hearing their cases individually was difficult and that a gathering in such numbers was also improper, the crowd dispersed and agreed to send their representatives the following day. The next day, according to Abdi Pasha, the people repented for their act the previous night and agreed to be heard individually. As it was difficult for them to appear one by one, they asked for the nomination of four deputies among them. Moreover, the people demanded the presence of four people from Muş's *ulema* to follow the case, while it was being heard by the Council. Abdi Pasha interpreted this demand as a lack of confidence in the council, yet the council accepted people's demand to avoid further trouble. Claiming that the people's petition was partly unreadable and incomprehensible, the council had the correspondence clerk rewrite the report and narrate the case and complaints of the people in front of the representatives and said ulema. The people were allowed to keep the rewritten report for twenty-four hours to cross-check. However, the representatives later notified the chief clerk that the inhabitants of Muş refused to sign the report prepared by the council and insisted on the submission of their own, original draft. Thereupon, the kaimakam and council members of Muş declared that they would not help the petitioners in their case. As they did not trust the local government, he suggested they should apply to either the provincial council or to Istanbul.[137]

The petitioners' reservations about the council of Muş shows not only the extent of the corruption of council members and the deterioration of the institution, but also the tensions between the peasants and the local government. Although the main issue was the nonpayment of money for provisions during the Crimean War, claimants specified many similar examples of extortion. For instance, council members neither paid for nor returned provisions collected and stored in certain villages of Muş for the troops, when there was no longer such a necessity. Similarly, the petitioners complained about over collection of the tobacco tax (*duhan*), double taxation, and practices of forced labor.[138]

---

137 BOA. MVL. 705/62, 29 Zilkade 1281 (25 April 1865).
138 Fehmi Yılmaz notes that the cultivation of tobacco increased in the Asian part of the Ottoman Empire in the first half of the nineteenth century. Among the eastern provinces Muş and Bitlis became important districts where tobacco was cultivated. Fehmi Yılmaz, "Osmanlı İmparatorluğu'nda Tütün: Sosyal, Siyasî ve Ekonomik Tahlili (1600–1883)" (PhD diss., Marmara Üniversitesi, 2005), 36. Increase in the cultivation of tobacco led to increase in its export in the empire throughout the nineteenth century. Donald Quataert, "The Age of Reforms," in *An Economic and Social History of the Ottoman Empire, 1600–1914*, eds. Halil İnalcık and Donald Quataert (Cambridge: Cambridge University Press, 1997),

In addition, while the people accused kaimakam Abdi Pasha of not paying for fuelwood and coal, the council prepared a report – without the consent of the people – to argue that the kaimakam had paid all his debts. On top of that, petitioners argued that the tribes around Muş would not dare steal and murder if they did not have the tacit consent of council members.[139] This last point is important, the semi-nomadic and nomadic tribes of Muş were usually singled out in the cases of the extortion and assaults on the peasantry. However, the peasants were aware of the role of the council members in their overtaxation and they put a special emphasis on their role.

The kaimakam of Muş, Abdi Pasha, argued that he had witnessed no abuse or atrocities on the part of council members during his term of office and that the claimants did not specify their allegations against council members. However, emphasizing the assaults on and persecution of villagers by the Kurdish tribes, he argued that this was the main reason for the emigration of villagers. The kaimakam further stated that unless the inhabitants of Muş believed that the government would get those tribes under control, they would not specify the individuals they were accusing. According to him, the people were afraid of further assaults by the Kurdish tribes should they openly accuse them and the government not successfully discipline them. For instance, Abdi Pasha argued, the Armenians of the village of Hars petitioned that they had suffered all kind of assaults by the Kurds of the neighboring village of Marinek, yet sexual assaults were the last straw. A certain Süleyman from the village of Marinek arrived in Hars with around fifty armed men for abduction of a woman. Despite the fact that some of the armed Kurds were caught, Süleyman had managed to escape. However, upon a demand to submit a register of assaults by the Kurds of Marinek, the Armenians of Hars emphasized that they did not want to bring up the past events; their wish was to prevent further assaults.[140]

Contrary to the allegations of the petitioners of Muş against local council members, tax farmers, moneylenders, and the kaimakam, both the council and the kaimakam's reports emphasized that the source of the people of Muş's grievances and the reason for depopulation were atrocities by Kurdish tribes, denying their own involvement. However, the following petition of Halil and Hüdaverdi, representatives of the commoners of Muş, summarizes how the people of Muş were greatly suppressed not only because of their aggravated

847–52. For a study of tobacco workers as a result of this expansion of tobacco cultivation and export, see Can Nacar, "Tobacco Workers in the Late Ottoman Empire: Fragmentation, Conflict, and Collective Struggle" (PhD diss., State University of New York, 2010).

139 "… ancak meclis-i mezkûrun hafiyyen ruhsat vukû'una istinâdından iktizâ eylediği …" BOA. MVL. 707/57, 6 Muharrem 1282 (1 June 1865).

140 BOA. MVL. 706/1, 5 Zilhicce 1281 (1 May 1865).

relations with Kurdish tribes but also because of a system of debt and dispossession established by the usurers (*murabahacılar*) that were, as the representatives alleged, protected by the council members:

> In the case one of our inhabitants needs a few hundred guruş, certain moneylenders and greedy usurers, who have been appearing in our region for a while, departing from sharia and contrary to the rule of His Majesty, add forty or fifty guruş for each hundred guruş in the name of inflation and they prepare bills of debt to be paid in kind. Within a decade, our inhabitants have become miserable and have migrated to other places. Today, in Istanbul, there are more than ten thousand [of our] people. Although they are busy with trade thanks to His Majesty, they could not escape the clutches of these cruel, ferocious people, and so they are in misery. It is obvious that this issue will subsequently impede imperial revenues because most of these usurers are influential people and the members of the local council. The kaimakam, and other officials are backing them instead of protecting poor inhabitants. When a poor inhabitant falls into the hands of the local government, he is not protected and is imprisoned for two months because of a few hundred guruş. And then all his property is sold off to pay his debts. Thus, our poor inhabitants are exhausted and dare not apply to the government. Thus, a hundred guruş debt can exceed a thousand guruş in the course of time.[141]

The emergence and expansion of the usury system was related to the monetization of economy and people's increasing need for cash to adapt to the transformation in the tax collection system.[142] This issue of indebtedness through usury is important as it aggravated the conditions of sharecroppers in Muş as discussed in *Envar-ı Şarkiyye*.[143] Not only usurers but also landowners were lending money to the sharecroppers with high interest rates. This led to endless

---

141   BOA. MVL. 476/77, 7 Rebiülevvel 1282 (31 July 1865).
142   In the later periods, this sytem was called as "selef/selem" system. Polatel, "Armenians and the Land Question," 138. As Pamuk states both small peasantry and sharecroppers were constantly indebted to usurers because of a set of reasons, suh as agriculture's being depended on climatic conditions, low productivity, taxes and the pressures of tax farmers. Pamuk, Türkiye'nin 200 Yıllık, 130–31.
143   *Envar-ı Şarkiyye* was the provincial official newspaper of Erzurum and published first in 1867. It was in Ottoman Turkish and also in Turkish in the Armenian alphabet. Muammer Yaşar, *Anadolu'da İlk Türk Gazetesi (Envar-ı Şarkiyye)* (Ankara: Türk Tarih Kurumu, 1971). Unfortunately, I could not find the first issues concerning the scope of this study. Yet, the study of Muammer Yaşar – that I have consulted here – provides both transliterations and original texts. The incomplete but available issues are for later periods.

chain of debt for the sharecroppers who became deprived of their money, lands and livestock at the end. To be saved from the assaults of creditors during the harvest time, the villagers had no option but to leave sharecropping. Thus, it was decided to establish a commission to fix interest rates at one percent per month and to protect the rights of sharecroppers against creditors, landowners and usurers. Another important step was to disseminate *memleket sandığı* (homeland boxes)[144] that were already established in Muş to other sanjaks and districts to alleviate the moneylending issue.[145] In spite of these precautions, this issue of indebtedness became aggravated in the following decades.[146] This phenomenon sheds light on the reasons behind the dispersion of the population of Muş. Having been dispossessed because of their debt, the inhabitants of Muş had to migrate. It also shows how council members and the kaimakam were involved in the poverty of the inhabitants of Muş, collaborating not only with tax farmers and moneylenders but also usurers.

The provincial authorities sought to ways to alleviate the grievances of the commoners of Muş. As understood from the anxiety of the kaimakam of Muş, Abdi Pasha, the governor of Erzurum had not replied to his any correspondence for a few weeks.[147] The reason for the lack of communication came out in the governor's report to the grand vizier about the misgovernment of Abdi Pasha. Accordingly, during the pasha's term of office, the order and control in

---

144 Memleket sandıkları that were the first examples of agricultural credit organizations in the Ottoman Empire emerged in the nineteenth century with initiatives of Midhat Pasha during his governorship in Niş, in 1863. It was a precaution against usurers and landowners who were lending money to the peasants with high interest rates. Sertaç Dokuzlu, "The Agricultural Credit System in the Ottoman Empire between 1863 and 1888," *Rural History* 28, no. 2 (2017): 179–80.

145 *Envar-ı Şarkiyye*, no. 105, 25 Rebiülahir 1286 (23 July 1869) in Yaşar, *Anadolu'da İlk Türk Gazetesi*, 59–60.

146 A report of the kaimakam of Muş at the beginning of the twentieth century points out the extent of the indebtness of the inhabitants of Muş under the selem system. "Kürdistân Ahvâli ve Mesele-i Islahât." *Mülkiye*, no. 8 (1 Eylül 1325): 1–18. In the same vein, Mehmet Polatel argues that "the commodification of land and expansion of debt relations were significant contributors to the erosion of small-scale Armenian peasantry and the transformation of agrarian relations." Polatel, "Armenians Furthermore, such forms of indebtness became mechanisms to bind the cultivators and sharecroppers to the soil in the other parts of the empire. Alp Yücel Kaya, "On the Çiftlik Regulation in Tırhala in the Mid Nineteenth Century: Economists, Pashas, Governors, Çiftlik-Holders, Subaşıs and Sharecroppers" in *Ottoman Rural Societies and Economies: Halcyon Days in Crete VIII A Symposium Held in Rethymno 13–15 January 2012*, ed. Elias Kolovos (Rethymno: Crete University Press, 2015).

147 BOA. MVL. 711/11, 25 Muharrem 1282 (20 June 1865).

the sanjak was not maintained and turmoil among Kurdish tribes increased. Therefore, the governor suggested the discharge of Abdi Pasha and the appointment of Osman Bey, a member of the Grand Council of Erzurum, by proxy.[148]

As the report to the Grand Vizier did not mention anything about the corruption of council members and tax farmers, it can be assumed that none were punished seriously. As a common precaution, the grievances of the petitioners were alleviated through the dismissal of the kaimakam. The problems concerning tax farmers, local notables or usurers did not diminish as reported in the pages of official newspapers in later years. An issue of *Envar-ı Şarkiyye*, dated 1869, is partially dedicated to the condition of the sanjak of Muş. One of the urgent issues was misdeeds of tax farmers. Officials (*şahne*) sent to villages by tax farmers to inspect the harvest became involved in corvée and overtaxation. It was stated in the newspaper that officials should not take anything without pay from the villagers except tithe, water and at maximum a bed. Otherwise, they would be punished. Moreover, it was required to inform the villagers about this fact. Similarly, it was reminded that councils of elders were established according to the Provincial Law in the villages and so people with the title of *kahya, kocabaşı, muhbir, and melik* – who were collecting money and grains for both their guests and livestock – should not be employed in village affairs and even these titles should be abolished.[149]

As these articles make clear, the problem of the depopulation of certain villages of Muş was part of the abuse and corruption of council members, moneylenders, and tax farmers. The rest of the chapter elaborates this issue of depopulation.

6.4.1 *The Migration and Depopulation*

As emphasized above, one of the more concerning problems in Muş was the decrease of the population of Muş due to the atrocities of Kürkçübaşı Agob, Manas, Vartan (the Armenian tax-farmer and his collaborators), council members and Kurdish tribes.[150] It was emphasized both in the petitions and official reports that the population of the sanjak had decreased from eighty thousand to twenty-five thousand. It is necessary to consider these numbers with caution. The existence of some population data in Ottoman records, consular reports and traveler accounts allows comparison despite its difficulty. For instance, in

---

148 BOA. MVL. 708/38, 23 Muharrem 1282 (18 June 1865).
149 Envar-ı Şarkiyye, no. 105, 25 Rebiülahir 1286 (23 July 1869) in Yaşar, Anadolu'da İlk Türk Gazetesi, 58–59.
150 BOA. MVL. 706/1, 5 Zilhicce 1281 (1 May 1865), BOA. MVL. 462/55, 16 Şaban 1281 (14 January 1865).

a record dated 1854, the non-Muslim population of the sanjak of Muş – including districts (*kaza*) of Muş, Bitlis and Malazgird and the sub-districts (*nahiye*) of Bulanıklar, Vartolar, Huyud, Mutki, Çukur, and Ahlat – was registered as 32,149 (31,030 Armenians and 1,119 Catholics).[151] If women are included by simply duplicating this number, it comes to 64,298. In the same vein, in the yearbook of the province of Erzurum of 1871, non-Muslim men were recorded as 29,104, and doubling this would be a population of 58,208.[152] Over these fifteen years, it can be seen that the non-Muslim population of the sanjak had decreased. If the unit of analysis is kept smaller – for instance, if the district (*kazâ*) of Muş is taken into consideration – it is also possible to observe a decrease in the non-Muslim population of Muş. The total non-Muslim population of Muş in 1854 was registered as 23,064.[153] In 1871 it was 9,238, after the inclusion of women.[154] The number given by British Consul of Erzurum, Robert Dalyell, for the total non-Muslim population of the kazâ of Muş in 1862 was even lower at 6,090.[155] Although these numbers are not completely reliable, they contribute to the claims of the inhabitants of Muş that the population was decreasing.[156]

Meanwhile, in May 1865 kaimakam Abdi Pasha, despite putting all the blame on the Kurdish tribes and putting an emphasis on the locusts which hit the harvest of the villagers, argued that a thousand and two hundred households had left over three years, but five to six hundred households from neighboring sanjaks and districts had settled in their place. The kaimakam was struggling to show the continuity of tax revenues rather than scrutinize the reasons for emigration. Abdi Pasha strikingly argued that, contrary to the claims of the petitioners, emigrated households were not be described as the traditional

---

151   BOA. NFS. d. 3868, 29 Zilhicce 1270 (22 Eylül 1854).
152   *Salnâme-i Vilâyet-i Erzurum*, 1288 (1871), 145.
153   BOA. NFS. d. 3868, 29 Zilhicce 1270 (22 Eylül 1854).
154   *Salnâme-i Vilâyet-i Erzurum*, 1288 (1871), 145.
155   Mr. Dalyell stated that the total population of the kazâ of Muş was 13,790 (7,700 Muslim and 6, 090 non-muslim). FO 78/1669, No:9, Dalyell, "Report on Eyalet of Erzurum," Erzurum, February 28, 1862. In the same vein, the account of Vital Cuinet penned in 1890–95 states the total population of Muş as 123,459. Cuinet, La Turquie d'Asie, 2, 573.
156   In consular reports the continuing decrease in the population of Muş was highly emphasized. FO. 195/227, No: 6, Brant to Stratford Canning, Erzurum, May 29, 1844. Besides, Cevdet Küçük also notes that in 1841, around eleven thousand Muslim and non-Muslim households of the province of Erzurum had dispersed due to famine and high costs. Cevdet Küçük, "Tanzimât Devrinde Erzurum'un Nüfus Durumu," *İstanbul Üniversitesi Edebiyat Fakültesi Tarih Enstitüsü Dergisi*, no. 7–8 (1976–1977): 187.

people of Muş; rather, they were those who had a tendency to migrate, leaving their houses for petty reasons and returning soon after.[157]

The migration pattern described by Abdi Pasha might have been true to some extent for the eastern provinces of the nineteenth-century Ottoman Empire. For instance, the migration of Armenian peasants to Russia temporarily was typical.[158] However, cases from certain villages in Muş also point out that in addition to migration to other countries, there were examples of being forced to settle in nearby villages. Thus, for the purpose of the current chapter and as an attempt to constitute a link with the following chapter, it is necessary to discuss the multiple reasons for migration and for being forced to leave one's villages in the 1850s and 60s.[159]

The migration of the inhabitants of Muş stemmed on one hand from the oppression of a network of kaimakams, council members, tax-farmers, money lenders, and usurers and on the other because of the conflicts with Kurdish tribes. To begin with the story of corruption – that is, abuse by the council members, moneylenders, tax-farmers, and usurers – the commoners and provincial authorities pointed out that the population of Muş had decreased by two thirds as a result. In fact, the issue of migration had aroused anxiety of provincial and central authorities in the last three years, as the former kaimakam of Muş, Abdi Pasha, had mentioned. The governor of Erzurum Mehmed Hayreddin Pasha informed the Sublime Porte that around six hundred inhabitants consisting of village kahyas and wealthy people (*ashâb-ı servet*) of Bulanık, a sub-district of Muş, had departed for Russia to perform a pilgrimage to Üç Kilise. However, the governor had received intelligence that this visit was a pretext for becoming subjects of Russia. After getting the necessary passports, they supposedly intended to return and dispose of their property as before (*emlâklarını kemâfi's-sâbık tasarruf itmek niyetinde*). Having been informed about this issue, the governor of Erzurum stated that in the case these people returned holding passports of another country, it would be required of them to cut relations with either the Ottoman Empire or Russia.

---

157 "... ahâlî-i kadîme hükmüne giremiyerek hoşnişîn makûlesinden oldukları cihetle bir 'ariza-i cüziye ile terk-i vatan ve ba'id müddete yine mevâ-yı kadîmilerine 'avdet itmek 'adet-i me'lûfiyeleri ..." BOA. MVL. 706/1, 5 Zilhicce 1281 (1 May 1865).

158 Wars between Ottoman and Russian Empires also triggered the migration of especially Armenian community. For the migration of Armenians to Russia during and after 1828–1829 Ottoman-Russian War, see Beydilli, *1828–1829 Osmanlı-Rus Savaşında*.

159 For a discussion of migration from the Ottoman East to United States and Canada from the 1880s to the 1910s, see David Edward Gutman, *The Politics of Armenian Migration to North America, 1885–1915: Sojourners, Smugglers, and the State and Dubious Citizens* (Edinburgh: Edinburgh University Press, 2019).

As a precaution, he immediately corresponded with the patriarch of Üç Kilise, demanding that these people should neither be granted Russian subjecthood nor provided with passports.[160]

The patriarch consulted with notables among the group that had arrived and responded to Hayreddin Pasha that theirs was just a visit; they would return after a few days. Not convinced by the answer of the patriarch, Hayreddin Pasha called for said notables after their return. When questioned about the reasons for trying to get Russian passports and subjecthood, it came out that the main cause was the above-mentioned council members, certain officials, and notables' embezzlement of money paid by the central treasury in return for provisions supplied by the people during the Crimean War. However, this was only a part of the story. The reasons for emigration and depopulation were actually a combination of practices that pointed to the continuation of pre-Tanzimat forced labor, over taxation, and indebtedness. As the governor of Erzurum, Mehmed Hayreddin Pasha wrote:

> Local tax farmers together with the members of the Council of Muş and notables assumed the collection of the revenues of tithe and tax through a secret partnership. [Similarly], they appoint officials to take subsistence and fodder without payment [from the villagers] and also they seize half or even more of the revenues like a shareholder and sharecropper. Likewise, council members and notables collect oil, cracked wheat, and milk from the villagers without payment for their own use by sending officials and transferring these goods to their houses by loading them on the animals and carts of the people without pay. Besides, the appointed zaptiehs and others take goods and fodder from the villages without payment, and also take fifty-a hundred guruş from each village in the name of a fee of the supervision. In addition, the various provisions required for the regular troops in Muş are levied on and collected from the villagers. Although the imperial army pays for them, a penny is not paid to the suppliers. When they appeal to the government, they are jailed and are not heard. Thus, they declared and responded that the atrocities and torment to which the inhabitants of Muş are exposed are extreme, so they had to obtain the subjecthood and protection of the Russian state.[161]

In addition to the statements of the notables of the non-Muslim population of Muş, the governor of Erzurum emphasized the role of provisions taken for the

---

160 BOA. MVL. 629/41, 20 Zilkade 1278 (19 May 1862).
161 BOA. MVL. 629/41, 20 Zilkade 1278 (19 May 1862).

Anatolian Corps in the suffering of the people. The governor pointed out how villagers had to transfer their surplus to the army instead of selling them and satisfying their necessities. When villagers were not paid in those days due to a shortage of cash, the governor argued, most among the non-Muslim population were migrating and considered settling in Russia and Iran given the provocation and instigation from those countries.[162]

The government had to keep up the deliveries of grain and fodder to the army, yet they could not pay the peasants for these supplies. As a result, local officials looked for other measures to prevent the migration of Armenian peasants. On one hand, the center of the kaimakamlık was transferred from Muş to Bitlis to facilitate reforms, and on the other, the kaimakam of Muş worked for the return of people who migrated to Russia and Iran and succeeded in arranging the return of a hundred and fifty houses to Ahlat, Çukur, and Bitlis.[163] Moreover, in Bulanık, a commission was constituted to investigate the allegations of Armenian peasants regarding tax-collection.[164]

The emigration of peasants on the periphery of Ottoman Empire was not specific to Muş. For instance, in other districts and sub-districts of the province of Erzurum, emigration – especially of non-Muslim peasants – was already on the agenda in the early 1850s. In the summer of 1852, it was reported that some villagers in the vicinity were considering migrating to Georgia.[165] Similarly, in the sub-district of Pasin, about three hundred Christian families together with some Muslim inhabitants were preparing to migrate to Russia. The route of the villagers was first to move to Kars, and if they could not live there, they fought to migrate to Georgia. The grievances of the villagers of Pasin were in line with those of Muş: unjust treatment, taxation, and oppression by Kurdish tribes such as plundering and burning loads of hay, which in turn led to livestock perishing.[166]

However, not all mobility was cross-border; people frequently moved to neighboring villages or provinces. In the village of Bazigan in Varto, it was reported that people left the village because of the atrocities of tax farmers and council members. Accordingly, in Bazigan, the tithe previously imposed by the tax-farmer was demanded in cash by the administrator of Varto, and council members oppressed the peasants during its collection. Some villagers were persuaded to turn back half way to Kars, yet the others reached their

---

162   Ibid.
163   BOA. MVL. 410/43, 7 Receb 1279 (29 December 1862).
164   BOA. A. MKT. MVL. 146/9, 8 Zilkade 1278 (7 May 1862).
165   FO. 78/906, No: 19, Brant to Malmesburry, Erzurum, 2 June, 1852.
166   FO. 78/906, No: 19, Brant to Redcliffe, Erzurum, May 31, 1852.

destination. Similarly, Armenian villagers from Hamza Şeyh and Şirvan Şeyh moved to Eleşgird, a district of Bayezid, due to oppression by tax farmers and some Kurdish tribes.[167] Nevertheless, migration and complaints about tax farmers and tribes was not specific to Muş. At the same time, in a dispatch from Istanbul to the governor of Erzurum, it was argued that in Çıldır and other sanjaks of Erzurum there was unease and a great many complaints about the administrators.[168] In the same vein, the commander-in-chief of the Anatolian Corps reported in correspondence with the patriarch of the Assyrian Yakubi and the murahhasa of the Armenians in Ottoman Kurdistan with regard to the disappointment of their communities. As their complaints about the oppression and injustice of tax farmers and Kurdish tribes was not heard by the central government, some left their homelands and others were considering emigrating.[169] Likewise, Armenians often demanded to move to villages with churches in order not to be deprived of their religious rites.[170] Nevertheless, such a requirement was generally followed by a complaint about either tax farmers or neighboring Kurds.[171]

The petitions discussed up to now bring forth the complaints of the peasants of Muş about murder, expropriation, and damage done by Kurdish tribes along with the overtaxation, indebtedness and continuation of corvée by local authorities since the 1850s.[172] However, in certain villages assaults were intended to force the evacuation of the Armenian population. According to a report of the Council of Armenian Community, Kurds occupied a few houses in the villages of Şeyhveli [Okçular], Purkaş [Oğlakkaya], Aryincek [Bostancılar], and Fındıklı in the sub-district of Lower Bulanık, and the situation was the same in the villages of Upper Bulanık, called Haçlu [Gölyanı], Pirane [Göztepe], and Kereğil [Karaağıl]. However, those Kurdish households

---

167 "Muş sancâğında kâin Varto kazâsına muzâfe Bazigan karyesi mülteziminin ahâli-i karyeye tevdiʻ eylediği hâsılât-ı ʻöşriyenin muahharen kazâ-i mezbûr müdiri maʻrifetiyle akçesi taleb olunmasından ve Muş meclis aʻzâsı tarafından ahâli-i merkûmeye muʻamele-i gadriye icrâ kılınmasından nâşi ahâli karyeyi terk …" BOA. A. MKT. UM. 494/92, 20 Safer 1278 (27 August 1861).
168 BOA. A. MKT. UM. 509/74, 18 Rebiülevvel 1278 (23 October 1861).
169 BOA. A. MKT. UM. 544/53, 28 Şaban 1278 (28 February 1862).
170 BOA. MVL. 116/86, 5 Ramazan 1268 (23 June 1852).
171 BOA. MVL. 634/41, 9 Safer 1279 (6 August 1862).
172 For instance, the governor of Kurdistan also reported that in addition to extortion and murder, the hay bales of inhabitants were burnt in Muş. In a village of Varto, a certain person called Arab had burned the hay and straw bales of the headman of the village, Süleyman. Therefore, not only Armenian but in addition Muslim villagers were suffering from the assaults of Kurdish tribes if not in the same degree. In order to prevent further occurrence of such acts, the Provincial Grand Council decided to sentence him to chains for a year. However, it is questionable to what extent such punishments were effective deterrents. BOA. MVL. 249/51, 13 Receb 1268 (2 June 1852).

were attempting to oppress the Armenians of those villages in myriad ways, confiscating their properties and churches in order to forcefully make them leave their villages.[173] On the other hand, the Kurds in the villages of Şahyolu, Aryincek, Haçaveh, Pirane and Kereğil, it was argued, were not natives, and they forced some native Armenians to leave and move to Porkaş and Fındıklı by seizing their properties and churches. The Council of Armenian Community demanded that the Kurds in Şahyolu be removed and settled in Porkaş and that those in Haçaveh, Pirane, and Kereğil also be expelled.[174]

As such examples show in the 1860s, the province of Erzurum in general and the sanjak of Muş in particular experience not only the depopulation especially of its non-Muslim inhabitants, but also the immigration of thousands of Muslims into the Ottoman Empire.

6.4.2   *Migration from Crimea and Caucasia*

In addition to hardships endured during the war, one of the most important socioeconomic results of the war was the mass migration of Crimean Tatars into the Ottoman domain. Drawing attention to population scarcity in the Ottoman Empire at the beginning of the nineteenth century, Kemal Karpat argues that the state regarded immigrants as human resources to cultivate large land areas.[175] In the same vein, the migration of Crimean Tatars in 1783/4, which began immediately after the incorporation of Crimea into Russia, was the first wave of Muslim migration to the Ottoman Empire.[176] Although the numbers could look exaggerated, Karpat claims that the number of Tatars that migrated to Ottoman lands between 1783 and 1922 was 1.8 million.[177] However, it was not only Crimean Tatars who migrated to the empire. Aftermath of Ottoman-Russian War of 1877–78 was a drastic phase in the migration of Muslim populations from Crimea, the Caucasus, and the Balkans. However, the effects of migration from the Caucasus started with the Crimean War and accelerated in the 1860s; the effects on the province of Erzurum and the sanjak of Muş, in particular, will be dealt with in this part.[178] By 1908, Muslim immigrants from

---

173   BOA. MVL. 261/15, 15 Zilhicce 1269 (19 September 1853). "... üçer beşer hâneden 'ibâret olan tâife-i ekrâd mevcûd olan re'âyâ ve berâyâ kullarını kurâ-i mezbûreden tard ve ihrâc itmek kasdıyla haklarında envâi' zulm ve ta'addî icrâsına ve kilisâ ve emlâkının tegallüben zabtına cür'et itmekde ..." BOA. MVL. 261/15, 15 Zilhicce 1269 (19 September 1853).
174   BOA. MVL. 261/15, 15 Zilhicce 1269 (19 September 1853).
175   Kemal H. Karpat, *Ottoman Population, 1830–1914: Demographic and Social Characteristics* (Madison: University of Wisconsin Press, 1985), 61–62.
176   Ibid., 65.
177   Ibid.
178   In 1859–60, three hundred thousand Crimean Tatars migrated to the Ottoman lands. See Nedim İpek, *İmparatorluktan Ulus Devlete Göçler* (Trabzon: Serander Yayınları, 2006), 40. The number for the years 1861 to 1864 was 227,627. See Karpat, Ottoman Population,

Crimea, the Caucasus, and the Balkans in the Ottoman Empire were estimated at about five million.[179]

At first issues like the transportation, expenses, and settlement of immigrants were carried out through the ministries of commerce, the zaptieh, and municipalities (Şehremaneti). Then a separate council, the Muhacirin Komisyonu (Commission of Immigrants) was established in 1860.[180] Moreover, immigrants were exempted from all taxes, including the tithe, as well as from conscription for twenty years.[181] However, Selim Deringil argues that immigrants arriving in the 1880s did not enjoy such exemptions from taxation and conscription, as governments began to regard immigrants not only as potential agriculturalists, but also as military forces.[182]

The decrease of population in Muş and its environs, particularly due to Armenians migration to Russia increased the need for new settlers. This explained the settlement of the Muslim immigrants in the Ottoman East. As indicated in various Ottoman documents, a group of immigrants was already settled in Erzurum, Kars, Muş, and Van by 1860, though the process accelerated throughout the 1860s. Muş was among the important places for the settlement of immigrants thanks to its large area. The immigrants who gathered on the coast of the Black Sea were transferred to these vast lands. In June 1861, it was reported that seven hundred immigrant households were transported to Samsun for settlement. However, due to the lack of land, their settlement in Samsun became difficult, and also upon the petition of some to be settled in the province of Erzurum, it was decided Muş would be suitable for their

---

1830–1914, 65. For further details about Muslim emigration from Russia after the Crimean War, see Alan W. Fisher, "Emigration of Muslims from the Russian Empire in the Years After the Crimean War," *Jahrbücher für Geschichte Osteuropas* 35, no. 3 (1987): 356–71.

179   Karpat, Ottoman Population, 55.
180   Abdullah Saydam, *Kırım ve Kafkas Göçleri* (Ankara: Türk Tarih Kurumu Basımevi, 1997), 105. Yet the council was abrogated in 1865. However different councils for the same aim would be established later. For details, Ibid.; Ahmet Cevat Eren, *Türkiye'de Göç ve Göçmen Meseleleri: Tanzimat Devri, İlk Kurulan Göçmen Komisyonu, Çıkarılan Tüzükler* (Istanbul: Nurgök Matbaası, 1966); David Cameron Cuthell, "The Muhacirin Komisyonu: An Agent in the Transformation of Ottoman Anatolia, 1860–1866" (PhD diss., Columbia University, 2005).
181   Kemal H. Karpat, "Ottoman Urbanism: The Crimean Emigration to Dobruca and the Founding of Mecidiye, 1856–1878," in Studies on Ottoman Social and Political History: Selected Articles and Essays (Leiden: Brill 2002).
182   Selim Deringil, "19. Yüzyılda Osmanlı İmparatorluğu'na Göç Olgusu Üzerine Bazı Düşünceler," in *Prof. Dr. Bekir Kütükoğlu'na Armağan-Istanbul Üniversitesi Edebiyat Fakültesi Tarih Araştırma Merkezi* (Istanbul: Edebiyat Fakültesi Basımevi, 1991), 437.

settlement.¹⁸³ Besides, some Nogai and Circassian families had been sent to Muş from Karahisar-ı Şarki in 1862.¹⁸⁴ Likewise, some immigrants settled in Biga, petitioned to be settled in Muş or Kars due to climate and the fact that most of their relatives had been settled there previously.¹⁸⁵

However, not all of these settlement decisions were implemented, or took place smoothly. In 1863, it was decided to send 222 immigrant households, previously settled in Muş, to Pasin-i Ulya and Sivas. The reason for this change was not specified, but another report of the provincial council of Erzurum that was transferred to the Immigrants Commission provides some information about the problems of the settlement of immigrants. The Provincial Council of Erzurum reported that during the settlement of Circassian immigrants in the sanjaks of Kars, Muş, and some other districts, the inhabitants helped them by offering the use of their carts. However, some of the immigrants returned to Russia and some did not stay in the places allocated to them. Rather, they were wandering about from village to village being a burden on the local people, and doing harm to their livestock. The governor Hayreddin Pasha, and the council members, emphasized that those immigrants were disorderly and did not heed any warnings, which led to their being a burden on the native people. The governor and the council emphasized that the province of Erzurum was a frontier region and consisted of tribal populations, so its situation was delicate; while the security and contentment of the local people was important. In another case, the provincial council emphasized that local people who had been living there for thousands of years, fulfilling their duties to the state, and paying their taxes, would be obliged to leave their lands and disperse. Therefore, they demanded that the immigrant groups who had already left or were going to leave Trabzon should no longer be sent to Erzurum.¹⁸⁶ Paying attention to the geo-political delicacy of the province of Erzurum, the governor of and the council members indicated the anxiety of possible troubles between local people, tribes and the immigrants.

In May 1865,¹⁸⁷ Nusret Pasha a member of the Dar-ı Şura-yı Askeri, who was appointed to transfer five thousand Chechen immigrant households from Muş

---

183 BOA. A. MKT. MHM. 221/10, 22 Zilkade 1277 (1 June 1861).
184 BOA. A. MKT. MHM. 238790, 18 Zilkade 1278 (17 May 1862).
185 BOA. A. MKT. MHM. 237/74, 16 Rebiülevvel 1278 (21 October 1861).
186 BOA. A. MKT. NZD. 385/59, 14 Cemaziyelahir 1278 (17 December 1861).
187 In 1864, after Russia annexed the Caucasses, a huge number of Caucassian peoples migrated to Ottoman lands. İpek, İmparatorluktan Ulus Devlete, 40. Also see Mehmet Hacısalihoğlu, ed. *1864 Kafkas Tehciri: Kafkasya'da Rus Kolonizasyonu, Savaş ve Sürgün* (Istanbul: BALKAR & IRCICA, 2014).

and Van.[188] However, by autumn of the same year, there were still problems regarding their settlement. Immigrants who had gathered in Muş and Erzurum refused to depart for places allocated for their settlement. However, there was order to collect their guns and send them to their places of settlement.[189] In a report by the newly appointed governor of Erzurum, Mehmed Reşid Pasha, details came to light. The pasha's report highlighted that most of the zaptiehs in the province of Erzurum were deployed for the transport and settlement of Chechen immigrants. He implied that this matter left other issues of the region in disarray; for example, cases of banditry had increased. It was first decided the Chechens would be settled in Van and Muş, yet upon the objection of Russia, it was decided to settle them in Diyarbekir and Harput.[190] Russia laid down the condition that immigrants should not be settled on frontier regions.[191] As the oxen and carts of the immigrants were not sufficient, necessary equipment was collected from the districts and villages of Erzurum Province by the zaptiehs. This matter also points to how the transport and settlement of immigrants were great burdens on local residents.[192]

Content with the previous decision concerning their settlement in Muş and Van, the immigrants – who amounted to eight thousand in Erzurum and fifteen thousand in Hasankale and Muş – refused to be dispatched to any other place. They caused difficulties and made up excuses. Upon the insistence of the immigrants, local inhabitants began to complain and demand that the immigrants should be settled in other, distant places. Governor Mehmed Reşid Pasha argued that if the immigrants were not sent to their places of settlement before winter and it became necessary to settle them in their current location, a great many problems would arise. Successive reports had already arrived from Muş complaining about the strife and conflict between the immigrants and the Kurds. The governor stated that unless necessary precautions were taken, such small disputes would result in greater troubles.[193]

Local authorities were not enthusiastic about the settlement of Muslim immigrants in the province of Erzurum in the 1860s. For the particular locality of Muş, which was already depressed because of the pressures analyzed in this chapter, the settlement of immigrants was considered an extra burden for the inhabitants.

---

188   BOA. A. MKT. MHM. 331/86, 17 Zilhicce 1281 (13 May 1865).
189   BOA. A. MKT. MHM. 345/63, 23 Cemaziyelahir 1282 (13 November 1865).
190   BOA. A. MKT. MHM. 344/94, 10 Cemaziyelahir 1282 (31 October 1865).
191   İpek, *İmparatorluktan Ulus Devlete*, 41.
192   BOA. A. MKT. MHM. 344/94, 10 Cemaziyelahir 1282 (31 October 1865).
193   Ibid., BOA. A. MKT. MHM. 346/1, 29 Cemaziyelahir 1282 (19 November 1865).

6.5 Conclusion

By looking at the locality of Muş in the 1850s and 60s through the cross-sectarian petitions of commoners, this chapter has examined the repercussions of the Tanzimat reforms. Although the first half of the nineteenth century, as discussed through the entire and partial careers of Emin and Şerif Pashas, respectively, was an era in which the employment of local notables for the implementation of reforms was deemed necessary, the most influential notables were actually seen as obstacles to an efficient collection of revenues in Ottoman Kurdistan. Thus, upon the first opportunity they were exiled from the region. Nonetheless, the primary outcome was that their elimination did not contribute to the implementation of reforms. Centrally-appointed administrators, deprived of the necessary knowledge of the region and influence over other local actors, failed to maintain security and order in the region. Thus, for two decades after the inclusion of the sanjak of Muş in the Tanzimat program, inhabitants filed petitions for the return of its historical administrators.

Such a desire on the part of local inhabitants does not necessarily mean the times when the dynasty of Muş was ruling was a "golden age." Rather, it emphasizes that the condition of the non-nomadic peasantry worsened in their absences. The main source of the displeasure of peasants consisted of two pillars. On the one hand, the extortion and the indebtedness of the peasants of Muş by a coalition of local councils, tax farmers, kaimakams, moneylenders, and local notables. On the other hand, conflicts they were experiencing with Kurdish tribes that increased due to the inadequacy of centrally-appointed kaimakams. As complaints mainly consisted of extortion, over taxation, and forced labor, it is possible to argue that the practices Tanzimat reforms sought to eradicate were still prevalent.

Especially when the sanjak of Muş became one of the suppliers for the Imperial Army during the Crimean War, its peasants frequently petitioned with regard to over taxation, extortion, and corruption by the kaimakams and council members. In fact, complaints about a range of local actors – not only kaimakams and council members but also tax farmers, moneylenders and Muslim and Armenian notables – continued for nearly a decade after the war. Thus, even though a reform edict, the Islahat Fermanı, was promulgated after the Crimean War to ensure the equality of Muslims and non-Muslims and to improve the conditions of the non-Muslim subjects of the empire, and even though there were important developments within the Armenian community, the Armenian peasants of Muş still sought for justice which had been denied to them by a network of local actors.

Complaints arrived mostly from the villages on the plain of Muş – the former yurtluk-ocaklık villages of the beys of Muş. Thus, these complaints also told of the fate of those villages and the economic power the notables of Muş once enjoyed. By the same token, petitions by local inhabitants shed light on the one of the main mechanisms of the dispossession of peasants: The monetization of the economy led to the emergence of *murabahacılık* (usury) in the 1860s. This system worsened the dispossession of the commoners of Muş through indebtedness that increased day by day. In this context, desperate peasants who were deprived of a competent, impartial governor could do nothing other than migrate. Thus, the native population of Muş decreased because of the immiseration the people endured. Nevertheless, the emigration of local inhabitants was not the only population movement of those years. An important number of Muslims immigrants displaced by Russian advances settled in the sanjak of Muş after the Crimean War. Although the issue of immigration worsened by the end of 1877–78 Ottoman-Russian War, the issue is foreshadowed in the 1860s.

At the end of 1860s, complaints about Muş's governance were not yet resolved. The particular inability of the kaimakams to control the Kurdish tribes resulted in the continuation of atrocities against peasants and the emigration of especially the Armenian population. Therefore, in 1869, drawing attention to the incapability of the kaimakams and their misconduct in the administration of the sanjak of Muş, provincial reports emphasized that Muş needed urgent reforms for which a competent kaimakam was essential. In search for a proper candidate, the chief treasurer (*defterdar*) of Erzurum even suggested someone from the dynasty of Erzurum, neither because of his administrative experience nor his knowledge of the area, but because he had always farmed the taxes of Muş. While correspondence between local and central authorities continued to debate an appropriate administrator for a region like Muş which was not only sensitively situated but was also the most fertile and productive sanjak of the province of Erzurum, it was reported that four to five hundred families of Armenians were considering emigrating to Russia.[194] The present chapter has focused on the one of the two pillars of discontent among the peasants of Muş and their migration; the following two chapters will focus on the second pillar, the tribes of Muş.

---

194   BOA. İ. ŞD. 12/567, 22 Şevval 1285 (5 February 1869).

CHAPTER 7

Governors, Tribes, and Peasants

In the 1850s–1860s, the people of Muş had two main sources of grievance. First, the coalition of kaimakams, moneylenders, usurers, tax farmers, and council members devastated the peasants of Muş with extortion, over taxation, indebtedness, and corvée, the account of which was elaborated in the previous chapter. Second, tensions arose from their relations with the seminomadic and nomadic tribes of Muş, which were equally disastrous for the peasants of Muş. While focusing on nomadic and semi-nomadic tribes in the context of the Tanzimat reforms, this chapter together with the next chapter will try to arrive at an understanding of why the relations between nomads and peasants worsened. The chapter analyzes in which ways nomad-peasant relations changed, while the Tanzimat state was settling nomads.

There is a growing literature which argues that the peasants-nomads relation was symbiotic. While not intending to refute this argument, this chapter argues that during the times when resources were insufficient, peasants and nomads got into conflict. Periods of significant transformation, such as the Tanzimat's attempts at the settlement of nomads would also result in aggravation of the relations between two groups. When the nomads were to be settled in or near villages – which had already had a settled population – in the framework of the Tanzimat in the sanjak of Muş, the tension between two groups became inevitable. This inquiry into the relations between peasants and nomads, in the transformation period, also provides a nuanced understanding regarding the insufficiency of tribal economy. The plunder economy, which was reflected in the official documents as the assaults and atrocities of nomads against peasants, signifies how the tribal economy was not self-sufficient, and was vulnerable to climatic and political fluctuations.

In the settlement of tribes the notables of Muş played crucial roles. Since the tribes were human resources in terms of both manpower and prospective agriculturalists, they were the target of the notables of Muş who were manipulating their influence over the tribes as leverage in the negotiation with the central and provincial governments to consolidate their power. Likewise, provincial and central authorities considered notables as the main controlling force over the tribes. The case of Emin Pasha and his brothers was such a story. They particularly used the settlement card as a leverage to bargain over their power with central and provincial authorities.

As a part of nineteenth century reforms designed to strengthen the central government's rule in the periphery, the hereditary rule of the Kurdish nobility, including the Muş notables, was forcefully eliminated by the Ottoman government. Pioneering works on Kurdish emirates and tribal organizations are generally unanimous concerning the "chaos" and "insecurity" in Ottoman Kurdistan, after the elimination of the emirates.[1] Nonetheless, this point requires some refinement. In the case of Muş, as discussed in the previous chapter, after the exile of Şerif Pasha together with his extended family, centrally-appointed administrators had difficulty in governing the region, controlling the tribes as reflected in the petitions of the commoners of Muş. However, this does not mean that the rule of the emirs was "peaceful" and "harmonious."[2] Even before the nineteenth century reforms, tribes were not passive actors simply subordinated to and controlled by the Kurdish emirs. They had their own agenda and played politics in the region. In addition, cases of extortion, usurpation, murder, and injury certainly also occurred during the rule of the mîrs. The difference lies in the negotiation, dialog, and coalition and/or contention between Kurdish notables and tribes. However, it is a fact that in the absence of the notables, the tribes found more opportunities to wreak havoc.

A related question is that of the nature of the rule that Tanzimat state sought to establish after the annihilation of the Kurdish emirates. As Bruinessen argued, the increasing control of the Ottoman central government and its successor states in the Kurdish periphery and the "breaking [of] the power" of Kurdish mîrs did not necessarily translate into "detribalization" and "simply" replacing "direct rule" with "indirect rule." On the contrary, the process was more complicated, and as he argues, it can be defined as "re-tribalisation."[3]

Thus, in a few generations, tribal organization in Bohtan has shown a rapid devolution from complex, state-like to much simpler forms of social and political organization-as if it has taken a few steps back on the evolutionary ladder. In this case it is clearly a response to central government interventions. The denser the administrative network of the state became, the smaller and simpler

---

1 Van Bruinessen, *Agha, Shaikh, and State*; Wadie Jwaideh, *The Kurdish National Movement: Its Origins and Development* (Syracuse: Syracuse University Press, 2006).
2 As Stephan H. Astourian also emphasizes that although, Armenians peasants "had not enjoyed a good life" under the rule of Kurdish emirates, "things had been predictable, fairly peaceful, and taxes [were] only due to the Kurdish lords." With their removal, he argues, "a free-for-all occurred." Stephan H. Astourian, "The Silence of the Land: Agrarian Relations, Ethnicity, and Power," in *A Question of Genocide: Armenians and Turks at the end of the Ottoman Empire*, eds. Ronald Grigor Suny, Fatma Müge Göçek, and Norman M. Naimark (Oxford: Oxford University Press, 2011), 63.
3 Martin Van Bruinessen, "Kurdish Tribes and the State of Iran: The Case of Simko's Revolt," in *The Conflict of Tribe and State in Iran and Afghanistan*, ed. Richard Tapper (London: Croom Helm, 1983), 371–2. Also Richard Tapper, "Introduction," Ibid., ed. Richard Tapper, 61.

the tribes. The state did not give up indirect rule altogether, but this took place at increasingly lower levels. After the mîrs, some government authority was delegated to tribe aghas, and later qabile aghas, village aghas.[4]

With regard to terminology, Bruinessen draws attention to the fact that it is "misleading" to designate all Kurdish tribes with a single term, when their variety "in size and forms of internal organization" is taken into consideration.[5] Despite its "notorious" ambiguity,[6] the term "tribe" has generally been employed in this study to describe nomadic and seminomadic groups in the eastern periphery of the Ottoman Empire.[7] Using the term "tribe" should not conceal the fact that tribes were "historically and situationally dynamic" rather than "static," and they were inclined to be both "centralizing and egalitarian" and "inegalitarian and hierarchical."[8]

For the earlier periods, one of the main approaches to theorize the tribes and state formation is an evolutionary perspective which simply envisages a development from small tribes to chiefdoms that eventually result in state or state-like formations. As Philip Khoury and Joseph Kostiner suggest, the main postulate of this approach is the view that chiefdoms are rooted in a "segmentary division of society in which tribes or tribal segments are bound together by a common identity based on kinship."[9] However, they rightly argue, kinship alone is not enough to understand chiefdom.[10] Albert Hourani also argues that tribes are not bound together by genuine kinship, rather "a myth of [a] common ancestor" held tribes together. In some cases "even this myth may not exist," he further argues.[11] Similarly, Bruinessen emphasizes that for Kurdish tribes,

---

4   Van Bruinessen, Agha, Shaikh, and State, 181–2.
5   "Kurds, States, and Tribes," in *Tribes and Power: Nationalism and Ethnicity in the Middle East*, eds. Faleh Abdul-Jabar and Hosham Dawod (London: Saqi, 2003), 178.
6   Tapper, "Introduction," 6.
7   For a discussion on the terminology to define the Kurdish tribes in the eastern periphery of the Ottoman Empire, see Yener Koç, "Nomadic Pastoral Tribes at the Intersection of the Ottoman, Persian and Russian Empires (1820s–1890s)," 32–70.
8   Beck, "The Tribes and the State," 190.
9   Philip S. Khoury and Joseph Kostiner, "Introduction," Ibid., eds. Philip S. Khoury and Joseph Kostiner (University of California Press, 1990), 8.
10 Ibid. The main tenet of the argument of kinship is embedded in the concept of "asabiyya" provided by Ibn Khaldun. Accordingly, tribal unity stems from asabiyya, "tribal bonding or the sentiment of group solidarity that results from kinship, blood ties, and common descent." Ira M. Lapidus, "Tribes and State Formation in Islamic History," Ibid., eds. Philip S. Khoury and Joseph Kostiner (Berkeley), 28.
11 Albert Hourani, "Conclusion: Tribes and States in Islamic History," in *Tribes and States in the Middle East*, ed. Philip S. Khoury and Joseph Kostiner (Berkeley: University of California Press, 1990), 304.

particularly larger ones what is more relevant than the significance of kinship is "political affiliation and loyalty to a common chieftain or chiefly lineage."[12]

As Richard Tapper argued, "a better understanding of the nature of tribal political organizations, and of relations between tribal and non-tribal society, must be sought in a closer examination of the social and economic basis of the tribal system."[13] While focusing on the tribes of the sanjak of Muş in the framework of the Tanzimat reforms, this chapter will partially deal with the social and economic organizations of tribes of Muş. However, a comprehensive historical analysis of the social, economic, and political bases of tribal societies is a subject for a further study.

In terms of state-tribe relations, Bruinessen argues, "neither the Kurdish emirates nor the large nomadic tribes were the creations" of the Ottoman Empire, as they predated the empire's influence in the region. However, the Kurdish emirates and tribes' "recognition and [the] delegation of powers to them by the Ottoman center fixated the state of affairs in the Kurdish periphery and solidified them as political units."[14] By the same token, Lois Beck underscores that states and tribes were "interdependent" throughout the history of Iran. They "maintained each other as a single system" and "did not function as two separate, opposing systems."[15] States required tribes for "military power, revenue, and regional security."[16] In the same vein, tribes "depended on state intervention in the case of regional competition and conflict, and their leaders drew sources of power, authority and wealth from their connections with states."[17] Beck's point is in line with Lisa Anderson's proposal in her piece on Libyan tribes and the Libyan state. She also argues that "tribe and state are not mutually exclusive analytical categories but rather summaries of characteristics more or less present in any society at any moment."[18]

Based on this literature of Middle Eastern tribes, this book partly contributes to the discussion on Kurdish tribes in the nineteenth century. An examination of the relations of the tribes of Muş with the provincial authorities, notables, and peasants in the nineteenth century is crucial to better understand the locality of Muş. In this framework, the following passage exemplifies how both central and local authorities related to tribes in the sanjak of Muş:

12   Van Bruinessen, "Kurds, States," 166.
13   Tapper, "Introduction," 7.
14   Van Bruinessen, "Kurds, States."
15   Beck, "The Tribes and the State," 192.
16   Ibid.
17   Ibid., 192.
18   Lisa Anderson, "Tribe and State: Libyan Anamolies," Ibid. (University of California Press, 1990), 289.

> Thirty years ago, the deceased commander-in-chief of the Anatolian Army, Gözlüklü Reşid Pasha, together with the late governor of Kürdistan, Esad Pasha, collected the present inhabitants of Malazgirt in Muş from the mountains and settled us in the district of Malazgirt. Thanks to the Sultan we received oxen and ploughs and have been busy with agriculture. We paid our taxes and performed our duties by fulfilling all the orders of the exalted state. The tribal chiefs of your humble servants joined in the past event [the Crimean War] with a thousand cavalrymen. They also served the state and the religion in the company of the governor of Diyarbekir, İsmail Pasha, in the Kozan war with seven to eight hundred cavalrymen and one of our influential aghas even passed away during this event. [Although] our services to the state were such, four to five months ago a few of our influential aghas were summoned to Erzurum and jailed in the army barracks since then without [having committed any] real offenses. Not only they but also the poor inhabitants of our districts have become destitute and miserable. We ask for our merciful majesty to rescue our aghas from jail and so rescue us from oppression and torment.[19]

The quotation is from a petition of the headmen of the villages of Malazgirt to Istanbul dated 1875. Having described the account of their settlement and their services to the state, they resented the imprisonment of the aghas of their tribe. Their tribe was the Hesenan, a seminomadic tribe of Muş that had already been settled in villages of district of Malazgirt by the 1870s to a large extent, if not completely. Although many frontier tribes like the Haydaran, Sıpkî, and Zilan had come to Muş mostly upon the effort of the beys of Muş at the beginning of the nineteenth century, the existence of the Hesenan was most openly felt in Muş during the second half of the century. Again, the nomadic tribes of Diyarbekir – namely the Reşkotan, Pençnar, Bekiran – and the tribes of Siird – Suluki – were still traveling to the mountains of Muş which were their summer quarters in the second half of the century. Central and local authorities not only embarked on accelerating the sedentarization of tribes like the Hesenan, but also tried to prevent passage of others about which locals were complaining throughout the second half of the nineteenth century.

Taking these facts into consideration, this chapter will focus on local tribes and nomadic tribes from neighboring provinces who preferred the mountains of Muş as summer quarters. The provincial and central authorities applied a

---

19   BOA. ŞD. 2884/54, 2 Zilhicce 1292 (30 December 1875).

range of policies to maintain control over and ensure the sedentarization of these nomadic and seminomadic groups.

After a brief introduction to Tanzimat reforms regarding tribal entities, the case of nomadic groups coming to Muş from Diyarbekir and Siird, like the Bekiran, Pençnar, Alikan, Reşkotan, and Suluki – whose story of settlement is more complicated as they long insisted upon keeping their summer quarters in Muş – will be discussed. The Hesenan, which was the most important local tribe of Muş and which, as noted above, were settled to a great extent by the end of the century. The account of the sedentarization of the Hesenan tribe, their confrontation and collaboration with central authorities, and their relations not only with peasants but also with other tribal groups in the vicinity of Muş, like the Sıpkî, and Haydaran, will be the main focus of the next chapter.

7.1 Implications of the Tanzimat Reforms for the Nomadic Groups

The inclusion of the province of Erzurum in the Tanzimat reform program envisaged a range of transformations not only concerning the provincial administration of the empire – from a new taxation system to the establishment of provincial and district councils – but also concerning nomadic and seminomadic entities. Despite the fact that the priority with respect to nomads was sedentarization, important novelties were carried out concerning their inclusion in the new taxation system. For instance, in Muş, like in other regions included in the Tanzimat program, the customary taxes peasants had been paying for centuries were abolished. In a report sent from Istanbul to the governor of Kurdistan, the *yaylakiye* tax, paid by the tribes for their summer quarters, was also described as "an ancien regime" (*usul-i kadime*)[20] Thus, the yaylakiye tax, which amounted to seventy-four hundred guruş, was abolished for nomads settled in the villages of Muş.[21] Instead, the settled tribes were to pay the "tax" imposed on them – which amounted to fifty thousand guruş in 1261 (1845) – according to their ability to pay, just like the sedentary inhabitants of Muş.[22] This modification to the taxation of the tribes is significant as a part of the new tax regime of the Tanzimat, yet it also suggests that the economic power of Muş's notables was gradually being curtailed, as they had been collecting the yaylakiye tax from the tribes.

---

20   BOA. A. MKT. MVL. 25/8, 25 Rebiülahir 1266 (10 March 1850).
21   Ibid.
22   BOA. MVL. 8/38, 15 Ramazan 1262 (6 September 1846).

The inclusion of Kurdish tribes in the new taxation and conscription systems could only be realized after their settlement. Thus, the settlement of tribes was the priority. The idea behind the settlement of nomadic groups was multifaceted. Sedentarization was idealized as a project to transform tribes from "bandits" who troubled the settled population into "civilized and peaceful" peasants and conscripts. Richard Tapper describes this perception of local and central authorities regarding nomads as such:

> While the city was the source of government, order and productivity, the tribes had a natural tendency to rebellion, rapine and destruction, a tendency which might be related to the starkness of their habitat and its remoteness from the sources of civilisation, and also to the under-employment inherent in their way of life.[23]

Such an argument, Tapper further argues, might have some "justifications," yet "it is superficial and over-simplified."[24] In his piece on Ottoman colonialism, Selim Deringil also emphasizes how nomadism was regarded as "an anathema for modernity." This perception of nomads included both "enmity" and "mild paternalism" to certain degrees. "Savagery," "wild nature," and "ignorance," were the most popular adjectives used to describe the nomadic groups. Nevertheless, what is unavoidable, for central and provincial authorities, is to "gradually include them in the circle of civilization (*pey der pey daire-i medeniyete idhal*)."[25]

For the Ottoman statesmen, the settlement of nomads and turning them into agriculturalists were depicted as their introduction to "the honor of civilization." In correspondence with İsmail Pasha, the temporary governor of Muş, the governor of Erzurum argued that they agreed that the reforms and the settlement of tribes in the sanjak would not only save the people from assaults by nomads but also that the tribes would abandon their savage ways, and become a part of "the circle of desired humanity" (*hey'et-i mergube-i insaniyete girub*), occupy themselves with agriculture and trade, and no longer need to steal or be involved in other kinds of mischief.[26]

23　Tapper, "Introduction," 6.
24　Ibid.
25　Selim Deringil, "'They Live in a State of Nomadism and Savagery': The Late Ottoman Empire and the Post-Colonial Debate," *Comparative Studies in Society and History* 45, no. 2 (2003): 317.
26　"hem ahâlî ve fukarânın dest-i ta'addîlerinden halâs olması ve hem de kendüleri tavır-i beyâbânîden çıkub hey'et-i mergûbe-i insâniyyete girub zirâ'at ve filâhet ve ticâretle

In the same vein, according to the governor of Erzurum, Mehmed Hamdi, tent-dwelling Kurds and tribes did not deal with agriculture and trade, so they were busy with thievery and similar mischief to survive. He emphasized that there were a great many tent-dwelling Kurds and tribes in the province of Erzurum and its neighborhood who not only made no contribution to the treasury, but were also a great burden on local inhabitants.[27] However, the data pointing out the tribal role in economic activities falsify this perception of Ottoman bureaucrats regarding the nomads. Many tribes in the Ottoman East were busy with sheep trade. They provided meat for the consumption of cities like Istanbul, Cairo, Damascus and Halep.[28]

With their settlement, seminomadic tribes would become engaged in either agriculture or trade and thus become productive subjects contributing to the treasury. Moreover, peasants of the province would be saved from assaults by those nomadic groups for whom they were not only forced to provide winter quarters, along with hay and straw for their livestock, but also because of whom they were exposed to murder, injury, and extortion.[29] This is how the Ottoman bureaucrats legitimized their settlement project. However, the settlement of the pastoral nomads in peasants' villages led to similar problems. When nomads were forced or convinced to settle and engage with an economic activity to which they had not been accustomed, their relations with the settled population – peasants – deteriorated.

The Ottoman authorities combined different kind of strategies for the sedentarization of the nomads. Acknowledging the relationship between the settlement of nomads and state centralization, Yonca Köksal, in her case study of the tribes of the province of Ankara, argues that "sedentarization shows how top down state policies of coercion or bottom up strategies of mediation with local authorities can be combined in state centralization."[30] As this chapter argues, the settlement of tribes was not only encouraged through the granting

---

meşgûl olub hırsızlık ve uygunsuzluklarına meydân kalmaması." BOA. A. MKT. UM. 239/26, 7 Şevval 1272 (11 June 1856).

27 "Her tarafda hayme-nişîn olan ekrâd ve 'aşâirin zirâ'at ve ticâretde beherleri olmayub kendülerine idârede lazım olduğu cihetle hırsızlık ve uygunsuzlukla idâreye alışmış ve şu hâl ile külliyen mugâyır-ı rızâ-yı badi ve 'ali bulunmuş olduğuna ve Erzurum eyâletinde ve civârı mahallerde pek çok hayme-nişîn ekrâd ve 'aşâir olub bunların hazîne-i celîleye bir güna menf'aatleri olmadığından başka ahâlî ve fukarâ ve ebnâ-yı sebil haklarından muzırratları başdan aşmış ve böyle hayme-nişînlik sûretinde kaldıkça zabt ve rabtlarıyla def'-i muzırratlarının istihsâli düşvâr olacağı derkâr bulunmuş ..." BOA. A. MKT. UM. 239/26, 7 Şevval 1272 (11 June 1856).

28 Koç, "Nomadic Pastoral Tribes," 241–242.

29 BOA. A. MKT. MHM. 293/10, 13 Ramazan 1280 (21 February 1864).

30 Köksal, "Coercion and Mediation," 469.

of salaries and exemption from taxes but was also imposed with military power when necessary. Yet, "coercion was employed only when mediation failed."[31] Along the same lines, "geopolitical location," "geographical boundedness," "tribal hierarchy," and the possibilities of trade between tribal and sedentary groups were factors that determined the degree of coercion and mediation, employed for the settlement of the tribes.[32]

According to Köksal, the Tanzimat project of the sedentarization of seminomadic and nomadic groups differed in many ways from previous efforts. At first, sedentarization was embarked upon widely from Anatolia to the Kurdish and Arab provinces. Then, among the previous strategies implemented, there was a settlement option when tribes created troubles for sedentary groups. The main method was to exile them to distant places like Rakka instead of intervening in tribal structures.[33] For instance, efforts to settle them did not drastically change seminomadism, as many tribes maintained their migratory routes. With the Tanzimat, not only was the seasonal migration of the nomads more determinedly prohibited, but there was a great effort to keep their property and population registers. Nevertheless, the settlement policies of the Tanzimat era were a combination of the state's "experience" with the tribes and new methods – among which "negotiation" was "the oldest" strategy.[34]

7.2 Peasants and the Nomads: Settlement of the Tribes

It is necessary to discuss the methods and motivations for persuading the tribes to settle voluntarily in the province of Erzurum, keeping in mind that resort to military force to ensure their settlement was also not unusual. For instance, in 1861 the governor of Erzurum received an order that either he or the commander-in-chief of the Anatolian Army should go to Muş in order to undertake the settlement of the tribes with as little force as possible.[35] Hence,

---

31 Ibid., 487.
32 Ibid., 472–73.
33 For early attempts to settle nomadic and seminomadic tribes, see Orhonlu, Osmanlı İmparatorluğu'nda; Yusuf Halaçoğlu, *XVIII. Yüzyılda Osmanlı İmparatorluğu'nun İskân Siyaseti ve Aşiretlerin Yerleştirilmesi* (Ankara: Türk Tarih Kurumu Basımevi, 1988), 1–20.
34 Köksal, "Coercion and Mediation," 477–78. Cengiz Orhonlu also argues that the difference with the Tanzimat lies in dealing with the matter of summer and winter quarters. Tribes no longer migrated to different places in summer and winter; instead their need for summer and winter quarters would be satisfied in the wastelands of districts and sanjaks. In other words, they would be settled in their winter quarters. Orhonlu, *Osmanlı İmparatorluğu'nda*, 114.
35 BOA. A. MKT. MHM. 279/36, 20 Rebiülahir 1280 (31 December 1863).

the most widely-used strategy was exemption from taxes and conscription for a certain period of time. For instance, it was reported in 1851 that five hundred households of certain tribes were settled in the sanjak of Bayezid, and that they were exempt from taxes for two years. Although the Meclis-i Vâlâ was asked to provide these tribal families with grain for a time – as the villages in which they were settled were in ruins – this request was turned down because of financial problems. In the same vein, one hundred families of the Zilan were among the sedentarized tribes in Bayezid, and salaries were granted to some tribal aghas, including the mother of one tribal leader, Kasım Agha.[36] Taking the Zilan's controversial situation between the Ottoman and Iranian states into consideration, it is possible to argue that the process of incorporating tribes changed according to their prominence.[37]

One of the most important methods was to seek for the "mediation" of tribal leaders by appointing them as administrators in the districts. As will be discussed, the notorious Rıdvan and Kulihan Aghas of the Hesenan were the müdirs (district governors) of the districts (kaza) Malazgirt and Bulanık, respectively.[38] Moreover, inclusion in provincial administration was also used as a method of reward in return for militarily contribution of tribes during wars. In this era, for instance, the members of the Hesenan and Cibran were rewarded with administrative positions for their participation in the army during the Crimean War.[39]

Although the sedentarization and incorporation of the tribes were realized through tax exemptions, salaries, and positions in the provincial administration, other previously applied methods were abolished. With the implementation of the Tanzimat, it was argued that tribal leaders should no longer be granted ceremonial robes (hil'at) and that their expenses should not be covered by the treasury. Instead, they should be encouraged and honored (taltifât-ı lisâniye).[40] In the same vein, the acceptance of gifts from the tribes

---

36 BOA. A. MKT. UM. 59/97, 18 Receb 1267 (19 May 1851).
37 For the Zilan, see Yener Koç, "A Tribal Confederation at the Intersection of the Ottoman, Russian and Qajar Empire: The Zilan Confederation and the Empires (1810–1860)," *Middle Eastern Studies* 59 No. 2 (2023): 181–192.
38 Ahmet Cevdet Pasha also focused on how tribal elders were granted official posts as a part of the mission of Fırka-i Islahiyye. Ahmet Cevdet Paşa, *Ma'ruzat*, ed. Yusuf Halaçoğlu, 4 vols., vol. 4 (Istanbul: Çağrı Yayınları, 1980), 136. Fırka-i Islahiyye was a military operation which was a part of the reform movement of the nineteenth century carried out in the Çukurova, Gavurdağı, Kürt Dağı, and Kozan mountains between 1865 and 1866. See Yusuf Halaçoğlu, "Fırka-i İslahiye ve Yapmış Olduğu İskan," Tarih Dergisi, no. 27 (1973): 1–20.
39 BOA. MVL. 646/81, 27 Şevval 1279 (17 April 1863).
40 BOA. A. MKT. UM. 75/1, 14 Zilkade 1267 (10 September 1851).

was also forbidden,[41] which was actually the extension of the legal code, treating gift taking as bribery, to tribe-official relations.[42]

The scope of the settlement of nomads is debatable. It can be argued that from the 1840s onwards, provincial and central authorities zealously attempted to settle as many tribes as possible. The first governor of the province of Kurdistan, Esad Pasha, together with the commander-in-chief of the Anatolian Army, Mehmed Reşid Pasha, embarked upon the arduous sedentarization of nomadic and seminomadic groups in Muş, as in other places. However, this was not a trouble-free process; rather it was uneven, complicated, and certainly gradual. In the case of Muş, the collaboration with the notables had always been crucial for maintaining control over Kurdish tribes, as has been emphasized throughout this study. Therefore, before his exile in 1849, Şerif Bey was nominated as the kaimakam of the sanjak to deal with the settlement of tribes in Muş. Similarly, upon Şerif Bey's exile, together with his immediate family, the search for a capable kaimakam stemmed from the necessity of maintaining control over nomadic groups, as has been discussed in chapter 6.

In a report by Esad Pasha during his governance of the province of Erzurum, the tribes of Muş were depicted as mostly tent-dwellers who spend their summers in tents on the mountains, and who had become accustomed to quartering themselves in certain villages of Muş in winter – assaulting the inhabitants and forcibly taking their hay and straw. Şerif Bey had been charged with preventing the tribes from arrogating the fodder and other property of the villagers, without payment. Nevertheless, in order to save the inhabitants of Muş from such tribal habits, their sedentarization was thought to be vital.[43]

The settlement of the nomads of Van and Muş was decided simultaneously and in Muş and Bitlis their settlement had already been embarked upon when these regions were included in the Tanzimat program. As Esad Pasha stated, the aghalıks of the tribes were abolished and the tribes were divided into four or five households and, if necessary, into even smaller units. They were settled in Muslim and non-Muslim villages. Places for them to build houses and engage in agriculture were allocated and they were registered in the population records of the villages where they were settled. Thereupon, they were regarded as settled populations, and in time they would be taxed as much as

---

41 BOA. A. MKT. UM. 229/54, 15 Receb 1272 (22 March 1856).
42 For a discussion on the Penal Code of 1840 in terms of bribery, see Kırlı, "Yolsuzluğun İcadı," 45–119.
43 "livâ-i mezbûrde kâin ekrâd ve 'aşâirin ekseri hayme-nişîn olub eyyâm-ı sayfde çadırlarla sahrâda ve mevsim-i şıtâda livâ-i mezbûrun hâvi olduğu münâsib karyelerde eğlenmekde olarak ahâlî-i fukarânın mine'lkadîm ot ve samânlarını almak misillû cebr ve taa'ddiye ibtidâr itmeği 'adet hükmüne koymuşlar." BOA. MVL. 8/38, 15 Ramazan 1262 (6 September 1846).

they could bear (*hal-i tahammüllerine göre*).⁴⁴ Besides, as they were not accustomed to settled life, they would have difficulty in maintaining a livelihood. Yet if the circumstances of Kurdistan were taken into consideration, it was sufficient if they got used to it, Esad Pasha argued. In the long run, once frontier matters and the Hakkari trouble (referring to the rebellion of Nurullah Bey) were settled, the plan was to settle tribes in the vast fields and abandoned villages of Muş, Bayezid, and Hakkari, equip them with the necessary tools for farming and building houses, and also give tribal leaders and aghas salaries. In this way, both the abandoned places would be improved and the revenues of the central treasury would be increased.⁴⁵

However, initial reactions proved that the settlement would not be an easy process. Some local authorities objected to the settlement of the tribes in the Armenian villages of Muş. Among them was the bishop of Çanlı Church, Zakarya. The governor of Kurdistan was of the belief that the settlement of the tribes would please and comfort the settled population and criticized the bishop for being so unreasonable as to oppose it. The pasha noted that as the bishop was a local, his replacement might be necessary in order to prevent any provocation in the region.⁴⁶ Zakarya had his own reasons in opposing the settlement of tribal households in the Armenian villages, as the accustomation of tribes to the settled life could not be succeeded overnight.

For instance, the Council of Muş reported that the settlement of the Elmanlı tribe was carried out with the help of Şerif Bey in 1845 and 1846.⁴⁷ The tribe was generally settled in the villages of Muş. Forty-two families of the tribe, the leader of which was Şero Agha, were likewise settled in the village Kasor [Suvaran] in Muş.⁴⁸ However, in a few years, complaints from the peasants of the village of Kasor reached the imperial center through a petition of the Armenian Patriarchate. The tribal leader Şero Agha was attacking Christian inhabitants on various pretexts. It was emphasized that as long as the agha remained, the inhabitants would have no peace and could do nothing but abandon their villages.⁴⁹ An investigation was carried out to warn him and in case he disobeyed, to exile him.

---

44   BOA. İ. MSM. 52/1343, 12 Şevval 1264 (11 September 1848).
45   BOA. İ. MSM. 52/1346, 4 Zilkade 1264 (2 October 1848).
46   BOA. İ. MSM. 52/1343, 12 Şevval 1264 (11 September 1848). It is possible that collaboration with Şerif Bey and his brothers was required to calm such reactions, as their exile had been suspended for a while.
47   In the meantime, it is necessary to emphasize that the family members describe relations between the tribe of Elmanlı and the Alaaddin Paşazades as intimate. Personal interview with Abdurrahman Yıldırım, Muş, 23 July 2014.
48   BOA. A. MKT. UM. 15/44, 5 Receb 1266 (17 May 1850).
49   BOA. A. MKT. 226/10, 5 Zilkade 1265 (22 September 1849).

According to a report of the Muş's council, when the Elmanlı tribe was settled in Kasor, the re'âyâ (Armenian peasants) of the village moved to neighboring re'âyâ villages, on the grounds that they would not get along with the tribe. Nevertheless, in 1848, while the settlements of other tribes were being carried out, the Elmanlı tribe was transferred from re'âyâ villages to other, more appropriate or abandoned (*harabe*) villages. However, Elmanlı Şero was allowed to remain in Kasor with permission of the murahhasa of the Armenians. Upon receipt of the complaint, Şero Agha was called before the council, and in the presence of the murahhasa, he argued that although his tribe had been involved in the acts described before the Tanzimat, they no longer dared to act in this way by virtue of the implementation of the Tanzimat in Muş. The agha continued that as they had become *meşta-nişin* (winterquartering tribes) they made peace and security due to the "auspicious rule" (*usûl-ı mehasinşumûl*) [of the Tanzimat]. Hereafter, he had not attacked anyone so that he could not be held responsible for any kind of misdeed.[50] The statement of Şero Agha indicates that tribal aghas also used the language of the Tanzimat to defend themselves.

In this confrontation, both the murahhasa and the re'âyâ confirmed the remarks of Şero Agha. They also emphasized that although some tribal members continued to steal for a few years they were being disciplined by officials. It is thus reasonable to question why the inhabitants of Kasor complained about the Elmanlı. It came out that despite the reality that Kasor was a Christian village and it had a church of its own, when the tribe was settled there in 1845/6 the Armenians had had to leave their village. Therefore, the council of Muş emphasized that the complaint of the re'âyâ about the tribe stemmed from their wish to remove the tribe from their village so that they could return. Having confirmed that the village of Kasor was a re'âyâ village, the council of Muş employed Emrah Agha to resettle the Elmanlı tribe. Consequently, Şero Agha and his tribal households would be resettled in the villages of Petar, Şeyh Bayram, Zorade, and Permuk to which the villagers of Kasor had emigrated previously. Thus, the latter could come back to Kasor. The tribe and the villagers of Kasor also settled financial issues among themselves.[51]

The settlement of the Elmanlı tribe was carried out more smoothly in comparison to that of tribes like the Hesenan, Sıpkî, and Haydaran. Certainly, the size and area of influence of the tribes played a crucial role in their settlement. Throughout the 1850s, there was a great effort to settle those tribes. In 1856, the decision was reported to settle the tribes of the Hesenan, Haydaran, and

---

50   BOA. A. MKT. UM. 15/44, 5 Receb 1266 (17 May 1850).
51   Ibid.

Sıpkî in five villages improved and ameliorated by the Şekaki tribe of Van, as well as four ruined neighboring villages.[52] Although it is difficult to determine the extent to which the settlement of those tribes in those villages was accomplished, the settlement process was modest and gradual.

In the same year, the governor of Erzurum, Mehmed Hamdi, informed the Sublime Porte that the Sıpkî tribe, consisting of more than seven hundred families,[53] was honorable (*ehl-ı ırz*) compared to other nomadic and semi-nomadic tribes and that it was willing to settle down if they were given proper reassurances. The villages suggested for the settlement of the Sıpkî were twenty-six ruined settlements in the districts of Malazgird and Bulanık in Muş. However, the Hesenan had already been settled in some of those villages. The governor of Erzurum, Mehmed Hamdi stated that those families of the Hesenan consisted of one or two hundred households, so it was possible for the two tribes to share the villages. Thus, after reassuring the administrators of both districts and the tribal leaders with necessary letters, Colonel Ali Bey from the Anatolian Army and Nuri Bey from the Provincial Council of Erzurum accompanied by necessary troops were entitled to allocate the twenty-six ruined villages between the Hesenan and Sıpkî.[54] The villages where each tribe was settled would be specified and their populations would be registered. If any empty villages remained, they would be reserved for the settlement of other tribes.[55] However, the settlement of the Sıpkî in the districts of Muş was temporary; in later years, they were generally settled in neighboring sanjaks like Bayezid.

The Suluki (Silukan) tribe[56] was also among the nomadic groups partially settled in Muş in 1850. In 1908, Mark Sykes described this tribe, which consisted of 900 families, as both "cultivators and nomads" who "migrate[d] in the summer to the Muş plain" at the beginning of the twentieth century.[57] Thus, the settlement in the case of Suluki meant turning from a nomadic tribe to a semi-nomadic one. The settlement of the tribe in Muş began with the opposition of Ferho Agha, the leader of the tribe who had been a tent dweller near

---

52   BOA. İ. DH. 358/23641, 28 Safer 1273 (28 October 1856).
53   According to Sykes, in 1908 the Sıpkî tribe consisted of 3000 families in total. Mark Sykes, "The Kurdish Tribes of the Ottoman Empire," *The Journal of the Royal Anthropological Institute of Great Britain and Ireland* 38 (1908): 477.
54   It is difficult to understand from archival documents whether those 'ruined villages' were used to be inhabited by the Armenians who had left after the 1828–1829 Ottoman-Russian War or not.
55   BOA. A. MKT. UM. 239/26, 7 Şevval 1272 (11 June 1856).
56   The Suluki tribe was also among the tribes coming from provinces in the vicinity of Muş.
57   Sykes, "The Kurdish Tribes," 460.

Bitlis, to the conscription lottery (*kura-i şeriyye*). The Agha was accused of misinforming officials about the number of his tribesmen by hiding them. It was decided in the Meclis-i Vâlâ to send him together with his family to Erzurum and to appoint a new agha to the tribe in his place.[58] However, during Ferho Agha's journey to Erzurum in the company of the commander-in-chief of the Anatolian Army, he was left in Muş as the route of the commander had changed. Upon the suggestion of Esad Pasha, Ferho Agha and his family were settled in Muş as the agha was of old age.[59] The ad interim kaimakam of Muş, Naim Efendi, was ordered to take all precautions to prevent his escape.[60]

The maintenance of harmony between the sedentary population – the peasants of the sanjak of Muş – and the newly settled nomadic groups proved to be hard. Below, some other cases of settlement will be discussed to better understand the reactions of the inhabitants of Muş to this process of settlement and their relations to the nomads.

In a petition dated 1853, the inhabitants of Muş emphasized that despite the relief they enjoyed thanks to the reforms of the Sublime State, they have become helpless due to more than fifteen hundred "black tent-dwellers" settled in the sanjak.[61] Although some other tribes like the Sıpkî and Elmanlı were settled in the villages of Muş, it was primarily the Hesenan who were settled there and could be regarded as a "local" tribe. Thus, the "black tent-dwellers" in question in this petition most probably referred to the Hesenan. This phrase was a formulation of the conflict between local peasants and nomadic groups. Although the settlement policy concerning the nomads was to settle them primarily in ruined or abandoned wastelands, it could not prevent them from attacking the neighboring villages and involving in plunder economy.

Consequently, some Muslim families from the village of Sipanun in the district of Kasor migrated to Bayezid. The kaimakam of Bayezid, Pertev Efendi, argued that there were even more reʿâyâ coming to live in Bayezid from certain villages of Muş, and in the case it was disallowed, they will immigrate to Russia. The Hesenan tribe from Malazgird, with the inducement of their headman (*muhtar*) Rızko (Rıdvan Agha) and his relatives Kulihan, Derviş, Umo, and Beyzade perpetually attacked on mostly Armenian but also Muslim villages. After one group of them went to the villages to forcefully take wheat, barley, cattle, money and other goods, another group would stop by the same villages twenty days or a month later with the same demands. The grain remaining

---

58 BOA. MVL. 227/38, 11 Ramazan 1265 (31 July 1849).
59 BOA. İ. MVL. 157/4486, 26 Muharrem 1266 (12 December 1849).
60 BOA. İ. DH. 212/12312, 5 Cemaziyelevvel 1266 (18 March 1850).
61 BOA. MVL. 131/20, 11 Cemaziyelevvel 1269 (20 February 1853).

after such extortion neither covered the needs of the villagers nor their livestock. Moreover, in the case of the slightest resistance to fulfilling the demands of tribal members, the stacks of hay and fodder which they had labored to collect in summer to feed their livestock in winter and even the houses were being burnt down. The tribal members were sharing goods seized from the villagers, as if they had bought them. In a similar line, burglary often occurred along the roadsides and village streets. The kaimakam of Bayezid, Pertev Efendi argued that the atrocities by Rızko and his relatives were similar or even worse than those of Han Mahmud who had tyrannized Van and been exiled to Rusçuk.[62] The allegory between Han Mahmud and Rıdvan Agha of the Hesenan actually indicates that the Ottoman authorities had not yet established their idealized rule in the region after the liquidation of the Kurdish emirates.

Apart from general complaints of settled habitants about the plunder economy, other problems arose due to the discrepancy between settled and nomadic lifestyles. The relationship between the houses of the Hesenan and the peasants of Kuştiyan [Şehittahir], a village of Malazgirt, best exemplifies this. The Kuştiyaners primarily complained that the families of the Hesenan who began living in their villages, namely Şero, Havzi, and Ferho, had many livestock that trespassed on and ruined the fields of the villagers. They demanded the removal of the three households from their villages and that they be resettled in other, ruined villages to open them to agriculture. Otherwise, they would themselves emigrate.[63]

Both the council of Muş and Esad Pasha emphasized that those three to five households were from among the Hesenan that had been settled in the villages of Muş, with the help of council members and notables in 1264 (1847–8). They were busy with agriculture, were no longer oppressing other villagers, and were considered locals (*yerli*). Thus, it would be wrong to remove them from Kuştiyan.[64] The case of Kuştiyan highlights two important points. Firstly, it points to the challenges of settling nomadic groups. Whether the sedentarization of the tribes was willing (by use of exemptions and privileges) or forced, the process thereafter was not trouble free. The transition of the tribes from nomadic modus vivendi to agricultural life did not happen overnight. In Kuştiyan, the Hesenan families also did not get along with other villagers, because of their great amount of livestock. Secondly, local and central administrators encountered the complaints of local inhabitants about nomadic groups differently. In this case, the Hesenan families were considered local and their

---

62   BOA. İ. MVL. 269/10320, 1 Receb 1269 (10 May 1853).
63   BOA. MVL. 92/98, 17 Şevval 1266 (26 August 1850).
64   BOA. MVL. 235/13, 18 Rebiülevvel 1267 (21 January 1851).

rights were protected. The main policy was to accustom tribes to settled life and not curb their enthusiasm by exiling or punishing them, except in cases of usurpation, burglary, killing, and assault.

Despite the determination of the central and provincial authorities to encourage the nomads' settlement, the villagers of Muş continued to file petitions against the houses of the Sıpkî and Hesenan that had been settled. For instance, the inhabitants of certain villages in Malazgird, namely Hıdır Şeyh, Reis, Kargalıh, Hayalverdi, and Atagel were reported to be in dire straits due to atrocities committed by someone called Yüzbaşı from the Sıpkî. Yüzbaşı together with his friends was attacking the villages, ravaging them, and burning grain mills. The villagers asked for compensation for the damage.[65] In order to protect the villagers and save them from these assaults, Istanbul ordered the governor of Erzurum to capture and question the perpetrators and to determine proper compensation and the extent of their crimes.[66]

In addition to the atrocities by the Sıpkî, the Hesenans not only continued to steal in Muş but also attacked Ahlat in Van. Although the kaimakam of Muş was informed of the issue, no measures had yet been taken. Thus, a *kır serdarı* (an official patrolling in the countryside) was appointed, together with regular troops, upon the petitions of the inhabitants.[67]

The examples discussed in the previous pages provide us with valuable information about the settlement of tribes in Muş. To begin with, it is important to understand the reasons for the migration of settled peasants to other places in the cases when tribal households were settled in their villages, as well as the peasants' insistence that the tribes be settled on uninhabited lands. The peasants, in the case of the villagers of Kasor for instance, believed beforehand that they could not get along with the semi-nomadic way of life, so they dispersed. In the case of Kuştiyan, the primary complaint was harm done to the cultivated lands by the large amount of livestock of the Hesenan. The local authorities attributed the thievery and unruliness of the tribes to their not being acquainted with agriculture. For pastoral nomads, transition to agricultural economy with which they had not familiar was difficult. The abundance of their livestock and the scarcity of the winter quarters led politically powerful tribes to plunder the peasants who were mostly Armenians. For instance, the burning of haystacks might be a strategy to force the settled peasants to abandon their villages.

---

65 BOA. MVL. 182/15, 3 Şaban 1273 (29 March 1857); BOA. A. MKT. UM. 278/48, 16 Şaban 1273 (11 April 1857).
66 BOA. A. MKT. UM. 278/48, 16 Şaban 1273 (11 April 1857).
67 BOA. MVL. 674/61, 16 Zilhicce 1280 (23 May 1864).

Despite the above mentioned motivations and efforts to sedentarize nomadic and seminomadic groups, sedentarization was a difficult process that continued until the end of the century. The following paragraph from a report dated 1863 importantly depicts the details of the settlement of tribes in the province of Erzurum some twenty years after its inclusion in the Tanzimat program:

> It is not necessary to repeat [that] the settlement of said tribes has not been fulfilled completely. Although some have built houses in Muş, Erzurum, and Bayezid, most are tent dwellers. Thus, the Hesenan tribe is migrating to pasturing grounds in the summer and, in the beginning of winters, to the villages of Malazgirt and Bulanıklar in the sanjak of Muş and to the villages of the districts and sub-districts of Ahlat in the sanjak of Van. In the same vein, the tribe of Cibran migrates in winters to the districts of Hınıs, Kığı, and Köynek in the province of Erzurum and plain villages in the districts of Muş and Vartolar. By the same token, the Sıpkî tribe, which was settled in the sub-district of Ayntab in the sanjak of Bayezid, has been coming out of their tents for a few years and in winter migrate to Patnos in the sub-district of Bayezid and to the villages of the sub-district of Malazgirt. The Zırki and Beliki tribes settled in the district of Hınıs and are also dispersing to districts and villages in the vicinity. Until the beginning of spring when the pasturages are sufficient to graze their livestock, some of those tribes feed their livestock by means of the inhabitants of said districts and villages without payment. As the inhabitants of those districts and villages were offended and tortured by said tribes, some have gone to the frontier to places like Kars and Bayezid with the intention of passing on to Russia. And the ones who found the opportunity actually did crossover to Russian lands and some of them are currently living there.[68]

Such settlement was carried out by the highest authorities. For example, the governor of Erzurum in the company of certain troops travelled from Hınıs, to Muş, Bulanık, Varto, and Malazgirt, and Bayezid, Eleşgird, and Ayntab with the aim of disciplining, settling and also registering the Zırki, Beliki, Mamanlı, Hesenan, Cibran, Seydanlı, Sıpkî, and Zilan tribes in the province of Erzurum. According to a report of the Provincial Council of Erzurum, although 1619 households from these tribes had been settled, by 1864 they had not yet been recorded in the population registries in their places of settlement. Moreover, among these tribes there were still 1055 households who were yet to be settled. Thus, it was decided to settle said families in the places where their tribes had

---

68   BOA. MVL. 646/81, 27 Şevval 1279 (17 April 1863).

already been living and move the remaining ones in ruined places and in *mevat* (uninhabited wastelands) lands. The land official of Erzurum, Şerif Efendi, was entitled by law to register the lands in the name of settled tribes. Furthermore, they were to be registered in the population records of the places they were settled together with the tribes who had not yet been registered. Moreover, the headmen of the villages where the tribal families were settled would stand as their guarantors in order to prevent their deserting the villages or assaulting the peasants and also to occupy them with agriculture. This was an ancient method applied in the sedentarization of the tribes. The council argued that the lands would be cultivated and that the treasury would get a contribution as high as two yük (200,000) guruş.[69]

Meanwhile, a multifaceted reform project was embarked upon in the sanjak of Muş to crush the resistance of the districts of Huyud, Mutki, and Sason which were most ostensibly opposing to the new taxation system, conscription lots, and the surrendering of guns.[70] Thus, for the government the sedentarization of the tribes in the provinces of both Erzurum and Kurdistan was a crucial part of this campaign of discipline. Only after their sedentarization could the tribes be included in the new taxation and conscription systems and their population and lands be registered according to the Land Code. This sedentarization campaign can be contextualized in the framework of establishing the state's infrastructural power. Through settlement of the tribes, the state capacity would increase as the tribal members would turn into taxable, legible and controllable subjects.

While local authorities were busy with settling the tribes of the sanjak of Muş and preventing them from continuing a plunder economy, the other prominent issue was the prevention of assaults by the tribes of neighboring provinces. The nomadic tribes of the provinces of Kurdistan, and later Diyarbekir, had been taking their herds to pastures in the mountains lying to the south of the Muş Plain in summer, and this became a source of tension.

7.3 Nomadic Tribes in the Vicinity of the Sanjak of Muş

In 1854 the council of Muş continued its fruitless correspondence with the governors of the provinces of Erzurum and Kurdistan concerning the prevention

---

[69] BOA. A. MKT. MHM. 293/10, 13 Ramazan 1280 (21 February 1864).

[70] BOA. A. MKT. MHM. 50/56, 5 Safer 1269 (18 November 1852); BOA. A. MKT. NZD. 71/19, 8 Rebiülahir 1269 (19 January 1853). For a study on taxation and conscription of the tribes of Mutki, see Yener Koç, "Taxing the Tribes in the Ottoman Empire: The Case of the Tribes of Mutki (1839–1908) in *Histories of Tax Evasion, Avoidance and Resistance*, (eds.) Korinna Schönhärl, Gisela Hürlimann, and Dorothea Rohde, (Abingdon: Routledge, 2023), 84–99.

of the tribes of Kurdistan from coming to the Muş pastures. The council wanted the governors to stop the tribes from coming to Muş due to the peasants' complaints.[71]

The tribes of the province of Kurdistan, namely the Reşkotan, Bekiran, Alikan, and Pençnar came to the pastures in the mountains to the south of Muş plain to graze their livestock from spring to autumn. Meanwhile, they attacked the villages in the plain and engaged in plunder economy. Tribes proved to be troublesome for persons who had been farming the taxes of the villages. They prevented officials from collecting products in due time and expelled them from the villages by beating them and swearing at them. As tax farmers had suffered a loss, no one dared to farm the revenues of the villages in 1270 (1854), so the council emphasized that this had in turn led to pecuniary damage for the treasury.[72]

Among the complaints against these nomads, the most outstanding issue that the Muş council emphasized was *hafırlik*. Hafırlik was roughly a system in which tribal members offered protection to villagers in return for grains and goods. In line with this, tribes from Diyarbekir tied the villagers of Muş to such a system, sending fifteen or twenty armed tribal members to each village to take grain and attack passers – by in the name of hafırlik. The lack of information about hafırlik prior to the nineteenth century begs the question whether it was a reformulation of kışlakiye, which was supposed to have been abolished with the Tanzimat.

The experience of previous years made local administrators of Muş feel obliged to call for higher authorities to keep the Bekiran, Reşkotan, and Pençnar tribes away from the pastures in Muş and partially if not completely relieve the villagers of the plain of Muş. Thus, the governor of Erzurum emphasized that especially that year – considering that the Crimean War with Russia had already begun – if said tribes were not prevented from returning, the inhabitants would become completely immiserated. For the same reason, using military force to detain those tribes was not an option either. As described by Muş council, if regular troops were dispatched to Muş, the tribes would immediately send news to each other and no less than two hundred men would league together and take up arms. Such an armed clash would take a long time, which was not desirable during the war. However, both the council of Muş and governor of Erzurum agreed that unless those tribes, all consisting of three to five thousand households, were disciplined and chastened, they would not abstain

---

71   BOA. MVL. 276/42, 17 Şaban 1270 (15 May 1854).
72   Ibid. Astourian also emphasizes that hafir was a continuation of "semifeudal practices" by arguing that it "often exceeded the amount of taxes levied by the government." Astourian, "The Silence of the Land," 60.

from mischief. The local authorities in Muş were desperate, and the governor of Erzurum suggested that the governor of Kurdistan summon tribal leaders and talk with them, or it would be required to dispatch regular troops.[73]

In the course of time, neither the arrival nor the assaults by the Bekiran and other tribes in Muş was prevented. On the contrary, these tribes did not obey the orders concerning their settlement, and around four hundred families fled to the mountains of Muş in summer 1859. The aim of some was to find places to shelter and that of others was to cross into Iran. Meanwhile, they did not refrain from plundering villages on their way. Although none of the leaders of these tribes came to Muş, they sent men to the members of Muş council to explain their situation. Heavy taxes were imposed on the tribes in the province of Kurdistan and they were being oppressed, so they came to Muş with the intent of being settled there. This statement of tribal men from the Bekiran, Pencinar and the Reşkotan was a discursive strategy to justify their coming to Muş during the summers. Although it is possible that those tribes were escaping from paying taxes, the concrete reason behind these tribes's migration to Muş was climatic. These tribes of Diyarbekir had very regular migration patterns which was shaped by climate. Their migration routes were seasonal and vertical between Upper Mesopotamia and Anatolian highlands. Obviously, the summer quarters of Muş provided a more favorable environment for the tribes of Reşkotan, Pencinar, Bekiran and Alikan to graze their livestock compared to dry, hot summers in Diyarbekir, Mardin and Urfa.[74]

As the governor of Kurdistan had not given any instructions on this issue, the best solution the kaimakam of Muş found was to host the tribes for a time and to warn district administrators to prevent tribes from passing into Iran, by deploying regular troops. However, the kaimakam emphasized, that if they emigrated in groups of three to five households, it would be easy to confront them. Otherwise, if they collectively moved from Muş, it would require using force, which depended on a decision of the commander-in-chief.[75]

The main inclination of the Ottoman government, with respect to the settlement of tribes, was to use military force as little as possible. This attitude decreased the financial costs, and provided for peace and security in the long run, when nomadic groups settled willingly. Thus, Istanbul ordered the

---

73 BOA. MVL. 276/42, 17 Şaban 1270 (15 May 1854).
74 Koç, "Nomadic Pastoral Tribes," 49. For the impacts of the climatic fluctuations on the pastoral nomads in the Ottoman Kurdistan in the late nineteenth century, see Zozan Pehlivan, "El Niño and the Nomads: Global Climate, Local Environment, and the Crisis of Pastoralism in Late Ottoman Kurdistan," *Journal of the Economic and Social History of the Orient*, 63 (3), 316–356.
75 BOA. A. MKT. UM. 361/54, 21 Muharrem 1276 (20 August 1859). From the governor of Erzurum to Istanbul.

governor of Erzurum not to oppress and torture either the aforementioned nomadic tribes of the province of Kurdistan or other tribal groups, for which settlement was being considered.[76]

Having been recommended to use force only as a last resort and to refrain from firing a tribesman and shedding blood, the kaimakam of Muş, İbrahim Edhem, dispatched council members to mediate with the notables of the tribes and to summon them to the local council. Consequently, either the headmen of the Alikan, Reşkotan, and Pencnar themselves or their agents arrived in Muş and were questioned by the council. The tribal notables argued that the climate of the places allocated for their settlement in the province of Kurdistan was not suitable in summer; neither they nor their livestock could survive. They proposed settling in those areas in winter, yet in summer they would move to the pastures as they used to. As their arrival in the summer pastures that year took place ten days later than in previous years, both their families and livestock had become sick and not yet recovered. Emphasizing that the summer pastures were a must for them, tribal notables insisted that unless some cool places were assigned for their settlement, to which they were accustomed, they could only choose to migrate to other countries.[77]

The statement of these tribal leaders can neither be considered merely as a condition for settlement nor as a threat. Rather, it provides clues about the nomadic way of life and patterns. The well-being of such transhumant communities depended on seasonal migrations between their summer and winter quarters. Accordingly, these nomadic tribes were inclined to a seminomadic rather than a complete sedentary life. Indeed, given their large amount of livestock, a sudden transition to sedentary life could not be carried out easily.[78] For the same reason, the breezy pastures of Muş were preferable to them compared with the hot summers of Diyarbekir. Hence, neither the settlement of these tribes nor the prevention of their coming to Muş was ensured. Although the main policy to control the tribes was negotiation, using military forces was not rare.

The Bekiran tribe was among those controlled by force. In spite of efforts to prevent the Bekiran and other tribes of neighboring provinces from committing assaults in Muş without bloodshed, armed encounters were inevitable.[79]

---

76 BOA. A. MKT. UM. 363/24, 30 Muharrem 1276 (29 August 1859). From Istanbul to the governors of Erzurum and Kurdistan.
77 BOA. A. MKT. UM. 367/94, 27 Safer 1276 (25 September 1859).
78 It is difficult to trace the trade activities of tribes with respect to their herds. Nevertheless, Brant states that "dealers come to buy sheep and drive them for sale to Syria, as well as Constantinople." Brant, "Notes of a Journey," 352.
79 BOA. A. MKT. UM. 423/55, 10 Safer 1277 (28 August 1860).

The Bekiran continued wandering around and sometimes plundering the villages of Muş despite warnings. Zaptieh soldiers were charged with capturing some of the tribesmen of the Bekiran who were involved in such mischief, yet tribesmen shot and injured some of them as well as their horses. Still, two criminals called Alo and Meto were arrested, and local forces were informed that around one hundred armed men from the tribe would come to the plain of Muş. As a result, regular troops and zaptiehs were deployed, some of whom encountered the tribesmen along their way, and a clash took place. The encounter resulted in casualties and pecuniary losses, but some tribesmen were arrested. It is noteworthy that the punishment of these tribesmen was to be based on the new Penal Code. This is the Penal Code of 1858, which was inspired by French Code of 1810. Together with the Penal Code of 1840, which was promulgated shortly after the Tanzimat Edict, it was among the main codifications in the sphere of the judicial reforms of the Tanzimat.[80] With reference to Article 62 of the new code (*kanun-ı cedîd*), it was argued that:

> whoever seizes, pillages the property, assets, and cash of the exalted state or of the property of the people, and leads or has a commanding role in a gang of armed bandits established with the aim of confronting the soldiers of the exalted state who are summoned against such criminals shall be executed. The ones involved in such gangs who do no lead or have a commanding role, if caught at the place of disorder, shall be sentenced to temporary hard labor.[81]

Because the leaders of the tribal group involved in the strife were killed in the clashes, the council sentenced the remaining tribesmen to hard labor for three years in Erzurum. Moreover, the properties and livestock that they had seized were returned to their owners. If their owners did not appear at the court, the assets were seized by the state. Moreover, the culprits also had to pay for livestock that had perished because of their actions.[82]

---

80   For details, see Omri Paz, "Crime, Criminals and the Ottoman State: Anatolia between the late 1830s and the late 1860s" (PhD diss., Tel Aviv University, 2010); Uriel Heyd, *Studies in Old Ottoman Criminal Law* (Oxford: Clarendon Press, 1973).

81   "her kim devlet-i 'aliyyenin emlâk ve emvâl ve nukûdunu veyâ ahâlîden bir cem-i gafir emlâkının zabt ve yağmâ ve garet itmek ve bu misillû cinâyât ashâbının 'aleyhinde hareket iden 'asâkir-i devlet-i 'aliyyeye karşu durmak zımnında teşekkül itmiş olan müselleh eşkiya cem'iyyetine baş olur veyâhud cem'iyyet içinde bir kumanda sâhibi bulunur ise anın i'dam olunması ve bu makûle eşkıyâ cem'iyyetlerinde dâhil bulunanlardan ol cem'iyyetlerde söz ve kumanda sâhibi olmıyanların mahal-i fesâdda tutuldukları hâlde muvakkaten küreğe konulması." BOA. A. MKT. MVL. 114/39, 29 Receb 1276 (22 March 1860).

82   Ibid.

Regardless of such punishment, throughout the 1860s, the Bekiran, Reşkotan and the other tribes neither abandoned their habit of coming to Muş for summer quarters nor of plundering the properties of the settled inhabitants of the plain of Muş, or they settled in the places determined for them in Diyarbakır and Siird. As emphasized above, the main inclination of the government was to control these tribes without incurring costs, in other words, without employing military troops. In this vein, there are examples of "mediation" applied to a subsection of those tribes. For instance, the tribe of Bekiran was composed of three clans, two of which compromised with the provincial authorities.[83] Nonetheless, the leader of the third subclan, Hamzo had escaped to Hıyan (between Muş and Diyarbekir).[84]

The above-mentioned tribes were not alone in their seasonal migrations. It was a long-standing habit of around eighteen tribes of Bohtan and Siird, like the Alikan and Dururi, to come to the sanjaks of Muş and Van in the summers. The meadows of both provinces were abundant. A military force of more than two thousand troops was required to make those tribes cease this old habit and settle in the sanjaks of Siird and Bohtan. However, the operation needed to be considered in detail as the tribes had already left for their summer pastures. Consequently, until there were suitable conditions for the deployment of military forces to control those tribes, the Meclis-i Vâlâ decided to appeal to influential tribesmen as intermediaries. After necessary warnings to prevent assaults by their followers, these tribesmen and leaders were held responsible for the further actions of their tribes via surety bonds.[85]

Despite the precautions to avoid coercion in the prevention of the migration of tribes of the province of Kurdistan to Muş and in their settlement, they were eventually settled by force.[86] The 4th Imperial Army reported that the cost of the military operation to prevent the Reşkotan, Bekiran and Pencinar from going to Muş amounted to 20,183 guruş 30 pare, and it was covered by the local treasury as before.[87] Nonetheless, the military operation neither intercepted sporadic migrations of those nomads to the plain of Muş nor completed their settlement. This was a process that continued up to the beginning of the twentieth century.[88]

---

83 BOA. MVL. 602/32, 17 Safer 1277 (4 September 1860).
84 Ibid., BOA. A. MKT. UM. 425/58, 19 Safer 1277 (6 September 1860).
85 BOA. MVL. 738/29, 25 Safer 1284 (28 June 1867).
86 BOA. İ. DH. 626/43528, 23 Şevval 1287 (16 January 1871).
87 BOA. İ. DH. 648/45054, 10 Muharrem 1289 (30 March 1872).
88 Actually, the tribes of Diyarbekir were neither kept from summer pastures in the mountains of Muş nor were peasant-nomad conflicts resolved. The relations among those nomadic Kurdish tribes and especially the Armenian peasantry was aggravated in

In contrast to the tribes discussed until now, one of the most important local tribes of the sanjak of Muş, the Hesenan had become sedentary to a great extent by the beginning of the twentieth century. The next chapter will focus on the story of the Hesenan.

---

ensuing years. Together with the influence of Armenian revolutionary movements that started to be felt in the region, the Hamidian regime came to a tacit agreement with Kurdish tribes regarding the assaults against the Armenian peasantry, which resulted in a series of massacres in the districts of Talori and Sasun, that was widely known as the Sason Massacre. Mehmet Polatel, "The Complete Ruin of a District: The Sasun Massacre of 1894," in *The Ottoman History in the Nineteenth Century: Socities, Identities and Politics*, eds. Yaşar Tolga Cora, Dzovaniar Derderian, and Ali Sipahi (London: I.B. Tauris, 2016), 179–98; Vahakn N. Dadrian, "The 1984 Sassoun Massacre: A Juncture in the Escalation of the Turko-Armenian Conflict," *The Armenian Review* 47, no. 1–2 (2001): 5–39.

CHAPTER 8

The Hesenan Tribe: The Cases of Rıdvan and Kulihan Aghas

The British envoy and traveler Mark Sykes reported that the Hesenan consisted of 3,300 households in 110 villages in Hınıs, Malazgirt, and Varto at the beginning of the twentieth century. Although some households were seminomadic, they were gradually abandoning their tents in later years.[1] Nonetheless, the settlement of the Hesenan was not a smooth process, just as the process with the other tribes was not. The story of the Hesenan, especially of the tribal leader Rıdvan Agha and his brothers and larger family sheds light on the fact that tribes, their relationships with governments, local administrators, notables, peasants, and other tribes are significant to understanding how a nomadic tribe became gradually incorporated into local administration.

The Hesenan were among the first tribes settled in the villages of Muş, following the Tanzimat reforms. It was a seminomadic tribe who were tent dwellers in the mountains of Muş in the summers and spent winters in its villages, which was a huge burden on the settled population. The Hesenan were among the important actors of the region. Their negotiations, collaborations, and conflicts with the beys of Muş were narrated in chapters 2 and 3. With the inclusion of Muş in Tanzimat, one of the main targets was to settle Hesenan households in its villages. The story of Rıdvan Agha started with this settlement phase of the reforms.

A year after the inclusion of Muş in the Tanzimat program, in 1846, the governor of Erzurum together with the provincial treasurer reported the assaults and misconduct of Rıdvan Agha. Having turned his back on Şerif Bey as an intermediary, the kaimakam of Muş at the time, Rıdvan Agha also turned a deaf ear to the warnings of the Colonel of Regular Troops in Muş, Mustafa Bey, and some other tribal leaders like Mustafa Agha of the Zırki. Then, Murad Bey, Şerif Bey's brother, was dispatched by the governor of Erzurum with a certain number of irregular troops and convinced some tribal elders (*ihtiyar*) among the accomplices (*'avene*) of Rıdvan Agha, if not Rıdvan Agha himself, to surrender. In response, Rıdvan Agha with his men and family withdrew to the castle of Malazgirt after plundering the villages of Bulanık on his way. Despite

---

1 Sykes, "The Kurdish Tribes," 476.

the mediation of certain tribesmen and military authorities, he did not submit. After clashing with the members of the Cibran tribe deployed against him, he escaped from the castle leaving his family and relatives behind. After his escape, his family was taken from the castle and sent to Muş, and the properties and livestock he left behind were registered with the help of the local council. The properties and livestock seized from the local people were returned by the local council if any claimant appeared, according to law.[2]

Rıdvan Agha wanted to avoid settlement in the plain of Muş, for which Şerif Bey and Mustafa Bey from the regular troops, were employed.[3] The agha was assured that he would not be oppressed and punished on the condition that he returned the properties and livestock seized from the inhabitants and agreed to settle down in the plain of Muş along with the tribal members he had gathered. The agha at first came to terms with local authorities and asked for reliable, impartial officials to carry out this case. Thereupon, two officials from Erzurum were employed.[4] Rıdvan Agha's insistence on impartial officials was a sign of the conflict between him and Şerif Bey. In Emin Pasha's rebel, Rıdvan of the Hesenan had defected to the side of Esad and Hüseyin Pashas. Nonetheless, the process resulted in a confrontation and the escape of Rıdvan Agha. As emphasized, the settlement of nomadic and seminomadic tribes was a process that involved both negotiation and force, the latter of which was employed as a last resort. Despite precautions to solve the matter of the Hesenan peacefully, Rıdvan Agha ended up sheltering with Han Mahmud after escaping from the castle of Malazgirt.[5] This was a precarious time when Han Mahmud was struggling against the inclusion of the sanjak of Van in the Tanzimat. Rıdvan Agha sided with Han Mahmud in order to avoid the settlement and the control of the provincial authorities. Accordingly, the provincial authorities were anxious about an alliance between a tribal leader like Rıdvan Agha and a rebel group. Şerif Bey was therefore tasked with preventing such a collaboration. Şerif Bey, who met with Han Mahmud in Adilcevaz, mediated on this issue and the latter promised to send Rıdvan Agha to Muş in a month.[6]

---

2   BOA. A. MKT. 59/80, 7 Muharrem 1263 (26 December 1846).
3   Şerif Bey had been appointed as kaimakam of Muş for the last time to deal with the settlement of nomadic groups and to intermediate in the revolt of Han Mahmud. For details, see chapter 4 in this book.
4   BOA. HR. MKT. 16/58, 2 Safer 1263 (20 January 1847).
5   BOA. HR. MKT. 17/41, 17 Safer 1263 (4 February 1847).
6   BOA. İ. MSM. 69/2010, 9 Rebiülevvel 1263 (25 February 1847).

Meanwhile, the properties and goods Rıdvan Agha left behind were registered; while the Muslim and non-Muslim inhabitants of the sub-districts of Bulanık-ı Ulya and Süfla and Ahlat filed a petition concerning assaults by Rıdvan Agha and his relatives. Having written the following lines, inhabitants asked for exile of Rıdvan Agha's family, who had by then been sent to Muş, to Sivas or Trabzon:

> All the Muslims and non-Muslims of each place sighed in relief thanks to their inclusion in the Beneficent Tanzimat. Although the inhabitants of the sanjak of Muş are willing to have relief from among the tribal aghas of the sanjak, Rıdvan Agha of the Hesenan together with his family, relatives, and ill-humored Kurds whom the agha persuaded with various promises have not accepted the rule of the Beneficent Tanzimat. They have prevented proper implementation of the reforms in our sanjak and overrode the local governments of the kaimakams. Although we have often submitted petitions regarding various kinds of violence, oppression, and assault committed by them upon the inhabitants of Muş, particularly those in the district of Malazgirt and the sub-districts of Upper Bulanık, Lower Bulanık, and Ahlat, the governors of Erzurum have turned a deaf ear. These tribal aghas and members are increasing their assaults upon the inhabitants day by day as they are of the opinion that they will remain unpunished whatever they do. In short, we have found no way out.[7]

Having emphasized that they were enslaved together with their families by tribal members of the Hesenan, the inhabitants of Malazgirt, Bulanık and Ahlat listed the goods seized by Rıdvan Agha and his relatives in 1261–2 (1845–6) on a village by village basis. Members of the Hesenan had extorted everything ranging from wheat to clothes from the local people. The total amount of embezzlement and damage amounted to 235,085 guruş.[8] In the same manner, the inhabitants of Malazgirt also submitted a petition regarding the money embezzled by Rıdvan Agha. In fact, this money was the equivalent of the taxes levied on the inhabitants of Malazgirt in the years 1845–6. He basically embezzled all the tax money. The following table indicates the details of Rıdvan Agha's embezzlement:

---

7   Ibid.
8   Ibid.

TABLE 5 The amount of money embezzled by Ridvan Agha from the inhabitants of Malazgirt

	Year	Amount (guruş)
The imperial taxes Rıdvan Agha took from *zımmî*. ... on the night he escaped	1261 (1845)	9350
The revenues of the sixteen villages, the tax farming of which was contracted to him by Kaşif Agha	1261	12500
The amount he seized from the revenues of the dye house (*boyahâne*) and syrup house (*şurubhâne*)	1261	250
The amount he took from the villages of Sofi in the name of *yaylakiye*	1262 (1846)	2309
The amount he embezzled from the revenues of sixteen villages of Sofi	1262	12500
The amount he took in the name of *baç* in Bitlis	1262	100
The amount he took from the *ihtisab* tax	1262	313
Total		37322

SOURCE: BOA. İ. MSM. 69/2010, 9 REBİÜLEVVEL 1263 (25 FEBRUARY 1847)

These articles show that a tribal leader, whom the peasants resented, was taxfarming the revenues of certain villages in the district of Malazgirt. Ferik Ahmet Pasha from the Anatolian Army reported that Rıdvan Agha claimed to have submitted all the taxes to the kaimakam of Muş, Şerif Bey, and that he had taken nothing from the inhabitants. The agha added that if he were to be heard and confronted with his complainants, he could prove his innocence. Nevertheless, his case was delayed until the termination of the Van issue.[9]

Rıdvan Agha surrendered in summer 1847, concurrent with the suppression of the revolt of Han Mahmud and Bedirxan Bey.[10] However, there was no trace that he was interrogated about the embezzlement case above. The documents indicate that the Hesenan tribe was settled in Malazgirt in 1848. Thus, it took at least three years to settle the Hesenan in Malazgirt. Soon after, new problems occurred. Instead of fulfilling the call of the commander-in-chief of the Anatolian Army, Rıdvan Agha arrived with two hundred families on the border

---

9   BOA. İ. MSM. 50/1278, 3 Ramazan 1263 (15 August 1847).
10 Kardam, Cizre-Bohtan Beyi Bedirhan, 326.

of Iran intending to pass to the other side.[11] However, his cousin Kulihan, at the head of another 150 households, became afraid and changed his mind while approaching the border. Having failed to deter his cousin, Kulihan left together with about 150 households and reported his cousin's intention.[12] After being informed about this issue, the kaimakam of Van, Mehmed Reşid immediately sent a letter to the agha. Consequently, Rıdvan Agha was persuaded to return to Bargiri, a district of Van, together with the two hundred households accompanying him. The kaimakam talked to Rıdvan Agha in person and convinced him to return and settle in Malazgirt.[13] The loyalty and efforts of Kulihan were rewarded with a stipend of 200 guruş until the issue of the demarcation of the border and the division of tribes (*tahdid-i hudud ve tefrik-ı aşair*) with the Iranian state was resolved.[14]

This attempt of Rıdvan Agha to cross over to Iran was not exceptional for the tribes on the eastern frontier of the Ottoman Empire. The "porous"[15] situation of the Ottoman-Iran frontier not only allowed nomadic groups to use either side as summer and winter quarters, but became a parameter in their negotiations with both governments. Migration to the other side became a form of threat, as the tribal issue was an important aspect of Ottoman-Iran border-making[16] on one hand and on the other, tribes were regarded as an important human resource. In this case, Rıdvan Agha's attempts to emigrate prompted local authorities to take precautions, as it would have impeded the demarcation of border and the allocation of tribes. Despite being persuaded to return, the mere fact of Rıdvan Agha's action created problems. The governor of Erzurum reported that the consul (*şehbender*) of Iran – when demanding the return of the Zilan tribe – referred to the fact that Rıdvan Agha was not accepted by frontier officials on the Iranian side. However, the governor emphasized that the Hesenan had been a tribe of the Ottoman Empire since

---

11 BOA. İ. DH. 206/11875, 20 Muharrem 1266 (6 December 1849).
12 BOA. İ. MVL. 185/5579, 17 Zilhicce 1266 (24 October 1850).
13 BOA. İ. HR. 60/2894, 26 Muharrem 1266 (12 December 1849).
14 BOA. İ. MVL. 185/5579, 17 Zilhicce 1266 (24 October 1850).
15 Sabri Ateş, "Empires at the Margin: Towards a History of the Ottoman Iranian Borderland and the Borderland Peoples, 1843–1881" (PhD diss., New York University, 2006), 69.
16 One of the important articles of the Treaty of Erzurum of 1847 was on this "tribal matter:" "The introduction, by both states, of measures to prevent acts of brigandage by nomadic frontier tribes, by establishing military posts and taking responsibility for the incursion of tribes into one another's territory; and a mutual agreement that tribes with an ambiguous dependency would permanently select their territory of residence, whereas those whose dependency was uncontested would return to their home state." Ateş, *The Ottoman-Iranian Borderlands*, 130.

time immemorial, living in Muş. Also, the return of Rıdvan Agha was the result of the insistence and efforts of Ottoman officials.[17]

Istanbul warned both the governor of Kurdistan province and the commander-in-chief of the Anatolian Army that such tribes were "savage" and "nomadic", that they were feared by the previous administration, and so they had yet to start to understand both just rule and imperial grace. Therefore, it was necessary to work towards accustoming them to civilization (*temdin etmek*) and settled life. Local authorities, meanwhile, were warned to be attentive, not to scare the tribes, to prevent their emigration to Iran, and to maintain control over them.[18] As discussed above, this 'civilizing mission' along with the stigmatization with 'savageness' were embedded in the discourse of Tanzimat bureaucrats, when dealing with transhumant communities.

As a result of all these efforts, the migration of Rıdvan Agha and his cousins to Iran was prevented. Their settlement was encouraged through their incorporation into the regional administration. Rıdvan was granted the administration of Malazgirt and his cousin Kulihan that of Bulanık. However, tribal members of the Hesenan under the leadership of Rıdvan Agha and his relatives continued to tyrannize the peasants of Muş by seizing money, wheat, barley, and cattle; plundering; and setting fire to stocks of fodder and houses. In addition to such lawlessness, they could extort and overtax with an authority stemming from their administrative positions. Due to the senility of İshak Pasha, the kaimakam of Muş at that time, and due to tribal members' collaboration with his deputy, İbrahim Efendi, the control mechanism over the tribes could not be maintained.[19] As discussed in chapter 6, as a result of both deteriorated relations between the tribes and peasants and the inability of administrators – and of extortion and corruption committed by a league that consisted of kaimakams, council members, tax farmers, notables, their Christian counterparts, kocabaşıs, moneylenders, and usurers – Armenian population of Muş in particular had no choice but to migrate.

Getting reports of the situation, Istanbul discharged İshak Pasha and exiled İbrahim Efendi. Likewise, the punishment of the leaders of the Hesenan was a topic under consideration. Meanwhile, having been appointed to carry out the reformation of Muş in 1855, the mutasarrıf of Kars, İsmail Pasha, also engaged in the questioning of Rıdvan and Kulihan Aghas, in particular, as the respective inhabitants of Malazgirt and Bulanık had brought charges against them. Apart from assaults and encroachments by tribal members, a register showing

17 BOA. HR. MKT 29.63/5.Ra.1266 (19 January 1850).
18 BOA. A. MKT. MHM. 18/83, 1 Zilhicce 1266 (8 October 1850).
19 BOA. İ. MVL. 269/10320, 1 Receb 1269 (10 May 1853).

the amounts embezzled by both aghas and their tribal members was prepared by the council of Muş and submitted to the Sublime Porte. Rıdvan and Kulihan Aghas were arrested and sent to Erzurum, yet their punishment was delayed due to an urgent development: the Crimean War had broken out.[20]

During the war, Rıdvan Agha and his sons and tribal members served in the army which was quartered in Kars.[21] The manpower tribes could provide to the army enabled them to negotiate with the central government. In this case, as they were located in a frontier region, the chiefs of the Hesenan remained unpunished thanks to their services to the army. Nevertheless, after the end of war, Rıdvan Agha and his cousins continued to be involved in the acts that had been matters of complaint. Thereupon, charges against the tribal members and registers submitted previously, resurfaced in 1860. The charges show not only the details of the extortion, double taxation, and authority that the tribal members enjoyed, but also provide clues about the extent of the settlement of the Hesenan and their incorporation into the administration system.

The charges by the inhabitants of Malazgirt and Bulanık indicated that Rıdvan and Kulihan had usurped almost everything – from wheat, barley, milk, and butter to fodder, cattle, and cows – from the villagers.[22] Actually usurpation, robbery, murder, and injury were common matters of complaint against nomadic groups. However, the difference lies in the fact that these tribal aghas and tribal members enjoyed the influence of being part of the administration of the region. Being entitled to collect and farm the taxes of Bulanık and Malazgirt strengthened the power of the leaders of the Hesenan.

According to the charges, Rıdvan and Kulihan aghas had extorted by adding to the taxes and poll taxes allocated to the districts and by over taxing inhabitants in collecting money in the name of their own expenses. Given that they were also tax farming some villages in the districts of Malazgirt and Bulanık, the collection of the tithe provided them with another channel of extortion. They were also accused of embezzling money and provisions collected in the name of the regular army. Among the accusations against Kulihan was the construction of a grain mill in Bulanık, while imposing corvée on the inhabitants by extorting the expense from the people and making them work there without pay. In the same vein, Rıdvan Agha also was still collecting the tax for winter quarters despite its abolishment.[23]

---

20   BOA. İ. MVL. 433/19083, 5 Zilhicce 1276 (24 June 1860).
21   BOA. A. MKT. UM. 205/94, 8 Zilhicce 1271 (22 August 1855).
22   BOA. İ. MVL. 433/19083, 5 Zilhicce 1276 (24 June 1860).
23   Ibid.

When questioned, Kulihan Agha admitted the debt amounted to 132,004 guruş, yet he denied responsibility for remaining 67,750 guruş. Moreover, he did not take responsibility for the debts of other tribal members which amounted to 66,006 guruş. He claimed that villagers should demand the amount from whomever they had provided with money and goods. Similarly, the former administrator of Malazgirt, Rıdvan Agha, admitted to a debt of 26,185 guruş, yet denied owing 9,753 guruş. Moreover, Rıdvan Agha promised to pay 40,680 that it was claimed had been usurped by his deceased son, Halid Agha, despite uncertainty about whether he had taken it or not. Like Kulihan Agha, Rıdvan Agha also did not accept responsibility for the money and the provisions seized by his tribal members, which amounted to 25,750 guruş.[24]

In addition to pointing out the extortion that tribal aghas and members were involved in given their privileges as administrators of the region, these accusations indicate the extent to which the settlement of the Hesenan had been accomplished. Tax farming the tithe of villages in Muş and building grain mills in the districts show that the aghas of Hesenan were becoming accustomed to sedentary life. However, they did not abandon their tents completely; when required, the tribal members reverted to and benefited from nomadic life. For instance, tribal members who had been accused by the peasants of Malazgirt and Bulanık could not be questioned following the detention of the tribal aghas. As it was summer, they had dispersed and migrated to the hills.[25]

Despite such accusations, these aghas participated in other aspects of economic life. Even if it is difficult to determine the extent of the trade in which these tribal leaders engaged, it is likely that they participated in some kind of trade.[26] In the cases of tribal members of the Hesenan, extortion and theft in the simple sense were related to the insufficiency of the pastoral economy, which has already been discussed. However, in the case of the tribal leaders of the Hesenan who had become part of the provincial administration and tax collection system, their extortion and double taxation cannot be explained only by the limits of the pastoral economy.

As a result in 1860, the Meclis-i Vâlâ discussed the tribal issue and emphasized that the inhabitants of a sanjak could not be left in the hands of a few mischievous, cruel people. Therefore, the exile of Rıdvan Agha and his extended family was required, yet as they were tribal leaders and had many supporters,

---

24 Ibid.
25 Ibid.
26 According to the data stated by Cuinet for the late 1880s, twenty thousand goat skins were exported annually from Muş and its environs. However, it is not certain that whether tribal share was included in this amount or not. Cuinet, *La Turquie d'Asie*, 2, 580.

their exile was depended on local authorities working in concert and taking necessary precautions.[27] Accordingly, it was decided that the tribal leaders of the Hesenan – not only Rıdvan and Kulihan but also İsa and Seyfi – should be removed from Muş, taken into custody, and summoned to Erzurum, with all precautions. As the questioning of Rıdvan and Kulihan had already been carried out, they were sent to Istanbul where they would be exiled to Edirne or somewhere in Rumelia. The same procedure would be implemented for İsa and Seyfi after their questioning was finished and their offenses clarified.[28]

Both local and central authorities were meticulous about the removal of Rıdvan Agha and his cousins from Muş. The kaimakam of the sanjak, Mahmut Paşa (who was appointed in November 1860[29]), was cautious about preparing a plan to arrest all four tribal aghas together. Indeed, the arrest of one would scare the others and cause them to hide. Among the aghas, İsa Agha was already in Muş, so the kaimakam tried to make excuses to summon the remaining ones. Resolving the conflict between the Hesenan and Cibran by summoning the parties to the Provincial Council was the pretext. However, Rıdvan Agha refused to appear claiming that as his tribe had many conflicts with the Haydaran and Sıpkî, he could not leave his family alone.[30]

Meanwhile, Kulihan and Seyfi were also visiting villages in Muş and Bitlis to collect their dues from the tithe. It is important to emphasize once again how tribal leaders of the Hesenan were incorporated into the provincial administration and played roles in the power network in the region. For instance, Kulihan was in the company of Colonel İsmail Bey for the reformation of Mutki and Sason, and he was sent to Erzurum by the colonel on some pretext.[31] In the same vein, the coming of Rıdvan to Erzurum was already realized on the pretext of settling some dues and debts with the moneylender Hoce Manas.[32] Hence, both Rıdvan and Kulihan were eventually arrested without use of force, which was a priority of local authorities. As they were the leaders of the tribe, the capture of the rest became easier. However, at first tribal members thought that the arrest of the two aghas was because of the murder of the Commander,

---

27 "bir sancâk ahâlîsinin böyle birkaç eşhâs-ı muzırra ve zalimede bırakılması tecvîz olunamıyacağından bunların oradan kaldırılması icâb-ı hâlde olub şu kadar ki kendüleri 'aşîret rüesası ve taraflı adamlar oldukları cihetle mahallerinden çıkarılmaları hakimâne-i re'y ve tedbîre mütevakkıf idüğünden ..." BOA. İ. MVL. 439/19491, 7 Cemaziyelevvel 1277 (21 November 1860).

28 Ibid.

29 BOA. A.MKT.MVL 115/49, 25 Şaban 1276 (18 March 1860).

30 Ibid.

31 BOA. MVL. 605/25, 20 Rebiülahir 1277 (5 November 1860).

32 BOA. İ. MVL. 439/19491, 7 Cemaziyelevvel 1277 (21 November 1860).

Reşid Bey, by the brothers of Kulihan in Bulanık.[33] Having benefited from this belief of the tribal leaders, the governor of Erzurum suggested that calling the families of Rıdvan and Kulihan to Erzurum should be delayed until the capture of Seyfi, so as not to excite them.[34]

Thereafter, the capture of İsa Agha of the Hesenan took place in rapid succession, again without force and in a proper style. İsa Agha was employed to persuade Seyfi Agha to surrender with several letters. As the kaimakam of Muş, Mahmut Pasha was concerned about employing military force for this issue as it might lead to a clash as these aghas were from the same family.[35] When the issue was discussed in the Meclis-i Vala, due to winter weather the employment of troops was ordered to be a second option after all assurances and persuasions failed.[36] The punishment for Rıdvan and Kulihan, according to the questioning carried out in 1855, was determined to be exile, and they would be settled in Edirne and prohibited from setting foot in Muş. Thus, both aghas were sent to Istanbul to which their families would also later be sent. However, this was delayed until spring. The questioning of İsa Agha was also cancelled in order to be carried out together with that of Seyfi, once he was captured.[37]

In summer 1861, Seyfi Agha was also captured with his men and family in a wooded, rocky place in the middle of the oak trees on Mount Nemrut while trying to escape with his family to Arab lands. The Meclis-i Vala decided to question him in Muş if any claimants showed up and then he was sent to Erzurum.[38] Thus, the chiefs of the Hesenan who were reportedly assaulting, extorting, and plundering especially Bulanık and Malazgirt, were eventually caught. However, only Rıdvan and Kulihan Aghas were exiled in Edirne, and neither the rest of their families nor Seyfi and İsa were sent to follow them

---

33   The brothers of Kulihan and Seyfi, namely Halef, Mısto, and Aki, had been residents of the village of Heftrenk in Bulanık. Their assaults on the inhabitants of Bulanık and usurpations were frequently complained about, so the commander Reşid Bey with around forty zaptiehs arrived in their houses in order to arrest and question them. Despite the fact that the commander guaranteed that as long as they surrendered they would be questioned according to the law and would not be hurt, tribal members took up arms. As a result of the clash, the commander was killed and some zaptieh were also injured. Besides, Mısto and his brothers escaped. Therefore, the kaimakams of Van and Bayezid were warned as Hesenan members might have collaborated with the Sıpkî and Haydaran. Despite conflicts among them, in such cases it was possible that they would protect one another. BOA. MVL. 605/8, 27 Rebiülahir 1277 (12 Novermber 1860).
34   BOA. İ. MVL. 439/19491, 7 Cemaziyelevvel 1277 (21 November 1860).
35   BOA. MVL. 606/29, 6 Cemaziyelevvel 1277 (20 November 1860).
36   BOA. A. MKT. UM. 441/82, 29 Cemaziyelevvel 1277 (13 December 1860).
37   BOA. A. MKT. UM. 449/81, 7 Receb 1277 (19 January 1861).
38   BOA. MVL. 611/41, 29 Zilkade 1277 (6 June 1861).

in exile. Meanwhile, both the aghas in exile started to file petitions about their loyalty and services to the imperial state with reminding the authorities of their employment in the army during the Crimean War.[39] Similarly, they emphasized how they revived the ruined villages of Malazgirt.[40] It is striking that the leaders of a pastoral nomadic tribe which had always been depicted in contrast to the settled life pattern and economy, emphasized their role in the enlivening of certain villages in the sanjak of Muş. In addition, drawing attention to the fact they had not been questioned and no claimants against them had appeared, Rıdvan and Kulihan asked to return to their homelands where their families and properties were unprotected.[41]

At first, Istanbul refused forgiveness for Rıdvan and Kulihan,[42] yet soon after – based on reports of the councils of Muş and Erzurum – Istanbul approved that Rıdvan and Kulihan could be allowed to return their homelands, as no claimants against them had appeared.[43] Given the above-mentioned lists showing the extortion and usurpation of Rıdvan and Kulihan Aghas, the only reason no claimants showed up must have been the fear of local people. Taking the fact that the Hesenan were still a strong tribe in Muş into consideration, the apprehension of the local people was reasonable.

The reports of the councils of Erzurum and Muş depicting the situation after the exile of Rıdvan and Kulihan, provide details about tribal organizations and state-tribe relations. Claiming that Rıdvan and Kulihan were among the most respected aghas of the Hesenan, the councils of Muş and Erzurum reported that the control over the tribe had been interrupted since their exile. Along the same lines, their services to the army and regional administration were appreciated. Besides, the councils argued that their exile had led to anxiety among other tribal leaders who were keeping away from the government (*nazar-ı barid ile bakmakda*). Having pointed out the absence of any claimants against them, both councils argued that the presence of men like Rıdvan and Kulihan who had an understanding of good and evil, who were recognized and influential among the tribes would be beneficial. Because of this, the local authorities saw no harm in the return of the Hesenan's aghas.[44] Once again, the existence of hierarchy in the tribal organization became the determinant in its management. Consequently, the period of exile of Rıdvan and Kulihan was determined to have been enough for their punishment and they were

---

39   BOA. MVL. 934/40, 13 Safer 1278 (20 August 1861).
40   BOA. MVL. 375/77, 14 Rebiülevvel 1278 (18 September 1861).
41   BOA. MVL. 934/40, 13 Safer 1278 (20 August 1861).
42   BOA. A. MKT. UM. 494/78, 19 Safer 1278 (26 August 1861).
43   BOA. A. MKT. MVL. 144/41, 14 Şevval 1278 (14 April 1862).
44   BOA. İ. MVL. 463/020917, 6 Şevval 1278 (6 April 1862).

allowed to return.⁴⁵ However, Rıdvan Agha passed away in Istanbul, and only Kulihan Agha managed to return to their homeland.⁴⁶

The case of Rıdvan and Kulihan Aghas indicates not only the details of the settlement of the Hesenan tribe, but also shows how they played politics in Muş and its environs. Despite their initial anxieties and attempts to cross to the other side of the border, the tribal leaders of the Hesenan were actually incorporated not only by means of imperial grants and employment in the provincial administration and army but by force and punishment when necessary. Moreover, the internal organization of the tribes played a decisive role in this process. The hierarchical importance of the tribal chiefs within the Hesenan tribe enabled government authorities to negotiate with them, so the influence of those tribal chiefs over the tribe facilitated not only control of the tribe but also their settlement.⁴⁷ Another factor in the relatively successful settlement of the Hesenan lies in the relatively short journey between the summer and winter pastures of the tribe. To put it differently, the Hesenan was already pasturing in the mountains of Muş in the summer and spending the winter in its villages. Hence, all that had to be done was to settle Hesenan families in abandoned, vacant, and uncultivated villages in large groups, or in populated villages in small groups, by implementing the same methods used in the settlement of other itinerant groups: exemption from taxes and conscription and favoring tribal elders, which proved to be effective in this case. Nonetheless, this process was not trouble-free. As will be discussed in the following pages, the conflict between the Hesenan and neighboring tribes like Sıpkî and Haydaran was regarded as a problem for security by the administrative authorities, and the solutions shed light on the perception of the

---

45 Ibid.
46 BOA. MVL. 949/17, 7 Zilkade 1278 (6 May 1862).
47 Köksal also emphasized that "hierarchical organization is the existence of a tribal chief who can coordinate tribal units and place semi-nomadic groups in contact with the state." Köksal, "Coercion and Mediation," 473. Albert Hourani also states that "there were three spheres of radiation from the cities, in particular the capital city" in Muslim states before modern times. First, the city itself and its "dependant hinterland," then there was the intermediate sphere "where the city and the government could exercise control, not through officials but through intermediate powers to which the government gave recognition," and third the "mountains, desert and distant agricultural land." It is the second, intermediate sphere where tribes "with effective leaders" are found. He further argues that "[I]t is generally accepted that the government plays an important part in creating and maintaining tribal leaders in these areas, as the intermediaries through which its authority is exercised, and thus in creating tribes of this kind." Hourani, "Conclusion," 304–5.

government about nomadic and seminomadic groups. Additionally, intertribal conflict provides clues about the social and economic organization of tribes.

8.1 The Tribes in Dispute: Conflicts between the Tribes of Muş and Those of Its Vicinity

Intertribal conflicts and confrontations mostly stemmed from struggle over resources, which is typical of how nomadic and seminomadic groups had to struggle over scarce resources in order to stay alive. Nonetheless, for central and provincial authorities, the reason for this struggle was clear: it was an inherent aspect of savagery and banditry. In this part, two cases of disputes with the Hesenan, one with the Haydaran and the other with the Sıpkî, will be discussed.[48]

In summer 1861, the local authorities reported that thirty cavalrymen from the Haydaran tribe of the sanjak of Van secretly stole a mare, three horses, and fifteen cattle, at night, from members of the Hesenan of Muş. After following the thieves some cavalrymen from the Hesenan retrieved the stolen properties. Yet the story did not end there. About twenty mounted men from among the Haydaran followed the Hesenan members to the village of Develik in Ahlat in Muş, where the two groups confronted one another. The clash between the two tribes resulted in deaths and casualties on both sides. Although the fight was ended and the members of both tribes were returned to their homes by means of the local force, the local authorities of Ahlat and the kaimakam of Muş expressed concerns about the recurrence of such incidents, emphasizing the longstanding hostility between the two tribes. Once again, central government warned the kaimakam of Van about the discipline of the Haydaran and the need to constrain them from such vicious behavior, as they had been the instigators of this fight.[49] For central authorities, that such groups would attempt to take revenge was certain because of their tribal nature and manners.[50]

The mutasarrıf of Van argued that although it was not appropriate to hold the Hesenan tribe responsible for the misdeeds of the Haydaran in this case, it was undeniable that the Hesenan had also long been attacking other tribes. However, the mutasarrıf pointed out the fact that the Haydaran tribe crossed the border with the encouragement of the imperial state and they had settled

---

48 BOA. A. MKT. MVL. 112/17, 4 Cemaziyelevvel 1276 (29 November 1859).
49 BOA. A. MKT. UM. 487/50, 20 Muharrem 1278 (28 July 1861).
50 "aşâir takımının ma'lûm olan hâl ve tab'iyyetleri iktizâsınca." BOA. A. MKT. MHM. 230/20, 30 Muharrem 1278 (7 August 1861).

down in the Ottoman lands for five or six years. The previous year they were included in the allocation of tax including cattle tax.[51] The mutasarrıf of Van felt it is necessary to emphasize that the Haydaran were also becoming a sedentary tribe who paid taxes like the Hesenan.[52] In a joint report of the council members of Muş, Erzurum, Bayezid, Van and the commander-in-chief of the Anatolian Army, it was stated that in this case Sıpkî and Milan tribes seduced the Haydaran to attack the Hesenan, murdering, stealing, and committing sexual assault, yet the reason behind this sedition was not specified.[53]

Hence, the governor of Erzurum and the commander-in-chief of the Anatolian Army decided to form a special commission to take precautions against attacks by the tribes on each other.[54] The commission was composed of two members from each council of Muş, Bayezid, and Van as well as aghas and reasonable members from each tribe. Assembling in Patnos, the commission embarked upon ensuring that both the Hesenan and Haydaran would not be involved in behavior and acts contrary to the law and not reclaim properties stolen by then, and not take revenge for men who were killed. Then tribal elders provided two written contracts (ta'ahhüd senedi), including the clause that if an offense was committed by a tribal member, the whole tribe would be punished. Moreover, in the case of the deployment of officials or troops to deal with troubles created by either tribe, double the expense would be charged to the tribes themselves.[55]

In a period when the Ottoman Empire was embarking on modernization, not only in the spheres of finance and administration but also in jurisprudence, the government had to follow the tribal customs of conflict resolution to prevent disturbances between the two tribes in this case – which had resulted in deaths and casualties – The most important codification immediately after the promulgation of Tanzimat was the Penal Code of 1840. However, on the periphery of the empire, the central government and local authorities still commonly resorted to tribal customs like obtaining commitments from tribal notables through contracts. Nonetheless, tribal members were punished according to legal codes in these cases, when their guilt was determined through investigation and questioning. A mixture of tribal customs and new articles was also commonly applied. The case of a conflict over brush between the Hesenan

---

51   BOA. A. MKT. UM. 509/79, 18 Rebiülevvel 1278 (23 October 1861).
52   However, as late as 1886 it was reported that unlike the Hesenans, conscription lots could neither be carried out among the Haydarans nor the Sıpkî. BOA. DH. MKT. 1377/62, 13 Safer 1304 (11 November 1886).
53   BOA. A.M. 26/32, 17 Cemaziyelahir 1278 (20 December 1861).
54   BOA. MVL. 410/92, 2 Şaban 1279 (23 January 1863).
55   BOA. A.M. 26/32, 17 Cemaziyelahir 1278 (20 December 1861).

and Sıpkî exemplifies the use of tribal customs in tribal disputes, rather than standing legal codes. The case also sheds light on the claims of tribal entities to land and property.

In 1868, the strife that stemmed from the "brush matter" (*çalı maddesi*) between the Feliki and Hesenan spread to the Sıpkî, resulting in around forty deaths. Brush was an important commodity for the pastoral nomadic lifestyle. It was used in making baskets to carry hay and make brushes and small utensils. It also used in making roofs for their tents. The dispute was at first between a few members of the Hesenan and Feliki tribes and then engulfed the Sıpkî. The Feliki were apparently a subsection of the Sıpkî, fifteen families of which had been settled in the village of Bane [Muratkolu] in Ayntab, a district of Bayezid the year before. The problem stemmed from the fact that Bane was an hour from the Hasanpaşa village of Malazgirt. When men from the Feliki were cutting brush near a stream called Kesik between Bane and Hasanpaşa, some people from the Hesenan noticed them and a quarrel started. The people of the Hesenan objected to the the Feliki cutting brush, claiming that it had belonged to them for twenty years. On the contrary, the Feliki members argued, it had belonged to Ayntab from time immemorial, so they could cut the brush as they wished. This polemic turned into a fight when some Hesenan cavalrymen led by one called Mîr Aziz joined them. The fight resulted in six casualties and a death among the Hesenan, four casualties and six deaths on the side of the Feliki. On top of that, the tribal members of the Hesenan raided the tents of the Feliki in the village of Bane and destroyed, seized, and plundered in some degree. The local government of Ayntab sent a mediator, and when it got dark, the fight ended and both parties took their casualties away.[56] This fight over the brushes indicates how the scarce source was the main reason for inter-tribal confrontations.

The mutasarrıf of Bayezid was informed about the strife and casualties; consequently, necessary precautions were implemented to maintain security and prevent the spread of the incident to the tribes of the Sıpkî and Hesenan as a whole. Hence, two people, one from the zaptieh and the other from among the notables were sent to Malazgirt to talk to Cezo and Fetho aghas of the Hesenan, to investigate, gain insight into the case, and determine the casualties. At the same time, the remaining tents of the Feliki were moved, to more distant villages as a precaution for their safety, after the casualties and financial damages were registered. Two squads of infantrymen were also employed and positioned in the village of Karaağaç between the two tribes. Hence, potential

---

56   BOA. ŞD. 2390/27, 29 Şaban 1285 (15 December 1868).

turmoil and a fight between the two tribes were prevented for a month. Then, the mentioned troops were called to Bayezid.[57]

Thereafter, the fears came true and conflicts between the Hesenan and the Feliki of Bane village spread to the Sıpkî tribe. The tribal members of the Hesenan and Sıpkî sought for revenge by seizing one another's properties and livestock. Moreover, they attacked villages which resulted in casualties as well as pecuniary damage. On one night in an attack of the Hesenan on tents in the village of Nuxtili [Dayıpınar] (in Ayntab), Sıpkî members responded with gunfire which ended with deaths and casualties. The following day, following correspondence between the two tribes, they started to gather, and cavalrymen from both tribes confronted each other in the village of Adakend [Adakent] of Ayntab. They started to attack each other to take their revenge. The fight continued until the withdrawal of the Sıpkî, resulting in fourteen dead and fourteen injured from among the Hesenan, with eighteen dead and fourteen injured from among the Sıpkî.[58]

The Meclis-i İdare-i Vilayet (Provincial Administrative Council) and the Meclis-i Temyiz (Provincial Court of Appeal) of Erzurum submitted a report about the incidents in Bane, Nuxtili and Adakend to the Divân-i Ahkâm-i Adliye (Council of Judicial Ordinances). The issue was transferred and discussed in the Şûrâ-yı Devlet (Council of State).[59] Two important dimensions of this case of murder and injury obstructed process of punishment. On the one hand, facts about the actors directly involved in the incident were ambiguous. Neither their names nor their physical characteristics were accurate. On the other hand, given the enmity between the tribes, the reliability of the statements of witnesses was doubtful. As the perpetrators were a group of unidentified people, it was difficult to carry out individual hearings and interrogations. Hence it was argued in the Divân-ı Ahkâm-ı Adliye that it was impossible to inflict the punishments of hard labor, retaliation or blood money on the tribes. Temporary precautions were to be taken to settle the disputes, and the enmity, between the Sıpkî and Hesenan, until the reform and discipline of the tribes throughout the whole province was finalized. In the meantime, direct and indirect perpetrators of the incident were to be investigated openly and secretly.[60]

Thus, punishment in this case was not individual but collective. First, the Sıpkî, Hesenan, and Feliki should pay restitution and compensate for each others' previously confiscated livestock, properties, and money. Although the

---

57   Ibid.
58   Ibid.
59   BOA. A. MKT. MHM. 456/35, 6 Zilkade 1285 (18 February 1869).
60   BOA. ŞD. 2390/27, 29 Şaban 1285 (15 December 1868).

expenses for the treatment of casualties were also deemed to be allocated to each tribe, this could not be done due to difficulty to determine the costs. Finally, the tribes were sentenced to pay blood money – seventy-five Mecidiye golden coins – for each death to heirs, with the help of the government. In return, bills of payment would be provided.[61]

As had happened in previous intertribal disputes, tribal elders and leaders also provided contracts. Accordingly, the tribes of the Hesenan, Sıpkî, and Feliki would not be involved in tyrannous and disagreeable acts against each other. If some tribal members dared to do so, tribal aghas and notables would submit them without hesitation to the government to be questioned and punished, by law and the sharia. If tribal leaders harbored, protected, or assisted the perpetrators, all the leaders and notables would also be held as responsible as the culprits themselves. In the same vein, inter or intratribal conflicts and cases would be solved by appealing to local governments through investigations and interrogations; neither of the tribes should try to solve them on their own. Again, if some of them attempted to do so they would be surrendered to the government. The expenses of troops dispatched to pacify disputes among said tribes were also to be allocated to the tribes involved.[62] However, the Şûrâ-yı Devlet decided that as the aggravation of the case partially stemmed from the withdrawal of troops situated between the Hesenan and Sıpkî-Feliki, it was not fair to burden the tribes with all the expenses. The tribes were only obliged to pay the blood money as determined previously. Meanwhile, the investigation of the case and the identification of the actors would continue.[63]

The case that stemmed from the "brush matter" between the Hesenan and Feliki and spread immediately to the tribe of the Sıpkî underscores tribal configurations on the periphery of the Ottoman Empire, during the second half of the nineteenth century. As discussed above, for provincial and central authorities this case first of all pointed to the urgency of settling and disciplining all the nomadic and seminomadic groups who were also to be incorporated into the circle of civilization. However, this case together with other intertribal conflicts, sheds light on the influence and power of nomadic and seminomadic groups and on the difficulty of realizing the authorities' projects.

Another important point is that, despite the attempts to modernize jurisprudence, the local government and central institutions had no choice but to apply tribal methods of punishment for intertribal crimes. Physical

---

61 Ibid.
62 Ibid.
63 BOA. A. MKT. MHM. 456/35, 6 Zilkade 1285 (18 February 1869).

accessibility was a factor in the difficulty in revealing the facts of crimes, along with the identities of perpetrators. The social organization of the tribes which protected tribal members, bore false testimonies against enemy tribes, and eventually solved intertribal disputes using their own methods, forced officials to seek the mediation of tribal notables and binding contracts to solve intertribal disputes.

By the end of 1869, according to reports of the province of Erzurum submitted to the Council of Judicial Ordinances, some tribal members of the Hesenan together with those of the Cibran, including a few members from other tribes, were sentenced to hard labor and temporary or permanent exile.[64] The governor of Erzurum, İsmail Hakkı, emphasized that despite ambiguity about their relation to the above-discussed dispute between the Hesenan and Sıpkî-Feliki, the tribal members from the Hesenan who had been captured and arrested had been attacking the inhabitants of Muş for a long time. He argued that the atrocities, usurpations and sexual assaults could not be described with pen and paper. Hence, it was necessary to expel them and punish said tribal members; if not, they would increase their attacks upon their return, as experience had proven.[65]

The governor emphasized that the punishment of the specified tribal members could be implemented in three categories relative to their crimes, once their interrogations were completed in Erzurum. The first should be sent into temporary exile in Sinop, then the second should be banished to Rumelia with all their connections to the region cut and the last should be sentenced to hard labor in the Tersane-i Amire (Imperial Shipyard). Moreover, tribal members not yet captured should be punished in the same way. According to lists prepared by a special commission consisting of the governor of Erzurum and top officials of the province, which dealt with the matter of the interrogation and punishment of the tribes, the tribal members of the Cibran and Hesenan, along with some other tribes whose sentences were prescribed, amounted to eighty-three persons.[66]

A report of the Special Council (*Meclis-i Mahsus*) of the Interior Ministry emphasized the chiefs were leading their kinsmen into misdeeds and brigandage. These aghas were leaders of a few tribal families and it was necessary to expel them from the province of Erzurum. Nevertheless, the sentence of hard

---

64   The Cibran tribe was consisted of approximately 2,000 families. As Sykes notes, it was during the governorship of Esad Pasha that the tribe was transferred from the south to near Bingöl and Muş and rapidly became sedentary like the Hesenan. Sykes, "The Kurdish Tribes," 476–7. As known, they were also settled in Erzurum.
65   BOA. İ. MMS. 38/1574, 16 Ramazan 1286 (20 December 1869).
66   Ibid.

labor could not be implemented, as the culprits had neither been questioned according to law nor had their punishment been applied according to law. If those tribal members took up arms against the military troops dispatched against their brigandage, then hard labor could be enforced. From now on, hard labor would be applied after details regarding their encounter with troops and the degree of the tribal members' crimes were clarified. Those to be exiled in Sinop, and those to be settled in Rumelia, with their families were to be sent to Istanbul to be dispatched to their places of exile.[67] To conclude, for the treatment and punishment of tribal groups, both traditional means and modern penal codes were implemented. In addition, provincial authorities like the governor of Erzurum were of the opinion that if the chiefs of the tribes were removed, it would be possible to control their tribesmen. However, this was not the case for all tribal disputes. As discussed in the cases of Rıdvan and Kulihan aghas of the Hesenan, the local authorities had difficulty in negotiating with the Hesenan in the absence of their chiefs. State projects regarding the tribes varied according to a variety of factor among which was the tribes' internal organization.

8.2 In Lieu of a Conclusion

Providing snapshots concerning the tribes of the sanjak of Muş, these two chapters have undertaken the tribal issue in terms of Tanzimat program with a special focus on nomadic-settled and intertribal relations. Within the reforms of the nineteenth century, the sedentarization of nomadic and seminomadic groups, upon which Ottoman governments embarked several times in previous centuries, was the important marker for the inclusion of these same groups in the new taxation and conscription system. Hence, the settlement of tribes had a manifold mission. On the one hand, tribes could be used as a human resource, as productive agriculturalists that would revive abandoned lands and as military conscripts. Such a way of life would "civilize these "nomads" and "savages" as the Ottoman bureaucrats defined them. As a result, their introduction to sedentary life would eliminate the sources of conflicts they experienced with settled populations.

The chapters 7 and 8 not only dealt with the Tanzimat state's project with regard to the nomadic and seminomadic groups, but also focused on the reception, negotiation, and contestation amongst the local and central authorities, Kurdish and Armenian peasants, and members of tribes. The leaders of the most prominent local tribe of Muş – the Hesenan – Rıdvan Agha and his

---

67 BOA. İ. MMS. 38/1574, 16 Ramazan 1286 (20 December 1869).

cousins that chapter 8 focused on, negotiated and pursued their own agenda in the settlement process, and were actively involved in the reorganization of the administration of the sanjak of Muş. Tribes in the vicinity of Muş like the Bekiran and Reşkotan fought to keep their summer pastures in the mountains in the south of Muş against the restraints of local and central authorities. The case of the Bekiran and other tribes' sheds light on the difficulties in the immediate transitioning of nomadic tribes to sedentary life and also points to how tribes negotiated to keep at least their summer pastures, which was a formulation for seminomadic life. Yener Koç argues that the pastoral nomadic economy depended on the tribes' regular seasonal migrations between their summer and winter quarters, and also on the maintenance of tribes' usufruct rights over their summer quarters.[68]

The literature on the tribal composition of the eastern provinces of the Ottoman Empire has until recently mostly engaged with the period beginning with the constitution of the Hamidian Regiments in 1891.[69] This period is infamous not only for extortion but also the land-grabbing practice of the Kurdish militia who enjoyed a range of privileges such as tax and conscription exemptions and impunity for their acts. The period of the Hamidian Regiments is outside the scope of this study. Nevertheless, one of the main purposes of this chapter was to offer a nuanced understanding of the relationship between Kurdish tribes and local peasants, in the decades before the establishment of the regiments. This book also draws attention to the common, cross-sectarian petitions of the peasants of Muş against tribal assaults (as well as against those committed by a variety of local actors) especially in the 1850s and 1860s. The foundation of Hamidian Regiments greatly aggravated peasant-nomad relationship. The obligation on the settled population of Muş to provide winter quarters to the nomadic and semi-nomadic groups was a custom implemented

---

68 Yener Koç, "Celali Aşireti: Üç İmparatorluğun Sınırında," in Tuncay Şur and Yalçın Çakmak eds, *Kürt Aşiretleri: Aktör, Müttefik ve Şaki* (Istanbul: İletişim Yayınları, 2022), 302. For environmental dependencies of nomads, see Anatoly Khazanov, *Nomads and Outside World* (Wisconsin: University of Wisconsin Press, 1994).

69 Klein, "Power in the Periphery"; The Margins of Empire, Kurdish Militas in the Ottoman Tribal Zone (Stanford: Stanford University Press, 2011); Stephen Duguid, "The Politics of Unity: Hamidian Policy in Eastern Anatolia " Middle Eastern Studies 9, no. 2 (May, 1973); Bayram Kodaman, Sultan II Abdülhamid Devri Doğu Anadolu Politikası (Ankara: Türk Kültürünü Araştırma Enstitüsü Yayınları, 1987); Joost Jongerden, "Elite Encounters of a Violent Kind: Milli İbrahim Paşa, Ziya Gökalp and Political Struggle in Diyarbekir at the turn of the 20th Century" in Social Relations in Ottoman Diyarbekir (1870–1915), eds., Joost Jongerden and Jelle Verheij (Leiden: Brill, 2012). For a recent edited volume on the Kurdish tribes which fills the lacuna in the literature with its articles focusing on different Kurdish tribes, see, Tuncay Şur and Yalçın Çamak (ed), *Kürt Aşiretleri: Aktör, Müttefik, Şaki* (Istanbul: İletişim Yayınları, 2022).

for many centuries, which the Tanzimat promised to end. However, the emergence of the hafırlık system, recorded in documents of the 1850s, was probably a continuation of the winter-quartering practice and was among the important dynamics that determined tribe-peasant relations.

Despite the promises of the Tanzimat and the alleged protection of the hafırlık system, tribal assaults on the peasantry gathered momentum and exploited the land reforms. This chapter ends with a case of land seizure in Muş to exemplify what would be called the "agrarian question" in later decades. The "agrarian question," as Janet Klein argues, "was a euphemism for the matter of the Armenian lands usurped during the previous decades mostly by Kurdish chiefs."[70] Nonetheless "the transformation in land tenure practices" had already been inaugurated before the foundation of the Hamidian Regiments which impacted the process.[71] The case of the village of Gemig [Beşparmak] was such an example.

In a petition submitted to the imperial center, the priest Gabriel from Çanlı Monastery in Muş, who was the representative of the inhabitants, depicted the process of the evacuation of the Armenians from the village of Gemig in Muş and later the usurpation of their lands. The priest's claims were based on another petition written by notables from villages in the vicinity of Gemig. The village of Gemig had been Armenian since time immemorial, yet the inhabitants had to disperse due to the assaults and cruelty of the Cibran and Hesenan tribes. The village was rich and large, with around two hundred fields and two churches.[72] The evacuation of villages, especially Armenian ones, due to the attacks and extortions of either the tribes or local authorities – that is to say, council members and tax farmers – was a trend observed since the early nineteenth century. However, the difference now lay in the extent of the power that Kurdish tribes enjoyed, after benefiting from the new reforms.

Accordingly, after being abandoned by its inhabitants, the village of Gemig was auctioned off without the knowledge of the villagers – neither those of Gemig nor those in the vicinity. The village, its fields and properties, and its churches were assigned (*ferâğ*) to the son of Resul Efendi of the Sıpkî, Abdurrahman Agha. Resul Efendi was described as among the perpetrators behind the dispersal of the villagers'. Abdurrahman Agha in turn delegated (*tefvîz*) the village in equal shares to Halid Agha from among the notables and to Nadir Agha on the local council. Neither the villagers of Gemig, nor those

---

70 Klein, *The Margins of Empire*, 131.
71 Ibid., 130. For the role of tax collection in the aggravation of the situation of the Armenian peasantry in the eastern provinces, see Özbek, "'Anadolu Islahatı,' 'Ermeni Sorunu,'" 59–85.
72 BOA. Y. PRK. AZJ. 10/73, 21 Zilhicce 1302 (1 October 1885). Priest Gabriel to Istanbul.

of other villages, were allowed by the agha to perform their religious ceremonies. The villagers were afraid to complain about this, but some dared to file petitions, though they remained inconclusive. The priest and villagers claimed that one of the churches was ruined and the other one ended up being used as a sheepfold. Drawing attention to the orders and codes regarding the protection of different religions and sects, Priest Gabriel asked for justice.[73]

Nevertheless, the governor of the province of Bitlis claimed that the charges of the priest were unfounded. The latter repeated his claims and the former continuously rejected them.[74] The case was heard in Muş and at the Court of Appeal in Van and it was decided that the village of Gemig, rather than being an Armenian village was a ruined village since time immemorial. The court also argued that Priest Gabriel's only evidence regarding the village being Armenian was just the ruins of the building which was supposed to be a church.[75] It is difficult to ascertain now whether the Gemig was a ruined village all along or not, as claimed by the local authorities of Muş and Bitlis. If we assume that Priest Gabriel was right, the case of Gemig would have been an example showing that tribal aghas were not the only culprits in the evacuation of the Armenian villages. Tribal leaders might have not dared to usurp Armenian lands if they had not been guaranteed the support of provincial authorities.[76]

---

73   Ibid.
74   BOA. DH. MKT. 1458/34, 9 Safer 1305 (27 October 1887).
75   BOA. Y.A. HUS. 195/76, 15 Muharrem 1304 (14 October 1886).
76   There were many cases of land usurpation which could not be solved. After the reinstitution of the Constitutional Regime, the Committee of Union and Progress (CUP) and the Armenian Revolutionary Federation (ARF) cooperated for restitution for the seized lands of the Armenian peasantry and also for the improvement in their living conditions. For the details and the failures of this collaboration, see Dikran M. Kaligian, "Agrarian Land Reform and the Armenians in the Ottoman Empire," The Armenian Review 48, no. 3, 4 (2003): 24–45. For an account of land disputes through an analysis of the petitions of peasants of certain villages of Diyarbekir in a post-revolutionary context, see Nilay Özok-Gündoğan, "A 'Peripheral' Approach to the 1908 Revolution in the Ottoman Empire: Land Disputes in Peasant Petitions in Post-Revolutionary Diyarbekir," in Social Relations in Ottoman Diyarbekir, 1870–1915, ed. Joost Jongerden and Jelle Verheij (Leiden: Brill, 2012).

CHAPTER 9

Conclusion

The sanjak of Muş had been granted to its mutasarrıfs as a yurtluk-ocaklık, which refers to hereditary rights over large plots of lands and their revenues accompanied by great immunities. The Ottoman-Safavid rivalry and the existing power of Kurdish dynasties in the sixteenth century determined the relations between the Kurdish beys and the imperial center. Although land tenure forms that were similar to yurtluk-ocaklıks and hükûmets were parts of an imperial policy applied on the frontiers, the course of the transformation of yurtluk-ocaklıks and their counterparts, hükûmet lands, differed from region to region. In the same vein, in spite of being similar to provincial notables all over the empire, yurtluk-ocaklık and hükûmet holders were also different as they had held hereditary, historical, political, and economic power far earlier than the eighteenth century, which was called the "age of the â'yâns." In the case of Muş, Alaaddin Pasha became influential by getting control of Muş in the eighteenth century during an era when the power of hükûmet holders of Bitlis was decaying.

Sources regarding their power prior to the eighteenth century are scarce, yet, based on the reference of family members during the nineteenth century to "a four-hundred-year dynasty" and from the fact that Alaaddin Pasha had been appointed as mütesellim of Muş by the khans of Bitlis, it is possible to deduce that the family had controlled certain plots of lands as yurtluk-ocaklık, mâlikâne, or mukâta'a under the rule of Bitlis khanate and they expanded their control with the fall of the khanate. Given that the family was originally from Bitlis and Rojki tribe, it is strongly possible that the family was part of the Bitlis khanate. From the eighteenth century onwards, the lineage of Alaaddin Pasha held the mutasarrıflık of Muş as yurtluk-ocaklık. Moreover, in the course of time, the family members increased their economic and political power by getting control over Hınıs, Tekman, and Malazgirt as mukâta'as, mâlikânes, or yurtluk-ocaklıks. This revealed that the yurtluk-ocaklık-type lands were not static and their limits were extended or narrowed according to negotiations carried out with central and provincial authorities.

The economic and political power of the yurtluk-ocaklık holders gradually decreased until the final abrogation of this land tenure form with the promulgation of the Tanzimat, which also took time. Thus, Emin Pasha from among Alaaddin Pashazades was the last member of his family to enjoy the economic and political power that yurtluk-ocaklık lands entailed, and he struggled to

CONCLUSION   275

keep these lands intact throughout the first half of the nineteenth century. His rise to power during the 1820s provides important clues about the sources of the power of the holders of yurtluk-ocaklık lands. Similarly, his oscillation between rise and fall in the same years casts significant light on the transformation of such types of land. By the early nineteenth century, Ottoman central and provincial authorities had already drawn attention to the potential of such lands should they be put under the direct control of the government. Thus, in an era when the central government was asserting its control over those lands, yurtluk-ocaklık holders adapted through negotiation, collaboration, and as a last resort, through contestation.

Throughout this book, I have emphasized the negotiation between local actors and provincial and central authorities as opposed to a binary opposition between them. Similarly, local actors and central and provincial authorities were heterogeneous – far from seeking the same agenda. The relation between the governor of Erzurum, Esad Pasha, and mutasarrıf/mütesellim of Muş, Emin Pasha, as well as the intrafamilial rivalry within the dynasty of Muş were the best examples of this heterogeneity. Emin Pasha voluntarily took part in military reforms during the reign of Mahmud II and in the settlement of the nomadic tribes; in return, he reclaimed the mukâta'as of Hınıs and Tekman. Similarly, the transformation of yurtluk-ocaklık types of land was also part of this negotiation. During the respective müşirliks of Reşid Mehmed and Hafız Pashas, Muş was granted to them. After the establishment of the müşirlik of Erzurum in 1836, the sanjak of Muş was annexed to it and the revenues of the sanjak were allocated to the Mansure Army. With this, the yurtluk-ocaklık status of the sanjak changed. During this process, Emin Pasha managed to keep twenty-four villages for himself and his immediate family. Those villages were among the most fertile in the plain of Muş; their limits and revenues would be contested even into the late nineteenth century. Thus, instead of being an abrupt process, the confiscation of yurtluk-ocaklıks was gradual. In the case of Muş, this process took place in two phases. The first was the abrogation of the yurtluk-ocaklık status of the sanjak of Muş in 1836 and its annexation to Erzurum Province. The second phase occurred with the confiscation of the yurtluk-ocaklık villages when the brothers of Emin Pasha were exiled along with their extended families in 1849, after the Tanzimat. Hence, one of the findings of this study is the difference between the granting of sanjaks vis-à-vis villages as yurtluk-ocaklıks. In the case of the granting of the sanjak, holders were also entitled to the mutasarrıflık of that sanjak. Referring to the usufruct right of the whole sanjak with its approximately four hundred villages, mutasarrıflık suggests a wider range of authority. On the contrary, in the mütesellimlik the sanjak was not granted as yurtluk-ocaklık. Thus, during his entire career, the post of Emin Pasha oscillated between mütesellimlik and mutasarrıflık, which at the same time reflects the fluctuating nature of yurtluk-ocaklık types of land in the nineteenth century.

After initial chapters discussing the strategies and conditions that led to the rise of a provincial notable and the composition of his political and economic power in the pre-Tanzimat era, the rest of the book focused on the implementation and reception of Tanzimat reforms and the transformation they brought about in the sanjak of Muş. The main purpose of the promulgation of Tanzimat was to increase the infrastructural power of the central state, so that more peripheral provinces would gradually be included in this circle. On the eve of the implementation of Tanzimat reforms in Muş, peasants were miserable and dispersed due to over taxation, corvée, and indebtedness as a result of the misdeeds by tax-farmers, governors, stewards, and Armenian notables as well as due to assaults by tribal members. Moreover, the rivalry within the dynasty of Muş over the mutasarrıflık of the sanjak aggravated this situation. By uncovering the network of power relations in the region, this book sheds light on both conflicting and congruent agendas of different local groups and their effects on the lives of the ordinary people of Muş.

The collaboration of yurtluk-ocaklık governors of Muş, Alaaddin Pashazades was vital in the fulfillment of the Tanzimat reforms. A proper governor with local knowledge and influence over the tribes who could be intermediate among regional power holders was required. This explained the Şerif Bey's appointment as the kaimakam of Muş to implement the Tanzimat reforms, settle the seminomadic tribes, and intermediate in the issue of Van, which had turned into a regional revolt that had merged with that of Bedirhan Bey in Bohtan. In this way, the book indicated that the Tanzimat reforms did not necessarily oust regional powerholders to establish direct rule. On the contrary, local knowledge, experience, and the intermediary role of local notables were essential in the implementation of a new system of rule. Thus, the incorporation of provincial notables in the new provincial administrations was not necessarily a failure of the reforms; on the contrary, it was a part of them. Rather than being a top-down process, the reforms were shaped and changed according to the necessities of given localities. Similarly, local power holders took part in new institutions of the Tanzimat, like the local councils, and were therefore the main implementers of the reforms. In the case of yurtluk-ocaklık holders, their power changed and in a sense was curtailed, but they also maintained their prominence as they were gradually incorporated into provincial administrations and participated in its politics.

The fiscal transformation that the Tanzimat reforms embarked upon initially required the annulment of the yurtluk-ocaklık system, which in turn would eradicate the economic and political power of provincial notables. Thus, the existence of the dynasty of Muş in the region, like those of their contemporaries, was a major obstacle in this new fiscal, administrative transformation. Despite their collaboration in the suppression of the revolt of Bedirhan Bey and Han Mahmud, Şerif Bey and his brothers, together with their immediate families, were exiled soon afterwards. However, the exile of those notables was not necessarily prescribed from the center and applied in the locality. In the case of Muş, the former governor of Erzurum – who had become the governor of the newly established province of Kurdistan – Esad Pasha, was influential in the exile of the local dynasty. In a sense, the suppression of the far-reaching revolt of Bedirhan Bey and his allies was a chance to govern the region without the interference of local power holders – a perception which had been on the agenda for many decades.

Nevertheless, exile did not exclude the option of incorporation. Some family members were employed in posts in imperial offices in the capital city. Similarly, negotiation and bargaining continued. The main negotiation after their exile was over the limits and revenues of their yurtluk-ocaklık villages, in return for which they had been put on salary. Despite being paid in return for their yurtluk-ocaklık villages, the notables of Muş lost a tremendous part of their power. The yurtluk-ocaklık land tenure system not only consisted of control of the revenues of certain plots of land, but also entailed considerable autonomy, including the right to collect taxes and have control over, including the taxation, of semi nomadic and nomadic groups. Furthermore, in addition to the yurtluk-ocaklık lands, the notables of Muş left behind landed properties, like mansions, mills, vineyards and orchards. They also had marks on the city life through religious endowments established as an extension of mosques built by the family members. In this situation, they did not cease for a moment to negotiate the terms of their return to their homeland through petitions. The contours of this negotiation changed, in the course of time, from challenging the limits and revenues of their villages to being content with sharecropping. However, the forgiveness of the family members was gradual and conditional. After the women and children of the family were allowed to return to Erzurum (not to Muş), Hurşid and Murad beys in the 1850s, and Şerif Pasha in the 1860s were also allowed to return.

The family members continued to take their salaries, in return for their yurtluk-ocaklık lands, until the breakout of the First World War. Both the sons and daughters of Şerif Pasha, Murad and Hurşid beys filed petitions for either continuation or increase in their salaries by referring to their ancestors' prominence in the Ottoman imperial system. Given that the descendants of the family are today living in their former contested yurtluk-ocaklık villages, it is possible to infer that family members returned to their homes in the course of time and that they were reincorporated into the state system. Some of the family members were employed in the administration of small districts in the province of Erzurum and were promoted in rank. The son of Hurşid Bey, Süleyman Bahri Pasha occupied significant positions in the Ottoman bureaucracy. After having been in the district administration in the province of Erzurum he was appointed to remarkable posts in the imperial capital from mutasarrıflık of Beyoğlu and Üsküdar to the Şûrâ-yı Devlet, one of the prominent institutions of the Tanzimat. Süleyman Bahri Pasha was governor of the province of Adana for ten years (1898–1908).[1]

This book is a monograph of the sanjak of Muş in the nineteenth century. Covering the period between the 1820s and 1880s, the study contextualized the milestones of the nineteenth century in Muş's locality. This book hopes to contribute to exploring the functions, sources of power, and the agency of Kurdish notables in the pre-Tanzimat era as well as how the transition to the Tanzimat era transformed their power and relations with different authorities. The book also hopes to discover the voices of the Muslim and Armenians commoners of Muş who sought to make themselves heard by filing petitions, a significant number of which was cross-sectarian. Finally, the book hopes to contribute to unveiling the active roles the nomadic tribes played in the politics and everyday life of a sanjak in the Ottoman East.

---

1 Yurdal Demirel, "Adana'nın Valisi: Süleyman Bahri Paşa (1898–1908)" in *Tarihte Adana ve Çukurova: Osmanlı Döneminde Adana ve Çukurova II*, eds. Yılmaz Kurt and Fatih Sansar, (Ankara: Akademisyen, 2016), 219–220.

Bibliography

Primary Sources

The Ottoman Archives of the Office of the Prime Minister -Istanbul

Bâb-ı Âlî Evrâk Odası (BEO): 4232/317336.

Cevdet Askerî (C. AS): 469/19549.

Cevdet Dâhiliye (C. DH): 65/3220, 98/4864, 117/5810, 133/6650, 142/7060, 187/9340, 201/10011, 217/13539, 229/11348, 270/13478, 279/13922, 279/13938.

Cevdet Mâliyye (C. ML): 269/11018, 299/14949, 410/16784, 585/24051, 654/26778.

Cevdet Zabtiyye (C. ZB): 27/1344.

Dâhiliyye Mektubî (DH. MKT): 1377/62, 1458/34, 1491/112.

Hâriciyye Nezâreti Mektubî Kalemi Evrâkı (HR. MKT): 16/58, 17/41, 29/63.

Hâriciyye Nezâreti Siyasî Kalemi Evrâkı (HR. SYS): 80/28.

Hâriciyye Nezâreti Tercüme Odası Evrâkı (HR.TO): 212/11.

Hatt-ı Hümâyûn (HAT): 96/3885, 175/7583-E, 308/18189, 309/18264, 314/18497, 314/18497-D, 314/18497-E, 329/19070, 377/204876, 381/20579, 381/20579-A, 446/22291, 447/22311-A, 449/22346-F, 450.22347-D, 450/22351, 450/22351-A, 450/22351-B, 450/22351-C, 450/22351-D, 450/22351-E, 450/22351-G, 450/22351-H, 450/22351-I, 450/22351-J, 450/22351-T, 450/22351-U, 451/22359, 461/22617-B, 533/26254-A, 625/30883, 634/31307-A, 634/31307-B, 634/313307-C, 637/31417, 637/31417-A, 659/32173-C, 703/33795, 703/33819, 718/34245-D, 721/34364-B, 721/34364-C, 721/34364-L, 721/34384 722/34418-A, 724/34457, 727/34640, 728/ 34650, 735/34903, 736/34932-F, 736/34992-B, 736/34992-C, 770/36176 789/36774, 790/ 36808-B, 790/36808-J, 790/36808-K, 790/36808-O, 793/36838-B, 794/36840-G, 795/36870, 795/ 36368-N, 802/27108, 811/37220-C, 818/37320-F, 819/37339-C, 819/37340-M, 826/37442-A, 892/39382, 892/39382-B, 1088/44264-B, 1088/44264-C 1011/42437-A, 1016/42520, 1023/42698-F, 1087/44245, 1229/47949, 1242/48291, 1242/48291-E, 1248/48350-A, 1248/48350-B, 1248/48350-C, 1315/51270-Ç, 1322/51635-B, 1364/53898, 1618/71, 1623/33, 1648/15, 22351 D, 22351 E.

İrâde Dâhiliyye (İ. DH): 7/298, 27/1305, 51/2557, 59/2950, 97/4852, 197/11181, 202/11557, 206/11875, 211/12262, 212/12312, 283/17817, 358/23641, 514/34990, 626/43528, 648/45054.

İrâde Hâriciyye (İ. HR): 60/2894.

İrâde Meclis-i Mahsûs (İ. MMS): 14/600, 38/1574.

İrâde Meclis-i Vâlâ (İ. MVL): 10/154, 27/430, 66/1254, 122/3116, 157/4486, 162/4718, 181/5442, 185/5579, 198/6184, 219/7325, 225/7675, 227/7731, 263/9985, 269/10320, 277/10774, 277/10796, 433/19083, 439/19491, 458/20546, 463/020917.

İrâde Mesâil-i Mühimme (İ.MSM): 49/1233, 50/1278, 52/1343, 52/1346, 69/2010.

İrâde Şûrâ-yı Devlet (İ. ŞD): 12/567.

Meclis-i Vâlâ (MVL): 2/18, 2/24, 2/26, 8/38, 9/38, 11/4, 24/56, 29/29, 81/37, 87/40, 87/41, 88/98, 90/65, 92/98, 93/62, 108/25, 108/52, 108/82, 116/86, 119/58, 121/24, 121/63, 131/20, 131/116, 133/55, 134/49, 180/9, 182/15, 226/61, 227/38, 229/37, 231/57, 235/13, 249/51, 251/64, 252/787, 261/15, 265/36, 276/42, 294/75, 300/89, 301/93, 302/21, 302/29, 304/10, 304/49, 306/44, 313/40, 314/42, 314/72, 315/46, 318/13462, 375/77, 410/43, 410/92, 425/136, 435/12, 462/55, 469/64, 476/77, 568/83, 577/47, 577/55, 602/32, 605/8, 605/25, 606/29, 611/41, 629/41, 634/41, 646/81, 674/61, 681/8, 694/7, 694/48, 705/62, 706/1, 707/57, 708/38, 711/11, 738/29, 934/40, 949/17.

Meclis-i Vâlâ Riyâseti Defterleri (MVL. D.): 2.

Meclis-i Vükelâ Mazbataları: 120/74.

Nüfûs Defterleri (NFS. d): 3868.

Sadâret Âmedî Kalemi Evrâkı (A.AMD): 34/38.

Sadâret Divan (Beylikçi) Kalemi Evrâkı (A.DVN): 17/62, 82/99.

Sadâret Meclis-i Vâlâ Evrâkı (A. MKT. MVL): 6/63, 33/4, 25/8, 48/46, 60/13, 72/36, 78/70, 106/25, 112/17, 114/39, 146/9.

Sadâret Mektubî Kalemi Evrâkı (A. MKT): 25/5, 28/84, 30/13, 59/80, 64/72, 79/82, 100/13, 143/66, 168/35, 213/51, 225/82, 226/10, 229/50, 231/15, 236/69.

Sadâret Mühimme Kalemi Evrâkı (A. MKT. MHM): 2/103, 18/83, 22/42, 49/101, 50/56, 86/75, 155/9, 221/10, 230/20, 237/74, 238/79, 279/36, 293/10, 331/86, 344/94, 345/63, 346/1, 367/96, 391/8, 456/35, 757/67.

Sadâret Müteferrik Evrâkı (A. AM): 26/32.

Sadâret Nezaret ve Devâir Evrâkı (A. MKT.NZD): 7/39, 71/19, 93/37, 132/22, 144/41, 206/80, 230/65, 385/59.

Sadâret Umûm Vilâyât Evrâkı (A. MKT. UM): 7/39, 15/44, 30/89, 42/94, 50/64, 59/97, 75/1, 85/46, 113/25, 113/69, 114/77, 131/19, 136/65, 157/38, 183/20, 200/26, 205/94, 229/54, 229/68, 236/24, 239/26, 240/98, 254/2, 241/15, 278/48, 287/24, 326/3, 330/1, 361/54, 363/24, 367/94, 423/55, 425/58, 441/82, 449/81, 487/50, 494/78, 494/92, 509/74, 509/79, 523/9, 544/53.

Şûrâ-yı Devlet (ŞD): 64/3763, 261/16, 295/35, 301/28, 308/26, 316/27, 358/16, 374/27, 2390/27, 2855/2, 2881/40, 2884/54, 2886/54.

Yıldız Perâkende Arzuhal Jurnal (Y. PRK. AZJ): 10/73.

Yıldız Hususi Mevzuat (Y.A. HUS): 195/76.

The National Archives of the United Kingdom – London

Foreign Office (FO): 78/366, 78/572, 78/797, 78/906, 78/955, 78/1115, 78/1669, 195/227.

Archive Diplomatiques du Ministère des Affaires Étrangères – Paris

Ministère des Affaires Étrangères (MAE): 69 CPC.

Provincial Yearbooks

Salnâme-i Vilâyet-i Erzurum. 1287, 1288, 1289 and 1290.

Books and Articles

Abadan, Yavuz. "Tanzimat Fermanı'nın Tahlili." In *Tanzimat: Değişim Sürecinde Osmanlı İmparatorluğu*, edited by Halil İnalcık and Mehmet Seyitdanlıoğlu, 57–88. Istanbul: Türkiye İş Bankası Kültür Yayınları, 2012.

Ágoston, Gábor. "A Flexible Empire: Authority and its Limits on the Ottoman Frontiers." In *Ottoman Borderlands: Issues, Personalities and Political Change*, edited by Kemal H. Karpat and Robert W. Zens, 15–32. Madison: University of Wisconsin Press, 2003.

Ahmed Cevdet Paşa. *Tarih-i Cevdet*. Translated by Dündar Günday. 6 vols. Vol. 6, Istanbul: Üçdal Neşriyat, 1983–1984.

Ahmet Cevdet Paşa. *Ma'ruzat*. Edited by Yusuf Halaçoğlu 4 vols. Vol. 4, Istanbul: Çağrı Yayınları, 1980.

Akgündüz, Ahmed. *Osmanlı Kanunnameleri ve Hukuki Tahlilleri*. Vol. 1, Istanbul: Fey Vakfı, 1990.

Akiba, Jun. "The Local Councils as the Origin of Parliamentary System in the Ottoman Empire." In *Development of Parliamentarism in Modern Islamic World*, edited by Sata Tsugitaka, 176–204. Tokyo: Toyo Bunko, 2009.

Alagöz, Mehmet. "Old Habits Die Hard, A Reaction to the Application of Tanzimat: Bedirhan Bey's Revolt." master's thesis, Boğaziçi University, 2003.

Anderson, Lisa. "Tribe and State: Libyan Anamolies." In *Tribes and State Formation in the Middle East*, edited by Philip S. Khoury and Joseph Kostiner. Berkeley: University of California Press, 1990

Anderson, Lisa. *The State and Social Transformation in Tunisia and Libya, 1830–1980*. Princeton: Princeton University Press, 1986.

Andıç, Fuat, and Süphan Andıç. *Kırım Savaşı Ali Paşa ve Paris Antlaşması*. Istanbul: Eren Yayıncılık, 2002.

Artinian, Vartan. *The Armenian Constitutional System in the Ottoman Empire 1839–1863: A Study of Historical Development*. Istanbul 1988.

Astourian, Stephan H. "The Silence of the Land: Agrarian Relations, Ethnicity, and Power." In *A Question of Genocide: Armenians and Turks at the end of the Ottoman Empire*, edited by Ronald Grigor Suny, Fatma Müge Göçek and Norman M. Naimark. Oxford: Oxford University Press, 2011.

Ateş, Sabri. "Empires at the Margin: Towards a History of the Ottoman Iranian Borderland and the Borderland Peoples, 1843–1881." PhD diss., New York University, 2006.

Ateş, Sabri. *The Ottoman-Iranian Borderlands: Making a Boundary, 1843–1914*. New York: Cambridge University Press, 2013.

Ateş, Sabri. "The End of Kurdish Autonomy: The Destruction of the Kurdish Emirates in the Ottoman Empire." In *The Cambridge History of the Kurds* edited by Hamit Bozarslan, Cengiz Güneş, and Veli Yadırgı. Cambridge: Cambridge University Press, 2021.

Averyanov, P.İ. *19. Yüzyılda Osmanlı İran Rus Savaşlarında Kürtler*. Translated by İbrahim Kale. Istanbul: Avesta, 2010.

Ayn-ı Ali Efendi. *Kanunname-i Âli Osman: Osmanlı Devleti Arazi Kanunları*. Translated by Hadiye Tuncer. Ankara: Resimli Posta Matbaası, 1962.

Aytekin, E. Attila "Hukuk, Tarih ve Tarihyazımı: 1858 Osmanlı Arazi Kanunnamesi'ne Yönelik Yaklaşımlar." *Türkiye Araştırmaları Literatür Dergisi* 3, no. 5 (2005): 723–44.

Badem, Candan. *The Ottoman Crimean War, 1853–1856*. Leiden: Brill, 2010.

Barkan, Ömer Lûtfi. "Türk Toprak Hukuku Tarihinde Tanzimat ve 1274 (1858) Tarihli Arazi Kanunnamesi." In *Tanzimat I*, 321–421. Istanbul: Maarif Matbaası, 1940.

Barkey, Karen. *Bandits and Bureaucrats: The Ottoman Route State Centralization*. Ithaca Cornell University Press, 1997.

Barkey, Karen. *Empire of Difference: The Ottomans in Comparative Perspective*. Cambridge: Cambridge University Press, 2008.

Barsoumian, Hagop. "The Eastern Question and The Tanzimat Era." In *Armenian People from Ancient to Modern Times*, edited by Richard G. Hovanissian. New York: St. Martin's Press, 1997.

Bayraktar, Bayram. *20. Yüzyılın Dönemecinde Rus General Mayevsky'nin Türkiye Gözlemleri: Van-Bitlis Vilâyetleri Askerî İstatistiği*. Istanbul: İnkılâp Kitabevi, 2007.

Bayraktar, Uğur. "Yurtluk-Ocaklıks: Land, Politics of Notables and Society in Ottoman Kurdistan, 1820–1890." PhD diss., Boğaziçi University and École des Hautes Études en Sciences Sociales, 2015.

Bayraktar, Uğur. "The Political Economy of Çiftliks: The Redistribution of Land and Land Tenure Relations in the Nineteenth Century Provinces of Ioannia and Trikala." master's thesis, Boğaziçi University, 2009.

Bebiroğlu, Murat. *Tanzimat'tan II. Meşrutiyet'e Ermeni Nizamnameleri*. Istanbul: Ohan Matbaacılık, 2003.

Beck, Lois. "The Tribes and the State in Nineteenth and Twentieth Century Iran." In *Tribes and State Formation in the Middle East*, edited by Philip S. Khoury and Joseph Kostiner. Berkeley: University of California Press 1990.

Ben-Bassat, Yuval. *Petitoning the Sultan: Protests and Justice in Late Ottoman Palestine*. London: I.B. Tauris, 2013.

Beydilli, Kemal. *1828–1829 Osmanlı-Rus Savaşında Doğu Anadolu'dan Rusya'ya Göçürülen Ermeniler*. Ankara: Türk Tarih Kurumu Basımevi, 1988.

Bozarslan, Hamit. "Kurdish Nationalism in Turkey: From Tacit Contract to Rebellion (1919–1925)." In *Essays on the Origins of Kurdish Nationalism*, edited by Abbas Vali. Costa Mesa: Mazda 2003.

Bragg, John K. *Ottoman Notables and Participatory Politics: Tanzimat Reform in Tokat, 1839–1876*. London: Routledge, 2014.

Brant, James. "Notes of a Journey through a part of Kurdistan, in the Summer of 1838." *The Journal of the Royal Geographic* X (1841): 341–434.

Budak, Mustafa, Önder Bayır, and Mümin Yıldıztaş, eds. *Tanzimat Sonrası Arazi ve Tapu*. İstanbul: Osmanlı Arşivi Daire Başkanlığı, 2014.

Ceylan, Ebubekir. *The Ottoman Origins of Modern Iraq: Political Reform, Modernization and Development in the Nineteenth-Century Middle East*. London: I.B. Tauris, 2011.

Chalcraft, John. "Engaging the State: Peasants and Petitions in Egypt on the Eve of Colonial Rule." *International Journal of Middle East Studies* 37, no. 3 (2005): 303–25.

Chesney, Francis R. *The Russo-Turkish Campaigns of 1828 and 1829: With a View of the Present State of Affairs in the East*. New York: Redfield, 1854.

Cin, Halil. *Mirî Arazi ve Bu Arazinin Mülk Haline Dönüşümü*. Ankara: Sevinç Matbaası, 1969.

Cora, Yaşar Tolga. "Transforming Erzurum/Karin: The Social and Economic History of a Multi-Ethnic Ottoman City in the Nineteenth Century." PhD diss., The University of Chicago, 2016.

Cora, Yaşar Tolga, Dzovaniar Derderian, and Ali Sipahi, eds. *The Ottoman East in the Nineteenth Century: Societies, Identities and Politics*. London: I.B. Tauris, 2016.

Cora, Yaşar Tolga, Dzovaniar Derderian, and Ali Sipahi. "Introduction: Ottoman Historiography's Black Hole." In *The Ottoman East in the Nineteenth Century: Societies, Identities and Politics,* edited by Yaşar Tolga Cora, Dzovaniar Derderian and Ali Sipahi, 1–15. London: I.B. Tauris, 2016.

Cora, Yaşar Tolga. "The Crimean War and the Armenian Elite in the Ottoman Empire." *Archiv Orientální* 87 (2019): 421–444.

Cuinet, Vital. *La Turquie d'Asie: Géographie Administrative: statisque, descriptive et raisonnée de chaque province de l'Asie Mineure*. 4 vols. Vol. 2, Paris: E. Leroux, 1891.

Cuthell, David Cameron. "The Muhacirin Komisyonu: An Agent in the Transformation of Ottoman Anatolia, 1860–1866." PhD diss., Columbia University, 2005.

Çadırcı, Musa. "Anadolu'da Redif Askeri Teşkilatının Kuruluşu." DTCF *Tarih Araştırmaları Dergisi* VII–XII, no. 14–23 (1975): 63–75.

Çadırcı, Musa. "II Mahmut Döneminde Mütesellimlik Kurumu." DTCF *Dergisi* XXVIII, no. 3–4 (1970): 287–96.

Çadırcı, Musa. *Tanzimat Döneminde Anadolu Kentlerini'nin Sosyal ve Ekonomik Yapısı*. 2 ed. Ankara: Türk Tarih Kurumu, 1997.

Çadırcı, Musa. *Tanzimat Döneminde Türkiye: Askerlik*. Istanbul: İmge Kitabevi, 2008.

Çakır, Coşkun. "Tanzimat Dönemi Vergi Uygulamalarında Karşılaşılan Güçlükler ve Vergi İhtilalleri." *İktisat Fakültesi Mecmuası* 51, no. 1 (2001): 71–95.

Çetinsaya, Gökhan. *Ottoman Administration of Iraq, 1890–1908*. London Routledge Taylor, 2006.

Çiçek, Talha. *Negotiating Empire in the Middle East: Ottomans and Arab Nomads in the Modern Era, 1840–1914*. Cambridge: Cambridge University Press, 2021.

Çiftçi, Erdal. "Fragile Alliances in the Ottoman East: The Heyderan Tribe and the Empire, 1820–1929." Phd. diss., Bilkent University, 2018.

Çiftçi, Erdal. "Osmanlıdan Cumhuriyet'e Hayalî bir aşiret olarak Heyderan Aşireti ve Değişimi." In *Kürt Aşiretleri: Aktör, Müttefik ve Şaki*, edited by Tuncay Şur and Yalçın Çakmak. Istanbul: İletişim Yayınları, 2022.

Dadrian, Vahakn N. "The 1984 Sassoun Massacre: A Juncture in the Escalation of the Turko-Armenian Conflict." *The Armenian Review* 47, no. 1–2 (2001): 5–39.

Dağlı, Murat. "The Limits of Ottoman Pragmatism." *History and Theory* 52, no. 2 (2013): 194–213.

Dankoff, Robert. *Evliya Çelebi in Bitlis: The Relevant Section of the Seyahatname/edited with translation, commentary and introduction*. Leiden: E.J. Brill, 1990.

Davison, Roderic H. *Reform in the Ottoman Empire, 1856–1876*. New Jersey: Princeton University Press, 1963.

Davison, Roderic H. *Essays in Ottoman and Turkish History, 1774–1923*. Austin: University of Texas Press, 1990.

Demirel, Yurdal. "Adana'nın Valisi: Süleyman Bahri Paşa (1898–1908)." *In Tarihte Adana ve Çukurova: Osmanlı Döneminde Adana ve Çukurova II*, edited by Yılmaz Kurt and Fatih Sansar. Ankara: Akademisyen, 2016.

Derderian, Dzovaniar. "Shaping Subjectivities and Contesting Power through the Image of Kurds, 1860s." In *The Ottoman East in the Nineteenth Century: Societies, Identities and Politics*, edited by Yaşar Tolga Cora, Dzovaniar Derderian and Ali Sipahi, 91–108. London: I.B. Tauris, 2016.

Deringil, Selim. "19. Yüzyılda Osmanlı İmparatorluğu'na Göç Olgusu Üzerine Bazı Düşünceler." In *Prof. Dr. Bekir Kütükoğlu'na Armağan-İstanbul Üniversitesi Edebiyat Fakültesi Tarih Araştırma Merkezi*, 435–42. Istanbul: Edebiyat Fakültesi Basımevi, 1991.

Deringil, Selim. "'They Live in a State of Nomadism and Savagery': The Late Ottoman Empire and the Post-Colonial Debate." *Comparative Studies in Society and History* 45, no. 2 (2003): 311–42.

Dokuzlu, Sertaç. "The Agricultural Credit System in the Ottoman Empire between 1863 and 1888." *Rural History* 28, no. 2 (2017): 177–88.

Doumani, Beshara. *Rediscovering Palestine: Merchants and Peasants in Jabal Nablus, 1700–1900*. Berkeley: University of California Press, 1995.

Duguid, Stephen. "The Politics of Unity: Hamidian Policy in Eastern Anatolia". *Middle Eastern Studies* 9, no. 2 (May, 1973): 139–55.

Duman Koç, Gülseren. "A Negotiation of Power during the Age of Reforms in the Ottoman Empire: Notables, Tribes and State in Muş (1820–1840)". *Middle Eastern Studies* 57 no. 2 (2021): 209–226.

Duman Koç, Gülseren. "Provincial Governors and Yurtluk-Ocaklık Holders on the Eve of the Tanzimat Reforms: The Embezzlement Case of Mehmed Esad Muhlis Pasha". *Archiv Orientální* 91 no. 1 (2023): 69–88.

Efe, Ayla. "Muhassıllık Teşkilatı." PhD diss., Eskişehir Anadolu Üniversitesi, 2002.

Eren, Ahmet Cevat. *Türkiye'de Göç ve Göçmen Meseleleri: Tanzimat Devri, İlk Kurulan Göçmen Komisyonu, Çıkarılan Tüzükler*. Istanbul: Nurgök Matbaası, 1966.

Erinç, Sırrı. *Doğu Anadolu Coğrafyası*. Istanbul: Sucuoğlu Matbaası, 1953.

Eser, Mithat. "Muş Adına Dair Bir Soruşturma." In *Muş Tarihi*, edited by Murat Alanoğlu, Mustafa Alican, and Mehmet Özalper. Istanbul: İdeal Kültür Yayıncılık, 2021.

Esmer, Tolga U. "A Culture of Rebellion: Networks of Violence and Competing Discourses of Justice in the Ottoman Empire, 1790–1808." PhD diss., The University of Chicago, 2009.

Esmer, Tolga U. "Economies of Violence, Banditry and Governance in the Ottoman Empire Around 1800." *Past & Present* 224, no. 1 (2014): 163–99.

Etmekjian, Lillian. "The Armenian National Assembly of Turkey and Reform." *The Armenian Review*, no. Spring 29 (1976): 38–52.

Evans, Peter B., Dietrich Rueschemeyer, and Theda Skocpol, eds. *Bringing the State Back in*. Cambridge: Cambridge University Press, 1985.

Evliya Çelebi, *Günümüz Türkçesiyle Evliya Çelebi Seyahatnamesi*, edited by Seyit Ali Kahraman and Yücel Dağlı, vol. 4 Istanbul: Yapı Kredi Yayınları, 2010.

Faroqhi, Suraiya. "Coping with the Central State, Coping with Local Power: Ottoman Regions and Notables from the Sixteenth to the Early Nineteenth Century." In *The Ottomans and the Balkans: A Discussion of Historiography*, edited by Fikret Adanır and Suraiya Faroqhi, 351–83. Leiden: Brill, 2002.

Findley, Carter Vaughn. "The Tanzimat." In *The Cambridge History of Turkey*, edited by Reşat Kasaba, 11–38. New York: Cambridge University Press, 2008.

Fisher, Alan W. "Emigration of Muslims from the Russian Empire in the Years After the Crimean War." *Jahrbücher für Geschichte Osteuropas* 35, no. 3 (1987): 356–71.

Gara, Eleni. "Popular Protest and the Limitations of Sultanic Justice." In *Popular Protest and Political Participation in the Ottoman Empire: Studies in Honor of Suraiya Faroqhi*, edited by Eleni Gara, Christoph K. Neumann and M. Erdem Kabadayı. Istanbul: İstanbul Bilgi University Press, 2011.

Gencer, Fatih. "Merkezileşme Politikaları Sürecinde Yurtluk-Ocaklık Sisteminin Değişimi." *Ankara Üniversitesi Dil ve Tarih-Coğrafya Fakültesi Tarih Bölümü Tarih Araştırmaları Dergisi* 30, no. 49 (2011): 75–96.

Gencer, Fatih. *Bitlis ve Muş'un Son Beyleri: Alaaddin Paşazadeler*. Istanbul: Libra Kitap, 2019.

Genç, Mehmet. *Osmanlı İmparatorluğu'nda Devlet ve Ekonomi*. Istanbul: Ötüken, 2000.

Gerber, Haim. *The Social Origins of the Modern Middle East*. Boulder: Lynne Rienner Publishers, 1994.

Ginio, Eyal. "Coping With the State's Agents 'from below': Petitions, Legal Appeal, and the Sultan's Justice in Ottoman Legal Practice." In *Popular Protest and Political Participation in the Ottoman Empire: Studies in Honor of Suraiya Faroqhi*, edited by Eleni Gara, Christoph K. Neumann and M. Erdem Kabadayı. Istanbul: İstanbul Bilgi University Press, 2011.

Gutman, David Edward. *The Politics of Armenian Migration to North America, 1885–1915: Sojourners, Smugglers, and the State and Dubious Citizens*. Edinburgh: Edinburgh University Press, 2019.

Güran, Tevfik. "19. Yüzyıl Temettüat Tahrirleri." In *Osmanlı Devleti'nde Bilgi ve İstatistik – Data and Statistics in the Ottoman Empire*, edited by Halil İnalcık and Şevket Pamuk. Ankara: T.C. Başbakanlık Devlet İstatistik Enstitüsü, 2000.

Güran, Tevfik. *Tanzimat Döneminde Osmanlı Maliyesi: Bütçeler ve Hazine Hesapları (1841–1861)*. Ankara: Türk Tarih Kurumu Basımevi, 1989.

Güran, Tevfik. "Temettuat Registers as a Resource about Ottoman Economic and Social Life." In *The Ottoman State and Societies in Change: A Study of the Nineteenth Century Temettuat Registers*, edited by Hayashi Kayoko and Mahir Aydın. Islamic Area Studies. London: Kegan Paul, 2004.

Hacısalihoğlu, Mehmet, ed. *1864 Kafkas Tehciri: Kafkasya'da Rus Kolonizasyonu, Savaş ve Sürgün*. Istanbul: BALKAR & IRCICA, 2014.

Hakan, Sinan. *Osmanlı Arşiv Belgelerinde Kürtler ve Kürt direnişleri (1817–1867)*. Istanbul: Doz 2007.

Halaçoğlu, Yusuf. "Fırka-i İslahiye ve Yapmış Olduğu İskan." *Tarih Dergisi*, no. 27 (1973): 1–20.

Halaçoğlu, Yusuf. *XVIII. Yüzyılda Osmanlı İmparatorluğu'nun İskân Siyaseti ve Aşiretlerin Yerleştirilmesi*. Ankara: Türk Tarih Kurumu Basımevi, 1988.

Hanssen, Jens. "Practices of Integration: Center-Periphery Relations in the Ottoman Empire." In *The Empire in the City: Arab Provincial Capitals in the Late Ottoman Empire*, edited by Jens Hanssen, Thomas Philip and Stefan Weber. Beirut: Orient-Institut der DMG, 2002.

Hewsen, Robert H. "The Historical Geography of Baghesh/Bitlis and Taron/Mush." In *Armenian Baghesh/Bitlis and Taron/Mush*, edited by Richard G. Hovannisian, 41–58. California: Mazda Publishers, 2001.

Heyd, Uriel. *Studies in Old Ottoman Criminal Law*. Oxford: Clarendon Press, 1973.

Hourani, Albert. "Ottoman Reforms and Politics of Notables," In *Beginnings of Modernization in the Middle East: The Nineteenth Century*, edited by William R. Polk and Richard L. Chambers, 41–68. Chicago: University of Chicago Press, 1968.

Hourani, Albert. "Conclusion: Tribes and States in Islamic History." In *Tribes and States in the Middle East*, edited by Philip S. Khoury and Joseph Kostiner. Berkeley: University of California Press, 1990.

İnalcık, Halil. "Centralization and Decentralization in Ottoman Administration." In *Studies in Eighteenth Century Islamic History, Papers on Islamic History* edited by Thomas Naff and Roger Owen, 27–52. Carbondale: Southern Illinois University Press, 1977.

İnalcık, Halil. "The Emergence of Big Farms, Çiftliks: State, Landlords, and Tenants." In *Landholding and Commercial Agriculture in the Middle East*, edited by Çağlar Keyder and Faruk Tabak, 17–34. Albany: State University of New York Press, 1991.

İnalcık, Halil. *Tanzimat ve Bulgar Meselesi*. Doktora Tezleri Serisi. Ankara: Türk Tarih Kurumu Basımevi, 1943.

İnalcık, Halil. "Autonomous Enclaves in Islamic States: Temlîks, Soyurghals, Yurdluk-Ocaklıks, Mâlikâne-Mukâta'as and Awqaf." In *History and Historiography of post-Mongol Central Asia and the Middle East: Studies in Honor of John E. Woods*, edited by Judith Pfeiffer and Sholch A. Quinn; in collaboration with Ernest Tucker. Wiesbaden: Harrassowitz, 2006.

İnalcık, Halil. "Military and Fiscal Transformation in the Ottoman Empire, 1600–1700." *Archivicum Ottomanicum* VI (1980): 283–337.

İnalcık, Halil. "Şikayet Hakkı: 'Arz-ı Hâl ve 'Arz-ı Mahzar'lar". *Osmanlı Araştırmaları Dergisi* 7–8 (1988): 33–51.

İnalcık, Halil. "Tanzimat Nedir?". In *Tanzimat: Değişim Sürecinde Osmanlı İmparatorluğu*, edited by Halil İnalcık and Mehmet Seyitdanlıoğlu, 29–56. Istanbul: Türkiye İş Bankası Kültür Yayınları, 2012.

İnalcık, Halil. "Tanzimatın Uygulanması ve Sosyal Tepkiler." In *Osmanlı İmparatorluğu: Toplum ve Ekonomi*, edited by Halil İnalcık. İstanbul: Eren, 1993.

İnalcık, Halil, and Donald Quataert, eds. *An Economic and Social History of the Ottoman Empire, 1600–1914*. 2 vols. Vol. 2. Cambridge: Cambridge University Press, 1997.

İnalcık, Halil, and Donald Quataert, eds. *An Economic and Social History of the Ottoman Empire, 1300–1600*. 2 vols. Vol. 1. Cambridge: Cambridge University Press, 1997.

İpek, Nedim. *İmparatorluktan Ulus Devlete Göçler*. Trabzon: Serander Yayınları, 2006.

İslamoğlu, Huri. "Modernities Compared: State Transformations and Constitutions of Property in the Qing and Ottoman Empires." *Journal of Early Modern History*, no. 5 (2002): 353–86.

İslamoğlu, Huri. "Property as a Contested Domain: A Reevaluation of the Ottoman Land Code of 1858." In *New Perspectives on Property and Land in the Middle East*, edited by Roger Owen, 3–61. Cambridge, Massachusetts: Harvard University Press, 2000.

İslamoğlu, Huri, and Peter C. Perdue. "Introduction." *Journal of Early Modern History* 5, no. 4 (2001).

Jongerden, Joost, and Jelle Verheij. "Introduction." In *Social Relations in Ottoman Diyarbekir, 1870–1915*, edited by Joost Jongerden and Jelle Verheij. Leiden: Brill, 2012.

Jwaideh, Wadie. *The Kurdish National Movement: Its Origins and Development*. Syracuse: Syracuse University Press, 2006.

Kaligian, Dikran M. "Agrarian Land Reform and the Armenians in the Ottoman Empire." *The Armenian Review* 48, no. 3, 4 (2003): 24–45.

Kardam, Ahmet. *Cizre – Bohtan Beyi Bedirhan: Direniş ve İsyan Yılları*. Ankara: Dipnot Yayınları, 2011.

Karpat, Kemal H. "Ottoman Urbanism: The Crimean Emigration to Dobruca and the Founding of Mecidiye, 1856–1878." In *Studies on Ottoman Social and Political History: Selected Articles and Essays*. Leiden: Brill 2002.

Karpat, Kemal H. "Comments on Contributions and the Borderlands." In *Ottoman Borderlands: Issues, Personalities and Political Changes*, edited by Kemal H. Karpat and Robert W. Zens, 1–14. Madison: University of Wisconsin Press, 2003.

Karpat, Kemal H. *Ottoman Population, 1830–1914: Demographic and Social Characteristics* Madison: University of Wisconsin Press, 1985.

Kaya, Alp Yücel. "Politique de L'enregistrement de la richesse economique: Les Enquetes Fiscales and Agricoles de L'empire Ottoman and de La France au Milieu du XIXᵉ Siecle." PhD École des Hautes Études en Sciences Sociales, 2005.

Kaya, Alp Yücel. "On the *Çiftlik* Regulation in Tırhala in the Mid Nineteenth Century: Economists, Pashas, Governors, *Çiftlik*-Holders, *Subaşıs* and Sharecroppers." In *Ottoman Rural Societies and Economies: Halcyon Days in Crete VIII A Symposium Held in Rethymno 13–15 January 2012*, edited by Elias Kolovos. Rethymno: Crete University Press, 2015.

Kévonian, Arménouhie. *Gülizar'ın Kara Düğünü*. Translated by Aslı Türker and Ece Erbay Istanbul: Aras Yayıncılık, 2015.

Khazanov, Anatoly. *Nomads and Outside World*. Wisconsin: University of Wisconsin Press, 1994.

Khodarkovsky, Michael. *Russia's Steppe Frontier: The Making of A Colonial Empire, 1500–1800*. Bloomington: Indiana University Press, 2004.

Khoury, Dina Rizk. "The Ottoman Center versus Provincial Power-Holders: An Analysis of the Historiography." In *The Cambridge History of Turkey*, edited by Suraiya Faroqhi, 135–56. Cambridge: Cambridge University Press, 2006.

Khoury, Dina Rizk. *State and Provincial Society in the Ottoman Empire: Mosul, 1540–1834*. Cambridge: Cambridge University Press, 1997.

Khoury, Philip S., and Joseph Kostiner. "Introduction." In *Tribes and State Formation in the Middle East*, edited by Philip S. Khoury and Joseph Kostiner. Berkeley: University of California Press, 1990.

Kılıç, Orhan. "Ocaklık Sancakların Osmanlı Hukukunda ve İdari Tatbikattaki Yeri." *Fırat Üniversitesi Sosyal Bilimler Dergisi* 11, no. 1 (2001): 257–74.

Kılıç, Orhan. *18. Yüzyılın İlk Yarısında Osmanlı Devleti'nin İdari Taksimatı: Eyalet ve Sancak Tevcihatı*. Elazığ: Şark Pazarlama, 1997.

Kılıç, Orhan. "Yurtluk-Ocaklık ve Hükümet Sancaklar Üzerine Bazı Tespitler." *OTAM*, no. 10 (1999): 119–37.

Kırlı, Cengiz. *Sultan ve Kamuoyu: Osmanlı Modernleşme Sürecinde "Havadis Jurnalleri" (1840–1844)*. Istanbul: Türkiye İş Bankası Kültür Yayınları, 2008.

Kırlı, Cengiz. "İvranyalılar, Hüseyin Paşa ve Tasvir-i Zulüm." *Toplumsal Tarih*, no. 195 (2010): 12–21.

Kırlı, Cengiz. "Yolsuzluğun İcadı: 1840 Ceza Kanunu, İktidar ve Bürokrasi." *Tarih ve Toplum Yeni Yaklaşımlar* 4 (2006): 45–119.

Klein, Janet. *The Margins of Empire, Kurdish Militas in the Ottoman Tribal Zone*. Stanford Stanford University Press, 2011.

Klein, Janet. "Power in the Periphery: The Hamidiye Light Cavalry and The Struggle over Ottoman Kurdistan, 1890–1914." PhD diss., Princeton University, 2002.

Koç, Yener. "Bedirxan Pashazades: Power Relations and Nationalism (1876–1914)." master's thesis, Boğaziçi University, 2012.

Koç, Yener. "Nomadic Pastoral Tribes at the Intersection of the Ottoman, Persian and Russian Empires (1820s–1890s)" PhD diss., Boğaziçi University, 2020.

Koç, Yener. "A Tribal Confederation at the Intersection of the Ottoman, Russian and Qajar Empire: The Zilan Confederation and the Empires (1810–1860)." *Middle Eastern Studies* 59 No. 2 (2023): 181–192.

Koç, Yener. "Celali Aşireti: Üç İmparatorluğun Sınırında." In *Kürt Aşiretleri: Aktör, Müttefik ve Şaki* edited by Tuncay Şur and Yalçın Çakmak. Istanbul: İletişim Yayınları, 2022.

Koç, Yener. "Taxing the Tribes in the Ottoman Empire: The Case of the Tribes of Mutki (1839-1908. In *Histories of Tax Evasion, Avoidance and Resistance*, edited by Korinna Schönhärl, Gisela Hürlimann, and Dorothea Rohde, 84–99. Abingdon: Routledge, 2023.

Koçunyan, Aylin. "Nizâmnâme-i Millet-i Ermeniyân Anayasa mıydı?". *Toplumsal Tarih*, no. 216 (Aralık 2011): 46–52.

Kodaman, Bayram. *Sultan II Abdülhamid Devri Doğu Anadolu Politikası*. Ankara: Türk Kültürünü Araştırma Enstitüsü Yayınları, 1987.

Köksal, Yonca. "Coercion and Mediation: Centralization and Sedentarization of Tribes in the Ottoman Empire." *Middle Eastern Studies* 42, no. 3 (May 2006): 469–91.

Köksal, Yonca. "Local Intermediaries and Ottoman State Centralization: A Comparison of the Tanzimat Reforms in the Provinces of Ankara and Edirne (1839–1878)." PhD diss., Columbia University, 2002.

Köksal, Yonca. *The Ottoman Empire in the Tanzimat Era: Provincial Perspectives from Ankara to Edirne*. Abingdon: Routledge, 2019.

Köksal, Yonca. "Tanzimat Döneminde Bulgaristan: Osmanlı'da Merkezi Devlet Oluşumu." *Toplum ve Bilim*, no. 83 (Kış 1999/2000): 241–64.

Köksal, Yonca. "Tanzimat ve Tarih Yazımı." *Doğu Batı: Osmanlılar I* 51 (2010): 193–216.

Köksal, Yonca, and Davut Erkan. *Sadrazam Kıbrıslı Mehmet Emin Paşa'nın Rumeli Teftişi*. Istanbul: Boğaziçi Üniversitesi Yayınevi, 2007.

Köksal, Yonca and Mehmet Polatel. "A tribe as an economic actor: The Cihanbeyli tribe and the meat provisioning of İstanbul in the early Tanzimat era." *New Perspectives on Turkey*, no. 61 (2019): 97–123.

Krohn-Hansen, Christian, and Knut G. Nustad. "Introduction." In *State Formation: Anthropological Perspectives*, edited by Christian Krohn-Hansen and Knut G. Nustad. London: Pluto Press, 2005.

Kunt, Metin İ. *Sancaktan Eyalete: 1550–1650 arasında Osmanlı Ümerası ve İl İdaresi*. Istanbul: Boğaziçi Üniversitesi, 1978.

Küçük, Cevdet. "Tanzimât Devrinde Erzurum." PhD diss., İstanbul Üniversitesi, 1975.

Küçük, Cevdet. "Tanzimât Devrinde Erzurum'un Nüfus Durumu." *İstanbul Üniversitesi Edebiyat Fakültesi Tarih Enstitüsü Dergisi*, no. 7–8 (1976–1977): 185–224.

Küçükoğlu, Lütfiye Sevinç. "Power Politics in Ottoman Provincial Administration: A Case Study of Gürcü Osman Pasha (1789–1807)" PhD diss, Bilkent University, Ankara, 2019.

Lambton, Ann K.S. "Two Ṣafavid Soyūrghāls." *Bulletin of the School of Oriental and African Studies* 14, no. 1 (2009): 44–54.

Lapidus, Ira M. "Tribes and State Formation in Islamic History." In *Tribes and State Formation in the Middle East*, edited by Philip S. Khoury and Joseph Kostiner. Berkeley University of California Press, 1990.

Lynch, H.F.B. *Armenia, Travels and Studies*. Vol. 2, London: Longmans, 1901.

Macid, Ahmed. "Kürdistân Ahvâli ve Mesele-i Islahât." *Mülkiye*, no. 8 (1 Eylül 1325): 1–18.

Makdisi, Ussama S. *The Culture of Sectarianism: Community, History and Violence in Nineteenth-Century Ottoman Lebanon*. Berkeley: University of California Press, 2000.

Mann, Michael. "The Autonomous Power of the State: Its Origins, Mechanisms and Results." *European Journal of Sociology* 25, no. 2 (1984): 185–231.

Mardin, Şerif. "Tanzimat Fermanı'nın Manâsı: Yeni Bir İzah Denemesi." In *Tanzimat: Değişim Sürecinde Osmanlı İmparatorluğu*, edited by Halil İnalcık and Mehmet Seyitdanlıoğlu, 145–65. Istanbul: Türkiye İş Bankası Kültür Yayınları, 2012.

Mardin, Şerif. *Türk Modernleşmesi*. 22 ed. Istanbul: İletişim Yayınları, 2013.

McGowan, Bruce. *Economic Life in Ottoman Europe: Taxation, Trade, and Struggle for Land, 1600–1800*. Cambridge: Cambridge University Press, 1981.

McGowan, Bruce. "The Age of *Ayans*, 1699–1812." In *An Economic and Social History of the Ottoman Empire, 1600–1914*, edited by Halil İnalcık and Donald Quataert, 638–79. Cambridge: Cambridge University Press, 1997.

Meeker, Michael E. *A Nation of Empire: The Ottoman Legacy of Turkish Modernity*. Berkeley: University of California Press, 2002.

Mehmet Süreyya Bey. *Sicill-i Osmanî*. 6 vols. Vol. 5, Istanbul: Tarih Vakfı Yurt Yayınları, 1996.

Meriwether, Margaret L. *The Kin Who Count: Family and Society in Ottoman Aleppo, 1770–1840*. Austin: University of Texas Press, 1999.

Migdal, Joel S. "Introduction: Developing A State-in-Society Perspective." In *State Power and Social Forces: Domination and Transformation in the Third World*, edited by Atul Kohli Joel S. Migdal, Vivienne Shue, 1–4. Cambridge: Cambridge University Press, 1984.

Migdal, Joel S. *State in Society: Studying How States and Societies Transform and Constitute One Another*. Cambridge: Cambridge University Press, 2004.

Minorsky, V. "A Soyūrghāl of Qāsim b. Jahāngir Aq-qoyunlu (903/1498)." *Bulletin of the School of Oriental and African Studies* 9, no. 4 (2009): 927–60.

Mundy, Martha, and Richard Saumarez Smith. *Governing Property, Making the Modern State: Law Administration and Production in Ottoman Syria*. London: I.B. Tauris, 2007.

Murphey, Rhoads ed. *Kanûn-nâme-i Sultânı li Aziz Efendi = Aziz Efendi's Book of Sultanic Laws and Regulations: An Agenda for Reform by a Seventeenth-century Ottoman Statesman*. Cambridge: Harvard University Press, 1985.

Nacar, Can. "Tobacco Workers in the Late Ottoman Empire: Fragmentation, Conflict, and Collective Struggle." PhD diss., State University of New York, 2010.

Nagata, Yuzo. *Muhsin-zâde Mehmed Paşa ve Âyânlık Müessesesi*. Tokyo: Institute for the Study of Languages and Cultures of Asia and Africa, 1982.

Nagata, Yuzo. *Tarihte Âyânlar: Karaosmanoğulları Üzerine Bir İnceleme*. Ankara: Türk Tarih Kurumu, 1997.

Okcu, Naci, and Hasan Akdağ. *Salnâme-i Vilâyet-i Erzurum (1287/1870–1288/1871–1289/1872–1290/1873), Erzurum İl Yıllığı*. Erzurum: Atatürk Üniversitesi Yayınları, 2010.

Orhonlu, Cengiz *Osmanlı İmparatorluğu'nda Aşiretlerin İskânı*. Istanbul: Eren Yayıncılık, 1987.

Ortaylı, İlber. *Tanzimat Devrinde Osmanlı Mahalli İdareleri (1840–1880)*. Istanbul: Türk Tarih Kurumu, 2011. 2.

Owen, Roger, ed. *New Perspectives on Property and Land in the Middle East*. Cambridge: Harvard University Press, 2000.

Öz, Mehmet. "Ottoman Provincial Administration in Eastern and Southeastern Anatolia: The Case of Bidlis in the Sixteenth Century." In *Ottoman Borderlands: Issues, Personalities, and Political Changes*, edited by Kemal H. Karpat and Robert W. Zens, 144–56. Madison: University of Wisconsin, 2003.

Özbek, Nadir. *İmparatorluğun Bedeli: Osmanlı'da Vergi, Siyaset ve Toplumsal Adalet (1838–1908)*. Istanbul: Boğaziçi Üniversitesi Yayınları, 2015.

Özbek, Nadir. "Defining the Public Sphere during the Late Ottoman Empire: War, Mass Mobilization and the Young Turk Regime (1908–1918)." *Middle Eastern Studies* 43, no. 5 (2007): 795–809.

Özbek, Nadir. "Modernite, Tarih ve İdeoloji: II. Abdülhamid Dönemi Tarihçiliği Üzerine Bir Değerlendirme." *Türkiye Araştırmaları Literatür Dergisi* 2, no. 1 (2004): 71–90.

Özbek, Nadir. "Policing the Countryside: Gendarmes of the Late-Nineteenth-Century Ottoman Empire (1876–1908)." *International Journal of Middle East Studies*, no. 40 (2008): 47–67.

Özbek, Nadir. "The Politics of Taxation and the 'Armenian Question' during the Late Ottoman Empire, 1876–1908." *Comparative Studies in Society and History* 54, no. 4 (2012): 770–97.

Özbek, Nadir. "'Anadolu Islahatı,' 'Ermeni Sorunu,' ve Vergi Tahsildarlığı." *Tarih ve Toplum Yeni Yaklaşımlar*, no. 9 (2009): 59–85.

Özkan, Fulya. "A Road in Rebellion, A History on the Move: The Social History of the Trabzon-Bayezid Road and the Formation of the Modern State in the Late Ottoman World." PhD diss., State University of New York, 2012.

Özkaya, Yücel. *Osmanlı İmparatorluğu'nda Âyânlık*. Ankara: Türk Tarih Kurumu, 1994.

Özkaya, Yücel. "XVIII. Yüzyılda Mütesellimlik Müessesesi." *DTCF Dergisi* XXVIII, no. 3–4 (1970): 369–90.

Özoğlu, Hakan. *Kurdish Notables and the Ottoman State: Evolving Identities, Compating Loyalties, and Shifting Boundaries*. Albany: State University of New York Press, 2004.

Özok-Gündoğan, Nilay. "The Making of the Ottoman Modern State in the Kurdish Periphery: The Politics of Land and Taxation, 1840–1870." PhD diss., State University of New York, 2011.

Özok-Gündoğan, Nilay. "A 'Peripheral' Approach to the 1908 Revolution in the Ottoman Empire: Land Disputes in Peasant Petitions in Post-Revolutionary Diyarbekir." In *Social Relations in Ottoman Diyarbekir, 1870–1915*, edited by Joost Jongerden and Jelle Verheij. Leiden: Brill, 2012.

Özok-Gündoğan, Nilay. "Counting the Population and the Wealth in an 'Unruly' Land: Census Making as a Social Process," *Journal of Social History* 53, no. 3 (2020): 763–791.

Özvar, Erol. *Osmanlı Maliyesinde Mâlikane Uygulaması*. Istanbul: Kitabevi, 2003.

Pamuk, Şevket. *A Monetary History of the Ottoman Empire*. Cambridge: Cambridge University Press, 2000.

Pamuk, Şevket. *Türkiye'nin 200 Yıllık İktisadi Tarihi*. Istanbul: Türkiye İş Bankası Kültür Yayınları, 2012.

Paz, Omri. "Crime, Criminals and the Ottoman State: Anatolia between the late 1830s and the late 1860s." PhD diss., Tel Aviv University, 2010.

Petrov, Milen V. "Everyday Forms of Compliance: Subaltern Commentaries on Ottoman Reform, 1864–1868." *Comparative Studies in Society and History* 46, no. 4 (2004): 730–59.

Philliou, Christine. "The Ottoman Empire's Absent Nineteenth Century: Autonomous Subjects." In *Untold Histories of the Middle East: Recovering Voices from the 19th and 20th Centuries*, edited by Amy Singer, Christoph K. Neumann and Selçuk Akşin Somel, 143–58. London: Rourtledge, 2011.

Polatel, Mehmet. "Armenians and the Land Question in the Ottoman Empire, 1870–1914." PhD diss., Boğaziçi University, 2017.

Polatel, Mehmet. "The Complete Ruin of a District: The Sasun Massacre of 1894." In *The Ottoman History in the Nineteenth Century: Socities, Identities and Politics*, edited by Yaşar Tolga Cora, Dzovaniar Derderian and Ali Sipahi, 179–98. London: I.B. Tauris, 2016.

Quataert, Donald. "The Age of Reforms." In *An Economic and Social History of the Ottoman Empire, 1600–1914*, edited by Halil İnalcık and Donald Quataert, 761–943. Cambridge: Cambridge University Press, 1997.

Quataert, Donald. *The Ottoman Empire, 1700–1922*. Cambridge: Cambridge University Press, 2005.

Reinskowski, Maurus. *Düzenin Şeyleri, Tanzimat'ın Kelimeleri: 19. Yüzyıl Osmanlı Reform Politikasının Karşılaştırmalı Bir Araştırması*. Istanbul: Yapı Kredi Yayınları, 2017.

Rogan, Eugene L. *Frontiers of the State in the Late Ottoman Empire, Transjordan, 1850–1921*. Cambridge: Cambridge University Press, 1999.

Salzmann, Ariel. "An Ancien Régime Revisited: Privatization and Political Economy in the Eighteenth-Century Ottoman Empire." *Politics & Society* 21, no. 4 (1993): 393–423.

Saraçoğlu, M. Safa. "Resilient Notables: Looking at the Transformation of the Ottoman Empire from the Local Level." In *Contested Spaces of Nobility in Early Modern Europe*, edited by Matthew P. Romaniello and Charles Lipp, 257–77. Burlington: Ashgate, 2011.

Saydam, Abdullah. *Kırım ve Kafkas Göçleri*. Ankara: Türk Tarih Kurumu Basımevi, 1997.

Schofield, Richard. "Narrowing the Frontier: Mid-Nineteenth Century Efforts to Delimit and Map the Perso-Ottoman Boundary." In *War and Peace in Qajar Persia*, edited by Roxane Farmanfarmaian. New York: Routledge, 2008.

Scott, James. C. *Seeing Like a State*. New Haven: Yale University Press, 1998.

Sertoğlu, Midhat, ed. *Sofyalı Ali Çavuş Kanunnamesi: Osmanlı İmparatorluğu'nda Toprak Tasarruf Sistemi'nin Hukukî ve Malî Müeyyede ve Mükellefiyetleri*. Istanbul: Marmara Üniversitesi Yayınları, 1992.

Seyitdanlıoğlu, Mehmet. *Tanzimat Devrinde Meclis-i Vâlâ, 1838–1868*. Ankara: Türk Tarih Kurumu Basımevi, 1994.

Seyitdanlıoğlu, Mehmet. "Tanzimat Dönemi İmâr Meclisleri." *OTAM*, no. 3 (Ocak 1992): 323–32.

Shaw, Stanford J. "Local Administrations in the Tanzimat." In *150. Yılında Tanzimat*, edited by Hakkı Dursun Yıldız, 33–49. Ankara: Türk Tarih Kurumu Yayınları, 1992.

Shaw, Stanford J., and Ezel Kural Shaw. *History of the Ottoman Empire and Modern Turkey*. 2 vols. Vol. 2, Cambridge: Cambridge University Press, 1976–77.

Shiel, J. "Notes on a Journey from Tabriz, through Kurdistan, via Van, Bitlis, Seert and Erbil to Suleymaniyeh, in July and August 1836," *Journal of the Royal Geographical Society of London*, vol. 8 (1838)" *Journal of the Royal Geographical Society of London* Vol. 8 (1838): 54–101.

Sinclair, Tom. "The Ottoman Arrangements for the Tribal Principalities of the Lake Van Region of the Sixteenth Century." In *Ottoman Borderlands: Issues, Personalities and Political Change*, edited by Kemal H. Karpat and Robert W. Zens, 119–44. Madison: University of Wisconsin Press, 2003.

Sipahi, Ali. "At Arm's Length: Historical Ethnography of Proximity in Harput." PhD diss., University of Michigan, 2015.

Sipahi, Ali. "Suburbanization and Urban Duality in the Harput Area." In *The Ottoman East in the Nineteenth Century: Societies, Identities and Politics*, edited by Yaşar Tolga Cora, Dzovaniar Derderian and Ali Sipahi, 247–67. London: I.B. Tauris, 2016.

Southgate, Horatio. *Narrative of a Tour through Armenia, Kurdistan, Persia and Mesopotamia: With an Introduction, and Occasional Observations upon the Condition of Mohammedanism and Christianity in those Countries*. Vol. 1, New York: D. Appleton, 1840.

Sykes, Mark. "The Kurdish Tribes of the Ottoman Empire." *The Journal of the Royal Anthropological Institute of Great Britain and Ireland* 38 (1908): 451–86.

Şaşmaz, Musa. *Kürt Musa Bey Olayı, 1883–1890*. İstanbul: Kitabevi, 2004.

Şener, Abdüllatif. *Tanzimat Dönemi Osmanlı Vergi Sistemi*. Istanbul: İşaret Yayınları, 1990.

Şeref Han. *Şerefname*. Translated by Mehmet Emin Bozarslan. Istanbul: Yöntem Yayınları, 1975.

Tapper, Richard. "Introduction." In *The Conflict of Tribe and State in Iran and Afghanistan*, edited by Richard Tapper. London: Croom Helm, 1983.

Thompson, Elizabeth. "Ottoman Political Reform in the Provinces: The Damascus Advisory Council in 1844–45." *International Journal of Middle East Studies* 25, no. 3 (1993): 457–75.

Tilly, Charles. *Coercion, Capital, and European States, AD 990–1992*. Cambridge: Blackwell, 1992.

Tilly, Charles. "Survey Article: Power-Top Down & Bottom Up." *Journal of Political Philosophy* 7, no. 3 (1999): 330–52.

Toksöz, Meltem. *Nomads, Migrants and Cotton in the Eastern Mediterranean: The Making of Adana Mersin Region 1850–1908*. Leiden: Brill, 2010.

Toraman, Ömer. "Tanzimat'ın Yurtluk-Ocaklık ve Hükümet Sancaklarda Uygulanması (1839–1864)." PhD diss., Fırat Üniversitesi, 2010.

Toraman, Ömer. "Trabzon Eyaletinde Yurtluk-Ocaklık Suretiyle Arazi Tasarrufuna Son Verilmesi (1847–1864)." *Uluslararası Karadeniz İncelemeleri Dergisi*, no. 8 (2010).

Ueno, Masayuki "'For the Fatherland and the State': Armenians Negotiate the Tanzimat Reforms." *International Journal of Middle East Studies*, no. 45 (2013): 93–109.

Ursinus, Michael. *Grievance Administration (Şikâyet) in an Ottoman Province: The Kaymakam of Rumelia's 'Record Book of Complaints' of 1781–1783*. London: Routledge, 2005.

Uzun, Ahmet. *Tanzimat ve Sosyal Direnişler: Niş İsyanı Üzerine Ayrıntılı Bir İnceleme (1841)*. Istanbul: Eren Yayıncılık, 2002.

Ünal, Mehmet Ali. "XVI. Yüzyılda Palu Hükümeti." *On Dokuz Mayıs Üniversitesi Eğitim Fakültesi Dergisi*, no. 7 (1992): 241–65.

Van Bruinessen, Martin. *Agha, Shaikh, and State: The Social and Political Structures of Kurdistan*. London: Zed Books, 1992.

Van Bruinessen, Martin. "Kurds, States, and Tribes." In *Tribes and Power: Nationalism and Ethnicity in the Middle East*, edited by Faleh Abdul-Jabar and Hosham Dawod. London: Saqi, 2003.

Van Bruinessen, Martin. "Kurdish Tribes and the State of Iran: The Case of Simko's Revolt." In *The Conflict of Tribe and State in Iran and Afghanistan*, edited by Richard Tapper. London: Croom Helm, 1983.

Van Voss, Lex Heerma. "Introduction." In *Petitions in Social History*, edited by Lex Heerma Van Voss. Cambridge: Cambridge University Press, 2002.

Veinstein, Gilles. "On the Çiftlik Debate." In *Landholding and Commercial Agriculture in the Middle East*, edited by Çağlar Keyder and Faruk Tabak, 35–53. Albany: State University of New York Press, 1991.

Verner, Andrew. "Discursive Strategies in the 1905 Revolution: Peasant Petitions from Vladimir Province." *The Russian Review* 54, no. 1 (1995): 65–90.

Von Moltke, Helmuth. *Moltke'nin Türkiye Mektupları*. Translated by Hayrullah Örs. Istanbul: Remzi Kitabevi, 1969.

Willbraham, Richard. *Travels in the Trans-Caucasian Provinces of Russia and Along the Southern Shores o the Lakes of Van and Urumiah in the Autumn and Winter of 1837*. London: J. Murray, 1839.

Yaşar, Muammer. *Anadolu'da İlk Türk Gazetesi (Envar-ı Şarkiyye)*. Ankara: Türk Tarih Kurumu, 1971.

Yaycıoğlu, Ali. *Partners of the Empire: The Crisis of the Ottoman Order in the Age of Revolutions*. Stanford: Stanford University Press, 2016.

Yaycıoğlu, Ali. "The Provincial Challange: Regionalism, Crisis and Integration in the Late Ottoman Empire." PhD diss., Harvard University, 2008.

Yazbak, Mahmud. *Haifa in the Late Ottoman Period, 1864–1914*. Leiden: Brill, 1998.

Yıldırır, Gökşen, Saim Erdem, and Hüseyin Erol, eds. *Muş İl Yıllığı*. Elazığ: Bingöl Matbaası, 1973.

Yılmaz, Bilal. "Muş Vakıfları." master's thesis, Yüzüncü Yıl Üniversitesi, 2009.

Yılmaz, Fehmi. "Osmanlı İmparatorluğu'nda Tütün: Sosyal, Siyasî ve Ekonomik Tahlili (1600–1883)." PhD diss., Marmara Üniversitesi, 2005.

Zens, Robert W. "The *Ayanlık* and Pasvanoğlu Osman Paşa of Vidin in the age of Ottoman Social Change, 1791–1815." PhD diss., University of Wisconsin, 2004.

Zürcher, Erik Jan. "The Ottoman Conscription System, 1844–1914." *International Review of Social History*, no. 43 (1998): 437–49.

Index

â'yânlık 29
Abbas Mirza (Qajar prince) 53, 61
Abdal Bey (nephew of Han Mahmud) 133, 138
Abdülfettah Bey (from Alaaddin Pashazades) 45, 58
Abdülmecid I (sultan) 148
Adakend (village) 267
Adil Bey 51
Adilcevaz 16, 40n67, 56, 253
Ahlat 16, 37, 40n67, 139n150, 216, 219, 243–244, 254, 264
Ahmed Kaşif Agha 114, 118, 121, 123, 125
Alaaddin Bey 32, 38–40, 65
Alaaddin Pasha 10, 27, 29, 31, 38, 94, 143
Aladağ Mountains 18
Alikan tribe 232, 246–248, 250
Alizurum (village) 156
Ardonk (village) 156
Armenian clergy 182n21
Armenian notables 14, 24, 118n58, 140, 206–208, 276
Armenian Patriarchate 119, 190, 192, 238
Armenian Peasants 21–22, 25, 136, 187, 190, 193, 195n71, 204, 217, 219, 225, 270
Armenians 1, 6, 14–15, 20, 106, 111, 117, 119, 154, 180, 192, 203, 206–208, 212, 216, 220–222, 226, 239, 243, 272
Asakir-i Mansure-i Muhammediyye (Victorious Soldiers of Muhammad) 50
Atak 74–79, 82–84
  beys 74
ayan 3, 45
Ayn-ı Ali Efendi 34
Ayntab 244, 266–267

Bane (village) 266–267
Bayburd 122
Bedirhan Bey 104, 129–134, 137–141
Behlül Pasha (Mutasarrıf of Bayezid) 43
Bekir Sami Pasha (governor of Erzurum) 114n37, 160
Bekiran tribe 231, 246–247, 249–250, 271
Beliki tribe 244
beys of Atak 67, 75, 77–78, 83

Bilbasi 31
Bitlis 16–19, 26, 32, 37–40, 43, 45, 73, 75, 92, 94, 99, 109, 119, 137, 167, 169, 174, 183, 208, 216, 219, 237, 241, 255, 260, 273–274
Bitlis khanate. *See also* Khanate of Bitlis 91, 274
Bostangend Village 157, 168–170
Burhan Han (khan of Bitlis) 32, 38–39
büyük meclis (large council) 104

Çanlı Monastery 74, 182, 191, 201, 209, 272
Castle of Hoşap 51
Caucasus 30n20, 194, 221
Celaleddin Pasha (governor of Erzurum) 55, 61
Cemaldini tribe 60–61, 65, 67, 70, 79, 81
Cennetzades 117
Cibran tribe 75, 77, 83, 125, 236, 244, 253
çiftlik (large farms) 28
Cihangir Mirza 50, 61, 63, 70, 80–81, 84
Çıldır 32, 219
Circassian immigrants 180, 223
Cizre-Bohtan 24, 105, 134
Cizye (*poll tax*) 90, 104n7, 109, 135, 205
corvée 6–7, 23, 25, 111–112, 154, 177, 181, 183, 188, 193, 202, 215, 227, 258, 276
Crimean War 164–165, 174, 180, 194–196, 204–210, 218, 225–226

Damascus 32, 105n9, 139, 143, 149, 153, 234, 294
Defter-i Hakani (Imperial Registers) 34
Divân-ı Ahkâm-ı Adliye (Council of Judicial Ordinances) 267
Duhan (tobacco tax) 211

Eleşgird 47, 220, 244
Elhac Şeyho Bey 41
Elmanlı Tribe 238–239, 241
Emin Pasha (from Alaaddin Pashazades) 26, 38–39, 44–67, 79–89, 91–102, 107, 110, 126, 139, 157, 275–276
  contested villages 168–171
  Revolt 67–79
Erciş 55n129, 56

Erişter (village) 157
Erzuru 53
Erzurum 1, 8, 11, 14, 16, 19–20, 22–24, 38–39, 46–47, 49–53, 56–59, 61n148, 80n44, 108, 114–126, 129, 136n139, 144, 145n6, 162, 164–165, 169–170, 174, 181, 185, 193–195, 201, 208n126, 209, 219–221, 223–226, 232, 234n27, 235, 244–245, 260–261, 269, 275, 277–278
Erzurum Treaty of 1823 54
Esad Pasha (governor of Erzurum) 51–52, 56–65, 67–87, 90–93, 127–128, 131, 136–139, 149–153, 163, 173, 187, 204, 231, 237–238, 241–242, 275, 277

Feliki tribe 266–269
Ferho Agha 241
fief (tımar) 27–29, 34, 98, 159
fiefs (tımar)
  Makrak and Gebre 157

Galip Pasha (governor of Erzurum) 43, 45–46, 48
Garzan 85–86, 88, 92–93, 135, 182n21
Garzan Kurds 85
Genç 16
Gürcü Osman Pasha 41
Güroymak 16, 18

Hacı Ahmed Bey (from Alaaddin Pashazades) 45, 139n150
Hacı Esad Agha (tax farmer) 208
Hacı Manok 119
hafirlik 6–7, 246, 271
Hafız Pasha 94–97, 100, 124, 143
Hafız Pasha 173, 275
Hakkari 36n45, 47, 95, 105, 109, 123, 132–133, 137–138, 238
Halil Kamili Pasha (governor of Erzurum) 99, 107, 124, 135
Hamidian Regiments 271–272
Hamparsum 119
Han Abdal (brother of Han Mahmud) 132–133
Han Mahmud 95–96, 104, 123, 125, 130–134, 136–137, 175
Hariciye Mektubi Kalemi (Foreign Correspondence Office) 144

Harput 224
Hars (village) 156, 212
Haydaran tribe 42, 48, 51, 60–65, 67, 70–71, 76–81, 231–232, 264–265
hayme-nişin (*nomads*) 60
Hesenan tribe 73, 75–77, 125–127, 135n135, 189n44, 197, 231–232, 236, 240–244, 251–254, 256–272
Hınıs 7n14, 26, 32, 37, 40n67, 41, 44n92, 47, 49n112, 50, 54, 59–60, 65, 71n11, 73, 86–87, 92, 94, 96, 98, 137, 152, 164, 174, 193n61, 238, 244, 252, 274–275
Hizan 160
hükûmet 27n8, 30n20, 36n45, 36n47, 37, 59n144, 75, 142, 148, 159, 274
Hurşid bey 277
Hurşid Bey 26, 73, 127, 140, 146, 153, 155, 157, 159, 165–166, 168, 170, 172, 174, 187, 192

İbrahim Efendi (kethüda) 106–113, 119–120, 188–189, 192
Ilıcanlu tribe 198
irregular cavalrymen (başıbozuk süvari) 87
Ishak Pasha 83
Ishak Pasha (Çötelizade) 77–78, 83
Ishak Pasha (kaimakam of Muş) 186
Islahat Fermanı (The Edict of Reform) 25, 104n7, 180, 204–206, 225
Ispir 122
Istabl-ı Amire (Imperial Stables) 131

Kanunnâme-i Hümayun (Imperial Law Book) 34
Karaağaç (village) 266
Karasu River 18
Kars 20, 32, 40, 61, 78, 81–82, 98–99, 113n34, 117n56, 121–122, 188, 194–198, 219, 222–223, 244, 257–258
Kasım Agha 62, 65, 81
Keban 74, 76–77
Kenan Pasha (son-in-law of Esad Pasha) 194
Keşişoğlu Ohannes (moneylender) 75
Khanate of Bitlis 65
Kiravi (village) 156
kışlakiye 7nn13–14, 62–63, 67, 70, 74, 79–81, 92, 111, 246, 265
Kömüs (village) 157, 168

Koro Agha
 of Cemaldini tribe 61, 65, 70, 79
Köseoğlu Kivork 117
küçük meclis (small council) 104
Kurdish emirates 228, 230
Kurdish peasants 2, 6, 20, 75n26
Kurds 1, 15, 47, 49–50, 54, 59, 86–88, 102, 120, 133, 135–136, 176, 189, 212, 220, 224, 234, 254
Kürkçübaşı Agop 208
Kuştiyan (village) 242–243

Land Code of 1858 13, 145, 147n13, 167, 169, 174, 287
Liz (village) 157, 168–170
local councils 3–4, 13, 24, 105n9, 113, 118, 128, 157, 179–180, 196, 203, 206, 225, 276

Ma'den-i Hümâyûn 75–76, 85
Mahmud II (sultan) 50, 85, 88, 96, 102n2, 275
Maksud Pasha (from Alaaddin Pashazades) 40
Malatya 74, 76–77
Malazgird 51, 53, 56–57, 59–60, 92, 126, 137, 216, 240–241, 243
Mâlikâne (life long tax farms) 28, 32, 58, 65, 123, 129, 143, 147, 151, 274
Mamanlı tribe 244
Mansure Army 50, 53–54, 56–58, 71, 86, 91, 98, 100–101, 274
Mansure Treasury 59n142, 90, 143
Mardin 133, 247
Meclis-i İdare-i Vilayet (Provincial Administrative Council) 267
Meclis-i Kebir-i Eyâlet (Provicial Council). *See also* local councils 200
Meclis-i Mahsus (Special Council) 270
Meclis-i Temyiz (Provincial Court of Appeal) 267
Meclis-i Vala (Supreme Council) 21–22, 102, 148
Mehmed Agha (Haydaran chief) 61
Mehmed Ali Pasha (governor of Egypt) 3, 69
Mehmed Bey (Şerif Bey's son) 137, 162, 168
Mehmed Bey (the brother of Selim Pasha) 45–46
Mehmed Ragıb Pasha (governor of Kurdistan) 192

Mehmed Salih Pasha (governor of Erzurum) 46
Mercimek Hill 39
Mirza Pasha (from Alaaddin Pashazades) 41
Mirza Rıza (Persian envoy) 79–81
Mosul 3, 4n3, 5, 130, 132, 288
Muhacirin Komisyonu (Commission of Immigrants) 222
muhallefat 41
muhassıl (tax collector) 7, 12, 113
Muhassılık councils 118
Müküs 95, 108, 133
murabahacılık (usury) 213, 226
Murad Bey (the brother of Emin Pasha) 44, 72–73, 76, 83, 86, 91–92, 96, 108, 138–140, 144, 155–156, 159–160, 162–166, 171, 174, 252, 277
Murad Pasha (the father of Selim Pasha) 41–42, 58
Murad Pashazade 42, 72–73
Muradoğlu Mattos 117
Murat River 1, 18
Muş plain 21, 37, 180, 240, 246
müşir (military governor) 90, 93, 131, 139
 of Anatolian Army 127n100
 of Erzurum 117n56
müşirlik (military governorship) 68
 of Erzurum 90, 101, 143, 275
mütesellimlik 93–94, 275–276
 of Muş 91, 94, 107
Mütesellimlik 28n12
Mutki 16, 186, 190, 216, 245, 260

Norşen (village) 157, 195, 200
Nurullah Bey 95, 105, 123, 132–133, 137–138, 238
Nuxtili (village) 267

Orginos (village) 156
Oseb (the milletbaşı of Bitlis) 119, 123, 128
Osman Pasha (commander in chief of the east) 49
Oşnam (village) 156
Ottoman-Iranian War of 1821–1823 42
Ottoman-Russian War of 1828–29 46

Palu 14, 32n27, 36, 122, 147, 161, 294
Penal Code of 1840 150, 237n42, 249, 265
Pençnar tribe 231–232, 246

INDEX

Province of Kurdistan   133–134, 136, 148–149, 154, 173, 175, 187, 192, 193*n*61, 237, 246–248, 250, 277

raiyyet (commoners)   152
Redif (reserve) Army   88–93, 99, 173
Reşid Mehmed Pasha   68, 84, 89–90, 143, 275
Reşkotan tribe   231–232
Rıdvan Agha (Hesenan chief)   269, 271
Rojki   32, 38, 75, 274

Safavid(s)   10, 27, 34*n*36, 65, 274
Salorik (village)   156
salyane   62
Sason   16, 186, 190, 245, 251*n*88, 260
Selim Bey (the son of Murad Bey)   153–154, 168
Selim III (sultan)   3, 11, 21, 58
Selim Pasha   42–44, 48, 55, 61
Şerafeddin Bey (bey of Hizan)   127, 160–161
Şeref Han   37, 294
Şerif Bey   26, 51, 73, 96, 100–101, 109, 118, 142, 145, 151–152, 161, 188, 192, 237, 254
    mansion   166–167
Şerif Pasha. *See also* Şerif Bey   166–167, 171–172, 188, 225, 228, 277
Şero Agha   238–239
Sharafnama   37–38, 172
sharecropper   213, 218
sharecropping (ortakçılık)   164, 214, 277
sheep tax (ağnam)   7*m*13, 114
sheep trade   234
Sheikh Abdülmelik   168–169
Sheikh Burhaneddin   169
Sıpkî tribe   15, 40–41, 53, 76–77, 79, 231, 244, 269
Sırrı Pasha (kaimakam of Van)   129
Sivas   43, 68, 70, 72, 83, 92–93, 101–102, 223, 254
soyurghal   33
Süleyman Agha (Sıpkî Chief)   53–54, 56, 76, 79
Süleyman Bahri Pasha   167, 278
Süleyman I (sultan)   34
Sultan Agha   51, 63–65, 70, 78–81
Suluki (Silukan) tribe   231–232, 240
summer quarters   81, 85, 183, 231–232, 247, 250, 271
Şûrâ-yı Devlet (Council of State)   22, 267

299

Tanzimat   3–7, 22–25, 31, 52, 54, 60, 99–100, 102, 104*n*5, 105–106, 108–109, 111–127, 129–131, 138, 144*n*5, 150, 159–160, 179–188, 192–193, 196, 198, 203–204, 206*n*117, 207, 227–228, 232–233, 235–236, 239, 244, 249, 252–254, 265
tax farming   12, 28, 104, 113, 118–119
    in the plain Muş   165
    of mineral springs   114
    the villages of Muş and Bitlis   94
Tayyar Pasha (governor of Trabzon)   40
Tebavenk (village)   156
Tekman   32, 40*n*67, 41, 46–47, 50, 53–54, 56–60, 65, 152, 274–275
temettuat   91, 113–114
Tersane-i Amire (Imperial Shipyard)   269
Tevnig (village)   157
The Ottoman-Iranian War of 1821–1823   48
Timur Pasha   56, 77, 79
    Revolt   49–51
Timur Pasha (the guardian of Van)   31

Urfa   247

Van   1, 17–18, 32, 37, 39, 42–43, 50–53, 56–57, 69, 82, 98, 109, 129–130, 134, 137–138, 222, 224, 237, 242, 250, 253, 255, 265, 273
Vartinis (village)   157
Varto   16, 58, 84, 219, 220*n*166, 220*n*171, 244, 252

winter quarters   62–63, 79

yaylakiye   232, 255
Yezdanşer   132–133
Yoncalı Village   157, 168–169
yurtluk-ocaklık   i, 3, 6–7, 11, 14, 16, 23, 27*n*8, 30*n*20, 32*n*27, 36, 40–41, 45–46, 52, 58, 65, 91, 93–94, 98, 100, 106–107, 119, 122, 161, 172*n*105, 178, 180, 186–187, 203, 226, 277
    salaries   171–172
Yusuf Kamer Pasha   40

Zilan tribe   15, 42, 79–81, 230, 235, 244, 256
Zinyaret (village)   156
Zirki Beys   14, 36, 77, 147, 161